First World War
and Army of Occupation
War Diary
France, Belgium and Germany

8 DIVISION
25 Infantry Brigade,
Brigade Machine Gun Company
and Brigade Trench Mortar Battery
5 June 1915 - 1 January 1916

WO95/1732

The Naval & Military Press Ltd
www.nmarchive.com
Published in association with The National Archives

Published by

The Naval & Military Press Ltd

Unit 10 Ridgewood Industrial Park,
Uckfield, East Sussex,
TN22 5QE England
Tel: +44 (0) 1825 749494

www.naval-military-press.com
www.nmarchive.com

This diary has been reprinted in facsimile from the original. Any imperfections are inevitably reproduced and the quality may fall short of modern type and cartographic standards.

© Crown Copyright
Images reproduced by permission of The National Archives, London, England, 2015.

Contents

Document type	Place/Title	Date From	Date To
Heading	8th Division 25th Infy Bde 25th Machine Gun Coy Jan 1916-1918 Feb.		
Heading	8th Division. 25th, Brigade. 25th, Machine Gun Co. January, 1916. Dec 1917		
Heading	25th Bde Mach En Co Jan Vol I		
War Diary	Sercus	30/12/1915	07/01/1916
War Diary	Sailly	19/01/1916	26/01/1916
War Diary	Trenches	27/01/1916	31/01/1916
Heading	8th, Division. 25th, Brigade. 25th, Machine Gun Co. February, 1916.		
War Diary	Trenches	01/02/1916	29/02/1916
Heading	8th, Division. 25th, Brigade. 25th, Machine Gun Co. March, 1916		
War Diary	Trenches	01/03/1916	27/03/1916
War Diary	Line of March	28/03/1916	29/03/1916
War Diary	Flesselles	30/03/1916	31/03/1916
Heading	8th, Division. 25th, Brigade. 25th, Machine Gun Co. April, 1916.		
Heading	War Diary of 25th Company Machine Gun Corps From 1st April 1916 To 30th April 1916 (Volume IV)		
War Diary	Flesselles	01/04/1916	04/04/1916
War Diary	St. Gratien	05/04/1916	05/04/1916
War Diary	Millencourt	06/04/1916	30/04/1916
Heading	8th, Division. 25th, Brigade. 25th, Machine Gun Co. May, 1916.		
Miscellaneous	To D.A.G 3rd Echelon		
War Diary	Millencourt	01/05/1916	18/05/1916
War Diary	Millencourt Trenches	19/05/1916	31/05/1916
Heading	8th, Division. 25th, Brigade. 25th, Machine Gun Co. June, 1916.		
Heading	To D.A.G. 3rd Echelon G.H.Q.		
War Diary	Henencourt	01/06/1916	04/06/1916
War Diary	Millencourt	05/06/1916	30/06/1916
Heading	25th Inf. Bde. 8th Div War Diary. 25th Machine Gun Company July 1916		
Miscellaneous	To D.A.G. 3rd Echelon. G.H.Q.		
War Diary		01/07/1916	04/07/1916
War Diary	Riencourt	05/07/1916	07/07/1916
War Diary	Burbure	08/07/1916	14/07/1916
War Diary	Bethune	15/07/1916	21/07/1916
War Diary	Trenches	22/07/1916	31/07/1916
Miscellaneous	Operation Orders For Offensive Operations.		
Heading	8th, Division. 25th, Brigade. 25th, Machine Gun Co. August, 1916.		
War Diary	Trenches	01/08/1916	06/08/1916
War Diary	Fouquereuil	07/08/1916	14/08/1916
War Diary	Vermelles	15/08/1916	31/08/1916
Heading	8th, Division. 25th, Brigade. 25th, Machine Gun Co. September, 1916.		
War Diary	Vermelles	01/09/1916	01/09/1916

War Diary	Fouquereuil	02/09/1916	07/09/1916
War Diary	Vermelles	08/09/1916	30/09/1916
Heading	8th, Division. 25th, Brigade. 25th, Machine Gun Co. October, 1916.		
War Diary	Vermelles	01/10/1916	11/10/1916
War Diary	Burbure	12/10/1916	20/10/1916
War Diary	Trenches	21/10/1916	31/10/1916
Heading	8th, Division. 25th, Brigade. 25th, Machine Gun Co. November, 1916.		
War Diary	Trenches	01/11/1916	01/11/1916
War Diary	Camp Citadel	02/11/1916	08/11/1916
War Diary	Trenches	09/11/1916	17/11/1916
War Diary	Sandpit	18/11/1916	30/11/1916
Heading	8th, Division. 25th, Brigade. 25th, Machine Gun Co. December, 1916.		
War Diary	Croquoison	01/12/1916	31/12/1916
War Diary	Trenches	01/01/1917	07/01/1917
War Diary	Camp. 117	08/01/1917	09/01/1917
War Diary	Croquoison	10/01/1917	23/01/1917
War Diary	Camp 12	24/01/1917	26/01/1917
War Diary	Camp 17 Trenches	27/01/1917	27/01/1917
War Diary	Trenches	27/01/1917	31/01/1917
War Diary	Rancourt Sector	01/02/1917	12/02/1917
War Diary	Camp 12	13/02/1917	21/02/1917
War Diary	Trenches	22/02/1917	28/02/1917
War Diary	Trenches	01/03/1917	25/03/1917
War Diary	Manancourt	26/03/1917	26/03/1917
War Diary	Riverside Wood	27/03/1917	31/03/1917
Operation(al) Order(s)	25th Machine Gun Company. Operation Order No 1		
Miscellaneous	25th Machine Gun Company Amendments and Additions to Operation Order No.22		
Operation(al) Order(s)	25th Machine Gun Company. Operation Order No. 2.		
Miscellaneous	25th Machine Gun Company. Amendments And Addition To Operation Order No. of 22		
Map			
War Diary	Equincourt	01/04/1917	07/04/1917
War Diary	Epinette Wood	07/04/1917	15/04/1917
War Diary	Heudicourt	16/04/1917	21/04/1917
War Diary	Gauchewood	21/04/1918	21/04/1918
War Diary	Heudicourt	21/04/1917	26/04/1917
War Diary	W 6 d.	27/04/1917	29/04/1917
War Diary	Sunken Road W.6.d.	29/04/1917	01/05/1917
War Diary	Lieramont	02/05/1917	05/05/1917
War Diary	Villars Guislain	10/05/1917	25/05/1917
War Diary	West World Moislains	29/05/1917	31/05/1917
Miscellaneous	8th. Division No. G. 30/ Appendix A	03/03/1917	03/03/1917
Map	Intelligence		
Miscellaneous	Group No. 6 R 27 c 35.80 Appendix A3		
Miscellaneous	Table "A" issued with 8th. Division Order No. 190 Appendix A4		
Map	8th Division		
Miscellaneous	Proposed Machine Gun Tactics For The Sector 22 Ravine-Targelle Ravine. Appendix B2		
Miscellaneous	Company Orders. by Captain J.M. Mood Commanding 25 Machine Gun Company. Appendix C.1.		

Miscellaneous	Company Orders by Capt. J.M. Mood Commdg 25 M.G. Coy.	30/05/1917	30/05/1917
Miscellaneous	After Orders		
Miscellaneous	8th Division.	21/05/1917	21/05/1917
War Diary	Sailly Lorette	01/06/1917	03/06/1917
War Diary	Strazeele	04/06/1917	14/06/1917
War Diary	Bosseboom	15/06/1917	26/06/1917
War Diary	In The Field	27/06/1917	30/06/1917
War Diary	Near Ypres H 14 C 5 8 (Ref Sheet 28)	01/07/1917	02/07/1917
War Diary	Near Ypres I 14 C 58 (Ref Sheet 28)	03/07/1917	06/07/1917
War Diary	Ypres I 8 c 3525 (Ref Sheet 28)	07/07/1917	09/07/1917
War Diary	Dominion Camp. G 24 c 36. (Ref. Sheet 28)	10/07/1917	10/07/1917
War Diary	Dominion Camp. G 24 c 36 (Ref Sheet 28) And Audenfort (Ref. Calais 13)	11/07/1917	11/07/1917
War Diary	Audenfort	12/07/1917	16/07/1917
War Diary	Audenfort (Ref. Calais 13)	17/07/1917	18/07/1917
War Diary	Audenfort and Tournehen (Ref. Calais 13)	19/07/1917	19/07/1917
War Diary	Tournehem	20/07/1917	23/07/1917
War Diary	Tournehem (Ref Hazebrouck) 1/100,000	23/07/1917	23/07/1917
War Diary	Reninghelst G.32. d. 7.3. (Ref. 28 N W)	24/07/1917	27/07/1917
War Diary	Reninghelst (G. 32 d 73) Ref Sheet 28 And "Dominion Area" G. 17. D. 8.4.	28/07/1917	28/07/1917
War Diary	Halifax And (G. 14.C. 6595) Ref. Sheet 28	29/09/1917	30/09/1917
Miscellaneous	25 Machine Gun Company Appendix I		
Miscellaneous	25th Infantry Brigade No. G. 1/11. Appendix I Relief Orders	30/06/1917	30/06/1917
Miscellaneous	H 13 Ant		
Operation(al) Order(s)	8th Division Order No. 241 Appendix IX	21/11/1917	21/11/1917
Operation(al) Order(s)	25 Machine Gun Company Relief Order No. 4 Appendix II	06/07/1917	06/07/1917
Operation(al) Order(s)	25 Machine Gun Company Relief Orders No. 5 Appendix III.	08/07/1917	08/07/1917
War Diary	Before Ypres	31/07/1917	31/07/1917
War Diary	In The Line Before Ypres.	01/08/1917	01/08/1917
War Diary	Afterwood At Vancouver Camp H. 14. a. 70	02/08/1917	02/08/1917
War Diary	Vancouver Camp H.14. a. 70 (Sheet 28)	03/08/1917	04/08/1917
War Diary	Moved To Steenvoorde (Hazebrouck Map)	05/08/1917	05/08/1917
War Diary	Steenwoorde	06/08/1917	09/08/1917
War Diary	Steenvoorde Ypres	10/08/1917	10/08/1917
War Diary	Halfway House	11/08/1917	12/08/1917
War Diary	Ypres	13/08/1917	18/08/1917
War Diary	Halifax Camp	19/08/1917	19/08/1917
War Diary	Pradelles Camp	20/08/1917	22/08/1917
War Diary	Pradelles Sheet 27-W. 21	23/08/1917	26/08/1917
War Diary	Greenjackets Camp Sheet 36 B.8.e 3.8.	27/08/1917	27/08/1917
War Diary	Greenjackets Camp Near Steenverck Sheet 28 B. 8.C. 3.8.	28/08/1917	31/08/1917
Miscellaneous	The Attack Before Ypres	31/07/1917	31/07/1917
Operation(al) Order(s)	25th. Machine Gun Company-Operation Order No. 6 Appendix I	23/07/1917	23/07/1917
Miscellaneous	25th Machine Gun Company. Operation Order No. 6 Appendix I		
Miscellaneous	25th Infantry Brigade Instructions No. 8	22/07/1917	22/07/1917
Operation(al) Order(s)	To 25th Machine Gun Coy. Operation Order No. 6 Appendix IV	25/07/1917	25/07/1917

Type	Description	Date 1	Date 2
Miscellaneous	Account of Operations At Ypres On 15/16 1917. by 25th. M.G. Company Appendix III	21/08/1917	21/08/1917
Miscellaneous	25 Machine Gun Company Appendix IV	30/08/1917	30/08/1917
War Diary	Greenjackets Camp Sheet 36 B.8.e.3.8.	01/09/1917	10/09/1917
War Diary	Greenjackets Camp B 8 C 3.8. Sheet 36 And Line Near Ploegsteert	10/09/1917	10/09/1917
War Diary	Sheet 28 T 27 a 55	11/09/1917	18/09/1917
War Diary	Wackland Camp B 13 b 39 (Sheet 36) And Line Opposite Warneton (Sheet 28)	19/09/1917	22/09/1917
War Diary	Wackland Camp B 13 b 39 (Sheet 36) And Line Opposite Warneton (Sheet 28)	22/09/1917	22/09/1917
Operation(al) Order(s)	25 Machine Gun Company Relief Order No. 7 Appendix I	05/09/1917	05/09/1917
Miscellaneous	8th Division No. 1/52/A. Appendix II	09/09/1917	09/09/1917
Miscellaneous	Reference Attached From 8th Division No. G 96/26 Appendix III	15/09/1917	15/09/1917
Miscellaneous	Extract From 8th Division No. G 96/26.	14/09/1917	14/09/1917
Map	8th Div 14-9-17		
Miscellaneous	Ref. Attached Copy of 25th Infantry Brigade Raid Orders Appendix IV	16/09/1917	16/09/1917
Miscellaneous	25th Infantry Brigade Raid Orders.	15/09/1917	15/09/1917
Miscellaneous	25th Infantry Brigade No. 294/G/14	16/09/1917	16/09/1917
Miscellaneous	Instructions In Connection With 8th Division No. G 96/30 Appendix V	16/09/1917	16/09/1917
Miscellaneous	8th Div. No. G. 96/30	15/09/1917	15/09/1917
Miscellaneous	Barrage Table For 25th Machine Gun Company Battery 'C'.		
Map	Map G 26		
Miscellaneous	25th Infantry Brigade No. A1018 Appendix VI	16/09/1917	16/09/1917
Miscellaneous	Instructions Regarding Practice Barrage Appendix VII	19/09/1917	19/09/1917
Miscellaneous	Ref. 8th Div. G 96/37 dated 17/9/17	19/09/1917	19/09/1917
Miscellaneous	8th Div. No. G. 96/37	17/09/1917	17/09/1917
Operation(al) Order(s)	29th M.G. Coy. Relief Order No. 7 Appendix IX	21/09/1917	21/09/1917
Miscellaneous	25 M.G. Coy. Relief Order No. 8	21/09/1917	21/09/1917
Miscellaneous	8th Division No. G. 96/44	20/09/1917	20/09/1917
Miscellaneous	Table "A" Issued With 5th Division No. G. 96/44		
Operation(al) Order(s)	25 M.G. Company Relief Order No. 9 Appendix X	29/09/1917	29/09/1917
War Diary	Wackland Camp B 13 b 3 9 (Sheet 36) And Line Opposite Warneton (Sheet 2.8)	01/10/1917	31/10/1917
Operation(al) Order(s)	25 Machine Gun Company Relief Order No. 19 Appendix I	01/10/1917	01/10/1917
Operation(al) Order(s)	25 Machine Gun Company Relief Order No. 11 Appendix II	07/10/1917	07/10/1917
Operation(al) Order(s)	25th Machine Gun Company Relief Order No. 15 Appendix III	16/10/1917	16/10/1917
Miscellaneous	Table issued With 25th M.G. Coy. Relief Order No. 15		
Miscellaneous	23rd Inf. Bde. (2)	13/10/1917	13/10/1917
Miscellaneous	Table 'C' 25th M.G. Company.		
Miscellaneous	25 Machine Gun Company No. X. 5 Appendix IV	18/10/1917	18/10/1917
Miscellaneous	Extract From Table "A"		
Map			
Operation(al) Order(s)	25th Infantry Brigade Order No. 245	18/10/1917	18/10/1917
Miscellaneous			
Miscellaneous	25th Infantry Brigade No. 294/G/33	18/10/1917	18/10/1917
Miscellaneous	8th Division No. G. 9/1/19	17/10/1917	17/10/1917
Miscellaneous	Table 'A'		

Miscellaneous	25th Infantry Brigade No. 294/G/48.	19/10/1917	19/10/1917
Operation(al) Order(s)	25th M.G. Company Relief Order No. 16 Appendix V	23/10/1917	23/10/1917
Miscellaneous	25th M.G. Company No. X. 6 Appendix VI	27/10/1917	27/10/1917
Operation(al) Order(s)	25th Infantry Brigade Order No. 248	26/10/1917	26/10/1917
Miscellaneous	25th Infantry Brigade No. 294/G/15	26/10/1917	26/10/1917
Miscellaneous	8th Division No. G. 9/1/25	26/10/1917	26/10/1917
Miscellaneous	Table "A"		
Miscellaneous	25th Infantry Brigade No. 294/G/19	27/10/1917	27/10/1917
War Diary	Wackland Camp B 13 b 3 9 (Sheet 36) And Line Opposite Warneton (Sheet 2.8)	01/11/1917	11/11/1917
War Diary	Wackland Camp B 13 b 3.9 (Sheet 36)	11/11/1917	11/11/1917
War Diary	La Motte D 30 Antial (Sheet 36 a)	12/11/1917	16/11/1917
War Diary	Saint Jean C 26 d 8.4 (Sheet 28)	16/11/1917	16/11/1917
War Diary	Passchendaele Sector Coy. H.Q. at D 13 d 8.2 (Sheet 28)	17/11/1917	18/11/1917
War Diary	Line By Passchendaele Coy. H.Q. Laamkeek D 10 b Central (Sheet 28)	19/11/1917	22/11/1917
War Diary	Brandhoek D S C 54 (Sheet 28)	23/11/1917	24/11/1917
War Diary	St. Jean I 3 c o s 95 (Sheet 28)	25/11/1917	30/11/1917
Operation(al) Order(s)	25 M.G. Company Relief Order No. 17 Appendix I	31/10/1917	31/10/1917
Miscellaneous	8th Division No. G. 96/103 Appendix II	05/11/1917	05/11/1917
Miscellaneous	Harrassing Fire Table.		
Miscellaneous	25th H. F. Company X 9	06/11/1917	06/11/1917
Miscellaneous	25c M.G Coy X 9		
Miscellaneous	25th M.G. Company X. 12	06/11/1917	06/11/1917
Miscellaneous	24th M.G. Coy. 25th M.G. Coy. Appendix III	07/11/1917	07/11/1917
Miscellaneous	8th Division No. G. 96/107	06/11/1917	06/11/1917
Miscellaneous	8th Division No. G. 96/10	08/11/1917	08/11/1917
Operation(al) Order(s)	25 M.G. Co. Relief Order No. 18	09/11/1917	09/11/1917
Operation(al) Order(s)	25th Infantry Brigade Order No. 249 Appendix IV	10/11/1917	10/11/1917
Miscellaneous	March Table "A" To Accompany 25th Infantry Brigade Order No. 249		
Operation(al) Order(s)	25th Infantry Brigade Order No. 250 Appendix V	15/11/1917	15/11/1917
Miscellaneous	Table "A" (Personnel)		
Miscellaneous	Table "B" (Personnel).		
Miscellaneous	Table "C"		
Miscellaneous	25th Infantry Brigade No. 282/G/17	16/11/1917	16/11/1917
Miscellaneous	25th Infantry Brigade No. 282/G/18	16/11/1917	16/11/1917
Operation(al) Order(s)	25th Infantry Brigade Order No. 251 Appendix VI	16/11/1917	16/11/1917
Operation(al) Order(s)	25th. M.G. Company Relief Order No. 19 Appendix VII	17/11/1917	17/11/1917
Operation(al) Order(s)	7th. Canadian Machine Gun Company Operation Order No. 34	16/11/1917	16/11/1917
Miscellaneous	8th Division No. G. 97/16 Appendix VIII	19/11/1917	19/11/1917
Diagram etc	Sketch "A" 8th Division Harassing Fire Nov 20th 1917		
Miscellaneous	8th Division No. G. 97/16		
Miscellaneous	List of Targets-Harassing Fire.		
Map	Message Map Harassing Fire		
Miscellaneous	Message Form.		
Operation(al) Order(s)	25th M.G. Coy. Relief Order No. 21	22/10/1917	22/10/1917
Miscellaneous	Appendix X		
Miscellaneous	Defence Policy For Sector At Present Held By 8th Division.	23/11/1917	23/11/1917
Miscellaneous	8th Division No. G. 22/16/35	23/11/1917	23/11/1917
Miscellaneous	Machine Gun Disposition Table		
Map	Map G 32 8th Division 23 A 17		

Type	Description	Date From	Date To
Miscellaneous	Message Form		
Miscellaneous	Appendix XI		
Miscellaneous	25th Infantry Brigade No. G. 2/70	22/11/1917	22/11/1917
Miscellaneous	Night Harassing Fire.	22/11/1917	22/11/1917
Miscellaneous	Counter Offensive Measures And Night Harassing Fire Table "B"		
Diagram etc	Diagram A-8th Division-Harassing Fire 23rd Nov 1917		
Map			
Miscellaneous	Message Form		
Operation(al) Order(s)	8th Division Order No. 245 Appendix XII	24/11/1917	24/11/1917
Miscellaneous	Appendix XIII		
Operation(al) Order(s)	8th Division Order No. 242	23/11/1917	23/11/1917
Miscellaneous	8th Division No. G. 97/38	24/11/1917	24/11/1917
Map	Map G 33		
War Diary	Line Near Passchendaele Transport Line Saint Jean (Sheet 28)	01/12/1917	03/12/1917
War Diary	Saint Jean & Road Buck To Wazerne Area	04/12/1917	04/12/1917
War Diary	Westbecourt V 14 (Sheet 27 a)	05/12/1917	26/12/1917
War Diary	Sheet 28 N.W.	27/12/1917	28/12/1917
War Diary	Sheet 28 N.W. C. 27. C. 7.5.	28/12/1917	31/12/1917
Miscellaneous	Appendix No. I		
Miscellaneous	25th Infantry Brigade No. G. 1/8.	23/11/1917	23/11/1917
Miscellaneous	No Map Issued With This Copy.		
Miscellaneous	25th Infantry Brigade No. G. 1/9	24/11/1917	24/11/1917
Miscellaneous	25th Infantry Brigade No. G. 1/13		
Miscellaneous	25th Infantry Brigade No. G. 1/10	24/11/1917	24/11/1917
Miscellaneous	25th Infantry Brigade No. G. 1/24	27/11/1917	27/11/1917
Miscellaneous	25th Infantry Brigade No. G. 1/12	25/11/1917	25/11/1917
Diagram etc	Tracks.		
Operation(al) Order(s)	25th Infantry Brigade Order No. 259	29/11/1917	29/11/1917
Miscellaneous	Addendum No. 1 To 25th Infantry Brigade Order No. 259	29/11/1917	29/11/1917
Operation(al) Order(s)	25th Infantry Brigade Order No. 255	27/11/1917	27/11/1917
Miscellaneous	Table "A" Attached To 25th Infantry Brigade Order No. 255		
Operation(al) Order(s)	25th Infantry Brigade Order No. 257	29/11/1917	29/11/1917
Operation(al) Order(s)	25th Infantry Brigade Order No. 258	29/11/1917	29/11/1917
Miscellaneous	25th Infantry Brigade No. 6 1/16	28/11/1917	28/11/1917
Diagram etc	Map. No. G. 6		
Miscellaneous	Appendix II		
Miscellaneous	25th M.G. Company Operation Order No.	30/11/1917	30/11/1917
Miscellaneous	Table "A" Right Half Battery		
Miscellaneous	Table "A" Left Hale Battery		
Miscellaneous	Table "B" Right Half Battery		
Miscellaneous	Table "B" Left Half Battery		
Miscellaneous	Table "C"		
Map			
Miscellaneous	8th Division Instructions No. 4	27/11/1917	27/11/1917
Miscellaneous	Table 'A' Attached To 8th Division Instructions No. 4		
Miscellaneous	Table "B" Attached To 8th Division Instructions No 4.		
Miscellaneous	Table "C" Attached To 8th Division Instructions No. 4		
Map	Map G 34 8-Division		
Miscellaneous	8th Division Instructions No. 6	28/11/1917	28/11/1917
Miscellaneous	8th Division No. G 97/1/22	28/11/1917	28/11/1917
Miscellaneous	8th Division No. G. 97/1/33	30/11/1917	30/11/1917
Miscellaneous	8th Div. No. G. 97/1/25	29/11/1917	29/11/1917

Type	Description	Date From	Date To
Miscellaneous	25th M.G. Company. App III	06/12/1917	06/12/1917
Operation(al) Order(s)	25th Infantry Brigade Group Order No. 260 Appendix No IV	30/11/1917	30/11/1917
Miscellaneous	Table "A" To Accompany 25th Infantry Brigade Group Order No. 260		
Miscellaneous	Addendum No. 1 To 8th Division Order No. 246 Appendix No. V		
Operation(al) Order(s)	25th M.G. Company Relief Order No 25	02/12/1917	02/12/1917
Miscellaneous	Addendum No. 2 To 8th Division Order No. 246 Appendix No. VI.	01/12/1917	01/12/1917
Miscellaneous	8th Division No. C/275/11/Q.	02/12/1917	02/12/1917
Miscellaneous	Appendix VII		
Miscellaneous	25th M.G. Company		
Miscellaneous	25th M.G. Coy Appendix VIII		
Miscellaneous	25th Infantry Brigade No. Q/6/32	25/12/1917	25/12/1917
Miscellaneous	25th Inf. Bde. No. Q/6/32	24/12/1917	24/12/1917
Miscellaneous	Dear Renny		
Operation(al) Order(s)	25th Infantry Brigade Order No. 261	22/12/1917	22/12/1917
Miscellaneous	Amendment No. 1 To 25th Infantry Brigade Order No. 261	22/12/1917	22/12/1917
Miscellaneous	March Table For Transport of 25th Infantry Brigade Group.		
Operation(al) Order(s)	25th Infantry Brigade Order No. 262	24/12/1917	24/12/1917
Miscellaneous	Location of Units On Arrival In New Area.		
Miscellaneous	Table "A" To Accompany 25th Inf. Bde. Order No. 262		
Miscellaneous	Programme of Entrainment		
Miscellaneous	Appendix X Relief Orders	30/12/1917	30/12/1917
Operation(al) Order(s)	25th M.G. Coy Relief Order No 22 Appendix X	30/12/1917	30/12/1917
Miscellaneous	Orders For move		
Miscellaneous	C Form (Duplicate) Messages And Signals.	25/12/1917	25/12/1917
War Diary	Sheet 28 N.W.	01/01/1918	31/01/1918
Miscellaneous	25th Machine Gun Coy Relief Order	08/01/1918	08/01/1918
Miscellaneous	24th M.G. Coy		
Operation(al) Order(s)	25th Infantry Brigade Order No. 266	06/01/1918	06/01/1918
Miscellaneous	March Table With 25th Infantry Brigade Order No. 266		
Operation(al) Order(s)	8th Division Order No. 251	05/01/1918	05/01/1918
Operation(al) Order(s)	8th Division Order No. 252	09/01/1918	09/01/1918
Operation(al) Order(s)	Relief Orders No 8 Operation Order No.8 By Capt. F.W. Robinson MC		
Miscellaneous			
Operation(al) Order(s)	25th M.G. Company Relief Orders No.28	15/01/1918	15/01/1918
Operation(al) Order(s)	8th Division Order No. 254	13/01/1918	13/01/1918
Operation(al) Order(s)	25th Infantry Brigade Order No. 267	14/01/1918	14/01/1918
Miscellaneous	Administrative Instructions	14/01/1918	14/01/1918
Miscellaneous	Table To Accompany 25th Infantry Brigade Order No. 267		
Operation(al) Order(s)	25th Infantry Brigade Order No. 268	16/01/1918	16/01/1918
Miscellaneous	Relief Table "A" To Accompany 25th Infantry Brigade Order No. 258		
Miscellaneous	Table "B" To Accompany 25th Infantry Brigade Order No. 268		
War Diary		01/02/1918	10/02/1918
War Diary	Ref. Sheet. Belgium 28 N.W.	11/02/1918	12/02/1918
War Diary	Irish Farm	12/02/1918	17/02/1918
War Diary	Dead End	18/02/1918	28/02/1918

Miscellaneous	8th Divisional Machine Gun Battalion Training Programme for the period 3rd Feb 1918-9th Feb 1918		
Operation(al) Order(s)	E Machine Gun Coy Relief Order. No. 1	18/02/1918	18/02/1918
Operation(al) Order(s)	C Machine Gun Coy Relief Orders No. 2	24/02/1918	24/02/1918
Heading	8th, Division. 25th, Brigade. 2nd, Rifle Brigade. November, 1915		
Heading	25 Trench Mortar Bty 1915 June to 1915 Dec		
War Diary	In the Field	05/06/1915	29/06/1915
War Diary		01/07/1915	29/07/1915
War Diary		03/08/1915	29/08/1915
War Diary		30/09/1915	30/09/1915
War Diary		05/09/1915	23/09/1915
War Diary		08/10/1915	31/10/1915
Miscellaneous	There is nothing to report this week.		
War Diary		10/11/1915	17/11/1915
War Diary		24/11/1915	24/11/1915
Miscellaneous	There is nothing to report this week.		
War Diary		12/12/1915	26/12/1915
War Diary		24/12/1915	01/01/1916

8TH DIVISION
25TH INFY BDE

25TH MACHINE GUN COY.
JAN 1916 - DEC 1917.
1918 FEB

8th, Division.

25th, Brigade.

25th, Machine Gun Co.

January, 1916.

Dec '917

25.- Rosa Morales Juan

tem

Vol 1

Army Form C. 2118

WAR DIARY
or
INTELLIGENCE SUMMARY

25th Brigade Machine Gun Company
8th Arm

(Erase heading not required.)

Instructions regarding War Diaries and Intelligence Summaries are contained in F.S. Regs., Part II. and the Staff Manual respectively. Title Pages will be prepared in manuscript.

Place	Date	Hour	Summary of Events and Information	Remarks and references to Appendices
Servins	30-12-15		Personnel of Machine Gun Company assembled to be fitted, etc.	
—	4-1-16		Personnel rejoined units for march to Trenches.	
SAILLY	19-1-16		Machine Gun Company formed whilst in Divisional Reserve.	
—	20-1-16		Officers visited Trust in LAVENTIE area.	
—	21-1-16		Posts in CROIX MARECHAL area occupied by Machine Gun Company	
	22-1-16		Nº 2 & 3 Sections took over gun positions in front line Trench from 70th Brigade.	
			Nº 2 Section with 3 guns in fire trench, 1 in CELLAR FARM. Nº 3 Section 3 guns in fire trench, 1 in BEE POST.	
			Two officers and 32 machine gunners of 2/Tyneside Scottish attached for instruction in Trench Warfare.	
Trenches	24-1-16		Enemy seen working up a communication trench flashing electric torches. Fire was opened on them by Nº 3 Section. Result not observed.	
			Indirect fire directed on FROMELLES. No observation possible.	
			Two howitzers fired on position.	
Trenches	25-1-16		Indirect fire used on FROMELLES. FME DELEVAL and adjacent roads fired on.	
			Enfilade fire was brought to bear on German Trench opposite Nº B.2 & Nº B.3	
			Hostile machine gun engaged and silenced.	
			One howitzer fired on position.	
Trenches	29-1-16		Enemy were observed to enter and leave a farm 1500 away. Indirect fire was brought to bear on them, also artillery co-operated and fired five rounds shrapnel. Machine gun fire observed to be too much to left.	
			It is thought that German relief took place about 4.30pm. Fire was opened on RUE DE TURKS. Fire was also opened on the vicinity of a burning house behind the enemy lines.	

Army Form C. 2118

No. 2 Continued

WAR DIARY
or
INTELLIGENCE SUMMARY
(Erase heading not required.)

Place	Date	Hour	Summary of Events and Information	Remarks and references to Appendices
Trenches	30-1-16		Two new loopholes placed in position in trenches and framework of two of the new casemates erected.	
			As the weather was very foggy - night dispositions were carried out during the day. The enemy's parapet and the ground behind their lines was swept by machine gun fire at frequent intervals during the day. No 1 and 4 Sections relieved No 2 & 4 Sections during the day.	
"	31-1-16		Work continued on new loopholes. Enemy's machine gun engaged and silenced. Indirect fire directed on Frommelles.	

1/2/16

W.E. Gray Captain
Machine Gun Company
25th Infantry Brigade

<u>8th, Division.</u>

<u>25th, Brigade.</u>

<u>25th, Machine Gun Co.</u>

<u>February, 1916.</u>

WAR DIARY or INTELLIGENCE SUMMARY

Machine Gun Company 25th Inf Brigade

Army Form C. 2118.

(Erase heading not required.)

Instructions regarding War Diaries and Intelligence Summaries are contained in F.S. Regs., Part II. and the Staff Manual respectively. Title Pages will be prepared in manuscript.

Place	Date	Hour	Summary of Events and Information	Remarks and references to Appendices
Trenches	1-2-16		Engaged hostile machine gun which was enfilading our trenches. Two guns fired on enemy working party. No observation possible. One dug-out constructed. Work continued on N°s 1, 1b Positions.	
	2-2-16		Prepared alternate position for indirect enfilade fire on hostile trenches. Fire of two guns concentrated on hostile parapet in conjunction with Lewis gun and rifle fire opposite N.T.5 – N.9.1. New emplacements for machine gun erected in CORDONNERIE POST. Engaged and silenced hostile machine gun opposite N.10.4. Traversed enemy parapet during night. Indirect fire used on hostile trenches opposite Guards Brigade.	
	3-2-16		Machine gun section 3rd Tyneside Scottish attached for instruction. N° 1, 1b sections relieved by N°s 2 & 3 sections at 2 p.m. Fire opened on hostile machine gun opposite N.9.2 and silenced. Work commenced on N° 2 position in CORDONNERIE POST. Fire from 3 machine guns concentrated on hostile working party reported opposite N.10.2.	
	4-2-16		Indirect fire from N.10.4 on ground behind hostile lines. Indirect fire from N.9.4 against enemy trenches opposite right brigade. Traversed RUE DE TURKS with two guns as trench was reported behind hostile lines as though works were in progress. FROMELLES ROAD searched by indirect fire. Enfilade fire directed by compass on hostile trenches from N.10.3. Bursts of fire directed at loopholes in hostile parapet at frequent intervals.	

Army Form C. 2118.

WAR DIARY
or
INTELLIGENCE SUMMARY
(Erase heading not required.)

Instructions regarding War Diaries and Intelligence Summaries are contained in F. S. Regs., Part II. and the Staff Manual respectively. Title Pages will be prepared in manuscript.

Place	Date	Hour	Summary of Events and Information	Remarks and references to Appendices
Trenches	5.2.16		During afternoon enemy fired about 30 5.9 shells at No 2 Position. No casualties. Heavy fire directed at night against enemy's fatigue & ration parties and communication trench.	
	6.2.16		Work continued on all positions and parapet close to No 2 position strengthened. Fire directed on breaches in hostile parapet; strand and ground tried. Indirect fire on trenches from 2 points. One of our guns compelled to cease fire owing to hostile sniper.	
	7.2.16		During night frequent bursts of fire on hostile parapet. About 12.30 pm No 2 position shelled with 5.9 Howitzer. No damage to emplacement and no casualties to gun teams. Two N.C.O of French garrison killed near gun position. Reply carried out about 2 pm. Detachment of 3rd Tyneside Scottish regiment unit. Fire opened on German working party opposite N 10.3 at 10 pm. Partly dispersed. Two hostile trench mortar shells were fired at gun.	
	8.2.16		During night occasional bursts of fire directed on enemy parapet to keep down his fire. Fire directed on gaps in enemy parapet opposite N 10.5 Fire opened on hostile machine gun in organisation with Trench mortar.	
	9.2.16		Indirect fire opened on enemy working party opposite N 10.4 partly dispersed. Indirect fire on enemy's communication trench opposite N 10.3. Occasional bursts of fire on enemy trench. Vertical sweeping 400x - 1300x employed. Hostile bombers at frequent intervals.	
	10.2.16		Working party opposite N 9.4 fire opened and partly dispersed.	

Army Form C. 2118.

WAR DIARY
or
INTELLIGENCE SUMMARY
(Erase heading not required.)

Instructions regarding War Diaries and Intelligence Summaries are contained in F. S. Regs., Part II. and the Staff Manual respectively. Title Pages will be prepared in manuscript.

Place	Date	Hour	Summary of Events and Information	Remarks and references to Appendices
Trenches	11.2.16		Relief carried out at 2 p.m. Snowing. Fire on trenches with 2 guns.	
	12.2.16		Working parties of enemy seen putting up sandbags or parapet. Fire opened and parties dispersed. Fired on hostile working parties during night. Hostile Trench Mortar fired at No 6 position. No casualties.	
	13.2.16		Engaged hostile machine gun which opened fire on our working party. Gun silenced. Hostile Sentinel. Searching fire on communication trenches behind hostile lines. It was reported that enemy was expected to attempt bombing raid. NO MAN'S LAND swept with machine gun fire at frequent intervals during night. Hostile machine gun engaged by two of our guns.	
	14.2.16		Hostile fire used on communication trenches and roads behind hostile lines as it was presumed his reliefs were in progress. Hostile machine gun searched for our guns behind lines but was not located. Casualties No 9345 Rfn Brown wounded Rifle Shot - forearm. Relief carried out. Company attached to 102 nd Inf Bde whilst 35th Inf Bde were in Divisional Reserve.	
	15.2.16		Co-operated with artillery, trench mortars, and swept roads and communication trenches behind enemy lines. Enemy retaliated by firing 12 Trench Mortar shells which caused no damage. Party of four Germans seen working behind their lines - dispersed by Machine gun fire at 9.20 am. Indirect fire from No 9.1 on hostile trenches in front of Left Brigade.	
	16.2.16		Co-operated with artillery on front and second line hostile trenches opposite N 10.1 between 11 p.m. &	

Army Form C. 2118.

WAR DIARY
or
INTELLIGENCE SUMMARY

(Erase heading not required.)

Instructions regarding War Diaries and Intelligence Summaries are contained in F. S. Regs., Part II. and the Staff Manual respectively. Title Pages will be prepared in manuscript.

Place	Date	Hour	Summary of Events and Information	Remarks and references to Appendices
Trenches	16.2.16		and 11.35 p.m. Enemy retaliated with artillery and Trench Mortars. No damage done. Machine gun fire brought to bear on hostile working party observed about 1500° behind hostile trenches opposite N.10.3. Observer with Brigade reported that about 15 men of our party were hit.	
	17.2.16		Indirect fire on enemy working party opposite N.10.1. Observer reports that enemy dispersed and took cover. Transverse hostile trench opposite N.10.3 and silenced machine gun. Working party reported by patrol to be opposite N.9.1 was fired on by machine guns and dispersed.	
	18.2.16		Relief carried out. Occasional bursts of fire opened on enemy footfast during the night. Roads behind enemy lines swept by fire during evening.	
	19.2.16		Enfilade fire was brought to bear on enemy trenches opposite right longrange machine fire on known approach to be used by enemy on ration and engineer dumps. Artillery fire from machine gun Corps gunned company. Indirect fire from Junction N.10.1 - N.10.2 on bearing 145° at 1900°. Roads behind hostile lines swept occasionally during night.	
	20.2.16		In co-operation with artillery and Trench Mortars swept roads and communication trenches with indirect fire. Particular attention was paid to trenches opposite N.10.1, N.10.2, N.10.3. Enemy retaliated with Trench Mortars and a few 4.2 shells.	
	21.2.16		Hostile working party in front of N.10.1 was discovered and driven in by machine gun fire. Relief carried out at 1.30pm.	

WAR DIARY or INTELLIGENCE SUMMARY

Army Form C. 2118.

Place	Date	Hour	Summary of Events and Information	Remarks and references to Appendices
Trenches	21.2.16		Machine gun company regained 25th Inf Brigade on departure of 102nd Bde from lines.	
	22.2.16		Two German machine guns silenced by flash and silenced. Hostile snipers swept with machine gun fire to prevent enemy firing at our working parties. Hostile working party opposite N.9.1 dispersed by machine gun fire.	
	23.2.16		Indirect fire used on MAISNIL CROSS ROADS. Small hostile patrol seen by our listening patrol in front of N.10.2 dispersed by machine gun and rifle fire. The machinery of the enemy opposite our trenches has never been so marked - trench mortars bursts of machine gun and rifle fire failed to draw them.	
	24.2.16		In co-operation with a Howitzer Battery and Field Battery we opened indirect fire on houses at N.16.c.1.2 and N.16.c.3.2. Two machine guns were used. This was fired simultaneously with the first salvo. About 1000 rounds used by each gun. Howitzer obtained direct hit on both farms, that at N.16.c.1.2 being set on fire. After our fire had ceased enemy fired 8 5.9 shells at our right gun. No casualties. At 5.20pm batteries fired another salvo we so opened with our machine gun. An message received and stood to arms 11.35 - 12 midnight. Indirect fire on MAISNIL CROSS ROADS.	
	25.2.16		Relief carried out about 7.20pm. Fired at in hostile parapet during night.	
	26.2.16		Enemy communication trenches behind FME DELAPORTE enfiladed from left of N.B.5. Road in rear also swept at intervals during night. Hostile machine gun located opposite N.10.2. Emplacement destroyed by fire of Field Battery.	

Army Form C. 2118.

WAR DIARY
or
INTELLIGENCE SUMMARY

(Erase heading not required.)

Instructions regarding War Diaries and Intelligence Summaries are contained in F.S. Regs., Part II. and the Staff Manual respectively. Title Pages will be prepared in manuscript.

Place	Date	Hour	Summary of Events and Information	Remarks and references to Appendices
Trenches	24.2.16		Enfilade fire brought to bear on hostile trenches from the TADPOLE to TURK'S POINT. During night fire opened on working party opposite N 10.1 shrubs and ground heard. Indirect enfilade fire was brought to bear on hostile trenches from left of N 9.1. Frequent bursts of fire opened on enemy's trenches during night.	
	25.2.16		Communication trench behind FME DELAPORTE was enfiladed at intervals from 4 pm to 8 pm. Roads and tracks behind enemy's lines frequently swept during night. Between 4 pm & 4 am indirect fire was used on supposed Hn. Headquarters and R.E. dump. From time behind hostile lines swept with indirect searching fire. Hostile snipers swept ground around gun position.	
	29.2.16		Relief carried out about 1.30 am. Four men from machine gun corps joined company. One gun put out of action by hostile rifle fire, bullet penetrated side plates and bored casing and broke link. Casualties Pte. Hann slightly wounded.	

W Byrne Captain
O.C. Machine Gun Company
25th Inf Brigade

<u>8th, Division.</u>

<u>25th, Brigade.</u>

<u>25th, Machine Gun Co.</u>

<u>March, 1916.</u>

WAR DIARY or INTELLIGENCE SUMMARY

Army Form C. 2118

25th Machine Gun Company
25th Inf. Bde.   March 1916

Place	Date	Hour	Summary of Events and Information	Remarks and references to Appendices
Trenches	1-3-16		Fired on enemy working party opposite N 10 2.	
			Indirect fire from N 10 2. No observation possible.	
			Heavy howitzers shelled hostile parapet and machine gun emplacement with fixed mounting revealed hostile machine guns active during night - parapet being frequently traversed.	
			At 3 am and 4.45 am hostile working parties were located and dispersed.	
	2-3-16		At least 3 hostile machine guns over the ground in front of N 10 3 and N 10 4.	
			Fired occasional bursts on hostile parapet where an enemy mortar had made breach opposite N 10 4.	
			Hostile working party dispersed opposite N 10 3.	
			Between 11 pm and midnight 6 rifle grenades and 6 heavy trench mortar bombs were fired into enemy trenches opposite N 9 4. At the same time machine gun indirect fire was directed on the approaches to hostile trenches. Enemy searched for our machine guns with indirect fire but we were not located.	
			There is a sally port at N 9.c.3.1 and close to it a very large loophole probably a m.g. emplacement.	
			Machine gun emplacements located at N 19.a.5.2½ and N 13.d.14.4	
			Hostile working parties opposite N 8.1 were fired at and worked apparently ceased.	
	3-3-16		Indirect fire directed at FROMELLES from N 10.3 and N 9 2.	
			Early in the evening a hostile working party was located on the parapet opposite N 10.4 and dispersed by M.G. fire.	
			The machine gun emplacement at N 5 d 8.3 has not been disturbed.	
	4-3-16		Relief carried out at 1.30 pm.	
			Frequent bursts of fire directed on hostile parapet.	
	5-3-16		A minor bombardment of the hostile trenches at N 8.d. 5.3.3 was carried out by our artillery in conjunction with 6 and 9.2" howitzers. Considerable damage was done, a large breach being made in the hostile parapet. Machine gun fire was kept up on the gap during night.	
			Parade behind hostile lines swept at intervals during night.	
			Fire opened from N 10.3 at hostile working party.	
	6-3-16		Barged hostile fort gun opposite N 9.4. The gun was silenced and fired no more during night.	
			Fire hostile working parties dispersed during night. Breaches in hostile parapet fired on at frequent intervals during night.	
			At 4 pm the enemy was seen to be scrounging out a relief. Men were seen filing into	

Army Form C. 2118

WAR DIARY
or
INTELLIGENCE SUMMARY
(Erase heading not required.)

Instructions regarding War Diaries and Intelligence Summaries are contained in F.S. Regs., Part II. and the Staff Manual respectively. Title Pages will be prepared in manuscript.

Place	Date	Hour	Summary of Events and Information	Remarks and references to Appendices
Trenches	6.3.16		into LES CLOCHERS communication trench opposite junction N.10.2 - N.10.3 with fourth on. Artillery rifle and machine gun fire was brought to bear on them.	
"	7.3.16		6 pm - 6.40 pm indirect fire brought to bear on road junction N.21.C.0.3 from N.9.1. Range 3350.ˣ 4 pm - 8.30 pm the roads, tracks, and communication trenches behind hostile lines swept with indirect fire from positions in rear.	
"	8.3.16		Relief carried out as usual. About 4.30 pm indirect machine gun fire was directed on a party of Germans in the communication trench at N.21.a.8.5 with 2 machine guns. A patrol reported that hostile working parties were repairing the breach opposite N.10.5. Machine gun played on this spot during night. Hostile machine gun from a new position enfiladed N.10.5 from the right and caused two casualties.	
"	9.3.16		Between 4.30 pm and 6 pm two Vickers guns firing from N.9.1 searched the following points :- TRAM DUMP N.21.6.3.1 - N.20.6.6.1 and N.20.B.6.6 - MOYAN FARMS, and the hostile trenches at TRIVELET. Fire directed at FARM DELANGRE in conjunction with Trench Mortars from TURK LANE. Whilst our parties were putting up wire round the mine crater outside N.9/4 we were met with a dog were seen approaching our party withdrew. and machine gun fire was turned on to the hostile patrol who retired.	
"	10.3.16		Between 6.30 pm and 8.30 pm indirect machine gun fire was directed on to the roads and communication trenches behind the hostile lines. Hostile machine guns retaliated searching our positions. We suffered no casualties. Fire opened on German working party opposite N.10.1. Worth searched for remainder of night. 6.30 pm - 7.30 pm indirect fire on TRAM DUMP - N.21.6. - HAYEM FARM and area N.16.C. At stand to till 6.0 pm we engaged enemys fort gun opposite N.9.2. and silenced it.	
"	11.3.16		Fired up TURK LANE and Examined RUE DE TURKS from N.10.4. Two hostile machine guns - one firing from the NEEDLE and the other from TURK POINT were very active	

1875 Wt. W593/826 1,000,000 4/15 J.B.C. & A. A.D.S.S./Forms/C. 2118.

Army Form C. 2118

WAR DIARY
or
INTELLIGENCE SUMMARY
(Erase heading not required.)

Instructions regarding War Diaries and Intelligence Summaries are contained in F.S. Regs., Part II. and the Staff Manual respectively. Title Pages will be prepared in manuscript.

Place	Date	Hour	Summary of Events and Information	Remarks and references to Appendices
Trenches	11-3-16		Active – Our artillery silenced them with one salvo.	
"	12-3-16		Engaged hostile machine gun at 10 pm and midnight. Their hostile working parties dispersed during night by machine gun fire.	
"	13-3-16		The enemy's machine guns were very active firing on to the roads behind our trenches between 5.45 pm and midnight.	
			At 11 pm a party was heard marching along the RUE DES TUNKS. It was fired on by our machine gun. Transport heard moving from west to east from N.9.1, bearing about 145°. Indirect fire from N.9.1 and N.8.6 was opened from two machine guns on road N.31 & N.C.	
"	14-3-16		Between 6.15 pm – 4.30 pm indirect fire from N.9.1 and N.9.5 – the following places being swept:– Area N.16 d & c – RUE DELEVAL, and also embanked trenches to right of SUGAR LOAF. Gun in N.9.4 was hit by bullet which smashed flash protector, front cone, tin dish and muzzle cup. An officer's patrol went up to the German wire opposite the junction of N.9.2 – 9.3 and saw a hostile party but with a covering party. Our patrol retired and machine gun fire was opened on the flares – result not known.	
"	15-3-16		At 8.30 pm heavy rapid fire was opened by the Germans opposite left of N.10.6. M.& Y was ready mounted in a new emplacement but hesitation and at once opened fire and traversed the hostile parapet from which flares could be seen. Two hostile machine guns later engaged this gun. One was silenced until "Stand To" – the other was taken on by M.6.b. The latter gun with a Lewis gun acting as decoy was successful in silencing no less than 3 guns opposite it. This is a further proof of the large number of guns opposite our front. Our machine gun used indirect fire on to the roads and communication trenches behind the enemy's front line from 6.30 pm – 8.30 pm. It is thought that we caught a German relief behind place as the enemy were very aggressive after this and shelled N.9.5 – N.9.1 from	

1875 Wt. W593/826 1,000,000 4/15 J.B.C.& A. A.D.S.S./Forms/C.2118.

Army Form C. 2118

WAR DIARY
or
INTELLIGENCE SUMMARY
(Erase heading not required.)

Instructions regarding War Diaries and Intelligence Summaries are contained in F.S. Regs., Part II. and the Staff Manual respectively. Title Pages will be prepared in manuscript.

Place	Date	Hour	Summary of Events and Information	Remarks and references to Appendices
Trenches	15.3.16		From about 5.30 pm – 11.30 pm with 10.5 c.m. gun. No damage done. Hostile machine guns were active at evening "stand to". At 9.30 pm a machine gun traversed our parapet at N.10.1 – our artillery fired two rounds and silenced it for the rest of the night. Several hostile working parties were fired on. One wiring party was caught by fire of guns in N.9.2. One belt was fired by gun and three magazines from a Lewis gun of Sussex Regt who were attached for instruction. Unfortunately the results could not be observed.	
"	16.3.16		Reliefs carried out at 1.30 pm. The enemy were very quiet during the night and appear to have been working very hard on their parapet and wire. Hostile working parties were dispersed several times by M.G. fire.	
"	17.3.16		Hostile machine guns very active during the night. Our guns were also very active during early hours of the night firing on to the roads and communication trenches behind hostile parapet. Hostile working parties opposite N.10.2 and N.10.5 were dispersed during night. Loud hostile working party opposite N.10.3 – shouts were heard also blowing of whistles. Indirect fire used on TRAM DUMP and enfiladed trench to right of SUGAR LOAF. Indirect fire with 9 guns – 4 in positions in rear of trenches and 5 in trenches. The following places were searched :- vicinity of FROMELLES – HAYEM – RUE DES TURKS – N.31.b – N.30.a.d – N.22.b.d and N.16.d	
"	18.3.16		Several hostile working parties dispersed by M.G. fire. Hostile aeroplane fired on by two machine guns. The plane turned back. Hostile machine guns engaged at various times during night. Indirect fire from TURKS LANE (N.10.4) on FROMELLES village and railway station where activity was reported. No observation possible. The enemy's crater opposite N.10.1 is certainly reopened as earth was seen thrown up	

Army Form C. 2118

WAR DIARY
or
INTELLIGENCE SUMMARY
(Erase heading not required.)

Instructions regarding War Diaries and Intelligence Summaries are contained in F.S. Regs., Part II. and the Staff Manual respectively. Title Pages will be prepared in manuscript.

Place	Date	Hour	Summary of Events and Information	Remarks and references to Appendices
Fromelles	19.3.16		up early in the evening. Machine gun fire from N 10.1 and rifle grenades were directed upon it. The hostile machine guns were active during the night. Several hostile working parties were dispersed by machine gun fire.	
"	20.3.16		Fire was directed at hostile aeroplanes at 4-30 a.m. and 10.0 a.m. Relief carried out at 1-30 p.m. Detachments from 11th Rifle Brigade and 14th K.R.R³ attached to company for instruction in Trench warfare	
"	21.3.16		Enemy extremely quiet. Our machine gun traversed his parapet at frequent intervals - but in very few cases did he reply.	
"	22.3.16		Gun at N 10.1 struck by bullet - front end of barrel casing muzzle cup, steam escape hole and securing portions damaged. Indented for new gun. Starched trenches and roads behind hostile lines.	
"	23.3.16		About 6.45 p.m. a hostile machine gun enfiladed N 10.1 apparently firing from a high position somewhere close to FME DELANGRE - it was silenced by our artillery. An officer's patrol from N q 3 met a German patrol which retired before any action could be taken. A stronger hostile patrol was reported later about the same place and was dispersed by rifle and machine gun fire. Relief carried out at 2 p.m.	
"	24.3.16		Detachments of K.R.R¹ & R.B³ rejoined their units. Indirect fire brought to bear on MARLAQUE FARM from N 10.5. Several hostile working parties dispersed by machine gun fire.	
"	25.3.16		Engaged two hostile machine guns during night. Fire opened from two machine guns on hostile aeroplanes flying very low over lines - they were apparently turned back by our fire.	
"	26.3.16		Indirect fire directed on trenches in front of TRIVELET - FME DELANGRE, TURKS LANE and FROMELLES	

Army Form C. 2118

WAR DIARY
or
INTELLIGENCE SUMMARY
(Erase heading not required.)

Instructions regarding War Diaries and Intelligence Summaries are contained in F. S. Regs., Part II. and the Staff Manual respectively. Title Pages will be prepared in manuscript.

Place	Date	Hour	Summary of Events and Information	Remarks and references to Appendices
Trenches	26.3.16		Fired on hostile working parties during night.	
	27.3.16		Three men from M.G. Corps joined company to replace casualties. Relieved in trenches by 106th M.G. Coy and proceeded to SAILLY	
Line of march	28.3.16		Commenced move to 4th Army area. Paraded 6.30 am and proceeded to entrain at MERVILLE and LESTREM	
"	29.3.16		Detrained at LONGEAU station and proceeded to billets at FIESSELLES. Lieut. Batchelor rejoined from leave.	
FIESSELLES	30.3.16		Thoroughly overhauled guns, limbers etc. One man admitted hospital broken shoulder blade.	
" "	31.3.16		Paraded 9am. Running and jumping drill. 9 am - 12 noon Overhauling ammunition, belts etc.	

W. E. Young Capt
O. C. 25th Coy Machine Gun Corps

8th, Division.

25th, Brigade.

25th, Machine Gun Co.

April, 1916.

Confidential

War Diary

of

25th Company Machine Gun Corps.

from 1st April 1916.   to 30th April 1916.

(Volume IV.)

R.U.Forbes. Lieut.
25th Company Machine Gun Corps.

Army Form C. 2118

WAR DIARY
or
INTELLIGENCE SUMMARY
(Erase heading not required.)

Instructions regarding War Diaries and Intelligence Summaries are contained in F.S. Regs., Part II. and the Staff Manual respectively. Title Pages will be prepared in manuscript.

Place	Date	Hour	Summary of Events and Information	Remarks and references to Appendices
FLESSELLES	1.4.16		Company Route March – distance about 9 miles. Route Flesselles – TALMAS – NAOURS – FLESSELLES	
"	2.4.16		Brigade Church Parade.	
"	3.4.16		7 a.m – 7.45 Running & Jumping drill. 9 a.m. – 12 noon Inspection, Standing etc. 3 p.m Company inspected by 9 O.C. Brigade	
"	4.4.16		Company commences move to divisional reserve area. Marched to M. Gratien and billeted. Lieut Talley proceeds on leave.	
St. GRATIEN	5.4.16		Marched to Millencourt & Collette	
MILLINCOURT	6.4.16		Cleaned billets. Clean Guns etc.	
	7.4.16		7 a.m – 7.45 a.m Running & Jumping drill. Visited 23rd Bde M.G. Coy to inspect billets in Collett	
	8.4.16		3 O.R. joined company from England. Section Officers visited trenches	
	9.4.16		Moved to trenches to relieve 23rd Brigade	
	10.4.16		No 2 & 3 sections in trenches No 1 in billets in Albert. Action in billets thoroughly cleaned billets and vicinity. During the morning ranging fire was opened on various points in the village of LA BOISELLE with excellent results. The enemy also two mines one at 6.40 a.m the other at 10.30 a.m. Between 10 & 11.30 a.m the Mobile Artillery bombarded our trenches, about 500 shells being fired. A great deal of damage was done to the parapet. The enemy support trenches were fired on during the night. LA BOISELLE was also fired on	

1875 Wt. W⁵593/826 1,000,000 4/15 J.B.C. & A. A.D.S.S./Forms/C. 2118.

WAR DIARY or INTELLIGENCE SUMMARY

Army Form C. 2118

Place	Date	Hour	Summary of Events and Information	Remarks and references to Appendices
	11.4.16		Further shelling was carried out on communication between LA BOISELLE & OVILLERS. At 6.55 p.m. the hostile Artillery commenced a heavy bombardment of our front's reserve and communication trenches in the right section, Trench Mortars, Machine Guns co-operating. A great many Lachrymatory shells were used. The bombardment lasted for about one hour, fifteen minutes & was particularly heavy about INCH STREET & RENCH St. Considerable damage was done to the trenches & great many casualties were caused. An infantry charge was made & parts of our enemy left flank trenches towards the end of the bombardment. 17 German hand Grenades were picked up in the front line & dug into our trench head, now 2 or 3 live guns are missing from all captures of the enemy. Heavy fire was brought to bear on the enemy's support & communication trenches & beyond intervals during the night. "Stop and observation on intervals. Every time hit gun from the enemy fired a heavy trench Mortar shell into the second line just in front of Jct gun.	
	12.4.16		No. 11th Sections relieved No. 2. 23rd in the trenches early in the afternoon. During the night the hostile front & support lines & communication trenches between LA BOISELLE & OVILLERS were frequently fired on. A German machine Gun was located by at flash was engaged & silenced by No. 2 gun.	
	13.4.16		1000 rounds were fired for harassing purposes in the vicinity of OVILLERS. The enemy front line was quiet at intervals during the night.	
	14.4.16 11am & 3.30pm		Five was opened on German trenches & communication trenches, about 500 rounds being fired. No MAN'S LAND & the enemy trenches were swept at intervals during the night. 4 Other ranks joined the Company from England	

Army Form C. 2118

WAR DIARY
or
INTELLIGENCE SUMMARY
(Erase heading not required.)

Instructions regarding War Diaries and Intelligence Summaries are contained in F.S. Regs., Part II. and the Staff Manual respectively. Title Pages will be prepared in manuscript.

Place	Date	Hour	Summary of Events and Information	Remarks and references to Appendices
	16.11.16	1.30 A.m & 9.30 p.m	About 500 rounds were fired at enemy Machine Gun near OVILLERS. Enemy communication trenches were heavily fired on during the earlier part of the evening	
	17.11.16		2/Lt True Ramadier reported company from Bure U.K. No. 2 & 3 sections relieved No. 1 & 4 in trenches. At frequent intervals during the night No. 1 Gun fired on a gap in the enemy wire made by our artillery during the day. No. 7687 Pte. Henry was wounded by a rifle bullet when acting sentry on No. 2 Gun.	
	18.11.16		No. 1 Gun engaged & eventually silenced a German Machine Gun in the enemy front line. The support line & communicating trenches round LA BOISELLE were fired on frequently during the night.	
	19.11.16		At morning stand-to-arms the sentry on No. 3 Gun saw the Germans dismounting a Machine gun in the third line. The Artillery were shewn the position of the Machine gun in the enemy front line & 2 Coy were fired on during the day. 3 other Scouts joined the company from the U.K.	
	20.11.16	12.10 p.m & 9.35 p.m	All guns in the front line system co-operated with our artillery in a minor bombardment of LA BOISELLE, & the trenches in the immediate neighbourhood	

Army Form C. 2118

WAR DIARY
or
INTELLIGENCE SUMMARY
(Erase heading not required.)

Instructions regarding War Diaries and Intelligence Summaries are contained in F.S. Regs., Part II. and the Staff Manual respectively. Title Pages will be prepared in manuscript.

Place	Date	Hour	Summary of Events and Information	Remarks and references to Appendices
	20.4.16	contd.	5,500 rounds were fired during the demonstration.	
	21.4.16		H.Q. 2/3 sections were relieved by H.Q. 1st H.Day. in the afternoon. Various points in OVILLERS were ranged on. Weather observation was very good. Enemy machine gun to the right of OVILLERS was engaged.	
	22.4.16	10.30 a.m.	250 rounds observed fire was directed on OVILLERS. The enemy shelled the gun with 77 mm shells but no damage was done. At 9.30 p.m. our artillery opened fire on the hostile trenches. Under cover of the bombardment a small party scaled the hostile trenches about 10 p.m. Two of the enemy were captured, as recruits fair it is believed some others. During however to heavy hostile machine gun fire the party was forced to return without obtaining any identification. From dusk till about 9.30 p.m. A.C.P. gun fired very frequently at the support to the enemy's wire made earlier in the day by our artillery. All the guns formed in the embrasured most of the fire being directed on ZIA BOISELLE & the trenches in the vicinity. About 9000 rounds were fired.	
	23.4.16	3.15 p.m.	Indirect fire was opened from Vena Redoubt on OVILLERS. The effect could not be observed as the ground was very wet. The enemy front & support lines & communication trenches were held on at intervals during the night.	
	24.4.16		Two Germans were seen to enter a dug-out. One gun was laid on the dug out & fired several bursts onto the door.	
	25.4.16		Relieved in the above trenches by 70th M.G. Coy. The company moved back to the Divisional Reserve Area & were billeted in MILLENCOURT. 2/Lt. H.W. Hobbs joined the company from U.K.	

1875 Wt. W593/826 1,000,000 4/15 J.B.C. & A. A.D.S.S./Forms/C. 2118.

Army Form C. 2118.

WAR DIARY
or
INTELLIGENCE SUMMARY

(Erase heading not required.)

Instructions regarding War Diaries and Intelligence Summaries are contained in F. S. Regs., Part II. and the Staff Manual respectively. Title Pages will be prepared in manuscript.

Place	Date	Hour	Summary of Events and Information	Remarks and references to Appendices
MILLENCOURT	26.4.16	7am	Running and Physical drill.	
		9 - 10am	Cleaning billets etc.	
		10 - 11am	Gun drill.	
		11 - 12noon	Arm drill.	
	27.4.16	7am	Running and Physical drill	
		9 - 10am	Gun drill	
		10 - 11am	Indication & recognition of targets.	
		11 - 12noon	Arm Drill	
		4pm - 5pm	Nos 3 & 4 Sections on range	3 Other Ranks joined company from U.K.
	28.4.16	7am	Running & Physical drill	
		9 - 10am	Arm drill and saluting drill	
		10 - 11am	Indication & recognition of targets	
		11 - 12noon	Gun Drill.	
	29.4.16	7am	Running & Physical drill	
		9 - 10am	Signalling.	
		10 - 11am	Tactical handling	
		11 - 12noon	Indication & recognition of targets.	

Army Form C. 2118.

WAR DIARY
or
INTELLIGENCE SUMMARY

(Erase heading not required.)

Instructions regarding War Diaries and Intelligence Summaries are contained in F. S. Regs., Part II. and the Staff Manual respectively. Title Pages will be prepared in manuscript.

Place	Date	Hour	Summary of Events and Information	Remarks and references to Appendices
MILLENCOURT	29.4.16	1-5 pm	No 1 & 2 Sections on range.	
	30.4.16		Captain W. B. Gray proceeded on leave to U.K. Church parades.	

M. F. Soles.
Lieut.
O.C. 25th Coy. Machine Gun Corps.

8th, Division.

25th, Brigade.

25th, Machine Gun Co.

May, 1916.

To/
D. A. G
3rd Echelon

Herewith War Diary of 25th Brigade
Machine Gun Company for May 1916.

2/6/16

M. Gray Capt
O.C. 25th Bde Mac Gun Coy

25 Bde M G Coy
Vol 5

Army Form C. 2118

25th Bde Machine Gun Company

WAR DIARY or INTELLIGENCE SUMMARY

(Erase heading not required.)

Instructions regarding War Diaries and Intelligence Summaries are contained in F. S. Regs., Part II. and the Staff Manual respectively. Title Pages will be prepared in manuscript.

Place	Date	Hour	Summary of Events and Information	Remarks and references to Appendices
MILLENCOURT	1-5-16	7 am	Running and Physical Drill.	
		9-11am	Tactical handling.	
		11-12 noon	Indication and Recognition of targets	
			O.C. Coy and Section commanders visited trenches & billets in ALBERT.	
	2.5.16	7am	Running and Physical Drill.	
		9-10am	Arm drill and Saluting drill.	
		10-11am	Gun drill.	
		11-12 noon	Tactical handling.	
			2/Lt. J.M.V. Buxton proceeded on leave to U.K.	
	3.5.16		Relieved 23rd Bde Machine Gun Company in trenches No.1/4 section in trenches remainder of company billeted in ALBERT. No.1. Gun in Bray St. registered on enemy trenches North of OVILLERS.	
	4.5.16		Indirect fire was brought to bear on the woods East of CONTALMAISON from OVILLERS POST.	
			Owing to the nature of the ground in this section of the line it is most difficult to get good machine gun positions to cover the front. Most of the new positions which were taken over are useless. Work is proceeding on new positions as fast as possible.	

1875 W: W593/326 1,000,000 4/15 J.B.C. & A. A.D.S.S./Forms/C. 2118.

WAR DIARY
or
INTELLIGENCE SUMMARY

(Erase heading not required.)

Army Form C. 2118

Instructions regarding War Diaries and Intelligence Summaries are contained in F. S. Regs., Part II. and the Staff Manual respectively. Title Pages will be prepared in manuscript.

Place	Date	Hour	Summary of Events and Information	Remarks and references to Appendices
	5.5.16	12 noon	Indirect fire was used from OVILLERS POST on OVILLERS 9 communication trenches.	
	6.5.16		Two Germans were seen walking on the sky line just before enemy stand to. A burst was fired at them & they threw themselves on the ground. After several minutes they got up & ran for it being followed by bursts of fire from the gun. Between 12 midnight & 1 am. our artillery bombarded the hostile trenches in accordance with a previously arranged scheme. The machine guns joined in & kept up a good fire on the enemy support & communication trenches. Several suspected dug-outs in the enemy's support line were fired on with good results. The communication trenches between OVILLERS & LA BOISSELLE were fired at intervals during the night.	
	7.5.16		A suspected field gun battery near OVILLERS was fired on from OVILLERS POST. After one felt low her fire the enemy commenced to search for its gun with 77 mm shells. Nos. 2 & 3 sections relieved Nos. 1 & 4 in the trenches.	
	8.5.16		During the night frequent bursts of fire were directed on the enemy's wire in front of OVILLERS were they were suspected to be working.	

Army Form C. 2118

WAR DIARY
or
INTELLIGENCE SUMMARY
(Erase heading not required.)

Instructions regarding War Diaries and Intelligence Summaries are contained in F.S. Regs., Part II. and the Staff Manual respectively. Title Pages will be prepared in manuscript.

Place	Date	Hour	Summary of Events and Information	Remarks and references to Appendices
	9.5.16		Indirect fire was used on OVILLERS during the day. At night the enemy wire & front line system of trenches were swept at frequent intervals.	
			Capt. W.B. Gray returned from leave.	
	10.5.16		During the morning and afternoon ranging fire was carried out on A.C. 2,9,3, guns 7 & 8 guns on OVILLERS. Rest firing indirect fire from an advanced position. Splendid observation was obtained on "Y" Sap. TABOISIERES & OVILLERS communication trenches & the prominent dugout.	
	11.5.16		2/Lieut. J.H.V. Buxton returned from leave.	
			Lieut. H.L. Heale proceeded on 7 days leave to U.K.	
			The company were relieved during the morning by 23rd Machine Gun Company and moved back to Divisional Reserve Area and billets in MILLENCOURT.	
MILLENCOURT	12.5.16		Cleaning guns kittts etc.	
	13.5.16	7 am	Running trenched drill	
		9-10am	Spectarian.	

Army Form C. 2118

WAR DIARY
or
INTELLIGENCE SUMMARY
(Erase heading not required.)

Instructions regarding War Diaries and Intelligence Summaries are contained in F. S. Regs., Part II. and the Staff Manual respectively. Title Pages will be prepared in manuscript.

Place	Date	Hour	Summary of Events and Information	Remarks and references to Appendices
METERENCOURT	13.5.16	10-11am	Semaphore & Signals.	
		11-12noon	Instruction recognition of targets.	
	14.5.16		Church Parade.	
	15.5.16	7am	Running & swedish Drill.	
		9-10am	Mechanism	
		10-11am	Semaphore & signals.	
		11-12noon	Indication & recognition of targets.	
	16.5.16		Pte McCarthy tried by F.G.C.M. for Drunkenness	
			2/Lieut. R.E. Howe proceeded on leave to England	
		7am	Running & swedish Drill	
		9-10am	Gun Drill	
		10-11am	Elementary instruction in Tactical Handling.	
		11-12noon	Indication & recognition of targets.	
	17.5.16	7am	Running & swedish Drill.	
		9-10am	Tactical handling across country with limbered wagons	
	18.5.16	7am	Running & swedish Drill	

Army Form C. 2118

WAR DIARY
or
INTELLIGENCE SUMMARY
(Erase heading not required.)

Instructions regarding War Diaries and Intelligence Summaries are contained in F. S. Regs., Part II. and the Staff Manual respectively. Title Pages will be prepared in manuscript.

Place	Date	Hour	Summary of Events and Information	Remarks and references to Appendices
MILLENCOURT	18.5.16	9-10am	Gun Drill.	
		10-11am	Indication & recognition of targets.	
		11-12noon	Fire orders at O.G. Coy revised Trenches to take over lines.	
MILLENCOURT	19.5.16	8am	Company moved to AUBERT and relieved 23rd Bde M.G Coy in Trenches	
Trenches			Indirect fire on OVILLERS. Direct fire on enemy communication trench	
			dug-outs & prominent objects	
	20.5.14		Indirect fire from OVILLERS POST on to DUMP east of OVILLERS.	
			Posts at work on alternative position for extreme right gun.	
			Traversed hostile parapet frequently during night also fixed bursts	
			at hostile communication trenches and Tramways. Cpl Lewin N°2 Section wounded	
			Rifle fire left hand	
	21.5.16		Fire directed on hostile reserve line frequently during night by indirect fire	
			Hostile communication trenches to left of NA 3 swept by fire at frequent intervals	
			Two Vickers guns taken up into the NA B in anticipation of hostile raid.	

1875 Wt. W593/826 1,000,000 4/15 J.B.C. & A. A.D.S.S./Forms/C. 2118.

WAR DIARY
or
INTELLIGENCE SUMMARY
(Erase heading not required.)

Army Form C. 2118

Place	Date	Hour	Summary of Events and Information	Remarks and references to Appendices
	22.5.16		Indirect fire on various points behind hostile lines.	
			No 5 Pavilion strengthened by concrete buttress.	
	23.5.16		Enemy's Machine guns very active during night.	
			Relief carried out about 1.45 p.m.	
			Fire directed on hostile trenches opposite NAB.	
			Indirect fire opened on various points behind hostile line.	
	24.5.16		Nothing of importance observed. A very quiet night.	
	25.6.16		Indirect fire position conducted on CONISTAN STREET.	
			Hostile trench mortars very active opposite left sector, several falling close to gun position.	
	26.5.16		Fire opened from concealed position in CONISTAN ST. on hostile communication trenches.	
			Very quiet night.	
			Hostile front line swept by traversing fire at frequent intervals.	
			Relief carried out. Company relieved by 70th Coy M.G.Cy.	
	27.5.16		Marched to HENNENCOURT WOOD to camp for training	

Army Form C. 2118

WAR DIARY
or
INTELLIGENCE SUMMARY
(Erase heading not required.)

Instructions regarding War Diaries and Intelligence Summaries are contained in F.S. Regs., Part II. and the Staff Manual respectively. Title Pages will be prepared in manuscript.

Place	Date	Hour	Summary of Events and Information	Remarks and references to Appendices
	28.5.16		Parade Church parade	
	29.5.16	7.7.45	Cleaning guns and equipment. Running sweedish Drill	
		9-10 am	Gun Drill and section drill. 10-11 am Mechanism 11-12.30 pm Wood fighting	
	30.5.16	7.7.45 am	Running sweedish Drill 9-10 am — 12.30 pm Tactical Handling	
			Visit Revt J.H. Butts preaches in camp to fire Macnamara admitted to Hospital	
	31.5.16	7.7.45 am	Running sweedish Drill 9.10 am Gun Drill 10-11 am Mechanism	
			11-12.30 pm Indication v recognition of targets	

8th, Division.

25th, Brigade.

25th, Machine Gun Co.

June, 1916.

To.
D.A.G. 3rd Echelon. G.H.Q.

Herewith the original copy of the 25th Coy. M.G. Corps' War Diary for the month of June 1916.

Walgray Capt.
O.C. 25th Coy. M.G. Corps.

25
2 Bde M G Coy
Vol 6

WAR DIARY
or
INTELLIGENCE SUMMARY

Army Form C. 2118

Place	Date	Hour	Summary of Events and Information	Remarks and references to Appendices
HENENCOURT WOOD	1.6.16	2.40.am	Company paraded for field operations in vicinity of TRANVILLERS & returned to camp about 11.30 am	
	2.6.16	7-7.45 am	Running & Swedish Drill 9-12.30 pm Tactical Handling. 2-3 pm Cleaning Guns. Lieut. A.H. Forbes returned from leave.	
	3.6.16	7-7.45 am	Running Swedish Drill 9-10 Belt-filling. 10-11 Fire Orders etc. 11-12.30 Signalling 2-3 pm Cleaning Guns.	
	4.6.16		Church parade. Company moved into billets in MILLENCOURT, vacated by 23rd M.G. Coy. being relieved in do. Wood by 70th M.G. Coy.	
MILLENCOURT	5.6.16	7-7.45 am	Running Swedish Drill 9-10. Semaphore Signals. 10-11. Gun Drill. 11-12 Indication & recognition of targets. 2-3 pm Belt-filling.	
	6.6.16	7-7.45 am	Running Swedish Drill 9-12.noon Tactical Handling. Pushing the attack 2-3 pm Cleaning Guns & Ammunition	
	7.6.16	7-7.45 am	Running Swedish Drill 9-10 am Gun Drill Section Drill. 10-11 am Indication & recognition of targets 11-12 noon Ammunition Supply 2-3 pm Gun Drill.	
	8.6.16	7-7.45 am	Running Swedish Drill 9-12 noon Cleaning Guns etc. Lieut. H.D. Batchelor proceeded on 7 days leave to U.K. 2-3 pm Elementary Instructions	

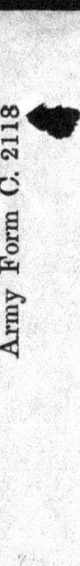

WAR DIARY or INTELLIGENCE SUMMARY

Army Form C. 2118.

Place	Date	Hour	Summary of Events and Information	Remarks and references to Appendices
MILLENCOURT	9.6.16		Running & Swedish Drill 9-10 a.m. Bell-filling 10-11 a.m. Mechanism 11-12 a.m. Immediate Action. 2-6 p.m. Range practice. Lieut J.L. Butler claims fire with 1X.	
	10.6.16	7pm	Running Swedish Drill 9-12 noon Tactical handling with Limbers	
	11.6.16		Church Parades	
	12.6.16		Relieved 23rd Bde Machine Gun Coy in Trenches. No 1 & 3 Sections in Trenches. No 2 & 4 Sections of the Company in billets in ALBERT. A noble working party was employed by 2 gun.	
	13.6.16		Very little firing could be done on account of the number of working parties in front of the trenches. Indeed fire was brought to bear on the enemy trenches in front of "NAB" also on supposed dumps in the enemy line. No 17589 Pte W. Kealty received a rifle bullet in the leg. During the night No 2 Gun was able to fire but no damage was done to danger to the enemy, shots were fired on at intervals.	
	14.6.16		No 3 Gun engaged an enemy Machine Gun which was firing from over LA BOISELLE Lieut H.V. Batcheloe believes from barrels the wire enemy was pushing	
	15.6.16		practically day & night at emplacements & dug out of an offensive very little firing was done during these four days	

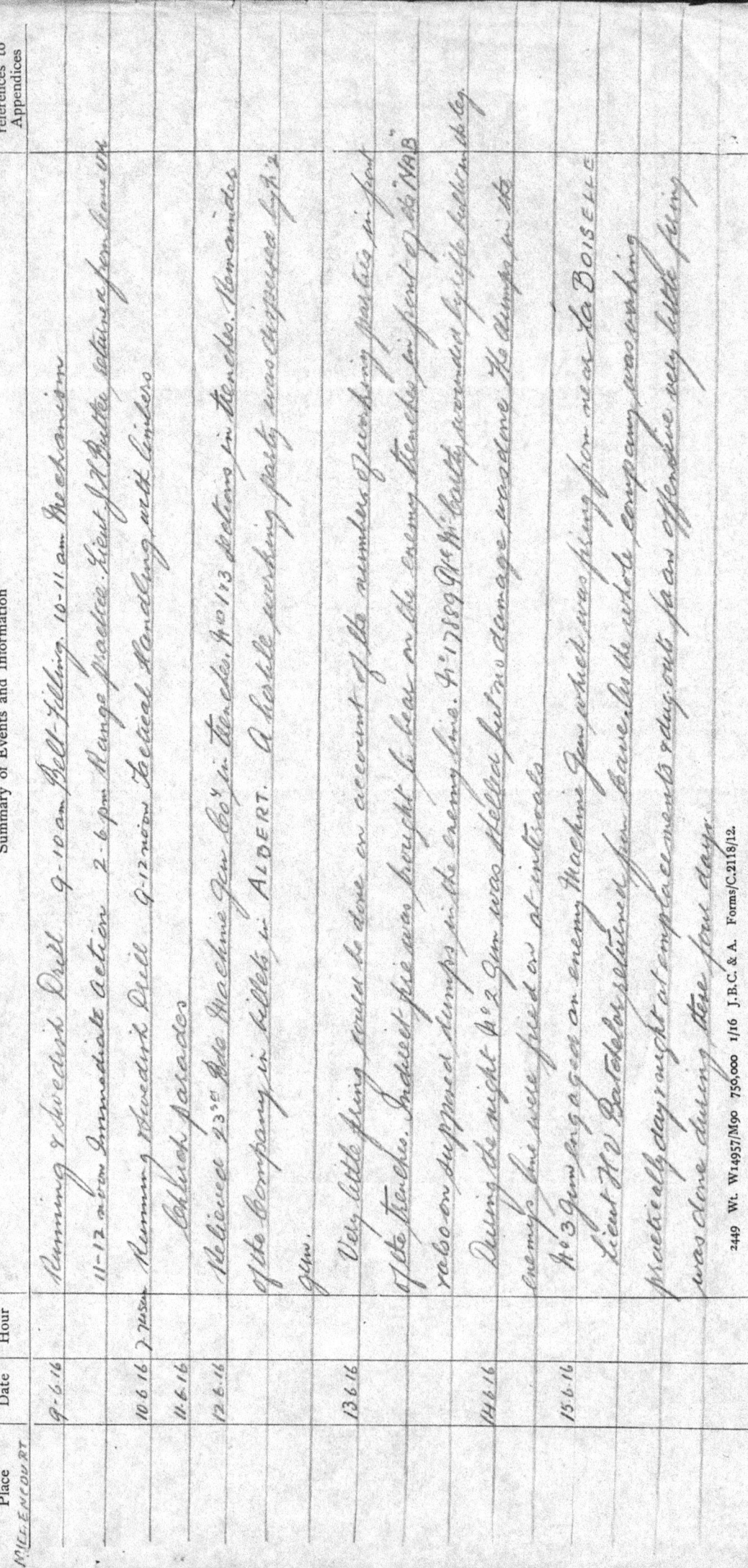

Army Form C. 2118.

WAR DIARY
or
INTELLIGENCE SUMMARY
(Erase heading not required.)

Instructions regarding War Diaries and Intelligence Summaries are contained in F.S. Regs., Part II. and the Staff Manual respectively. Title Pages will be prepared in manuscript.

Place	Date	Hour	Summary of Events and Information	Remarks and references to Appendices
	16.6.16		No 2 T.H. Section relieved No 1 & 3 in the trenches	
	17.6.16		Fire was brought to bear on German communication trenches at 1700+. Good observation was obtained. The enemy's wire was also swept at intervals. Working parties from the division in the trenches strengthened & improved the new battle positions & bombardment dug outs	
	18.6.16		Working parties were clearing away the earth in front of the loopholes of the new positions, having only 6 inches of dirt to be cleared away	
	19.6.16		There was no thing of any importance. The enemy was very quiet. Work was carried on of the new positions as before.	
	20.6.16		A rifle pointed was fired on with great effect. At enemy's "stand to" parties of the enemy were observed on their parapet in front of Ovillers. The cross fight & tear on them but the effect couldn't be observed to the light was too failing rapidly.	
	21.6.16		Work was still carried on on the positions & dug outs. The more thing of importance	
	22.5.16		Nothing of importance to report. Work as usual.	
	23.6.16		The two battle positions were taken over in X.7.C.9.5.2. X.7.C.9.4 X.7.a.15.5. X.13.a.3.37 X.14.53 X.7.b.15.75 X.7.d.11.8, X.7.C.4.9 15. Ref Maps 57d. S.E. 1/2000. The old positions were taken over as battle positions by the 23rd M.G. Coy on the night & the 10th M.G. Coy on the left. All the loopholes of the new positions were closely disguised with grass, sandbags etc. Nothing was broken out, except to test the positions. The remainder of the company moved from Killah in ALBERT at 10 pm. Bivouac in LONG VALLEY W1 & G. Ref Map 57 D. S.G. 2000. It was very wet & the men were very wet & most uncomfortable as the ground was wet & nobody had any cover except from their sheets.	

2449 Wt. W14957/Mgo 750,000 1/16 J.B.C. & A. Forms/C.2118/12.

Army Form C. 2118.

WAR DIARY
or
INTELLIGENCE SUMMARY

(Erase heading not required.)

Instructions regarding War Diaries and Intelligence Summaries are contained in F. S. Regs., Part II. and the Staff Manual respectively. Title Pages will be prepared in manuscript.

Place	Date	Hour	Summary of Events and Information	Remarks and references to Appendices
	23.6.16	cont.d	1 O.R. was wounded by Machine Gun fire on the left knee & left arm.	
	24.6.16		First day of the bombardment. Fire was kept up during the hours of darkness on the wire cut by our artillery & also on the communication trenches & Hoop trench & keep fires. There was very little retaliation.	
	25.6.16		Second day of bombardment. Nos 2 & 4 sections were relieved in the trenches by No. 1 & 3 at night. The men being conveyed to & from the trenches in G.S. Wagons. One N.C.O. of N.4 section was wounded by shell fire in the trenches at No 2 N.4 section were coming out of the trenches they were caught by lachrymatory shells at Ficheux Farm. There were no casualties the ordinary gas goggles found to be useless by the goggles of the box respirators were very effective. Lieut J.R. Butler L.G. Rifles & N.G. Corps was wounded in the wrist by splinter. Between the hours of 9 a.m. & 5 a.m. all the guns kept up a heavy fire on the enemy wire which was cut by the Artillery. No 5 gun in Kingsclere was killed frequently & on the 29th the enemy got a direct hit on it but there was no damage done to either gun or personnel.	
	26.6.16 27.6.16 28.6.16 29.6.16			
	30.6.16		At 10 p.m. the Company left the Lone Valley & marched to its assembly position in RIBBLE ST.	

25th Inf.Bde.
8th Div.

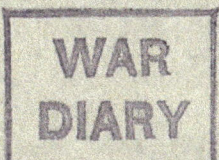

25th MACHINE GUN COMPANY.

J U L Y

1 9 1 6

2/

D.A.G. 3rd Echelon. G.H.Q.

Herewith original copy of the War Diary (A.F.C 2118) for the month of July 1916.

A copy of orders for the operation of 1st July is also enclosed.

W．．．．．． Capt
25th Machine Gun Company.

25th M G Coy

Vol 7

		Summary of Events and Information	Remarks and references to Appendices
7.16		The Company went into action with 9 Officers & 116 other ranks including the attached men. 1 Section was occupying the latter positions in RYCROFT ST. & CONISTON ST. 2 Section in LONGRIDGE ST. & 1 Section in BURY AVE. The guns kept up a heavy fire during the bombardment & after two hour (2.30am) moved into RIBBLE ST. 2 Section & Company Hd. Qrs. were in assembly positions in RIBBLE ST. At -0.20 No 2 Section moved to the front line trench to support the assaulting battalions and at -0.10 No 4 Section moved to FURNESS ST. preparatory to moving forward in support of the troops attacking the second objective. Owing to the very intense shell fire machine gun fire only two guns of No. 4 Section under 2/Lt. J.R.V. Buxton Rifle Brigade attd. to Machine Gun Corps, was able to carry on. Under 2/Lt. J.R.V. Buxton the two gun teams being covered. The guns & equipment were brought in after dark. 2/Lt Buxton was buried	

Army Form C. 2118

WAR DIARY
or
INTELLIGENCE SUMMARY
(Erase heading not required.)

Instructions regarding War Diaries and Intelligence Summaries are contained in F.S. Regs., Part II. and the Staff Manual respectively. Title Pages will be prepared in manuscript.

Place	Date	Hour	Summary of Events and Information	Remarks references to Appendices
	1.7.16	Cont⁴	am by his servant under very heavy fire. Although the servant was wounded himself in three places.	
			At 1.30 p.m. orders were issued by the Brigade for N°s 2 & 3 sections to go back to their battle positions & keep up a heavy fire on the battle line in rear & to reach communication trenches etc to prevent the enemy reinforcements coming up. Parties of the enemy were caught coming up over the open were swept out.	
			N° 2 & 4 sections were ordered to return to their positions in RIBBLE ST. The casualties of the Company during the action were 2 Lt. J. A. S. Preston wounded. 1 O.R. killed & 12 wounded.	
	2.7.16		About 6 a.m. the Company was relieved by the 34th Co. M.G. Corps & marched to the Long Valley. At 5 p.m. the company marched to DERNANCOURT & entrain	
	3.7.16		The Company entrained & detrained at AILLY-SUR-SOMME & marched	

Army Form C. 2118

WAR DIARY
or
INTELLIGENCE SUMMARY
(Erase heading not required.)

Instructions regarding War Diaries and Intelligence Summaries are contained in F.S. Regs., Part II. and the Staff Manual respectively. Title Pages will be prepared in manuscript.

Place	Date	Hour	Summary of Events and Information	Remarks and references to Appendices
	3/7/16	night	to ST. SAUVEUR where they bivouacked for the night	
	4/7/16	9 am	Company marched to RIENCOURT	
RIENCOURT	5/7/16		Cleaning guns, billets etc	
	6/7/16		The company marched to LONGEAU by sections at three hours interval & proceeded by train to PERNES, from there marched to MARLES-LES-MINES. The last section arriving at 6 a.m. on the 7th	
	7/7/16	5 pm	Company marched to BURBURE & then went into billets	
BURBURE	8/7/16		Cleaning billets &c. Clothing inspection. 2/Lt B.P. Ashurst joined company from base	
	9/7/16		Church parade	
	10/7/16	6 pm	Moved into other billets in the same village. Paraded under section officers. The company was inspected & addressed by the G.O.C. 8th Division.	
	11/7/16	7 am	Running the dirt drill. 9 am Semaphore, the Chavan. 2 am the Company Paraded for inspection of the Brigade by the G.O.C. 1st Army.	

Army Form C. 2118

WAR DIARY
or
INTELLIGENCE SUMMARY
(Erase heading not required.)

Instructions regarding War Diaries and Intelligence Summaries are contained in F.S. Regs., Part II. and the Staff Manual respectively. Title Pages will be prepared in manuscript.

Place	Date	Hour	Summary of Events and Information	Remarks and references to Appendices
BUR DURE	12/7/16		7am Running & Physical Drill 9am 12.30pm Elementary Training	
			No.1 Section on the range from 9am - 12.30pm	
	13/7/16		7-7.45am Running & Physical Drill 9am -12.30pm Tests of Elementary Training	
			No.2 Section on the range.	
	14/7/16		7-7.45am Running & Physical Drill 9am-12.30pm Occupation of various positions	
			by Machine Guns. No.3 Section on the range	
		2pm	Company matches v. BETHUNE & lifted there	
BETHUNE	15/7/16		7-7.45am Running & Physical Drill. 9am Cleaning billets generally.	
			Company paraded for Divine Service with remainder of Brigade	
			in the Municipal Kuiste. Service conducted by C.O.G 1st Army	
	16/7/16		7-7.45am Running & Physical Drill 9am-12.30pm Gun Drill, Indicanes & Signalling	
	17/7/16		7-7.45am Running & Physical Drill 9am-7.30pm Gun Drill 1.30pm-3pm Belt filling	
	18/7/16		7-7.45am Running & Physical Drill 9am-12.30pm Gun Drill Company Drill & Semaphore.	
			The Commander in Chief has awarded the Military Cross to 81472 L.C.G. Ashton for setting in the commencement of the action of gallant conduct in the presence of the enemy from the commencement of the action.

Camp a Oye in France to 25th June 1916.

WAR DIARY
or
INTELLIGENCE SUMMARY
(Erase heading not required.)

Army Form C. 2118

Place	Date	Hour	Summary of Events and Information	Remarks and references to Appendices
BETHUNE	20-7-16	7 - 7.45 am	Running shueduit Drill. 9am - 12.30 pm Elementary tactical handling	
	21/7/16		The Company marched to VERMELLES & relieved the no 60 M.G Corps. 12.9mo going into the line 2 Hd Qts & the remaining 4 guns kept in the Brewery	
TRENCHES	22.7.16		Indirect fire was carried out on the following points :- Cross roads & Junction south of HAISNES. Cross Roads S.E of AVCHY. Road from HAISNES to AVCHY. LE2-LA BASSÉE. The enemy's snipers machine guns were very active during the night	Map Ref: France 36ᵗʰ NW Sultan 7A. 1/20 000
	23-7-16		1 O.R wounded rifle fire Indirect fire was carried out on the following points :- A.30.a.0.4 - A.30.b.5.2 - A.29.a.6.7 - A.30.a.2.9, A.6.a.2.9 - A.6.d.5.9, A.29.a.3.2 - A.23.a.5.2. A.29.a.5.1.- A.29.a.2.2, A.5.b.4.4 - A.6.a.1.5 In conjunction with machine fire was directed on cross roads at G.6.c.69.	
		10am	The Dump was also fired on frequently. The enemy's snipers & M.Gs were	

WAR DIARY or INTELLIGENCE SUMMARY

Army Form C. 2118

Place	Date	Hour	Summary of Events and Information	Remarks and references to Appendices
TRENCHES Contd			intermittently. Active during the night. One of our guns was shelled out	
	24/7/16		H.E. & Shrapnel was fired to cover firing. Indirect fire was called against :- A.30.d.45.H., B.25.c.7.2. - H.10.75.b, S.6.B.0.8. Fire was also directed against :- A.29.c.H.6, The DUMP, S.6.a.3.5, S.6.B.0.8, S.6.D.7.5.9, S.6.a.9.5.	
	25/7/16		During the night, there was a very marked decrease in the amount of enemy MG fire. Between 10 pm & 11.30 pm transport was heard behind the enemy lines. Bursts of fire were directed on the roads behind the enemy lines. The DUMP was fired on at frequent intervals. In case of fire was called out on the following points :- S.6.L.0.8, S.6.a.2.9 - S.6.a.5.9, S.6.a.7.5 - S.6.a.9.5, A.29.a.3.2. - A.23.a.5.2, B.5.L.H.H. S.6.a.1.5	Ref. Maps 36ᴺᵂ Sketch 7ᵃ Zone
	26/7/16		Two of our gun positions were heavily shelled during the night. Indirect fire was called out in sonce direction & enemy commenced to open his behind his own lines. The DUMP was also fired on.	

Army Form C. 2118

WAR DIARY
or
INTELLIGENCE SUMMARY
(Erase heading not required.)

Instructions regarding War Diaries and Intelligence Summaries are contained in F. S. Regs., Part II. and the Staff Manual respectively. Title Pages will be prepared in manuscript.

Place	Date	Hour	Summary of Events and Information	Remarks and references to Appendices
TRENCHES	27.7.16		Indirect fire was carried out on the following points:- G30 b 52, G29 d 00, x junction G5a26, G6t08, G30 a04 - G30 b 52	
			One Gas engagement was tried. Hostile finally closed in	
	26.7.16		Lieut. H. Hollis Macrectis Bdg. one MG Coy & one OR were killed by a shell in the Form Indirect fire was carried out on the following points:- G6 a 65 - G30 a 35.4, G6 d 4.25. G6 a 6.5, H 7 a 3.6. H6 7 a 7.7, A 30 a 45.4, G6 39, G6 e 88	M 1/4 map Sheet 36 NW S. Ection 7A.
			The Quarry was heavily shelled during the day. Hostile MGs were more active in searching the Sunken Village lines	
	29.7.16		Hostile Machine Guns were again more active than usual. Heavy transport was heard near the DUMP between 10.30pm - 11 pm. The Quality was generally possibly hostile indirect fire was carried out through the night on roads & communications to the front line enemy line	
	30.7.16		About 9pm the enemy commenced a bombardment of the left of the brigade area. Two guns immediately came into action from their arrived positions shortly afterwards another did shrine rotty kept up a heavy fire on the enemy Trenches. The enemy tank employing harassing fire. When the bombardment appeared to be telling another gun formed in and also swept the enemy land. Indirect fire was also kept up on the hostile communications behind the DUMP. It was	

Army Form C. 2118

WAR DIARY
or
INTELLIGENCE SUMMARY

(Erase heading not required.)

Instructions regarding War Diaries and Intelligence Summaries are contained in F.S. Regs., Part II. and the Staff Manual respectively. Title Pages will be prepared in manuscript.

Place	Date	Hour	Summary of Events and Information	Remarks and references to Appendices
TRENCHES	30/7/16	cont.	Learned afterwards that the enemy attempted a raid but was unsuccessful. The gun in the huay was hit by a shell but worked out through into action in the reserve line. Over 11,000 rounds were fired.	
	31/7/16		Indirect fire was kept up to keep up fresh communication trenches behind the enemy lines. The enemy were very quiet. Hotch. M.G.s were actively between 12 mid-night & 2 am.	

Wellington Craft
O.C. 25th Company Machine Gun Corps

1875 Wt. W593/826 1,000,000 4/15 J.B.C. & A. A.D.S.S./Forms/C. 2118.

Operation Orders for Offensive Operations.

I.

8 Guns will be used during the 5 days bombardment previous to the Infantry Assault.

These guns will be distributed as follows.

4. Guns of No 3 Section (Lieut J.H. Butler & 2/Lieut H.W. Hobbs) will be in RYECROFT STREET.

2. Guns of No 1 Section (Lieut J. Halley) will be in LONGRIDGE STREET.

2. Guns of No 1 Section (Lieut A.H. Neale) will be in BURY AVENUE.

These guns will keep up a fire on the hostile trenches in rear of Front line and special points at night to prevent enemy repairing wire.

The hostile front line trenches will be swept by rifle fire and Lewis Guns to prevent wire mending.

When the infantry has reached the 1st line of trenches and covering fire is no longer practicable the 8 guns mentioned above will be moved as rapidly as possible by the shortest routes to reserve positions in RIBBLE STREET. Those from RYECROFT STREET moving via CONISTAN - RIVINGTON to RIBBLE STREET Those from LONGRIDGE STREET, via LONG STREET RIVINGTON STREET to RIBBLE STREET. Those from BURY AVENUE via ROCK STREET - GLASGOW Rd - CONISTAN STREET. RIVINGTON STREET.

During preliminary bombardment No 2 & 4 Sections will be in dug-outs in RIBBLE STREET.

At -05 No 2 Section will move to front line via JOHN O'GAUNTS. BARROW STREET and FURNESS STREET. After the two assaulting Battalions have taken the German front-line trench, these guns will advance to positions in hostile line from which covering fire can be brought to bear on 1st Objective the best positions will probably be between points (55). (71). (88). (95) & (02). Strong points to be consolidated in first objective are Pts. 44, 47, 78. Also in rear Pts. 10 & 56

2.

When the infantry have reached the first objective these guns will move there and support that line

No 4 Section will move to the front line via WENNING STREET & PENDLE HILL STREET immediately following "C" Battalion and follow in rear of that Battalion to the 1st Objective

O.C. No 2 Section must bear in mind that it may not be advisable to move his guns right to the 1st Objective immediately, as opportunities may occur of better covering fire being directed from positions in rear to cover the advance of our infantry to the 2nd Objective

When the infantry have reached the 2nd Objective No 4 Section will move forward and support them constructing positions so as to be able to bring a heavy fire on any counter attack the enemy may make. Strong points will be. 22. 28. 46 & 43

No 3 section will receive orders to move forward and take up positions occupied by No 2 Section No 2 Section will then move forward to 2nd Objective and consolidate that line.

When the 3rd Objective has been reached No 4 Section will move to that position and consolidate

No 1. Section will move forward immediately in rear of "D" Battalion moving to the 3rd Objective when it has been taken by the infantry and consolidating their guns in that position. Strong points will be. 91, 09, trench junction near point 80 and east corner of orchard near 97 Pt.

Lieut R.H. Forbes will move forward immediately behind No 2 Section and establish advance Company

Headquarters first at point (88) thence to (144) then to (28)

O.C. Company will be at Brigade Headquarters until the last section has moved, after that he will move forward and take up the above mentioned advance Company Headquarters as the operation progress.

Carrying parties will begin to move belt boxes forward as soon as advance Co. H.Q. has been established thus a continual chain of ammunition will be moved up by short stages

The Sergt Major will be in charge of the Ammunition supply from Company Headquarters Four Belt filling machines will be in use there. Empty belt boxes to be sent back by carrying party after leaving full boxes with guns.

Very pistols to be stored at Coy H.Q. also Cartridges for same. A supply of water and oil will also be at H.Q. and sent forward to guns as necessary

O.C section will ensure that each N.C.O. and man carries his oil bottle in his haversack full of oil.

Section officers will ensure that all N.C.O's understand the scheme of attack thoroughly and that the Special Map issued has been thoroughly explained to them.

8th, Division.

25th, Brigade.

25th, Machine Gun Co.

August, 1916.

23rd Machine Gun Coy

Army Form C. 2118

WAR DIARY
or
INTELLIGENCE SUMMARY
(Erase heading not required.)

Instructions regarding War Diaries and Intelligence Summaries are contained in F.S. Regs., Part II. and the Staff Manual respectively. Title Pages will be prepared in manuscript.

Vol 8

Place	Date	Hour	Summary of Events and Information	Remarks and references to Appendices
TRENCHES	August 1st		Indirect fire was carried out on the following points: O.x.g.e.7.3., O.30.d.6.4., G.6.d.4.3., H.7.O.36 – H.7.a.7.7, PARSIVAL ALLEY, GERMAN TRENCH, DUMP, SLAG ALLEY, ZEPPELIN ALLEY, MAD ALLEY, LONE TARM, AUCHY. Over 11,000 rounds being fired.	Maps Refs 36" NW 70000 Edition 7A
	2nd		Indirect fire was carried out on single score points & communication trenches through out the night. Over 10,000 rounds were fired.	
	3rd		Fire was brought to bear on various points & communication trenches behind the enemy lines. 10,000 rounds were fired.	
	4th		10,000 rounds were fired on various junctions etc behind the enemy lines.	
	5th		Indirect fire was carried out on AUCHY & CO on various tactical spots & communication trenches in the enemy lines. 10,000 rounds were fired.	
	6th		Indirect fire was carried out on tactical points & communication trenches in the enemy lines. The company was relieved by the 23rd Machine Gun Company & marched to billets in FOUQUEREUIL.	

Army Form C. 2118

WAR DIARY
or
INTELLIGENCE SUMMARY

(Erase heading not required.)

25th Machine Gun Coy

Instructions regarding War Diaries and Intelligence Summaries are contained in F.S. Regs., Part II. and the Staff Manual respectively. Title Pages will be prepared in manuscript.

Place	Date	Hour	Summary of Events and Information	Remarks and references to Appendices
FOUQUEREUIL	7th		Cleaning guns & billets etc.	
	8th	7.7.45 am	Running & Swedish Drill. 9-12 noon Gun Drill. Semaphore Signals	
			Squad & Coy Drill. No. 1 Section on the range	
	9th	7.7.45 am	Running & Swedish Drill. 9-12 noon Judging distances & tactical handling	
		12-12.30 pm	Lecture & demonstration of sights etc. No. 1 Section on the range.	
	10th	7.7.45 am	Running & Physical Drill. 12-12.30 pm Lecture & Demonstration of	
			Range cards & Tactical Handling. Construction of sketch & distance	
			Indirect fire. No. 2 Section on the range.	
	11th	7.7.45 am	Running & Physical Drill. 9-12.30 pm Range taking & tactical	
			Handling. No. 3 Section on the range	
	12th	7.7.45 am	Running & Physical Drill. 9-12.30 pm Indication & recognition	The Rich DFT (wounded) and Spr Parker awarded Military Medals
			targets. Tactical Handling. No. 4 Section on the range.	
	13th		Church Parade at 10.35 am. C.S.M. Sexton presented with Military Cross ribbon & Pte Parker	
			and Military Medal by Major General Hudson C.B. C.I.E. G.O.C. 8th Division	

Machine Gun Coy

WAR DIARY
or
INTELLIGENCE SUMMARY
(Erase heading not required.)

Army Form C. 2118

Instructions regarding War Diaries and Intelligence Summaries are contained in F.S. Regs., Part II. and the Staff Manual respectively. Title Pages will be prepared in manuscript.

Place	Date	Hour	Summary of Events and Information	Remarks and references to Appendices
FOUQUEREUIL	13th		LIEUT. R.H. FORBES proceeded to CAMIERS for an advanced course at the Machine Gun School.	
	14th		Nos. 2 & 3 Relievo proceeded to VERMELLES. Hence to the QUARRIES SECTION of the Trenches & relieved the guns of the 20th M.G. Coy in the Trenches. During the night these reliefs maintained Indirect fire on hostile communication trenches. The DUMP, also on G.6.B.t S.t. & G.5.B.4t.2	Map Ref. SHEET 36 N.W. TRENCH MAP SCALE 1/10,000 Edition 2.A
			2nd Lt. Goodwin & 7th Lt. King joined the Company.	
VERMELLES	15th		H.Q. No. 1 & H. Section relieved 2nd M.G. Co. at VERMELLES. H.Q. Cellar in STREET No. 6 near VERMELLES.	
			CHURCH. Indirect fire was carried out as follows: SLAG ALLEY, PARSEVAL, ZEPPELIN, CITE ST ELIE & HULLUCH & other communication trenches; also on CROSS ROADS at H.13 D.6.5, G.6.B.t.8t.	
			A.29 B.3½.5½, H.13 A.6.8, H.7 D.5.4.1, H.13 B.3.5.9. 10,000 rounds were fired.	
			2nd Lt. Mackenzie joined the Company.	
	16th		During the night Indirect fire was carried out on the following points. Communication trenches. The DUMP, LA BASSEE ROAD, CITE ST ELIE, G.6.c.5.8 & G.6.A.7.5 6.5. 17,150 rounds fired.	
	17th		Indirect fire was brought to bear on tramway at G.5.D.5.65 communication trenches between CITE ST ELIE & HULLUCH CROSS ROADS at A.29 A.4.5, 3.4 Junction of ROAD & RAILWAY at A.28 D.7.5.7 also on G.6 C.6.8.t. A hostile M.G. was located firing over G.185 & silenced by one of our guns which fired at the flash.	

Army Form C. 2118

23rd Machine Gun Coy

WAR DIARY
or
INTELLIGENCE SUMMARY
(Erase heading not required.)

Place	Date	Hour	Summary of Events and Information	Remarks and references to Appendices
VERMELLES	18th		Indirect fire was employed against ZEPPELIN ALLEY ROAD at G.5.a. & CROSS ROADS at C.6.B.5.t. v at A.29.D.2.3. Four German M.G's firing from the Dump swept the HULLUCH ROAD. 6,750 rounds were fired.	
	19th		During the night indirect fire was maintained on following points behind enemys lines:- ROAD at G.6.C.3.1, PEKIN TRENCH H.7.A.2.9, G.5.B.5.1, B.6.A.7.3, CROSS ROADS at A.29.B.3½.5½ & C.5.D.4.2. Trench at C.6.C.3.1 was enfiladed. 7,250 rounds were fired. The enemy made use of a searchlight at 9.30 p.m. from behind the Dump. Hostile M.G's worked to HULLUCH ROAD. Lieut. R.H. Forbes appointed to command 102nd Machine Gun Company.	
	20th		Gas was released at 11.30 p.m. to right left of HULLUCH ROAD. No of our guns fired to conceal the noise of escaping gas & sweep any supports coming up over the open. Fire was directed on the following points B.17.A.3.5, C.5.D.2.2, C.5.D.3.5, & H.13.A.6.5. H.7.D & H yielded German trenches 10,250 rounds were fired. No enemy used a combination red & green rocket as a gas alarm. Search lights were again seen behind the enemys lines. 10 R prevented during the night.	

WAR DIARY or INTELLIGENCE SUMMARY

Army Form C. 2118

25th Machine Gun Coy

Place	Date	Hour	Summary of Events and Information	Remarks and references to Appendices
VERMELLES	21st		Throughout the night our M.G' played on points behind the enemy's lines nearly 5000 rounds were fired. The night was normal	
	22nd		Indirect fire was maintained on the following points LOOS-AUCHY ROAD; FOSSE 8 & PARSONS ALLEY & PEKIN TRENCH HOUSE N.E. again swept the HULLUCH ROAD. Three sielllights were observed E. of HULLUCH.	
	23rd		Indirect fire was maintained on the following points. All the communication trenches mentioned under 22nd unit also H1 D.61 Mobile B. G's were not M active as usual. It was noticed that the 2 M G's which swept HULLUCH ROAD Regularly also kept up nightly Indirect fire was kept up behind the enemy's lines on other side of the HULLUCH ROAD being that position where the 2nd RIFLE BRIGADE attempted to raid German trenches	
	24th		At CHQR H.7.C, H.7 & H.13.A & H.13.B followed actively fire was returned. In LA BASSEE ROAD H.8.A.1.15, H.1A.6.1 About 37,000 rounds were fired.	
	25th		One M G emplacement at junction of 7.0.6 & CHAPEL ALLEY was hit by truck shell. 5 0.C. from 6.30 p.m. to 9.30 p.m. No damage was done Indirect fire was brought to bear on various enemy communication trenches & on CROSS ROADS at H.1.D, & S.N.V.CITE ST ELIE the night was remarkably quiet.	

23rd Machine Gun Coy

Army Form C. 2118.

WAR DIARY
or
INTELLIGENCE SUMMARY.
(Erase heading not required.)

Instructions regarding War Diaries and Intelligence Summaries are contained in F. S. Regs., Part II. and the Staff Manual respectively. Title pages will be prepared in manuscript.

Place	Date	Hour	Summary of Events and Information	Remarks and references to Appendices
VERMELLES	25th Sept		Hostile M.G. activity was fairly normal on A.G. swept the HULLUCH ROAD.	
	26th		Indirect fire was carried out against hostile communication trenches & CROSS ROADS at A30 D 3 4. At 5.30 pm a party of Germans was seen at A7 A15 making N.E. Indirect fire on German 2nd line trench, support trench at H8.A.10.15. TRACK across fields from HAISNES to CITE E.2.1.E. 8 yards from N.E. between 5.10 pm & 6.50 pm	
	27th			
	28th	1 pm	Indirect parties of Germans were seen moving N.E. between 5.10 pm & 6.50 pm. Indirect fire was maintained during the night on HAISNES-AUCHY ROAD, AUCHY-CORONS & PEKIN ROAD & tramway running South communication trenches leaving tracks & shunting noises at H.8.A.O.7.	
	29th	7.30 pm	Indirect fire against path in Cité ST ELIE at A.7.A.3.3. HAISNES-AUCHY ROAD, G.6.B.3.7.1. The night was quiet. LIEUT. M.E. COOPER appointed 2nd in command of the Company	
	30th		Indirect fire on HAISNES-AUCHY ROAD, AUCHY-CORONS on PEKIN ROAD & tramway at A.29. D 2 2 2 double communication trench.	
	31st		The 23rd M.G. Company believed the Guards gun Company in the trenches. Two sections proceed to REBECQ to FOUQUEREUIL	

W.E. Turner
CAPT
O.C. 23-M.G. Coy

8th, Division.

25th, Brigade.

25th, Machine Gun Co.

September, 1916.

25th Machine Gun Company
Army Form C. 2118.

WAR DIARY
or
INTELLIGENCE SUMMARY
(Erase heading not required.)

Place	Date	Hour	Summary of Events and Information	Remarks and references to Appendices
VERMELLES	Sept 1st		The remaining two sections of the Company & Headquarters relieved by the 23rd Machine Gun Coy. Proceeded to billets at FOUQUEREUIL. Rest of the Company at FOUQUIERES & charge of interlocking M.G. Company.	
FOUQUEREUIL	2nd		Clothing Inspection & Gun equipment by the O.C. Sections marching over inspected by Section Commanders. Six men from each Battalion of the Brigade attached to the Company	
	3rd	9-10 am	Cleaning of Equipment Church Parade (C of E) in the Field at 11.15 am R.C. in billets at 9 am	
	4th	Paid at 7 am	Running & Physical exercise cancelled owing to weather.	
		9.12.30 pm	Immediate action Gun mounting Semaphore During the night of 3rd/4th heavy bombardment was heard from south of 2nd Divl. front & early morning parade for Running & Sweeper Drill 7.45 — 9.12.30 pm	
	5th		Drill, Inspection & practice in using Gas Helmets & Box Respirators. Baths at FOUQUIERES allotted to the Company from 2-6 pm	
	6th		Running & Swedish exercise from 7-7.45 am 9-12.30 pm Lecture handling of Gun (Vin v Div y D2h) MAP of places BETHUNE (continued next) 36.B.N.E. Lecture on	

Army Form C. 2118.

WAR DIARY
or
INTELLIGENCE SUMMARY.
(Erase heading not required.)

Place	Date	Hour	Summary of Events and Information	Remarks and references to Appendices
FOUQUEREUIL	6th		Identification by Patrol Officers Horse Racing Competition, 12 Bn Coy. H.Q. also contest between Pte. ISSETT and Cpl. ROGERS. (ISETT won on points)	
	7th		Early parades for running, swedish exercise from 7 to 7.45 am Cleaning billets. 10-12.30 pm Indication & Recognition. Making of attack. Defence of Post. Lt. BATCHELOR posted to 9th Bn 9 Coy. on arrival in Command of Coy. company today. Final of Horse Racing Competition. Pte. BELL winning. Tens & other Contests won by Cpl. DEVEREAUX & SGT. LEONARD.	
VERMELLES	8th		Relieved the 24th Machine Gun Company in the HOHENZOLLERN SECTOR. Sections 1, 2 & 3 with H.Q. parading at 8. a.m. Section 4 paraded at 12.30. p.m. Relief complete by 3.30 pm. Twelve guns in Reserve Village lines. Four guns in Brewery (VERMELLES) also H.Q. Paid by E LANCS. on German front line.	
	9th		Partially successful. One gun press lifted by 24th Bn 9 Co's on top of offensive purposes during the raid. Indirect fire was carried out on the following points. Tramways at G.4.c.3. 3½. G.3.a.8½. 8½. & 12.b.77 Railway crossing head at A.26.d.77. Cross Roads A.29.d.2. 2½. & Dumps at G.5.L.8.8. Relief taken by E. LANCS. took place	

Army Form C. 2118.

WAR DIARY
or
INTELLIGENCE SUMMARY.
(Erase heading not required.)

Place	Date	Hour	Summary of Events and Information	Remarks and references to Appendices
VERMELLES	9th Cont.d		The enemy sent up one Green rocket. Retaliation consisted chiefly of Trench Mortar bombs. Very little machine gun fire on the part of the enemy. Bombs fired 11,500 Rds.	
	10th		Indirect fire was carried out during the night on Dumps at G5 c 87 and C6 b 63. Tramways at A29 c 65.2. A29 a 37. C6 c 4 92. Cross Roads South of HAISNES A30 d 45. 4 x C5 b 52 & Trenches C5 b 63, f C6 L C5 d 8, H7 a 36 ξ H7 a 77. TIRPITZ TRENCH who also marched. During the night 9th-10th enemy machine guns showed more activity. Weather still somewhat muggy, 9/I N.C.O's & men supplied last day for work on Salvage Dumps all spent time now the effort on providing more comfort in the building for want... Rounds fired 10,000.	
	11th		At 2.30 AM heavy bombardment by our guns supporting a raid made by the 32nd Div on our left. Indirect fire at intervals throughout the night on Dumps at G5 c 87 x G5 b 63. x Roads at C5 b 62. Tramways at G2 d 77. A29 c 65.2. x C6 c 4 92. x Roads between G5 L 385 x G1 C E 8. x H7 a 36. H7 a 77. Also on enemy communication & support trenches opposite G5.3. G5 4. G55 x G56.	

Army Form C. 2118.

WAR DIARY
or
INTELLIGENCE SUMMARY.
(Erase heading not required.)

Instructions regarding War Diaries and Intelligence Summaries are contained in F.S. Regs., Part II. and the Staff Manual respectively. Title pages will be prepared in manuscript.

Place	Date	Hour	Summary of Events and Information	Remarks and references to Appendices
VERMELLES	11th and 12th		Ammunition expended 12,750 Rds. Enemy machine gun activity normal.	
	12th		The following points received attention by machine gun fire. Tramway Junction B.12.L.77. Dumps at B.5.C.8.7 & B.29.C.23.35. Heads of A.30.b.52. A.29.a.20.25. A.51.b.52. Roads B.5.C. 40.25. A.29.a.43. Communications & Support trenches opposite C.53. C.54. C.55 & C.56. Rounds fired 13,750. Enemy Snipers pretty active. Enemy machine gunfire normal. On right front unregistered aerial shots in neighbourhood of M.G. emplacement R.2 (near junction of "O.B." & "Gordon Alley") Notes reinforcement of parapet	
	13th		Ctr. treat hampered by Bt. H.Q. to map making. Baths for below R.Y. H.Q. in Breury. Recent fire was kept up through the night on the following points & areas A.29.a.20.25. x A.30.a.5.2. Brickwork at A.28.a.30.45. Tramway Junction B.12.d.77. & roads B.5.C.94. & A.29. & A.19. Enemy very quiet	
	14th		Quiet & field in shelling & sniping of the railway embany A.28.d.77. & on C.5.I. 40.25. Road traversed from A.28.C. 36 & A.29.a.77 & track junction H.I.C.8.5. A.30.C.99 & A.24.C.75.40.	

WAR DIARY
or
INTELLIGENCE SUMMARY.

(Erase heading not required.)

Army Form C. 2118.

Instructions regarding War Diaries and Intelligence Summaries are contained in F. S. Regs., Part II. and the Staff Manual respectively. Title pages will be prepared in manuscript.

Place	Date	Hour	Summary of Events and Information	Remarks and references to Appendices
VERMELLES	15th		Indirect fire maintained on road junction & communication trenches in vicinity of A.23.c.90.65. A.29.L.85.50 & A.28.d.77.65.a.9.9. supply dumps near between C.5.c.80.25 & C.6.b.05.80 & A.29.b.20.75 F.A.20.b.15.24. also received attention.	
	16th		Indirect fire on hostile trenches A.28.d.77.65 A.99. Bomb stores A.3.1.N.N.5. A.29.d.22L Strathcona Communication trenches A.30.b.52.3 and A.30.a.32.5. W 400 & 500 at A.30.L.52.2 and West from A.29.L.27.75. F.A.30.L.15.25. Watch Tower mortars.	
	17th		Considerable movement of enemy transport heard. Indirect fire on French tramways A.29.a.7.3. & A.29.L.3.7 and roads B.5.L.4.2 tramways, roads and communication trenches at B.6.L.4.3. & A.23.C.1.2L. Tramway on CORONS DE MARON & ROAD. W. of HAISNES. Enemy transport heard on CITE ST ELIE-DOUVRIN. Several heavy mortars fell in QUARRY. Open emplacement in square below rev building dug out.	
	18th		Indirect fire on supply dumps C.5.C.88. VERMELLES-AUCHY rd. A.29.a.10.6. A.29.a.9.6L. 6000 rd. Tramways & trenches A.30.L.5.2.3. and A.30.A.3.2.5. 6000 rd. HAISNES. 5000 rd. N. of CITE ST ELIE. 1 round fired 1500 Mobile machine gun mine below Watch story trench mortar caserne may retire by night between two lights near building support.	

Army Form C. 2118.

WAR DIARY
or
INTELLIGENCE SUMMARY.
(Erase heading not required.)

Place	Date	Hour	Summary of Events and Information	Remarks and references to Appendices
VERMELLES.	18th		Captain W.E. Grey M.C. proceeded on leave to United Kingdom.	
	19th		Indirect fire on cross roads and trenches S. of HAISNES A.30.b.55.25 & A.30.d.4.55. Tench Tramway A.29.c.7.3. & A.29.a.3.7. Cross roads 3 INNS A.29.c.22.2. Road Junction S. of HAISNES A.20.a. N. of C.т.E. St ELIE Avenue fired 21000. Hostile trenches guns were more active than usual during the early part of the night. When our bombardment became intense the enemy sent up 35 rockets and fired bursts in two & fours 2 Red 1 Red & green. 2 Red. Enemy building dugouts under R.E. trenches & gun positions repaired.	
	20th		Indirect fire on Tramway A.29.d.05 Tramway A.29.a.70.05 Track and Junction of communication trench A.29.d.7.3. Road & Trench Junction at G.5.C.9.2.4. Tramway Junction at C.12.d.77. Road Junction S. of HAISNES at A.30.d.3.4. Sixteen new Building dugouts under R.E. for Employment built at entrance to QUARRY ALLEY. Rounds fired 13500.	
	21st		Indirect fire on Trench Tramway junction A.29.d.75.75. Cross Roads A.29.c.35.55. Tracks and junction of communication trenches A.29.a.7c.8 Junction of communication trenches and road at A.29.a.9.7. Road N. of C.т.E. St ELIE H.7.a.7.7 & H.1.c.8.5.	

2353 Wt. W2544/1454 700,000 5/15 D. D. & L. A.D.S.S. Forms/C. 2118.

Army Form C. 2118.

WAR DIARY
or
INTELLIGENCE SUMMARY.
(Erase heading not required.)

Instructions regarding War Diaries and Intelligence Summaries are contained in F. S. Regs., Part II. and the Staff Manual respectively. Title pages will be prepared in manuscript.

Place	Date	Hour	Summary of Events and Information	Remarks and references to Appendices
VERMELLES	22nd		Rounds fired 12.00. Machine Gun Fire on hostile new building dug-outs under R.E. supervision, alternate positions chosen. Indirect fire on tramway 856 & H. 77 mm battery at A.23.6.4.6. Battalion Head quarters & horse loading post A.29.a.15.20. Dump at A.29.a.15.80 C.12 & 77.A.30.d.3.4. Rounds fired 12,000. Sixteen new building dugouts under R.E. Trench disposed at R.56. Alternate positions chosen. Gun emplacement at V.M.1 completed.	
	23rd		Indirect fire on tramway crossroads and reported 77 mm battery position at A.23.C.4.6. Gun battery position A.29.B.2.2 & G.5.2.8.8 A.23.C.4.6. C.6.a.40.05 and indirect firing A.29.6.0.0.95. Considerable activity throughout the night early morning. Indirect fire on trench junction at A.29.65.0 A.29.6.7.3.6 A.29.a.3.7 along tramway. Emplaces enforced trenches one fence A.23.C.1.d. The enemy showed considerable activity, but with artillery.	
	at 24		LEFT BOYAU were shelled by 5.9 howitzer. They gave particular attention to the exit house in the line. Enemy machine gun fire was normal. Couple of battle emplacements increased. Stone & alternate emplacement to VILLAGE LINE piecewise. After latter half Allegacy & R.55 position putted down rebuilt & placed fresh.	

2353 Wt. W2544/1454 700,000 5/15 D. D. & L.   A.D.S.S./Forms/C. 2118.

Army Form C. 2118.

WAR DIARY
or
INTELLIGENCE SUMMARY.
(Erase heading not required.)

Place	Date	Hour	Summary of Events and Information	Remarks and references to Appendices
VERMELLES	24th Cont'd		2/Lt MACNAMARA proceeded to England on 10 days leave. Lead cover put on light men supplied for work under R.E on dug out near QUARRY ALLEY and also new dug out. O.B.H. party at work putting in billets.	
	25th		Indirect fire suspected H.O. at A29 L 5.2. Railway junction A29 a 3.6.5. Railway road A28 d 7.7. L.6.5. 2.9.9 Crossroads 6.5 L 4.2 Watts machine gun very active during the night traversing to right half of zone data apparently looking for our ration parties & Ammo carriers various lights at 11 p.m. Capt CRAY rejoined from base.	
	26th		Indirect fire was carried out on Railway junction A29 a 3.6.5. Road N. of HAISNES at A29 f 3.5.5. Trench Ramway A29 b.7.3. & A29 d 3.7 VERMELLES-AUCHY Road A29 a 10 & 29 a 9.6.5. Slight fire & enemy Machine gunfire normal. Indirect fire was carried out on suspects battery position A23. C.4.6. Road and Ramway b.12 L 7.7. Supply dump 65. C.8.5. Crossroads 3 INNS A29 d.	
	27th		2.25. Rounds fired 10,000 enemy Machine Guns were more active than usual during the night. At 10.30 P.M. sat 12 midnight the enemy were seen to sending tars and lights. 8 Men building dug outs under R.E.	
	28th		Indirect fire maintained on x roads A65 L 4.2 tramway CORONS on PERIN A29 C.93	

Army Form C. 2118.

WAR DIARY
or
INTELLIGENCE SUMMARY.
(Erase heading not required.)

Instructions regarding War Diaries and Intelligence Summaries are contained in F. S. Regs., Part II. and the Staff Manual respectively. Title pages will be prepared in manuscript.

Place	Date	Hour	Summary of Events and Information	Remarks and references to Appendices
VERMELLES	28th Sept		16 A29 c 37 also at G6 a 40.05 x G5 A 8 x Seacliw HAISNES A30 b 52 75. 9 Junction of trench & tramway G2 b 77. Last night complete frames for Antigas blankets at entrances to dug outs & replacements to existing trenches & sumps in dug out near RIO.	
	29		Special attention was paid during the night to be unknown dwellings near the DUMP. Other points fired on were Tramway from A29 a 20.05 & A29 L 05.90 & the CORONS in A29 c. Also tramway from G5 @ 05.90 Back & X roads at A29 d 60.15. Enemy machine gun fire hit French mortar wire cable near position R-54. 2 Enemy aeroplanes driven off. Two flying low were turned. Indirect fire was aimed all on B5 VERMELLES-AVENY Rd. Supply Dumps at C6.c.67.80 in A23 c.6 + on Junction of Tramways at A19 L 20.95.	
	30th			

2-10-16

M??grey Capt
O.C. 25th Mar gun Company

8th Division.

25th, Brigade.

25th, Machine Gun Co.

October, 1916.

WAR DIARY
or
INTELLIGENCE SUMMARY.
(Erase heading not required.)

Army Form C. 2118.

25 M G Coy
Vol X

Place	Date	Hour	Summary of Events and Information	Remarks and references to Appendices
VERMELLES	Oct. 1	1	Indirect fire was carried out on the M.G. HAISNES A.29 X.20.75. & A.30.F.15.74. Also supported 77mm on VERMELLE-AUCHY Rd. on junction of Fosseway & Happy Day. Enemy Machine Gun fire much below normal. Three enemy aircraft crossed our lines	
		2	Indirect fire was maintained at intervals throughout the night on the junction of Fosseway & 11000 Second was fired. Extremely quiet on our front. One enemy aeroplane attempted to cross our lines. Wind was strong West.	
		3	At 7.55 P.M. 8.40 P.M. & 10.79 P.M. 5 minute bursts of rapid fire on "Tricks spots" believed the enemy support line. Intermittent fire at other times throughout the night. 23 reconnaissance fires. This was in conjunction with the scheme [...] way. In reply to our bursts of rapid fire the enemy shells to reserve trench [junctions] in Railway & new partie at T.1. completed much continuous on new dug-out at R60.	
		4	Three 5 minute bursts of rapid fire carried out as above from midnight. Enemy reply was active, here machine guns were more active, with sweeping harsh fire on parapets of support reserve trenches. Most continuous overt fire at R60 & on depairing trenches which our [...] on 21500 [...] over fire on gun fire intermittently through the night until 3.5 minutes bursts of rapid fire	

WAR DIARY
or
INTELLIGENCE SUMMARY.
(Erase heading not required.)

Army Form C. 2118.

Place	Date	Hour	Summary of Events and Information	Remarks and references to Appendices
VERMELLES	Oct 5.	7.55 P.M & 11.45 P.M & 1.10.32 P.M	In Front of the trench, Enemy up behind the enemy's support line opened a distant.Lewis fire to the CORONS DE PEKIN. 23000 rounds were fired. Enemy machine guns were more active at 10.30 p.m. The enemy put up one Red Very light, on which numerous special chopper attacks near the QUARRY Keep jeopardy. Twenty rifles fire was aimed on Rennie trench. Lt. HOBBS proceeded to hand it over.	Nº 12860 Pte TAYLOR O. accidentally self inflicted whilst Keep whilst asleep.
	6.		Ten guns carried reproduced fire until 3 & 5 minute bursts at same time to persuade enemy 40,000 rounds were fired. Enemy fire was feeble. During the morning fire opened on a party of German near CORONS DE PEKIN at 11.30 A.M. 7.	
	7.		Indirect fire was carried on at intervals on VERMELLES AUCHY North & CORONS DE PEKIN. Two German aeroplane flying low over enemy trenches were not fired at. This on the recent time Enemy machine gun were active. Order received to Dump all surplus rifles + SAA SQI. 8. 3. By. 5. p.m Oct 8th	
	8.		Lt. Brennan was relieved from leave.	
	9.		Indirect fire carried out throughout night. Mobile Machine Guns very active.	
	10.		Company relieved in the trenches by 110 Machine Gun Company was later to billets at NOEUX LE MINES.	

Army Form C. 2118.

WAR DIARY
or
INTELLIGENCE SUMMARY.
(Erase heading not required.)

Instructions regarding War Diaries and Intelligence Summaries are contained in F. S. Regs., Part II. and the Staff Manual respectively. Title pages will be prepared in manuscript.

Place	Date	Hour	Summary of Events and Information	Remarks and references to Appendices
BURBURE	11th		Company marched from NEOUX LE MINES to BURBURE arriving about 4.30 p.m.	
	12th		Inspection of Gun Equipment etc. Company en Marching Order.	
	13th		Company paraded at 1.45 a.m. marched to LILLERS Station and entrained. Arrived at LONG PRE about 12.30 p.m. Detrained and marched to billets at AIRAINES. Reached billets about 3 p.m.	
	14th		Company at AIRAINES. Inspecting kit etc. also fighting order.	
	15th		Paraded at 7 a.m. and proceeded by Hired Motor Bus to MEAULTE, then marched to Camp at CITADEL.	
	16th		Company parade 8 a.m. - 7.30 p.m. Physical training etc.	
	17th		Company parade 9 a.m. - 12.30 p.m. Gun Drill etc.	
	18th		O.C. Company proceeded to Trenches, preparation to taking over.	
	19th		Company paraded 7.30 a.m. marched to Transport Lines at MONTAUBAN. 12 noon paraded and proceeded to take over trenches from 10th Machine Gun Company 60th Brigade during relief.	
	20th		Trenches shelled intermittently during day and night especially at "Stand To"	

Army Form C. 2118.

25th Machine Gun Company

Vol 10

WAR DIARY
or
INTELLIGENCE SUMMARY.
(Erase heading not required.)

Instructions regarding War Diaries and Intelligence Summaries are contained in F.S. Regs., Part II. and the Staff Manual respectively. Title pages will be prepared in manuscript.

Place	Date	Hour	Summary of Events and Information	Remarks and references to Appendices
TRENCHES	21st		Morning & evening during day. Aeroplanes very active flying at low altitude during day. One O.R. reported sick.	
	22nd		Fairly quiet in trenches. Nothing of importance happened.	
	23rd		Company moved into assembly positions previous to Division making attack on ZENITH TRENCH. One O.R. reported sick. Division attacked at 2.30 p.m. 23rd Brigade obtained their objective. 25th Brigade held up by machine gun fire. Our guns explained hostile trenches during assault, also swept ground in rear of our objective. Casualties 2/Lt. King killed. One O.R. killed. five O.R. wounded.	
	24th		Night attack on ZENITH was not successful. The O.C. formed Company from base. 2/Lt. H. Mackenzie slightly wounded, remained at duty. One O.R. wounded.	
	25th		Heavy hostile shelling of reserve and support trenches. One O.R. wounded. two O.R's missing. Both O.R. reported sick fast rept.	
	26th		Weather extremely bad. Continuous rain. Heavy hostile shelling 2/Lt. H. Mackenzie reported missing.	

Army Form C. 2118.

WAR DIARY
or
INTELLIGENCE SUMMARY.
(Erase heading not required.)

Instructions regarding War Diaries and Intelligence Summaries are contained in F. S. Regs., Part II and the Staff Manual respectively. Title pages will be prepared in manuscript.

Place	Date	Hour	Summary of Events and Information	Remarks and references to Appendices
	27th		Indent for carried out throughout night. 8 Germans surrendered to Machine Gun Company. 2/Lt. B.M. Jones 2 i/c Company wounded 10 a.m. Evacuated. 5 a.m. Jones from Base.	
	28th		Relief between Reliefs. 2 a.m. avoided.	
	29th		2/Lt. 8? Macnamara sent to Transport lines sick. 4 O.R. reported sick.	
	30th		Brigade relieved by 51st Brigade. Machine Gun Company remained in trenches. O.C. 51st M.G. Company visited trenches to take over. Relieved by 51st M.G. Coy 9.60 Relief not completed 11 a.m. 1st November. 4 O.R. missing during relief.	
	31st		2/Lt. Hundrick. & own staff together with 33 O.R.'s Joined Company from Base. Company proceeded to Camp at CITADEL.	

Wrayney Captain
O. C. 25th Machine Gun Company

8th, Division.

25th, Brigade.

25th, Machine Gun Co.

November, 1916.

Army Form C. 2118.

25 - M G Coy

Vol XI

WAR DIARY
or
INTELLIGENCE SUMMARY.
(Erase heading not required.)

Instructions regarding War Diaries and Intelligence Summaries are contained in F. S. Regs., Part II. and the Staff Manual respectively. Title pages will be prepared in manuscript.

Place	Date	Hour	Summary of Events and Information	Remarks and references to Appendices
	NOVEMBER			
TRENCHES	1st		Company relieved in trenches by 51st Machine Gun Company and proceed to Camp at CITADEL.	
CAMP CITADEL	2nd		Company cleaning up etc. Inspection of arm and accoutrements.	
	3rd		Company marched to billets at MEAULTE.	
	4th		Company inspected by Divisional Commander.	
	5th		Cleaning Gun Equipment etc. Coy Orders. Ole Waite & Pte Saunders rejoined Company.	
	6th		Company parade 9–12.30 pm Cleaning Guns at Sect G.S. took over No 1 & No 2 Gun Command from No 1 M.G.Co.	
	7th		Company parade 9–12 noon Cleaning Guns, packing limbers etc. 2 pm–5 pm Inspection of arms and accoutrements No 7360 Pte Taylor o. tried by 39 G.C.M.	
	8th		Company parade 9–12 noon Cleaning Gun preparatory to going into the trenches.	
TRENCHES	9th		Company moved to Sord Kamps Carroy on de way up to LES BOEUFS Sect. Company relieved 24th Machine Gun Company in LES BOEUFS SECTOR Distribution of Guns. 2 Guns in front line BENNETT TRENCH H. Guns in	

2353 Wt. W2544/1454 700,000 5/15 D.D.&L. A.D.S.S. Forms/C.2118.

Army Form C. 2118.

WAR DIARY
or
INTELLIGENCE SUMMARY.
(Erase heading not required.)

Instructions regarding War Diaries and Intelligence Summaries are contained in F. S. Regs., Part II. and the Staff Manual respectively. Title pages will be prepared in manuscript.

Place	Date	Hour	Summary of Events and Information	Remarks and references to Appendices
TRENCHES	9th		ANTELOPE TRENCH. 1 gun in OX TRENCH. 6 guns in reserve Rampart.	
	10th		Heavy shell fire. S.O.P. Hebbe and S.O.P. invaded by shell fire. Intense relief. 1 O.R. missing	
	11th		Built day ten shelling due [mostly] to recent sky and difficulty in observation.	
	12th			
	13th		Intense relief.	
	14th		2 Emplacements dug at T.M. A.2.S. 12. 2 Emplacements dug in FROSTS TRENCH 11 Emplacements dug in ANTELOPE TRENCH	
	15th		O.C. 67th Coy to Headquarters and arranged relief. 3 men per gun. Relieving Coy moved in for night.	
	16th		Coy Coy relieved by 67th Coy. Moved to NORTH CAMP CARNOY.	
	17th		Moved to SANDPIT CAMP	
SANDPIT	18th		Guns & equipment drawn and ammunition inspected. 2 S.W. gun in look out moved out. Hangar. Officers by road to CROQUOISON.	
	19th		Company moved to CROQUOISON. Billetting party by tactical train leaving EDGE HILL at 10 am and alighting at AIRAINES at 4 pm.	

2353 Wt. W2544/1454 700,000 5/15 D. D. & L. A.D.S.S. Forms/C. 2118.

WAR DIARY
or
INTELLIGENCE SUMMARY.
(Erase heading not required.)

Army Form C. 2118.

Instructions regarding War Diaries and Intelligence Summaries are contained in F.S. Regs., Part II. and the Staff Manual respectively. Title pages will be prepared in manuscript.

Place	Date	Hour	Summary of Events and Information	Remarks and references to Appendices
	19th		Company entrained at EDESSA at midnight & arrived at RAMANS at 6 am	
	20th		Company arrived at CROUOISON about 3pm	
	21st		O.C. Major and troops Coys arrived 10am. Parade for general change 9am – midday. 2pm – 3pm.	
	22nd		PARADE 9.6. Cleaning equipment & guns 2–3. Inspection of C.S.C. by O.C. Company	
	23rd		Parade 9.10. In accordance with training orders issued by Division to training statts with musketry work. 9 am Aim drill by statts 10–11am Gun Inspection and Fire-arms. 11–12am Gun Drill. 2 & 3pm Gas exercise immediate action.	
	24th		9.10.30am Right half Company on the Range. Left half Company Aim Drill &c. Each half cycle morning. They changed rooms 2–3 Gun Drill.	
	25th		Parade 10. Used for manœuvres training 9am Gun Drill. 10.11am Mechanism. 11am. Cleaning of guns 11–12am Mechanism. Immediate action 2.3pm. Aim Drill	
	26th		11am. Inspection of Company Store with Lieutenant of Newcast	

Army Form C. 2118.

WAR DIARY
or
INTELLIGENCE SUMMARY.
(Erase heading not required.)

Instructions regarding War Diaries and Intelligence Summaries are contained in F. S. Regs., Part II. and the Staff Manual respectively. Title pages will be prepared in manuscript.

Place	Date	Hour	Summary of Events and Information	Remarks and references to Appendices
	27th		Parade before breakfast started 7.15 7.45 am. Physical Drill 9.30 am Freshroom. 10-11 am. Gun Drill. 11-12 noon Msg. 2.3 pm. Gun Drill. Mr transport to Hospital Amiens	
	28th		Captain W.E. Gray left for En. Grand 7.15 7.45 am Physical Drill 9.30am Range Practice. Reveille off Company Smith and Anderson separately Company. 10.2 non Rifle Exerc. half temporaries changed	
	29th		Reveille 2.3 pm. Gun Drill. 10. C.D. formed temporary. Hill to Rehuts arriving from Base. 7.15 - 7.45 am Physical drill 9.10 on Inspection 10-11.30 am Gun Drill. 11.30-12 noon Cleaning Guns. 2.3 am Gun Drill.	
	30th		2.40-7.45am. Physical Drill. 9- 9.30 am. 7.45-1. Photos of Hospital at Amiens. 9.45-7.45 am. Physical Drill. 9.30-11.30 Marches to open up Notice by Actin officers a morning scheme 11.30-12 noon Lectures on at morning scheme Station. 2.3 pm. Practice in guard mountings. Both started	

C.P. Cook. Lieut.
O.C. No. 25 A.A. G. Co.

<u>8th, Division.</u>

<u>25th, Brigade.</u>

<u>25th, Machine Gun Co.</u>

<u>December, 1916.</u>

Army Form C. 2118.

Vol 72

25 Machine Gun Company.

WAR DIARY
or
INTELLIGENCE SUMMARY.
(Erase heading not required.)

Instructions regarding War Diaries and Intelligence Summaries are contained in F. S. Regs., Part II. and the Staff Manual respectively. Title pages will be prepared in manuscript.

Place	Date	Hour	Summary of Events and Information	Remarks and references to Appendices
CROUVOISON	1.12.16		Parade by sections 7.15. 2.45pm. No Physical Drill. First half of the morning Right half Company on the Range. & Left half Company had Helm Drills. Lecture & fatigues morning & too half Company's Interchanged. Paraded at 7.5 No Physical Drill. The morning was spent by Section practicing attacking a village under Section Officers. Arms drill to afternoon.	
	2.12.16		Physical Drill at 7.15. Under Section Officer. No.1 + 2 Sections took use of the Range in the morning the 3rd half Company practiced action from the Range in the morning the 4th half Company practiced action from Limbers and digging in on a number road. Remainder given Rum Drill.	
	4.12.16		Physical Drill 7.15. 7.45 under Section Officers. Right half Company spent the morning on the Range. The Left half practicing action from the limbers and digging in & Section roads. Lecture by Section Officers in use of overhead fire and elevation and directing Drills.	
	5.12.16		7.15 - 7.45. Physical Drill. 9 - 1 p.m. Company any where except from VERDEES in the FRONT WOOD and afterwards in the village of CROUVOISON ended & of afternoon was spent on Arms Drill.	
	7.12.16		7.15 - 7.45. Physical Drill.	

WAR DIARY or INTELLIGENCE SUMMARY

Army Form C. 2118

Place	Date	Hour	Summary of Events and Information	Remarks and references to Appendices
	7.12.16		Cadre, No. or Lieut Right half Company were on the Range, while No 3 & 4 Pelotons practised skirting and consolidation in a wood.	
		01.10.30	The Company was inspected by the M.O. from 25th F.A. for any cases of scabies. Only two cases were discovered.	
			All the inspection the Peloton returned their Postes. Football match in the afternoon on the terrain Rennes que Bugeaud. Competition Company played 4th Zouaves and lost 0-7 although the team was quite hors of proportion to the game which was fairly evenly contested.	
		7.15. A.m.	Played Drill.	
	8.12.16		Whole Company and the Range during the morning the Right half Company firing scheme for sections in a wood. The Deflection arcs with one inspection by the Brigadier at 2.30. Lieut Gaubis returned for leave and took over the Company.	
		7.3.	Company Drill.	
	9.12.16		The morning was devoted to Company volume in attack in ETREPIGNEY WOOD from BELOY. The afternoon Company Drill.	

2333 Wt. W2544/7454 700,000 5/15 D. D. & L. A.D.S.S.Forms/C 2118

WAR DIARY or INTELLIGENCE SUMMARY

Army Form C. 2118.

Instructions regarding War Diaries and Intelligence Summaries are contained in F. S. Regs., Part II. and the Staff Manual respectively. Title pages will be prepared in manuscript.

Place	Date	Hour	Summary of Events and Information	Remarks and references to Appendices
	10.12.16		C.O. Voluntary service. Holy Communion & Church Service at 8.0 am.	
	11.12.16		In morning a Company scheme was worked out. 1st Foot Guards Division from DROMESNIL and BEHINCOURT unfortunately time did not allow of a completion of the scheme. Powder Practice and Drill in the afternoon. Brigade Cinema Opera at MESTIENY.	
	12.12.16		Early morning preliminaries of Warning of flights and Equipment. Parade showing to Inspection by G.O.C. 8th Division Major General Hickie D.S.O. 80 companies marched to Company parade ground I MESTIENY on account of the very inclement the forenoon scheme could not be materialis... Powder Practice in the afternoon.	
	13.12.16		Church Drill under Section Officers 9.15 am. During the morning No.2 Platoon with a demonstration platoon from Lewis 2.3rd Company Drill. Remainder a Route March and attack from Lewis 2.3rd Company Drill. Bayonet Drill 7.15–7.45 am.	
	14.12.16		In the morning Operations Company did a scheme of approach march in Lectures Ammunition. Co. Range Practice. Bayonet Practice, P.3. Company Drill.	

WAR DIARY
or
INTELLIGENCE SUMMARY

Army Form C. 2118.

Place	Date	Hour	Summary of Events and Information	Remarks and references to Appendices
	15.12.16		Physical Drill 7.15-7.45 a.m. Whole of Company paraded and marched to Corporation Rifle Range. One company firing on Long Range, the other half Company on the Range. 2-3 Musketry Practice.	
	16.12.16		Company Line Attack 9.10 a.m. from PIERS to BOIS DU ROYE CORNER. BOIS DE CAMBOS thence into village of HEUCOURT. 2.3 p.m. Rapier Practice.	
	17.12.16		11 a.m. R.C. Church Parade at HEUCOURT CHURCH.	
	18.12.16		Physical Drill 7.15-7.45 a.m. No 1 & 2 Platoons Range Practices with Small Helmet. 3-4 Lectures. Letters from Sisters. 2-3 p.m. Revolver Practice.	
	19.12.16		8 a.m. Company Scheme. A Recd Guard Allow from MIDX HEUDONS through BOIS DELA PROVE are 16 PLATES which was encircled. On Duck in afternoon.	
	20.12.16		7.15-7.45 a.m. Physical Drill. 9-0-12 noon Route March. CROQUOISON-METIANX-ETRETUST-AVESNE-Home. Company Drill in afternoon.	
	21.12.16		7.15-7.45 a.m. Packing Limbers.	

Army Form C. 2118.

WAR DIARY
or
INTELLIGENCE SUMMARY.
(Erase heading not required.)

Instructions regarding War Diaries and Intelligence Summaries are contained in F. S. Regs., Part II. and the Staff Manual respectively. Title pages will be prepared in manuscript.

Place	Date	Hour	Summary of Events and Information	Remarks and references to Appendices
	21.12.16 (Wed?)		Remain all the morning 2.0.0 tobacco sent round to be allowed. Instructors & Gotts fortnight match V 24th Bn of RES. NEVILLE lost 0-3.	
	22.12.16		Physical Drill 7.15 - 7.45 a.m. 9 -12 noon off half Company & Carpentering at pickets. Rest half Company attack in the open 2-3.30. Stocks & Gunbox Right Flying.	
	23.12.16	8.30 - 1 p.m. 2 p.m.	Company & Platoon taking up position in Outpost line and advancing from the supports of a flank guard. In the afternoon photo was taken of the 6 officers. Play was held. Very there was a gale blowing. The day was not good for sport. Relay race transport v. Hy. Coys and football. No 3 Platoon won Relay race. Nothing similar.	
	24.12.16		C of E Church Parade	
	25.12.16	11 a.m.	Christmas day. Voluntary Church Parade HQ Commander officers then	
	26.12.16	6 a.m.	Transport moved	
		12.30 p.m.	Col. McDowan inspects 18 Brigade and pinned on to medal ribbon had in the Brigade who had been awarded an honour to all rest day	
	27.12.16	9 a.m. 11-12 noon	Roll Match cleaning Billeting area	

Army Form C. 2118.

WAR DIARY
or
INTELLIGENCE SUMMARY.
(Erase heading not required.)

Instructions regarding War Diaries and Intelligence Summaries are contained in F. S. Regs., Part II and the Staff Manual respectively. Title pages will be prepared in manuscript.

Place	Date	Hour	Summary of Events and Information	Remarks and references to Appendices
	26.12.16		Parade at 8.30 a.m. move to AIRAINES, to entrain – train was late. Starting out we did not reach Rest Sta. about 3 p.m. at EPEC HILL. Bivouac to Camp 12 where we spent the night.	
	27.12.16		Marche to Camp 16.	
	28.12.16		Moves by Motor bus from Camp 16 to MAUREPAS, where Company marched and took over from 10th Company on Bgde. Front. 10 Guns in front area. 2nd d.H.Q. and H. in COMBLES.	
	31.12.16		A very quiet part of the line indeed. A quiet cold day but no rain.	

W. Moore Lieut
W/C 25 Sp. 9. Co.

2353 Wt. W2544/1454 700,000 5/15 D. D. & L. A.D.S.S./Forms/C.2118.

Vol 15

Army Form C. 2118.

WAR DIARY
or
INTELLIGENCE SUMMARY.

(Erase heading not required.)

75th Machine Gun Company.   January 1917.

Instructions regarding War Diaries and Intelligence Summaries are contained in F.S. Regs., Part II. and the Staff Manual respectively. Title pages will be prepared in manuscript.

Place	Date	Hour	Summary of Events and Information	Remarks and references to Appendices
TRENCHES	1.1.17		A quiet day. No firing was done owing to work in hand. No. 4 Section relieved No. 3 Section and half No. 3 relieved the other half.	
	2.1.17		Another quiet day. During the night BULLET CROSS ROADS was shelled heavily.	
	3.1.17		Quiet day. Company relieved by 61st Company. H.Q. Heavily shelled about 6.30. Just after relief.	
	4.1.17		Company moved from MAUREPAS by Motor Lorry (Emp.11) was BRAS. Day was spent in cleaning guns, equipment etc.	
	5.1.17		Made full Kit Inspection exclusive of whole Kit which we did not have supplies in de Vie.	
	6.1.17		Wet Day. Arm. Drill and instruction in Belts.	
	7.1.17		Church Parade 9 a.m. 11 o'clock R.C. 3.30 pm Packing limbers.	
	8.1.17		Company moved off early in the morning for the Bath line. Inspection both O.C. 2 Pl arrived at 10.30 followed by Gun Drill until 12.1 Return to H.Q. for dinner in company and set our Command Company Parades at 1.45. Move to entraining Station at Bray-Sur-Somme Station. Sp. 691.6 entrained 10 a.m. Detained at PIRAINES. 3.30pm Marched to CROUISON	

Army Form C. 2118.

WAR DIARY
or
INTELLIGENCE SUMMARY.
(Erase heading not required.)

Instructions regarding War Diaries and Intelligence Summaries are contained in F. S. Regs., Part II. and the Staff Manual respectively. Title pages will be prepared in manuscript.

Place	Date	Hour	Summary of Events and Information	Remarks and references to Appendices
Camp H7	9.1.17		Arr: billets and tybes. The transport had clearly arrived	
Dioppain	10.1.17		The morning was spent in cleaning guns & getting up pay. In the afternoon the Company was supplied by the Coo	
	11.1.17		The tomy of transport vehicles occupied the whole of the morning parade. In the afternoon was good bath & a lecture was given by a Canadian Officer	
	12.1.17		Physical training commenced 7.30-7.30. In the morning the Platoon Comdgs. Proctors & Sergts. the company Lectures attended ammunition & equipment	
	13.1.17		The afternoon were formed in Gas Drill and Respirator Inspection. Drill & lecture programme for the platoon in the dining Gym. for every morning.	
	14.1.17		Capt Scarper & et St Geo. R.O.R.	
	15.1.17		M.T. detail relieve apport in a Football Scheme with the Royal Irish. In-Lieut. B.Hd. joined on the Comps. Company Sector aboard Sills and	

Army Form C. 2118.

WAR DIARY
or
INTELLIGENCE SUMMARY.

(Erase heading not required.)

Instructions regarding War Diaries and Intelligence Summaries are contained in F. S. Regs., Part II. and the Staff Manual respectively. Title pages will be prepared in manuscript.

Place	Date	Hour	Summary of Events and Information	Remarks and references to Appendices
Fienvillers	15.1.17		Tactical Exercise. Company Drill in the afternoon	
	16.1.17		No 3 Section in the Range. Lewis Gun Recon. Section Gun Drill. Tactical Schemes. Bombing instruction in afternoon. Lecture by Officer at 5.15 p.m.	
	17.1.17		Half the Section continued their Musketry Course & Bombing in afternoon. No. 1 & 2 Section on the Range. Remainder Gun Drill in huts. Did not turn out of huts.	
	18.1.17		No 3 Section went with Regt. Not Gun. Party & Coys. into a Scheme. Remainder of Company Route marched. Mechanism. Msyqaas. Lecture in afternoon.	
			½ Section went to Eclimeu to cooperate in a Tactical Scheme	
	19.1.17		No. 3 & 4 Sections Range Practice. No 2 Gun Drill. Remainder Gun Drill.	
			Into afternoon Bombing, Rifle & Mortar Service Exemptions from Base.	
	20.1.17		No 4 Section went to Rifle Brigade to cooperate in a Scheme	
			Remaining Section Gun Drill, Gun Drill and Mechanism.	
			Transport were inspected at 10am at EVREUST Company Stables	
			Arrived at BELLOY	
	21.1.17		Coys. Paraded at CROUY SON 2 a.m. R.C. at HERCOURT 7.45 p.m.	
	22.1.17		In the morning the Company paraded by Section for the Ann Drill. Bombing Night Practice	

Army Form C. 2118.

WAR DIARY
or
INTELLIGENCE SUMMARY.

(Erase heading not required.)

Instructions regarding War Diaries and Intelligence Summaries are contained in F. S. Regs., Part II. and the Staff Manual respectively. Title pages will be prepared in manuscript.

Place	Date	Hour	Summary of Events and Information	Remarks and references to Appendices
PROYOISON	22.1.17		All transport moved off for PICK Y SUR SOMME at 7 a.m. Inspection in full marching order by C.O.	
	23.1.17		Company paraded at 8 a.m. and marched to AIRAINES where it entrained at 10.30. Detrained at EQUE MHL at 3.15 p.m. and marched to Camp 12. Weather stormy and did not arrive till 4 a.m.	
Camp 12	24.1.17		Weather severe in Camp 12 and Company parade for preparing the Camp for the time, since they were mostly frozen.	
	25.1.17		Reconnoitring party went up to the RANCOURT SECTOR and arranged dispositions 119 Bn.	
	26.1.17		Company left Camp 12 at noon & marched to Camp 17. Very slow progress was made owing to transport being on the move, but at 5.30 GRAY the march was greatly curtailed. 17 was started at 4.30 p.m.	
Camp 17	27.1.17		Company left Camp 17 & proceeded by Lorry to MAUREPAS from the Regny marched and took over from 119th Company Welsh Regts 4 y 0 & th Division were in the front support Position N.2 Strongpoint & Fort Rience posting N.3 section were taken Coys Headquarters of position NS. Better tent Guns up was relieved	
TRENCHES			Co. H.Q. Coy Hd. Lieut Auslegh Williams	

Army Form C. 2118.

WAR DIARY
or
INTELLIGENCE SUMMARY.
(Erase heading not required.)

Instructions regarding War Diaries and Intelligence Summaries are contained in F. S. Regs., Part II and the Staff Manual respectively. Title pages will be prepared in manuscript.

Place	Date	Hour	Summary of Events and Information	Remarks and references to Appendices
TRENCHES	27/12		Relieved H.Q. near ADELPHI DUMP. Bss H.Q. at LE FOREST near Lt. Gen H.Q.	
	28/12		A quiet morning. Reconnoitering positions was done. In afternoon our artillery bombarded heavily the enemy trench system. There was very little retaliation.	
	29/12		Yesterday Inspection showed little damage to the enemy. Position. No other shelling. Something to their former positions.	
	30/12		RANCOURT was shelled during the morning but otherwise the day was quiet. Arranged for employment of ready made LINK GUN.	
			Indication given. ST. PIERRE VAAST WOOD was much cut up & CEMETERY RANCOURT. Y6 QUARRY was shelled with S.O.S. shells by the enemy.	
	31/12		A quiet day. O.C. D? Coy inspected Sub-tunnels in RANCOURT shelled during the night.	

V. Bootsical and Adjt.
73rd Machine Gun Coy.

Army Form C. 2118.

Vol 14
25. Aeroplane Gun Coy.

WAR DIARY
or
INTELLIGENCE SUMMARY.
(Erase heading not required.)

February 1917

Place	Date	Hour	Summary of Events and Information	Remarks and references to Appendices.
RANCOURT SECTOR	1/2/17		A quiet day with mutual intermittent shelling as usual.	
	2/2/17		Another quiet day. In the evening No 3 detm. relieved No 4 detm. in the S positions	
	3/2/17		No 4 detm. returning to the H positions	
			7/4 to 8 am enemy planes flew over Physical Dell annexe and reconnoitred at AVESNE German aeroplane flew over RANCOURT at a very low altitude and flew away. Very fire seen he brought to bear but ineffectively. Guns allotted to fire on M.G. movements	
	4/2/17		Quiet day. No Lewis Gun replaced No 3 detm in S positions	
	5/2/17		Enemy aircraft active over RANCOURT- encouraging emergency on our aircraft guns at M.E. 20.B.	
	6/2/17		Quiet day with the usual shelling and aircraft activity. No 2 detm. relieved No 2 detm. in S positions	
	7/2/17		A very quiet day with slight artillery activity in left front. Our attack on the left of MIRAUMONT FOSSILLS at 7.30 am	
	8/2/17		Everything was very quiet over front. Lewis Gun was in position and an extra gun was put in the right flank on our B's front by No 3 N° 10	
	9/2/17		Quiet day and usual work with Travelling to same	

Army Form C. 2118.

WAR DIARY
or
INTELLIGENCE SUMMARY.
(Erase heading not required.)

Instructions regarding War Diaries and Intelligence Summaries are contained in F. S. Regs., Part II and the Staff Manual respectively. Title pages will be prepared in manuscript.

Place	Date	Hour	Summary of Events and Information	Remarks and references to Appendices
RONCOURT	12/5/17		Quiet day. Usual Carsloff activity.	
SECTOR.	14/5/17		Relieved by 19 Co's at army cost marched to Camp 11 arriving at 1 am.	
Rest			Left Camp 11 and marched to Camp 12. arrived abt 7.30 a.m.	
CAMP 12.	15/5/17		Gas mask inspection. Equipment paraded.	
	16/5/17		Gun Drill and Cleaning gun equipment. Inspection Officer	
	17/5/17		Bath for Company in morning. Mon Enterior Salvo for Ration supplies.	
	18/5/17		Placed on instructional camps.	
	19/5/17		Range practice by 1 & 2 Sect of 1 Co. Instruction in use of army masks	
	20/5/17		Range practice in morning & Range Practice for 3 & 4 of 1 Co.	
	21/5/17		Bath for Company in morning.	
			Church Parade at 5.30 p.m. R.C. 9.30 a.m. at CHAPEL OF CHURCH.	
			No. 3 Section went out Thursday during the day.	
			Returned about 9 p.m. Strength of Co.	
	22/5/17		One O'clock Parade as usual & instruction in L.G. & Rifle tube Loaded platoon	
			Remainder of brie marked out Company move for Camp 12. to Camp 17, where it stayed the night	

Army Form C. 2118.

WAR DIARY
or
INTELLIGENCE SUMMARY.
(Erase heading not required.)

Instructions regarding War Diaries and Intelligence Summaries are contained in F.S. Regs., Part II. and the Staff Manual respectively. Title pages will be prepared in manuscript.

Place	Date	Hour	Summary of Events and Information	Remarks and references to Appendices
TRENCHES.	22/2/17		Moved by feet from Camp 17 to take over Grassy Farm sector. Reliefs to be complete by 10 p.m. 4 guns dropped into one pannier & (after their reliefs) went back to H.Q. caves	
	23/2/17		Work on to Goldfish Redan commenced during the night	
	24/2/17		Right half of Bridge Return completed & offensive commenced. Work. There was very urgent and a working party from Signals was obtained	
	25/2/17		Redans completed. Dump shells. Aeroplane activity. Machine Gun fire from Hussar Wood very heavy.	
	26/2/17		2 guns received orders for M.O.O. 153 R5. Aeroplane open fire dots 3.O.B. mounted and Redon Red.	
	27/2/17		Raid by Bosche at 10.10. 1 Gen— dropped in centre of trench.	

Major
for O. 25th M.G. Co.

WAR DIARY or INTELLIGENCE SUMMARY

Army Form C. 2118.

25. Machine Gun Company.

Vol /5

Place	Date	Hour	Summary of Events and Information	Remarks and references to Appendices
TRENCHES.	1.3.17.		Two Gun teams of 18". Section at F.5. d.6. relieved. Preparations for Barrage positions completed.	
	2.3.17.		A very quiet day. During the morning a hostile aeroplane was lighted and engaged from MARRIERE WOOD. During the night eight positions at ALDERSHOT were manned.	
	3.3.17.		The day was again quiet. In the evening the remaining eight guns moved up to their Barrage Positions and F. Guns were vacated.	
	4.3.17.		Company H.Q. moved up to REBECCA on the BETHUNE ROAD. At 5.45. am the Division attacked. Machine Gun Barrage was established from 2+6 & SEE Appendix A. I+16.	
	5.3.17.		Guns remained in their Barrage Positions. Enemy shelled heavily round the Positions. In the evening 4 guns from each group moved to relieve 8 guns of 73rd M.G.Co. near QUARRY BOUCHAVESNES.	
	6.3.17.		All guns remained in their positions — in case of counter attacks.	
	7.3.17.		Four guns from rear the QUARRY took over normal positions at RUTH, RACHAEL. and two Cape Intermediate Line guns R.7. v 8. Remaining guns still manned at ALDERSHOT.	

Army Form C. 2118.

WAR DIARY
or
INTELLIGENCE SUMMARY.
(Erase heading not required.)

Instructions regarding War Diaries and Intelligence Summaries are contained in F. S. Regs., Part II. and the Staff Manual respectively. Title pages will be prepared in manuscript.

Place	Date	Hour	Summary of Events and Information	Remarks and references to Appendices
TRENCHES.	8.3.17.		All guns relieved to normal Positions. No.2. Section went to F. Positions F.5.6.7.8. No.3. Section took over ROTH, RACHAEL and both REBECCA Positions	
	9.3.17.		No.4. Section took over the four Intermediate line R.5.6.7.8. Cat. No. 4. Section was in reserve. Capt. Roleston M.C. returned from Division. Lieut. Godeve went on 10 days special leave to U.K.	
	10.3.17.		A quiet day. Two enemy aeroplanes came over and were engaged by our guns from MARRIERE WOOD.	
	11.3.17.		Ridge behind MARRIERE WOOD shelled, during the evening otherwise the day was quiet and dull	
	12.3.17.		A hot day. Artillery was quiet and several aeroplanes were sighted. Fires on	
	13.3.17.		A very chat warm day. Several aeroplanes were up and two hostile cameras and were fired on by our guns in MARRIERE WOOD	
			A fair day. Indirect fire was carried out from in front of MARRIERE WOOD by No.1. Section. 6000 rounds fired. Lieut Malide. proceeded to "P" Anti-aircraft Battery, for a course.	
	14.3.17.		A wet day. Situation quiet on account of bad visibility	
	15.3.17.		A Misty day. Situation quiet. Enemy aeroplanes fired at several times from Anti-	

Army Form C. 2118.

WAR DIARY
or
INTELLIGENCE SUMMARY.
(Erase heading not required.)

Instructions regarding War Diaries and Intelligence Summaries are contained in F. S. Regs., Part II. and the Staff Manual respectively. Title pages will be prepared in manuscript.

Place	Date	Hour	Summary of Events and Information	Remarks and references to Appendices
TRENCHES.	15.3.17.		Aircraft Patrons:- MARRIERE WOOD.	
	16.3.17.		Into Section Relief orders issued:- uneventful day - enemy unusually quiet on out-post - Lieut. Cook & 4. O.R. proceeded to Transport Lines prior to going on a course of Machine Gun School CAMIERS.	
	17.3.17		A fine clear day enemy aeroplanes appeared over our front during forenoon & were engaged by our Anti-aircraft Machine Guns - In the afternoon No. 4. Section relieved No. 4. Section in positions F. 5. 6. 7. 8 & No. 1. Section relieved No. 3. Section at REBECCA, RAPHAEL & RUTH after which No. 4. Section occupied (as Subsidiaries) the positions and No. 3. Section was in Company Reserve during day night 17/18. Enemy very exceptionally quiet.	
	18.3.17.		A fine day, during early morning enemy retired from this flat's evacuated MORLANCOURT Village, was occupied by our troops during the day and out-posts were established along the Canal du NORD	
	19.3.17.		A very quiet day, enemy still reported with drawing from our front. Cavalry patrols later reported BUSSU & AIZE HAUT-LE-HAUT clear of enemy but NURLU held	

2353 Wt. W2544/1454 700,000 5/15 D.D.&L. A.D.S.S./Forms/C. 2118.

Army Form C. 2118.

WAR DIARY
or
INTELLIGENCE SUMMARY.
(Erase heading not required.)

Place	Date	Hour	Summary of Events and Information	Remarks and references to Appendices
TRENCHES	20.3.17.		A very wet morning - situation uneventful. Men awaiting movement orders.	
	21.3.17.		Uneventful. Capt. ROBERTON. M.C. and Lieut MacNAMARA reconnoitred the new Divisional main line along Canal du Nord EAST OF MOISLAIN. Company worked on trenches all afternoon.	
	22.3.17.		Again uneventful. Capt. ROBERTON. M.C. and Lieut. HARKWORTHY again reconnoitred Bgd's ground EAST OF MOISLAIN. Company worked on Bivvies again in the afternoon.	
	23.3.17.		Had uneventful. Received warning orders to relief of 3rd Guards Brigade was working parties on roads.	
	24.3.17.		At 2.16 p.m. Company marched off to relieve 3rd Guards Brigade Machine Gun Coy. in the trenches. Coy of 73rd Brigade. Relief completed about 7.30 p.m. Lieut. GOODEY evacuated to Hospital.	
	25.3.17.		Capt. ROBERTON. M.C. reconnoitred artillery line running S.E. from MANANCOURT towards NURLU - N°. 4 Section occupied positions in line which now became the main Line of Resistance.	W₁ 9105/15 Cue 3/c/se f/70000
MANANCOURT.	26.3.17.		N°.2 Section relieved N°.3 Section of the Machine Gun Company and GOVERNMENT FARM after relief N°.3 Section proceed to Res Roads V.20 a. 7. 7. East of MANANCOURT relieved cooked foods over	

2353. W⁺. W2544/1454 700,000 5/15 D. D. & L. A.D.S.S./Forms/C. 2118.

Army Form C. 2118.

WAR DIARY
or
INTELLIGENCE SUMMARY.
(Erase heading not required.)

Instructions regarding War Diaries and Intelligence Summaries are contained in F. S. Regs., Part II and the Staff Manual respectively. Title pages will be prepared in manuscript.

Place	Date	Hour	Summary of Events and Information	Remarks and references to Appendices
MANANCOURT.	26.3.17	Cont?	In the evening it advanced to High Ground about V.16.a. overlooking EQUANCOURT taking up position at 6.0.p.m. and subsequently co-operated with the Cavalry which attacked EQUANCOURT by harassing Western edge of WOOD. S.E. of EQUANCOURT. This operation included successfully about 1000 rounds, being fired after operation N°3 Section came under orders of O.P. Hines who established a new outpost line from about V.21.a.b. V.H. Patrol on [?] found EASTERN edge of the village swept. Company Headquarters and N°4 Section moved forward to Eastern edge of RIVERSIDE WOOD about V.20.C.1.5. – In the afternoon service section orders N°3 Section went forward with Royal Irish Rifles about 6.p.m. but established a new outpost line after our Cavalry before the village of FINS. and SORELLES GRAND – N°1 Section recurred [?] position vacated by N°3 Section – In the Coys Hair Line N°4 Section became local reserve up to Coy H.Q. – In the evening Lce Corporal FOR GOVERNMENT FARM.	
RIVERSIDE WOOD	27.3.17		Fine day. Capt ROBERTON MC. reconnoitred NURLU MANANCOURT line with N° Bays. Machine Gun Officer – 3.0 p.m. a conference with G.O.C. 76 Inf. Brigade to discuss operation. will attack outpost FINS and SOREL-LE-GRAND. N°1. Section moved forward in the evening to V.10 C.C.I.5 came under orders of O.C. Y°Rifle Brigade. – N°4. Section	
	28.3.17			

2353 Wt. W2544/1454 700,000 5/15 D. D. & L.   A.D.S.S./Forms/C. 2118.

Army Form C. 2118.

WAR DIARY
or
INTELLIGENCE SUMMARY.
(Erase heading not required.)

Instructions regarding War Diaries and Intelligence Summaries are contained in F. S. Regs., Part II. and the Staff Manual respectively. Title pages will be prepared in manuscript.

Place	Date	Hour	Summary of Events and Information	Remarks and references to Appendices
RIVERSIDE WOOD 28.3.17.	Cont.d		moved forward night 28/29th under orders 1000yds South of SOREL.	
	19.3.17.		No.1 Section fired intermittently from 5.30 a.m. & 8.30 a.m. into North & Eastern edges of SOREL and western edge of FIRS respectively to help cavalry who attacked SOREL at 8.30 a.m. Attack failed held up by enemy M.G. fire. Sq. Vanney nos.1, day & moved quietly after above operations. O.C. reconnoitred with Lieut. WOLDIE the new main line from EQUINCOURT to NURLU. Relieved French ordered for Brigade to do 30th inst. At 11.30 a.m. 7. Section 210th Machine Gun Company joined the Company to understudy & in the evening were attached to Rifle Brigade & Royal Berks for forthcoming operations – 8th Section proceeded forward in the evening & joined Lieut. GEORGE of 218th Company as ordered – the evening 7/Lt. LAMWORTH Y.I.O.R. proceeded – line L/724.	
	30.3.17.		A fine day. Capt. RUDERT O.R. M.C. met G.O.C. 75 Inf. Brigade and did preliminary reconnaissance for operations. In the afternoon No.2 Section & No.3 Section 218 Co. were attached to Rifle Brigade for Queants' & Pherire No.5 Sect.n & attached to Royal West Kent Rifles. No.1 Section and No.2 Section 218 Co. relieved the main line in the evening.	Ref. Map Sheet 57e SE Trankhoop

2353 Wt. W 2544/1454 700,000 5/15 D.D.&L. A.D.S.S./Forms/C. 2118.

Army Form C. 2118.

WAR DIARY
or
INTELLIGENCE SUMMARY.
(Erase heading not required.)

Instructions regarding War Diaries and Intelligence Summaries are contained in F. S. Regs., Part II. and the Staff Manual respectively. Title pages will be prepared in manuscript.

Place	Date	Hour	Summary of Events and Information	Remarks and references to Appendices
RIVERSIDE WOOD	30.3.17	cont'd	In the afternoon Rifle Brigade attacked DESSART WOOD and were supported by covering into the wood from the 2 sections attached to them. After the operation No. 1 Section moved forward took up position protecting DESSARD WOOD & the new outpost line established by Rifle Brigade. Royal Irish Rifles attacked the ridge running S.E. from DESSARTWOOD EAST of HEUDICOURT – the 2 sections attached to them supported this advance & after establishing the new outpost line No. 4 Section took up defensive position with the outpost Company. No. 3 Section became a supporting section with the support Company. Late No. 3 Section 218th Coy. withdrew from the Covering parties and took up supporting Position with support Company. Left patrols around the outskirts of Trons Being strong operation I.O.R. was killed. For the operation advanced Company Headquarters were established about V.10. C. O. I. near EQUANCOURT in the afternoon.	
	31.3.17		Night 30/31st passed uneventfully in the morning received reports that all our objectives had been taken. New outpost line established. Capt. TAYLOR O.C. 218th Company ordered Company Headquarters about 10.30 a.m. and afterwards do reconnected left outpost line with Capt. ROBERTON M.C. Day passed uneventfully.	

W.R. Wurk, Capt.
O/C 26th An. G. Co. V.

SECRET APPENDIX A Copy 2.

26th Machine Gun Company.
Operation Order No 1.

Amendments.

1.

On Z day 23rd, 24th, 25th and 120th Machine Gun Companies will be prepared to establish a barrage on the flanks and front of the objective.
The objective will be FRITZ TRENCH C10c 9.32 to C16a 60.10

2.

The following dispositions will be made:—

(a) Company H.Q. will be at REBECCA POSITION at C8C32.
O.C. Coy and C.S.M. will be at Coy H.Q. throughout the operations.

(b) No 1 and No 2 Sections will form the right Group Guns and will be in positions dug about C8 d 6.4 and will form a frontal barrage by sub-sections at intervals of 50 yds from C10 a 7.5 – C10 a 67 to C10 a 10.25 – C10 b 3.4.

(c) No 3 and No 4 Sections will form the Left Group Guns and will be in positions dug about C8 d 78.07 forming a frontal barrage by sub-sections at intervals of 50 yds from C 16 b 2.9 – C 16 b 60.75 to C16 b 16 – C16 55.45

(d) In every case each sub-section will use condenser lights no gas diffusers being used.

(e) Ammunition.
At every emplacement there will be
b. 24. Belt Boxes
2. Petrol Tins of Water

(f) — Duties

(2)

(f) DUMPS.

No 1 and No 2 Sections will form a dump at ROSE II position in the sunken road near ALDERSHOT.
No 3 and No 4 Sections will form a dump at ROSE I position C8 d 65 90.

At each of these dumps there will be two Belt filling Machines. These will be put together and ready for immediate use.

There will also be 16 Boxes S.A.A. at each Section Dump.

COMPANY DUMP.

The Company Dump will be at Coy HQ C8 c 32. Four Belt filling Machines will also be kept at the Coy Dump and the following Stores:

  S.A.A. 64 Boxes.
  WATER. 40 Tins
  RATIONS. 180.
  SOLIDIFIED ALCOHOL. 5 Tins.

380.
10 tins

(g) Brigade H.Q. will be at ALDERSHOT

3.

(a) SMOKE will be discharged as follows:—
  1. at Z—2+5 by 40th Div on the left and by 23rd Div on the right.
  2. at Z—2+15 on 5th Div front onto C10 a 42.

GAS will be discharged as follows
  1. at Z—2+50 by 42nd Divs onto C17 and C11.
  2. at Z—2+1 ⎫
     Z+90 — ⎬ by 202 Special Coy R.E. onto C4 and
     Z+91 ⎭   C10

In event of a stand between X pls and ss all between no discharge will take place. This applies to (ii) and (iii)

4.

Before Z day only gun per section will be manned. Section NCO i/c and rest of the gun teams will be at section dump.

On Z day

O.C. Coy will be at Coy HQ

2nd in Command will be at right group gun Dump.
Lieut. Searcy will be in command of right group guns and Lieut. Winton will be in command of left group guns

Lt Goodeve of Vi Section Dump. 2nd/Lorthwaite at Coy HQ MARLORE Wood.

Lieut. Winton will be at their respective Section Dump.

Two men at each gun No 3 at Dump' persons after each 10 minutes and collects empty belt

Three men will man each gun up around of section at the action point.
One man per section will be detailed to be at Coy HQ for Coy lining
The two Company Runners and Signaller will be at Coy HQ unless otherwise ordered.
A sentry will be detailed by each section to be at the Section Dump and send up spare men in case of casualties.

5.

SAFETY PRECAUTIONS

(a) Allowance for climatic conditions of the day must be made.

(b) Auxiliary Winning Mark lamps will be used by day and night.

(c) Worn barrels will not be used.

(d) Plugrods will be used.

(e) Depression stops will be used.

OPEN FIRE

4. OPENING FIRE

All guns will fire from zero to zero at the rate of 25 rounds per minute.

After that they will only open fire when they receive a signal from the infantry.

The following signals will be used by the infantry:

1. One Green over Red Very light
2. One Red and White rocket
3. Square flag yellow and black being displayed
4. SOS on the Lamp

On any of these signals being observed guns will fire for ten minutes at the rate of 4 rounds a minute, when they will cease fire until the signal is repeated, or a ...

The Infantry will only send up the signals for a barrage when the enemy is believed to be massing for a counter attack, or about to deliver a counter attack, or in case of a counter attack.

5.

The following Observers will be detailed:

A. Officer of No 1 Section and one private to be detailed by O.C. No 1 Section, will be observers for Very Light signals. On observing any one of the Very light signals, they will fire one Green Very light and inform ... from their position at ...

B. N/Cpl Farrell of 3 Section and one private to be detailed by O.C. No 3 Section will be observers for Life Buoy Flash signals. On observing any Life Buoy flash signal they will fire one Green Very light and inform ...

7. ...

All guns will fire from zero to ...

2Lt Lashworthy will be at Renting in MARICRE WORK with Coy details.
They will be responsible for the safe custody of all stores left at Rear H.Q.
Following O.R.s will be left at Rear H.Q.

Cpl Topham
Cpl [illegible]
Pte Stenson
Pte Kershell.

Attention is drawn to Standing Order ref gas "All troops in any part of the line within [illegible] mile of the nearest point where gases being discharged must **wear** their Box Respirators.
This order will be stringently obeyed.

The following are the Medical Arrangements for Operations LENZ No. 6

Regtl Aid Post. C 8 d 30 Alpha Lane
C 9 a 42 Agile avenue
Collecting Post [illegible] Bearer Post C 8 [illegible] 94 Junction Agile avenue & Alf Cut.
Avenue.

SECRET

Copy 8.

25th Machine Gun Company

Amendments and Additions to Operation Order No. 1 of a. 1917

Para 2. for SECTION 180 read SECTION 380
    Sandbags allotted to the read sentries & concentration
    These bottles will be issued out 3 tins per lewis gun, for
    use in battle positions only.

3. para: 4.
    For 2nd LIEUTENANT and JB SECTION read B COMPANY and
    Y SECTION, and after SECTION DUMP add
    "2nd LIEUTENANT" will be at ZERO OT in ORCHARD
    WOOD, where all surplus kit will be stored.

    The fatigue O.Rs will be left at REAR namely J Section:—
    L/Cpl Watson, H/g Dawson, Pte Harries, Pte Davies,
    Pte Harding.

    These details will be safeguard first shift at [illegible]

4. para 4. For three men will man each gun read — two
    men will man each gun. and add Drs of each
    section will be at Dump and will gun for at
    intervals at the direction of Officer at the Dump.

5. ORS: Attention is drawn to Standing Orders of GOC:
    All troops in any part of the line within half a mile
    of the nearest gas is being discharged must
    wear SB Box Respirator.
    This order will be strictly adhered to.

A. SIGNALS
    ZERO ORS: Roll and Post, ——————————
    SNIPER HOT: ————————
    ————— POST, ————— BATTERY and ————

Copies to all officers of C.C. No 1.
G Coup Coy & MG in Officers only.

SECRET

25th Machine Gun Company.   Copy 7

Operation Order No 2.

1. In continuation of O.O. No1 dated 22nd February 18 these operations will take place in March 18 at a Zero hour to be issued later.
   Attacks are being made by Divisions of 1st Army North and South of 5th Division front.

2. OCCUPATION OF BARRAGE POSITIONS.
   Eight Barrage Positions will be occupied on the night 2nd/3rd.
   Remaining Barrage Position will be occupied on the night 3rd/4th.

   A. On the night 2nd/3rd following moves will take place:
      1. The 8 positions requiring the use of Depression Stops will be occupied.
      2. No 2 Section will take over No 1 and No 3 Gun positions of their own position, and will temporarily take over No 1 and No 3 Gun positions of No 1 Sections position.
      3. Half No 3 Section will take over No 1 and No 3 Gun positions of their own position.
      4. Half No 4 Section will take over No 1 and No 3 Gun positions of their own position.

   No positions are to be vacated before 6 p.m. on the night 2nd/3rd.

   B. On the night 3rd/4th following moves will take place:
      1. Remaining positions will be occupied. Company HQrs will move to REBECQ POSITION.
      2. No 1 Section will vacate their positions in support line at 6 p.m.
         F3 and F4 will proceed by LONDON AVENUE

C.20.b.15.40 (end of LONDON AVENUE) where a guide will meet them and guide them to their positions. Nos 5 and 6 will proceed by LADDER AVENUE to point C.14.c.8.5 (where LADDER AVENUE crosses the BETHUNE ROAD) where a guide will meet them and guide them to their positions. A carrying party will be sent to 2/Lt. LUCKWORTHY and Sergt. LEONARD to report at 5.45 p.m. on 8th.

3. The remainder of Nos 3 and 4 Sections will vacate their positions and move to their barrage positions. They will not vacate the Corps line before 6 p.m. on 8th.

4. O's C 3 and 4 Sections may arrange with O.C. DECAUVILLE RAILWAY at LITTLEDALE DUMP for use of trucks on the railway.

3. Firing lines will be laid out by Section Officers as soon after each move as practicable.

4. Prior to Zero hour 1 gun per Section only need be manned.
The relief of these guns will be made by Section Officers: in daytime, if the light is clear, reliefs should be as seldom as possible as all positions are under observation by the enemy.

5. Completion of moves will be reported to Coy HQ by wire, the following codes being used:
    Night 2/3rd : BRENT'S NIL
    "   3/4th : NCC COMPLETE.

6. Separate instructions re rations are being issued to the Transport Officer.

7. Copy to list of stores at Section Dumps:

RM...

RATIONS:
        45 Rations per Section at each dump.
        10. Additional tins of Water at each dump.

8. Lieut: Macnamara will be at Brigade H.Q. at ALDERSHOT at 3 p.m. 5 p.m. and 9 p.m. on Y day to synchronise watches.

9. PLEASE ACKNOWLEDGE.

Copies to all recipients of O.O. No 1.

                                  G. A. Foote Lieut.
                                comdg: 251 Machine Gun Coy

1. 3. 17.

SECRET (M)

25th Machine Gun Company.

Amendments and Additions to Operation Order No. 1 of 21...

1. para. 2. f. for: Sections to read: 28 thus 380
   [illegible line]
   These belts will be issued out & taken per half day, for use in battle position only.

2. para. 4.
   For 2/Lt LANGWORTHY and 2/Lt WESTON read Pioneer Lt. Ferguson; and after section aim add
   2/Lt Langworthy will be at rear HQ or in reserve, where all surplus kit will be stored.
   The following O.Rs will be left at rear HQ namely, Pte Hickman, L/Cpl Topham, L/Cpl Harvey, Pte Morris, Pte [illegible], Pte Bentley.
   These O.Rs will be responsible for all [illegible]

   para 4: For Three men will man each gun read: two men will man each gun. and add: the 3 extra men will be in the Lamb and cart guns per at intervals at the direction of Officer at the Piano.

3. GAS: Attention is drawn to standing order of SSO2
   no troops in any part of the line will say awake but the sentries going when gas is being discharged avoid wearing their Box Respirator.
   [illegible line]

4. MEDICAL ARRANGEMENTS
   LEFT BN: Regtl Aid Posts: CROSBY ALPHA LEFT
                              OPQ N2 REGT AVENUE
            RIGHT BN: WINDSOR
            COLLECTING POST LANCASTER BATTERY AND ONGOVER

Copies to all recipients of O.O. No.1. & Regtl Headquarters.
1:5000 map to Section Officers only.
                                        Major 25th Machine Gun Company

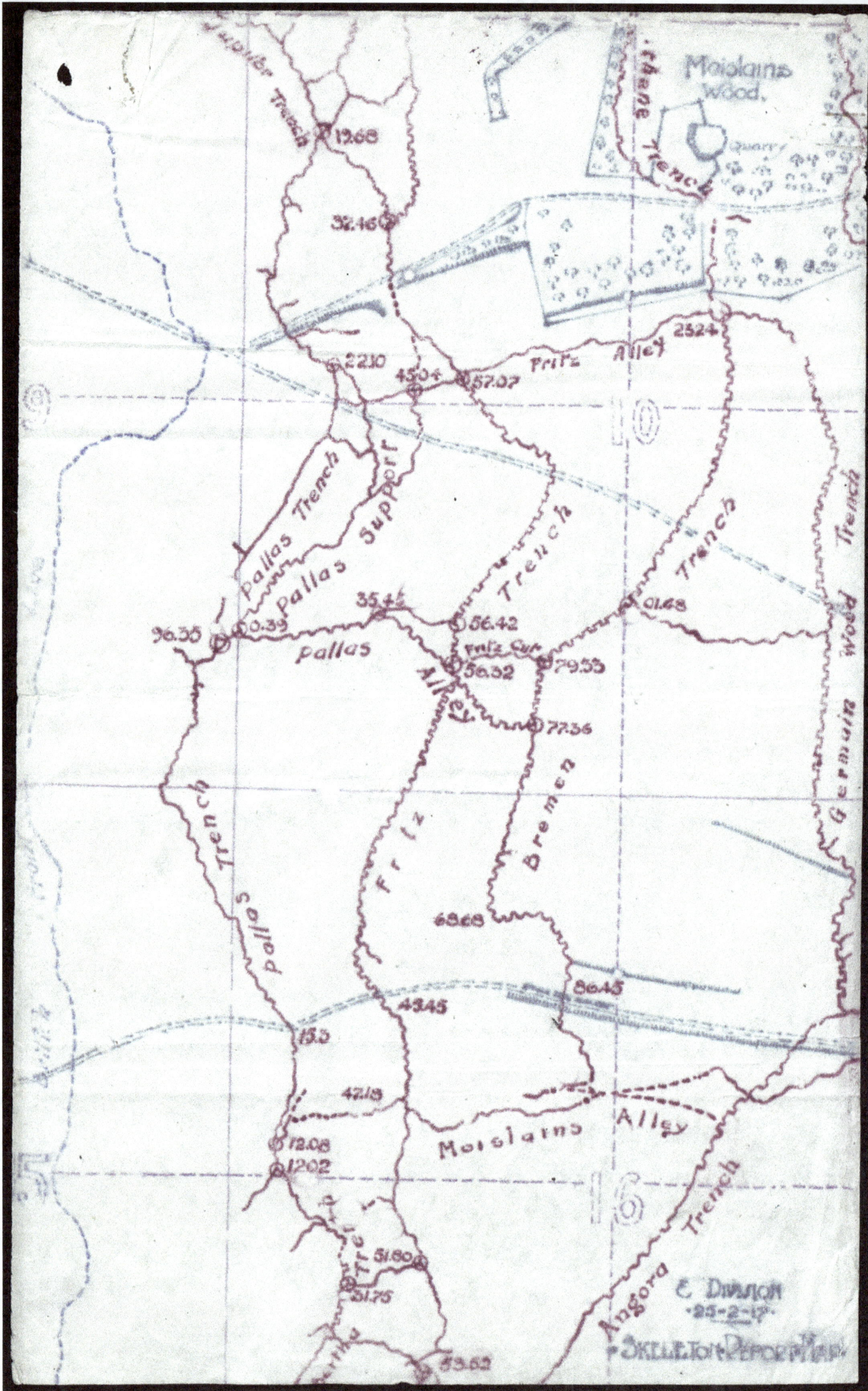

WAR DIARY or INTELLIGENCE SUMMARY

Army Form C. 2118.

April [March crossed out] **1917**

25 Machine Gun Coy.

Place	Date	Hour	Summary of Events and Information	Remarks and references to Appendices
Equincourt	1st		Meet O.C. 59 MGC to discuss co-operation in ensuing operations	
	2nd		No 1 Sect relieves No 4 Sect right sector outpost line – No 2 Sect/216MGC relieves No. 2. in left Section; & No 3/218 MGC relieves No 3/25 MGC in Roy.n.R. Support Coy. & No 3/218 MGC attached Lincolns Support Coy. No 2/25 to FINS . No 3/25 GOUZEL-LE-GRAND to positions in line of defence. CAPT. J.M MOOD joins Coy.	
	3rd		Reconnaissance for positions SOREL–FINS both inclusive.	
	4th		XV Cps M.G.O. inspects this line. Attack on GOUZEAUCOURT WOOD to a line south of this 2 Sect/7 25 to R.Berks.R. Nos 2 & 3/25 to Rifle Brigade – attack commenced at 2.15AM in very snowy & cold weather and by dawn 5th objective was gained except for a Mill in centre of Hill 135 on the right. 1 Officer /216 MGC wounded (D. Taylor since died of wounds).	
	6th		Coy relieved by 129 M.G.Cy. and moved to EPINETTE WOOD (less No 3/25 which was relieved by te Nos 2&1 Sects from FINS & SOREL moved to nebulous Corps line of futures. Return SOREL (Sx elusion) and GUYENCOURT (inclusion). W. WESTON to SGT Maling comm.	
	7th		Reconnaissance for positions on the above line. Coy move from EPINETTE	

WAR DIARY
or
INTELLIGENCE SUMMARY.

Army Form C. 2118.

Page 2.

25 Machine Gun Coy

April 1917

Place	Date	Hour	Summary of Events and Information	Remarks and references to Appendices
EPINETTE WOOD	7th		WOOD to Roadside Shelters at D 4 c. just South of NURLU. 2 horses died from exposure and fatigue.	
	8th		½ No 4/25 under L/NARDIE to anti-aircraft position at TIEREMONT. ½ No 4/25 to MOISLAINS for same purpose under Lt MACNAMARA. Work done shelters constructed gun belts outfits etc cleaned.	
	9th		The Coy's arrangements to the 8th review line GUYEN court - SOREL annex. Recconnts about witnesses.	
	10th			
	12th		Nos 1 & 2/25 returns to Coy H.Q. LL ARKWORTHY arriv from Rear.	
	13th		23 & 24 B⁰/F Div take MEUNIER HOUSE GAUCHE WOOD GOUZEAUCOURT Ry Sta;	
	15th		25 Coy relieve 24 & 25 B⁰. 25 MG Coy moves to HEUDICOURT East end Coln over 6 guns /2 & 8 mg Coy M East end of GOUZEAU COURT relieves 2 guns in QUENTIN MILL ½ No 1/25, No 3 Sect fire to position on proposed Brown Line of Offence ½ No 4/25 also to Brown Line ½ Matt/25 East of HEUDICOURT No 2 finding 2 anti-aircraft guns in HEUDICOURT. Support Line also acquired by ¼ N of QUENTIN MILL & GOUZEAU COURT STATION. Enemy on high ground just East of VILLARS GUISLAIN - All this period enemy counter attack expected.	

2353 Wt. W2544/1454 700,000 5/15 D. D. & L. A.D.S.S./Forms/C. 2118.

WAR DIARY or INTELLIGENCE SUMMARY

Army Form C. 2118.

Pay 3

April 1917

Place	Date	Hour	Summary of Events and Information	Remarks and references to Appendices
HEUDICOURT	16th		119th Bde Tale are on line North of FINS, GOUZEAUCOURT, main road (sub sect/218) return to 218 Cy.H.Q. (sect/218 ltsud court at night fall. The 23rd Brig: being about tale VILLARS GUISLAIN to Dot/25 more of QUENTIN MILL the direct purpose of assisting R.BERKS.R. & Som Fans during the attack on Seizing any Strong Points of retreating GERMANS East of VILLARS GUISLAIN – (This move promised excellent results but failed through lack of Berks in the morning).	
	17th		On further preparation for this attack not 24/25 more at dusk to GAUCHE WOOD from whence (an arrangements being made) they were to kl from the fire which the Enemy way th Burkley from GONNELIES Defences against the 2 3rd B's left positions dug, carefully emerald, line of fire laid off, zero hour for attack 4.25 AM 18th Thurs was established Light Fires the clinmouths on portion being on looks from the knees of Villars Guis LAIN by Cy lts comes to c.i.j. Shine at until 4.59 AM that out fire opens – This silenced all fire which was beginning to break out from GON & VILLd – The Enemy put up flare lares &	
	18th			

WAR DIARY or INTELLIGENCE SUMMARY

Page 4
25 Machine Gun Coy
April 1917

Place	Date	Hour	Summary of Events and Information	Remarks and references to Appendices
HEUDICOURT	18th		In about 20 mins. and then after shells the wood with outside our 2/3rd Bde. firing this objective with ease. fire was ceased at 6 AM Rounds fired 3000 - Enemy shelled wood 100 yds in front of HEUDICOURT between 11 AM & 3 P.M. In the evening No 4/25 E.M.G/s returned to HEUDICOURT. Fire was resumed on the same target by No 2 Sect as it was decided to try and shoot the enemy - Co-op de main by Coup de main by Corps de Nord - fire continued intermittently until midnight. GONNELIEU attack failed owing to hurried being too hurried the Enemy shooting a good light.	
	19th		Front No 2/25 interests continue firing on this night in large t until 2 enc. hour meanwhile No 1 Sect was relieved by Sect No 15 returning QUENTIN MILL and a succession of schemes have to be completed with repairing the defence line BROWN to the intermediate found between it and ST QUENTIN Mill line. (Mass known as the BLUELINE) 2 hostile aeroplanes rewarned in successfully to attack the Wood firing No 4 Sect arrd 6 am LINCOLNS. No 1 Sect firing moved to GAUCHE WOOD digs in N.E. 2nd & lays out lines of fire on the Eastern approaches of GONNELIEU - 23 Bn. & Coy co-operated by Lay 7	
	20th		a belt of fire East of the village or enemy wire 2 ens hour 4.20 AM - 1 hour before Zero LINCOLNS reach a taped line op- posite Westap and in the wire SW S.R. of the defences - at this hour thinks the Zero Sect the East LINCOLNS swung rifles through the village & came	
	21st			

WAR DIARY
or
INTELLIGENCE SUMMARY.

Army Form C. 2118.

Page 5

23 Maxim Gun Company

April 1917

Place	Date	Hour	Summary of Events and Information	Remarks and references to Appendices
APACHE WOOD	21st	4.20 AM	No 1 Sect then opened fire which fire is Volume until zero + 20 AM 23 M.G. Coy. concentrated fire then ceased. From Prisoners information this fire appears to have been well placed in most parts. Our men were greatly heartened by it. No 4 Sect meanwhile westward "PLOCKHART Though the village Turning 1 M.G. and 12 Enemy establishing his own guns in position East of the village When he was in the act of firing on a German M.G. getting into position taken a pre-emptying to unspat message from an inf. Coy Comdr sent him off to the right when as a matter of fact his fire were on an opposite that of war DIE'S front.— This I consider an instance of too great control being exercised by inf. Comdrs over the M.G.s attached to them. As this was due to the point of a triangle with two broad Valleys running into it from East & Northopposite. No 3 Sect is brought up & Sects are moved forward. The resulting formation being 4 guns attacked with 2 guns in echelon on each side & 2 guns on each side further back on a BLUE line. The flanking sub sections being of the same unit able to get up with a Counterattack from the flanking valleys.	

WAR DIARY
or
INTELLIGENCE SUMMARY

Army Form C. 2118.

Part 6   2St Machine Gun Coy

April 1917

Instructions regarding War Diaries and Intelligence Summaries are contained in F. S. Regs., Part II. and the Staff Manual respectively. Title pages will be prepared in manuscript.

(Erase heading not required.)

Place	Date	Hour	Summary of Events and Information	Remarks and references to Appendices
HEUDICOURT	21st		Pte CRABTREE wounded accidentally	
	22nd		Pte CRABTREE transferred to W.6.d. in a sunken road west of GOUVRE WOOD No 1 Sect burst Coy HQ. moved to W.6.d in a sunken road. No 2/25 relief 1 Sect 2/8 Coy which returns to 2/5 Coy HQ. Lt GOODEVE reports from Sick leave	
	23rd		Lt MACNAMARA with No 3 Sect attacked (with R.Ir. Rifles) an outwork of pain Trench (taly'u) with 40th Div when they take VILLARS PLUICH	
	24th		40th Div gain their objective. No 3 Sect with R.Ir. Rifles gain a line in front of N of GONNELIEU — No 1 Sect. construct strong points around QUENTIN MILL — No 2 Sect relieve No 4 Sect — The enemy for some reason shelling heavily Cpl ISSETT Pte ELLIS wounded Pte BANNISTER (No 2) killed Anniversary of Lt landing on GALLIPOLI — Division has now reached so far as necessary towards HINDENBURG Line and approaching	
	25th		was being wired (sensational). An outpost Coy (known as the green line) 656 in. Supporting Tps on BLUE line to work in rear. Cpl MANATE got slightly wounded No 3 Sect latter fiery position on QUENTIN No 1 Sect relieves No 3 Sect	
	26th		Men - Yesterday (Sect/28 Coy relieving not very gun shy stood No 4 returns to Coy HQ Division was fresh Lyell, Sask of GONSLIEU	

T2134. Wt. W708—776. 500000. 4/15. Sir J. C. & S.

WAR DIARY
or
INTELLIGENCE SUMMARY

April 1917

Army Form C. 2118

Place	Date	Hour	Summary of Events and Information	Remarks and references to Appendices
Wbd.	27th		The advance crosses town and Blue and Green lines in force. 6be Bug Systematicly Corps M.G.O inspects Blue line for M.G Emplacements - Coy System of Relief two section Green line 4 days, 1 sect Blue line 2 days so called rest Coy HQ.	
	28th		Lunch drive Some of Blue night position dug in material allotted. B.P. Major inspects line with B.G officer & O.C/s R.Q.L. also 1st Squadron C.E.F.&V.B. "Shall be "Shaped" - arrangements made. 4 guns in valley South of GOV[?]26A 4 copies (along which Ry Embankment runs) from out section for anti aircraft firing. No 2 sect loses 2 wounded. Tripod ?? broken shooting burned by shell fire in outpost position W having reached this position began to dig in the Enemy has settled down with the aid of Superior aircraft to shell by systematically both back forward area - In the further he has been excellent line Minenwerfer Like miniature howitzers firing shell very similar to this Bang's 6 secs 130m water range	
	29th		Arm period of several Guns included A.7k'd three Minenwerfer also fire shrapnel. Between A&76RM approximately the Northern end of an H.Q. heavy (W.6.d) was shelled by 5.9. A very sly report on the Railway Embankment -	

Army Form C. 2118

WAR DIARY
or
INTELLIGENCE SUMMARY.
(Erase heading not required.)

Page 8.

April 1917   25th Life

Instructions regarding War Diaries and Intelligence Summaries are contained in F.S. Regs., Part II. and the Staff Manual respectively. Title pages will be prepared in manuscript.

Place	Date	Hour	Summary of Events and Information	Remarks and references to Appendices
In W6d	Ap 29		Went first east of his about 100 shells. In only few with road wounding some men & 1 mule — Our own wounds in the trenches - Riper - My action especially from The Barracks & SUNNIST FARM ? as seen to its advantage to fire on with the 18 pdrs — perhaps they have bolted of in case of emergency. to first no cases with — Col Watson and they of the evening – Jas. Wolpamam the letter by Col Watson and they of the ORMS battle — He said no — I walter beowen at OMens	
"	30.5		Col Clark WWSGO & Capt Taylor arrived at Cry. Hqp to the Chief certain Sent wallop + barrage for schemes. OC 2 sqs + this Offeren can to take over by Line — Capt Bourne OC 13 sqs & RH recommends Grunruless position in accordance with barrage schemes — Isgt wounded to outpost line — It Ashway MC injured eye with trench fever	

1/4/17

J.M. Hood
Capt & Adjt
25 Dr. R. Wo.

Army Form C. 2118

WAR DIARY
or
INTELLIGENCE SUMMARY.
(Erase heading not required.)

25th Machine Gun Company

May 1917

Page 1.

Place	Date	Hour	Summary of Events and Information	Remarks and references to Appendices
			Reference FRANCE sheet 57 C SE Edition 3.A. 20,000	
Sunken Rd W.6.d.	1st		Change in strength.) 1st April 10 offs 164 O.R. 10 sick 16 OR. hosp 10 OR. leave 1 to 30 wounded 9 or killed 1 OR. actual strength } Schools 15. Hosp. Evacuated 1 or. Draft 19 OR. Strength 1st May 10 offs 174 OR. XV Corps M.G.O. discussed advance from the outpost line by Gonnelieu & by the Division and cooperation by M.G.s with an extended barrage on the HINDENBURG line. Reconnoitered for positions – Coy relieved by 23rd M.G. Coy. at dusk. Coy marched back to TIERAMONT	
TIERAMONT	2nd		Billets very foul. Every village has been left a rubbish heap by the enemy probably for the purpose of spreading disease. Reconnoitred material & 1 Km SE of Coy. billets & tin town in a clean open grass field. No 3 Section on A.A. duty, 2 guns	
	3rd		HEUDICOURT 1 gun SOREL 1 gun LIERAMONT. Transport remains at SOREL LE GRAND. Tin town finished and fly proofed on new premises. Orders received concerning M.G. Barrage APPENDIX A.1. MAP A.B. APPENDIX A.3. 10 gun Barrage moves up to QUENTIN MILL with 6 limbers with camouflage material amongst the other equipment. After dark gun positions R.31.c.1.b. settled and work commenced upon them. The material being left at QUENTIN MILL until afterwards announced. Lieut. Mills Crawshaw M.C. is a conference of C.O.Coy Commanders at	

WAR DIARY
INTELLIGENCE SUMMARY.

25th Machine Gun Coy.

Page 2

Place	Date	Hour	Summary of Events and Information	Remarks and references to Appendices
HERAMONT	May 5th 1917		Map FRANCE sheet 57 F S Edn 3 A 1/20,000 - sheet 62 C NE 1/10,000	
		3PM	Order at 3PM concerning recce & attack on the OPPY-GAVRELLE ROAD. It appears though enemy MGs.	
			Teams move up from QUESNY mill & Section B at 8:30PM. No A.L.G. yet up. Appears since first orders issued. Attack on a big scale on LAVACQUERIE 0.5mm ET	
			FARM by 4 Off. & 5 Divs. Cancelled & raid on large scale substituted. Thirty MRAA 3.74	
			officers on the line to BE. Great difficulty occurred over the non-appearance of the carrying party. Ammunition was eventually brought up from the BCS	
			dump by spare men of the 7 W F YORKS and our transport also brought up ammunition to the S.A.A. dumps at LEVEE	
			GONNELIEU. At 9 PM the enemy barrage starts. the Infantry went forward	
			The Company opened its barrage lines at the appointed hour and continued according to programme until ammunition ran rather short. All guns	
			worked well except two - one getting many repeated cases shifting the Buffers	
			from a sniper of thick mud. — No casualties — at 2AM the Teams was the	
			gun in the Infantry trench in front — at 2AM the enemy was not by Lewis	
			guns to LEVEE CROSSING at K.1.C. 15.65 where they were cut by Lewis	
			gun fire at close fire. M.G. telescopic sight captured.	

WAR DIARY
INTELLIGENCE SUMMARY

Army Form C. 2118.

25 Woolwich Siege Coy.
May 1917. Page 3.

Place	Date	Hour	Summary of Events and Information	Remarks and references to Appendices
VILLARS GUISLAIN.	16th		Last night relief complete of No 24 M.G.C. According to orders the Coy developed fire all along the front with as many guns as possible. The artillery put down a barrage. All this apparently for the purpose of bringing up hostile balloons. The 4th Brigade R.F.C. came on to do this but no balloons appeared. The result was several casualties — one from planes who forced down, flew past VILLARS GUISLAIN 30 ft up & went behind VAUCEL LETTE FARM.	App. B.1. M.P.P
			Positions of guns today wind not suitable: propose scheme for battle defence (M.Toll?) The line is now becoming more the normal Trench System, but owing to the ground the immediate front especially the west edge of HONNE COURT COPSE cannot be covered except by M.G.'s in the front line — The scheme is an illustration of the use of ground & of trajectories & very necessary point in this undulating country, of taking into account when guns & offrs will fall away from as for as possible. Offrs. use of support guns firing indirectly as a further defence of the front line. This extra "band of cross-fire" is most important. It fields of unammunition rifles" I can anyhow support to coming up with their types on the artillery	App. A.2

WAR DIARY or INTELLIGENCE SUMMARY

Army Form C. 2118.

25 Machine Gun Coy

May 1917

Page 4

Place	Date	Hour	Summary of Events and Information	Remarks and references to Appendices
VILLERS	10th		Ranges also of the weather into my long range fire without leaving it	
GUIS I PMCuD	11th		No work went possible during the day, guns known fire on suitable targets at night. O.C. 121 Coy came to see the line preparatory to taking over	
	12th		Battery in valley X 8 a put out special harassing fire was carried out – 2 guns M.G. came into M by 5 – In the evening the fire was carried out by a balloon officer G.U.I.S 4.4N	
	14th		121 M.G. Coy relieves 25 MGC. Battn. returning to N U R L U together with 1/R Ir R, Rifle Brig S. + Trench mortars – Training programme carried on	APPX C
	15th		Division placed in Corps Reserve and ready to support any part of the front. 25 M.G. Coy in such an event (shown by F.QUANCOURT – Road running through V4 – P 34 q Trolley in P 28 a 6	
	18th		2 Cooker paraded at VILLE wood for Corps Commander	
	25th		8" naval gun firing at long range fired 25 rounds half often into our camp 3 W.Royal Irish R when casualties were inflicted. That was the adjutant first lost of Coy Coy was broken up ?	

T2134. Wt. W708—776. 500000. 4/15. Sir J. C. & S.

Army Form C. 2118

25 Machine Gun Co[y]

WAR DIARY
or
INTELLIGENCE SUMMARY.
(Erase heading not required.)

May 1917 Page 5

Place	Date	Hour	Summary of Events and Information	Remarks and references to Appendices
WEST NORD	29th		Company moved to Moislains training on Railway. Training.	app 1. & App C3.
MOISLAINS	30th			app c 2 App C.
—	31st		March 8th to SUSANNE.	App D 1

J. Moore Capt.
1/6/17.
OC 25 MGC

Appendix A1

Secret   8th. Division No.G.30/

1. (a) In the forthcoming operations against SONNET FARM, the following Machine Guns of the Division will take part and will be placed under the orders of G.O.C. 23rd. Inf.Bde. for the operations on "Z" Day.
   (b) Captain C.W.Taylor 218th. M.G.Coy. will act as Machine Gun Staff Officer to G.O.C. 23rd. Inf.Bde. for the operations.

2. The 23rd. M.G.Coy. 24th. M.G.Coy. less two Sections 25 M.G.C less 1 Section and 1 Subsection and 218th. M.G.Coy. less two Sections will put down a Barrage in front and to Right Flank of the objective as shewn in the attached Map G.4.

3. The Gun positions as shewn on the attached Map are not to be taken as exact. O's.C.M.G. Coys. will insure that the positions selected give the necessary safety clearances. Gun positions will be reconnoitred forwith by O's.C.M.G.Coys. the positions and lines of fire will be so marked that there will be no difficulty in occupying them after dark.

4. Guns are divided into Groups and may be referred to by the number of the group during operations.

5. Depression Stops will be used as far as the supply permits.

6. Any special instructions for linking up M.G.Coys. by Telephone with Battalions or Brigade H.Q. will be issued by G.O.C. 23rd. Inf.Bde.

7. Carrying parties up to 24 men per M.G.Coy. will be provided on "Y" or "Z" day as required as follows:-
   23rd. Inf.Bde. for 23rd. and 25th MG.Coys.
   24th. Inf.Bde. for 24th. and 218th. M.G.Coys.
   To minimise labour, full use will be made of M.G.Limbers.

8. The Normal rate of fire will be at the rate of 150 rounds a minute, except for S.O.S. signal when the rate will be increased to 250 rounds a minute.

9. Orders as to when fire will be opened except for an SOS. Signal will be issued later.

10. There will be no special M.Gun S.O.S. Signal

11. The following will be stored at each Gun:-
    14 Belts S.A.A.   3 Boxes S.A.A.   2 Tins Water.

12. Remaining Guns of the 23rd. and 24th. M.G.Coys. will be at the disposal of G.O's.C. 23rd. and 24th. Inf.Bdes.

13. No. 1 Group will withdraw and come under orders of G.O.C. 24th. Inf.Bde. at 3.45 am. on "Z"+1 Day.
    Nos. 6 and 7 Groups will withdraw and come under orders of GO.C. 25th. Inf. Bde. at 4.30. am. on "Z"+1 Day.
    Nos. 2 and 3 Groups will withdraw to their positions in Green Line at 4.30 am. "Z"+1 Day.

14. In case of No5. Group the three cones of fire shewn in Red on attached Map G.4, will only be fired on up to a centain time to be notified later. These three Guns that were firing on these localities will then switch on to the targets shewn in R.16.d which will be their barrage lines.

15. The 40th. Division will be continuing the barrage to the North and will also be bringing M.G. fire to bear on the HINDENBURG LINE just South ofm R.16.d. central.

8th. Division.
3rd. May 1917.

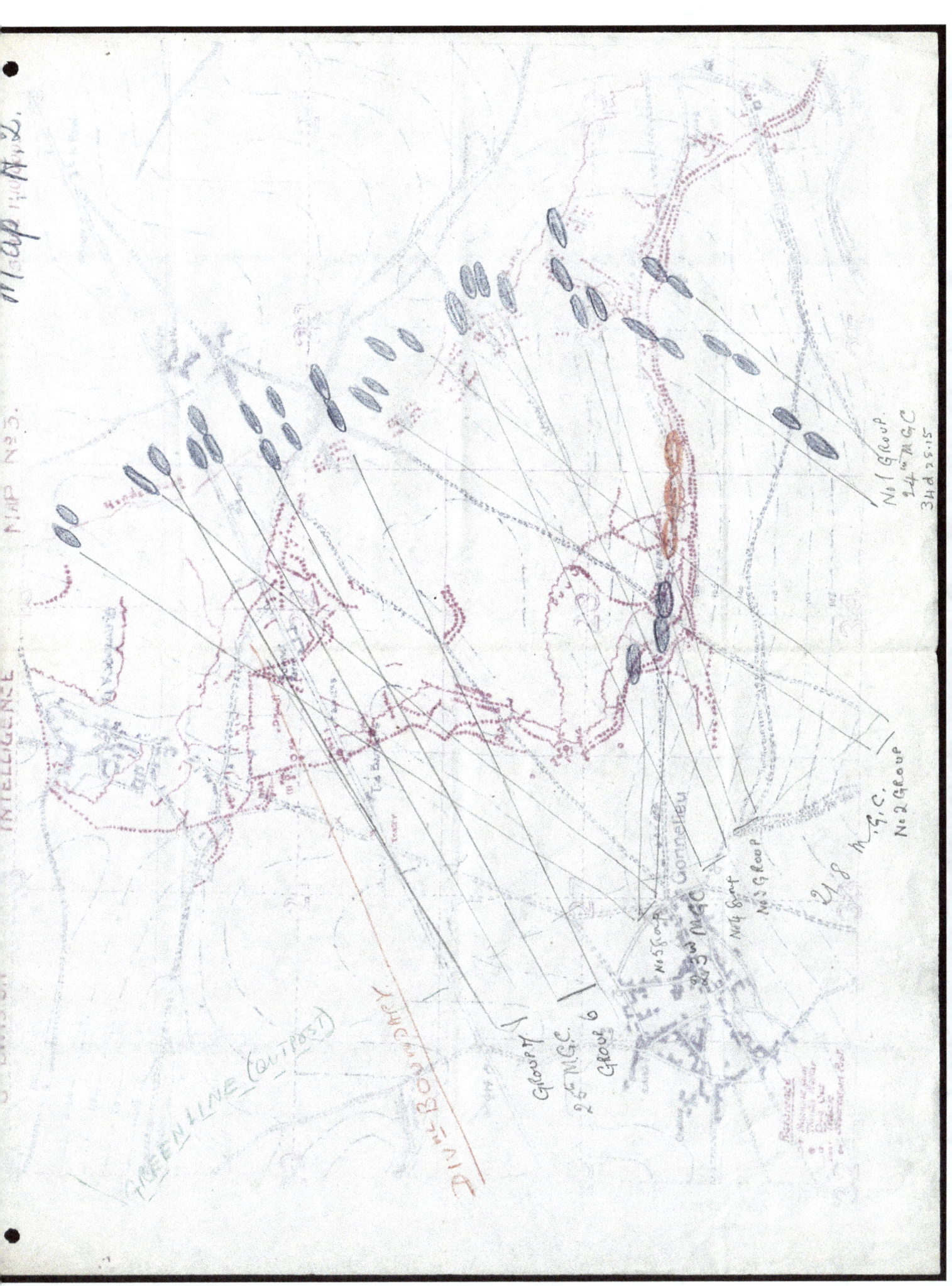

Appendix A 3

Group No. 6   R 27 c 35.80

Gun No.	Targets.	Map Bearing	Actual Range	Q.E.
1	R23c 35.82	72.30	2300	5.14
2	R23a 70.00	72.30	2350	6.13.
3	R23a 25.10	70.18	2225	5.31.
4	R23a 25.50	70.18	2375	6.30
5	R23a 20.60	~~2200~~/ 77.50	2200	5.30
6	R23a 40.75	77.50	2350	6.28.

Group No. 7.   R 27 a 27.30

Gun No.	Targets	Map Bearing	Actual Range	Q.E.
7	R23a 20.63.	72	2325	6.10
8	R23a 40.75	72	2450	7.4
9	R23a 15.75	72.18	2350	6.20
10	R17c 06.06	68.18	2400	6.27

Coy. H.Q. R26 b 9.2.

APPENDIX A 4

Table 'A' Issued with 8th. Division Order No. 199.

The following will be the time table of the Machine Gun Barrage:-

Series No.	Time.	Groups Engaged.	Target.	Rounds per gun per minute.	
1	11 p.m. to 11.18 p.m.	No.5	R.28.c.&d. R.29.c.	75	
2	11.18 – 11.40. p.m.	No.5 Nos.1,2,3,4.	Barrage Lines	100 50	
x 3	11.40 – 11.55. p.m.	All	Barrage Lines	150	22500
4	12.midnight– 12.5 a.m.	All	: :	100	5000
5	12.11.a.m. 12.15.a.m.	All	: :	100	2000
6	12.19.a.m. 12.25.a.m.	All	: :	50	3500
7	12.29.a.m. 12.35.a.m.	All	: :	50	2000
8	12.36.a.m. 12.42.a.m.	All	: :	50	3500
9	12.45.a.m. 12.48.a.m.	All	: :	50	1500
10	12.52.a.m. 1.0. a.m.	All	: :	150	12000
11	1.10.a.m. 1.20.a.m.	No.5 Nos.1,2,3,4.	R.28.c.&d. R.29.c. Barrage Lines	50	53500 32500 21000
12	1.25.a.m. 1.33.a.m.	No.5 Nos.1,2,3,4.	R.28.c.&d. R.29.c. Barrage Lines	50	
13	1.38.a.m. 1.45.a.m.	No.5	R.28.c.&d. R.29.c.	50	
14	1.55.a.m.	No.5	R.28.c.&d. R.29.c.	50	

x Barrage lines of No. 5 Group are shown on map G.4. by three Blue Cones of fire in R.29.c.&d. and 3 Blue Cones of fire in R.18.d.

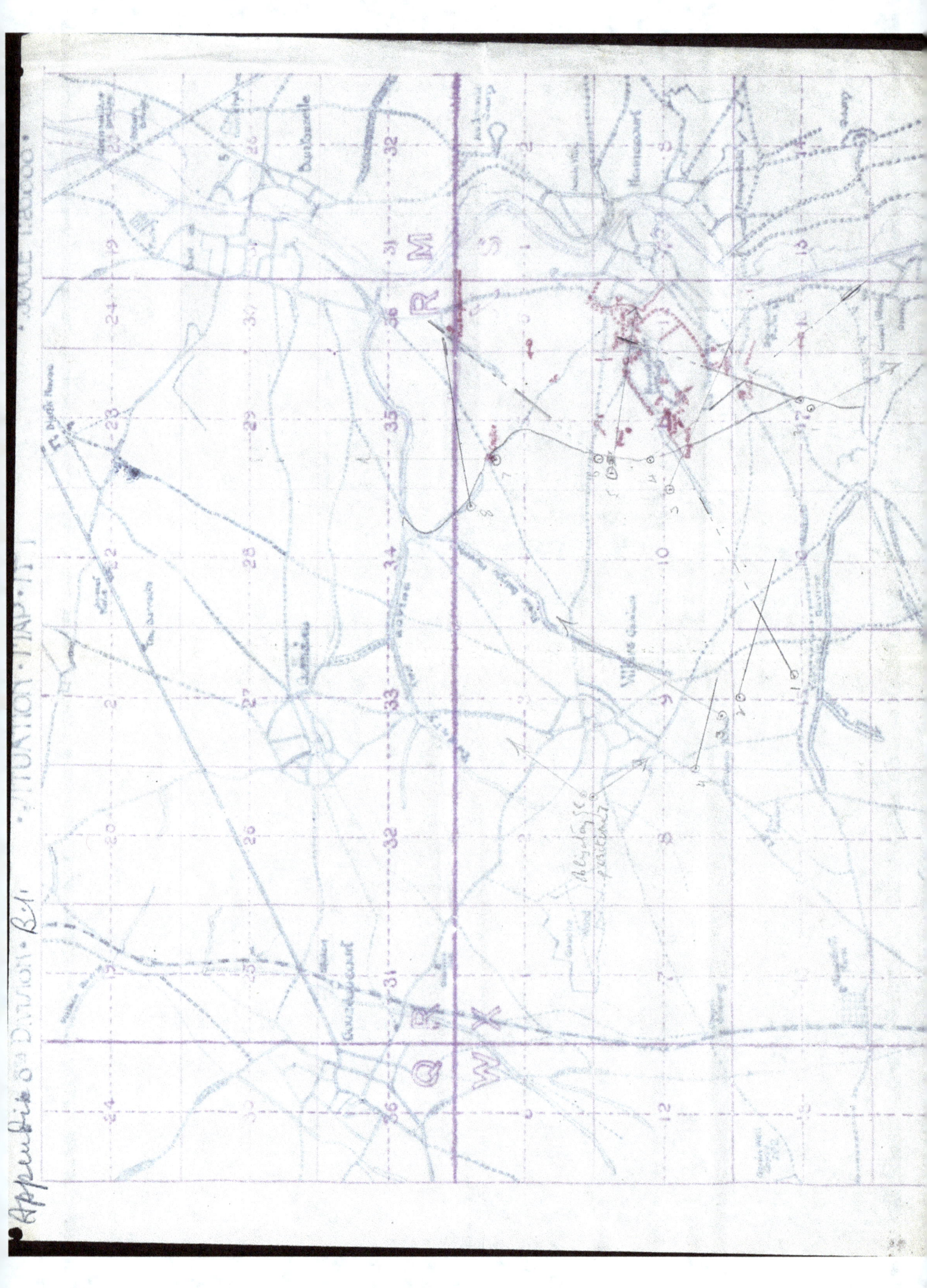

Appendix B 2

PROPOSED MACHINE GUN TACTICS FOR THE SECTOR 22 RAVINE--TARGELLE RAVINE.

THE BLUE (front) LINE.

Three areas of fire. The front one, as will be seen below, by the support guns; the middle band where the cones of fire and further limits of searches will fall on important places; The inner belt, which is formed into spear-heads of cross-fire, so that the men of an advancing line will fall under the fire in succession. The two last are put down by the front line guns.

No of gun	position	Mag:Line of Fire	Nature of fire.
No 1 gB	X.17.d.15.82.	164 degrees	Searching slightly.
No 2 gB	X 17 b 30 02	30	Q E for 400, grazing fire for 900, cone falls N E end HONNECOURT WOOD.
No 3 gB	X 11 c 04 91	24	Searching across valley
No 4 gB	X 11 a 53 10	152	QE for 1300, grazing fire from 500-900 cone falls valley N of CANAL WOOD.
No 5 g B	X 11 a 30 75	110	Searches N edge of HONNECOURT WOOD.
No 6 g B	X 11 a 5 9	51	QE for 1300 grazing fire 500-900 cone falls ravine junction R 36 c.
No 7 g B	X 5 a 5 4	12	Searching across ravine 22
No 8 B	X 4 b 83 72	92	QE for 1000 grazing fire for nearly 1200.

Outer band by guns on GREEN LINE as an extra defence or for "strafing"

No of gun	position	Mag:Line of Fire	Nature of fire.
No 1 G	X 15 b 35 10	114	QE for 2300 to traverse CANAL WOOD & track N of it
No 2 G	X 15 b 0 9	100	QE for 2525 traverse in front of LES TRANCHEES
No 3 G	X 15 b 45 55	104	QE for 2475 traverse BOSQUET FARM.
No 4 G	X 15 b 0 9	100	QE for 2600 traverse LES TRANCHEES and Northwards
No 5 218 coy	X 9 b 0 6	99	QE for 2600 traverse over roads in X 12 a 35 80
No 6 218 coy	X 3 d 2 3	69	QE for 2100 traverse over bend in ravine R 35 d 9 8

THE GREEN (support) LINE.

No of gun	position	Mag:Line of Fire	Nature of fire.
No 1 G	X 15 b 35 10	74	QE for 1400 grazing fire 700 conefalls X 10 d 7 3
No 2 G	X 15 b 0 9	117	QE for 500 grazing fire for about 1200
No 3 G	X 9 c 70 15	42	Searching valley E of VILLARS GUISLAIN.
No 4 G	X 9 c 00 55	116	QE for 500 grazing fire for about 900
No 7 218 coy	X 2 d 6 0	157	Belt of fire behind village.
No 8 218 coy	X 2 d 6 15	48	.. ..

N B 5 & 6 guns/218 coy are behind my line and useless. By Day 7 & 8 guns aree employed covering GONNELIEU from near Cemetary N of GUISLAIN.

Appendix C.1.

COMPANY ORDERS.

By Captain J M Mood commanding
25 MACHINE GUN COMPANY.

MAP REF
1/40000 Sheets 62 C & D   28/5/17

    Orderly officer   2/Lt. E.M. Lockhart
    Orderley Sergeant   Sgt. Templeton R.

MOVE   The company will move to MOISLAINS To-morrow

Parades Reveille 6.30 A M. Orderley room 7.30 A M. Staff parade 8.30 PM
            8/A M   Packing limbers.
            9 A M   Open warfare with fighting limbers.
            2 P M   P T   MOISLAINS
            3 P M   Combined drill

TRANSPORT   Reaches Coy H Q NURLU at 7 A M
              Leaves at 10.15 A M
              Passes starting point at 10.35 A M exactly
              Marches on MOISLAINS
              Formation :- 4 S A A limbers, H Q limber, COOK's cart, water
              cart 2 Sanitary men behind water cart ; Cooks, cooks
              cart, L/C Topham and storeman, H Q limber ; Armourer,
              saddler, shoemaker and C O's batman Brakesmen for S A A
              limbers . Transport officer commands ; Transport sgt
              supervises in rear .

Advanced   2nd in command, mounted, C Q M S", Signalling cpl, L/C Sanson
party   on bicycles to take over at MOISLAINS from 24 M G C
              Requisite signalling equipment to be carried on cycles

Camps   NURLU and SOREL camps must be left scrupulously clean.

Marches   March discipline must be strictly carried out and enforc-
            -ed on all occasions . The Divisional commander had
            cause to find fault with the company on the subject the
            other day

                                                   Lieut
                                  2-in-C . 25 M . G . Coy

Appendix C 2

COMPANY ORDERS BY CAPT. J.M.WOOD
COMMDG 25 M.G.Coy.

Company Orderly Officer   Lieut. E.T.Macnamara
Company Orderly Sergeant   Sgt. Finch J.

Reveille at   3.30 am

Parades

    4.0 am   Loading up
    4.15 am   Breakfasts
    5.15 am   Parade
    5.30 am   March off

1. All tents will be struck this evening by 7pm at Headquarters. Transport officer will arrange to transport them to Town Major.

2. Signalling equipment on to H.Q. limber with H.Q. and Stationary stores

3. Certain C.Q.M.S. stores on G.S. wagon.

4. No. 4 Section will lend half a limber to No. 3 Section.   Crossed

5. Full equipment carried tin helmets on pack with pack straps crossed on top and below no tin helmets to be worn

6. Breakfast as for yesterday.

7. Advanced party as before will report to Town Major's office SUZANNE Chateau at 6 am.

8. 2 Men as unloaders will be detailed to go with the lorry as unloaders

9. Blankets on lorry labelled by Sections.

10. 1 N.C.O. and four men to be detailed by A/C.S.M. to report to the officer in charge of the rear party of the Trench Mortar Battery behind as B.G.C.

11. All billets must be left scrupulously clean.

12. Order of March dismounted party ...200 yds. ...fighting limbers and transport

13. Route past MOISLAINS CHURCH...HAUTE ALLAINES...starting point I 5a-6.6 at 6.30 am...CLERY...MARICOURT A 28 c 8.5 ...SUZANNE CAMP no. 1 O 24 d 5 ?

14. Water point at Suzanne near Chateau.

15. Brigade H.Q. at Suzanne..Chateau.

16. **Discipline.**
Units are reminded that the Area into which the Brigade Gr up is proceeding is occupied by French civilians, and that they must show such consideration and respect to property as will result in claims being reduced to a minimum.

This applies particularly to Transport lines. On no account are horses to be allowed to wander on pasture land, and all Transport lines are to be selected after consultation with the Town Major or Maire as the case may be

25.3.17   Capt.
                                              Commdg. 25 M.G.Coy.

Appendix C 2
Cntd.

After Orders.

(a) Billeting party only O.Q.M.S. & L/Cpl. Sanson. report on Bicycles at junction NOIRLAIRS--HAUTE--ALAINE and AZIZCOURT-Le Haut--HAUTE ALLAINE ROAD (3 miles) by 4.45 am and report to senior officer on the spot.

(b) Additional rear party detailed by Sgt. Major will be left to clean billets 1 Cpl. 3 Men They will leave billets by 7.30 am so as to reach above road junction at 8.30 am and report there to senior officer of rear party. They must however not be armed with brooms.

Appendix D.1.

Fourth Army No. G.S.698.

8th Division.

    Before the 8th Division leave the Fourth Army I desire to express to all ranks my appreciation of the good services they have rendered during the past seven months.

    Their capture of ZENITH Trench in October, 1916, and of PALLAS and FRITZ Trenches in March, 1917, were operations requiring careful preparation and bold leadership. The success attained on both these occasions deserves high praise.

    The successful operations carried out during March and April, 1917, including the capture of HEUDECOURT, FINS, GOUZEAUCOURT and GOUZEAUCOURT WOOD, VILLERS GUISLAIN and GONNELIEU were conducted with a gallantry and a skill which was wholly admirable and shows that the Division has been brought to a high state of fighting efficiency.

    I regret that the Division is leaving the Fourth Army, but I hope that on some future occasion I may again have the good fortune to find them under my Command.

H.Q., Fourth Army,
21st May, 1917.

H Rawlinson
General,
Commanding Fourth Army.

Instructions regarding War Diaries and Intelligence Summaries are contained in F.S. Regs., Part II. and the Staff Manual respectively. Title pages will be prepared in manuscript.

25 Machine Gun Co.
Army Form C. 2118.
Page 1.

WAR DIARY
or
INTELLIGENCE SUMMARY.
(Erase heading not required.)

June 1917

Vol 18

Place	Date	Hour	Summary of Events and Information	Remarks and references to Appendices
SAILLY LORETTE	1st		March from SUSANNE to SAILLY LORETTE (Camps 24) commenced gear not been in billets since. Made + clean	
			Ending Army 10 Officers 176 men. Hospital 10 men June 2 Off Strength 5 O.R. Reinforcement 1 Off 14 men Evacuated 1 Recommended 1	
	2nd		Morgt 1st June 11 Offs 180 O.R. Company played at Camp 124. Today was pay inspection cleaning limbers and guns and getting — to Camp	
	3rd		Morning spent cleaning up Company paraded at 6.10 p.m. marched to the NEUVES entrained. Transport went out at 4.40 p.m. and entrained afterwards. Train left at 8.45 p.m.	
STRAZEELE	4th		Company arrived early. morning on at CAESTRE. Billeting Party, 2nd Lieutenant — and C.Q.H.S. went on ahead to STRAZEELE which is Company arrived about 11.0 a.m. Remainder of day spent in settling into billets. Training carried out about long paid + School fire drill.	
	5th			

WAR DIARY or INTELLIGENCE SUMMARY

Sheet 11.

Place	Date	Hour	Summary of Events and Information	Remarks and references to Appendices
STAZEELE	5th		Baths at Puttestreet at 8 am. Reveille to be at 4.30 a.m. Lieuts Lockhart and Pitworth took the parade	
	6th		Training was carried on from 10 to 12 and 2 to 4. Packs were packed in British and Training carried on.	
	7th		Company Conference re the billeting area and readiness to move up at any moment. Training carried on as usual. Church Parades C of E. 11.30 a.m. Presbyterian and R. Non. Conf: 11.30 at R.I.R. Transport Lines.	
	8th		Company paraded at 6.15 to march to HONDEGHEM - Billeting party went on as usual -	
	9th		Training carried on. Equipments cleaned.	
	12th		Marched to EECKE and stopped the night there	
	13th		Reveille 2 a.m. Marched off at 3.45 - Company marched to Scottish	
	14th		Camp BUSSEBOOM. Transport went Brigaded - Billeting Party, 2nd - in - Command and C.Q.M.S. went on with R.T. billeting parties - Captain Wood to Division as D.M.G.O.	

WAR DIARY
or
INTELLIGENCE SUMMARY.
(Erase heading not required.)

Army Form C. 2118.

Place	Date	Hour	Summary of Events and Information	Remarks and references to Appendices
BUSSEBOOM	15th		Foot Inspection and Training Carried on. Deficiencies in equipment and kit made up.	
	16th		Training Parade carried out by Section Officers.	
	17th		All Officers on Coys. inspected by Coys Commander.	
	18th		C of E Church Parade 11.30 a.m. in Church Hut. Training Carried on — Lieut Macnamara to DIV HQ to attend Companies —	
	19th		Company marched with 26th Infantry Brigade to STEENVOORDE SOUTH Training area — Reveille was at 2.15 and Coy moved off at 3.45, arriving at the Camp about 9.15. Rest of day was spent in cleaning the Camp — Baths at Steenvoorde — Company went in two parties under Lieut Farthwaite and Lieut Dolatic —	
	20th		Training by Company was carried out — 22.1 and 114 Lectures cooperation with 2nd Rifle Brigade —	
	21st		11. Coy 3 went to 1st A.I.R. but were not required and so returned	

Army Form C. 2118.

WAR DIARY
or
INTELLIGENCE SUMMARY.
(Erase heading not required.)

Place	Date	Hour	Summary of Events and Information	Remarks and references to Appendices
	22nd		As they were not required and carried on section training – Indirect Fire Drill and bomb drill in afternoon –	
	23rd		A wet day and cooperation with battalion impossible – Instructional parades in billets.	
			No. 1 and No. 4 Section cooperated in practice attack with 2nd Lincolns. No. 2 and 3 Section cooperated with 11th Brigade. Corps Machine Gun Officer visited the Company. Indirect Fire Drill and Arm Drill in afternoon.	
	24th		Inspection of Transport by O.C. A Coy Divisional Train and Staff Captain Divisional Commander came in the afternoon and found the Officers shooting on the range. The guns not	
	25th		Firing from 7.30 to 10.20. Parades under Section Officers	
	26th		Brigade field day – Company came into barrage positions and then advanced in support of the infantry for the attack. Corps M.G.O. came and watched the attack. Pte Frost A.S.C. attached tried for P. by C.M. and then consolidation.	

Army Form C. 2118

WAR DIARY
or
INTELLIGENCE SUMMARY.
(Erase heading not required.)

Instructions regarding War Diaries and Intelligence Summaries are contained in F. S. Regs., Part II. and the Staff Manual respectively. Title pages will be prepared in manuscript.

Place	Date	Hour	Summary of Events and Information	Remarks and references to Appendices
Whitefield	27th		Brigade Rifle Meeting – Company Teams came out second in both events – The Officers in the Shooters Tent was successful both teams being knocked out –	
	28th		Parades by Section for Instruction – Wet morning and no cooperation with S's Instruction was given in use of the Yukon Pack. –	
	29th		Half the Brigade moved up to Divisional area. Representation of 2.25 Coy. came round to take over. Parades by Sections preparing for moving	
	30th		Company moved off from STEENVOORDE at 5.25 a.m. and marched to HALIFAX CAMP (H14 c4.8 – Ref Sheet 28) arriving at 9.0 a.m., The Huts taken over were previously occupied by the 24th M.G. Coy. LIEUT A. SIMMONDS joined from 21st Coy. to take Command. [Gone O.R. from 25th Coy.]	

A Simmonds, Capt.
Commanding 25th M.G. Coy.

WAR DIARY

25th M.G. COMPANY from 1st JULY 1917 to 30th JULY 1917

Place	Date	Hour	Summary of Events and Information	Remarks and references to Appendices
Near YPRES H14.c.68 (Ref. Map Sheet 28)	1/7/17		Voluntary Church Parade. Two guns of No. 2 Section under 2nd Lt. LOCKHART relieved two guns of the 218th M.G. Coy on anti-aircraft duty at Ammunition Dumps at H.13.d.22 and H.8.d.81 (Ref. Map Sheet 28). Relief complete at 7.30 pm. 3.O.R. to C.C.S. A.S.	
	2/7/17		Nos. 3 & 4 Sections training under Section Officers 9.0 a.m. to 12.30 p.m. On the night of the 2nd/3rd July, Nos. 1 & 2 Sections relieved two Sections of the 218th M.G.Coy in the line held by the 24th BDE. Relief complete at 2.30 a.m. Upon completion of relief the two sections on the line (i.e. Nos. 1 & 2) came under the orders of the G.O.C. 24th BDE. and the senior Section Officer, LIEUT. GOODEVE was in charge of the guns and responsible to the O.C. 24th M.G. Coy. On the night of 2nd/3rd the Brigade Transport commenced to form a dump of S.A.A. at I.9.c.76 (Ref. Map Sheet 28). This S.A.A. is for the use of M.G's in future operations, and will be moved into forward dumps in the trench system by Transport and carrying parties from this Company during the next few nights. 2nd Lt. K.V. WESTON rejoined from M.G.C. Base Depot. A.S.	APPENDIX I RELIEF ORDERS

Army Form C.2118

WAR DIARY
or
INTELLIGENCE SUMMARY.
(Erase heading not required.)

Instructions regarding War Diaries and Intelligence Summaries are contained in F.S. Regs., Part II. and the Staff Manual respectively. Title pages will be prepared in manuscript.

Place	Date	Hour	Summary of Events and Information	Remarks and references to Appendices
Near YPRES I.14.c.5.8 (Ref. Sheet 28)	2/7/17		6534 PTE. F. BAGNALL tried by F.G.C.M. A.S.	
	3/7/17		The teams at Coy. H.Q. overhauled their equipment during the morning. At night a carrying party was sent out and also transport to transfer S.A.A. from Bde. Dump at T.9.c.75.4 forward Coy. Dump at T.17.b.5.4 (Ref. Sheet 28). 80,000 rounds were fed into forward Dump. 1 O.R. proceeded on leave to U.K. A.S.	
	4/7/17		At night transport and a carrying party again worked on S.A.A. A further 73,000 rounds were transported to forward dump, making 153,000 rounds in all. Sentence of G.C.M. on PTE F. BAGNALL promulgated. Sentence 6 months I.H.L. remitted. 1 O.R. killed. 1 O.R. from hospital. 1 O.R. joined Coy. 1 O.R. to Base. 1 O.R. additional duty. A.S.	
	5/7/17		The subsection on A.A. duty at ammunition dumps in M.13.4 and M.8.d (Ref. Sheet 28) was relieved by a subsection of the 218th Coy. Relief complete at 11.0 a.m. Upon relief subsection returned to Coy. H.Q. A further 47,000 rounds of S.A.A. were fed into forward dump, making 200,000. 1 O.R. from hospital. 1 O.R. to hospital. 1 Off. from leave.	
	6/7/17		On the night of 6/7th July Nos. 3 & 4 Sections relieved two sections of the 210th M.G. Coy. in the left subsector of the 13th. Bde. front. Relief complete at 2.0 a.m. Upon completion of relief the command of the Machine Guns in left subsection passed from O.C. 24th Coy. to	APPENDIX II Relief Orders.

WAR DIARY or INTELLIGENCE SUMMARY

Army Form C. 2118.

Place	Date	Hour	Summary of Events and Information	Remarks and references to Appendices
Near YPRES I.14.c.58 (Ref. Sheet 28)	6/7/17		O.C. 25th M.G. Coy. Coy HQ moved from HALIFAX CAMP and took over the H.Q. of the 24th Coy in YPRES at I.2.c.3525, (Ref. Sheet 28). The Company has now 16 guns in the line. The transport lines remained for the time being at HALIFAX CAMP. 1 O.R. leave to U.K. 16 Officers and 5 O.R. from Rest Camp. 1 O.R. from Hospital. A.S.	
YPRES I.2.c.3525 (Ref. Sheet 28)	7/7/17		Transport moved from HALIFAX CAMP to DOMINION CAMP. Move complete at 11.0 am. The night of 6/7/7th was quiet on the line except for intermittent shelling of HELLFIRE CORNER and a slight enemy bombardment on the right about midnight. During the day CAMBRIDGE & TRENTON were shelled heavy, with 15 c.m. shells, and MUD TRENCH received most attention throughout the day. During the afternoon a H.V. gun shelled RIFLE FARM. The junction of BEER TRENCH & WESTLANE was shelled during the night. E.A. were very active all day. They brought down three of our aeroplanes and five were brought down by our batteries. On 19 prisoners our A.A. guns fired on them, driving in at 4,500 yards, bringing down the nearest three. The 15th Div. on our left carried out a raid on night of 7th/8th. There were no relief. Casualties among M.G. Coy — Lieut. F.B. COOTE & 2nd G.C. struck off strength - wounded 2/7/17. 1 O.R. to England. 2 Cadets Units. A.J.	

WAR DIARY or INTELLIGENCE SUMMARY

Army Form C. 2118

Place	Date	Hour	Summary of Events and Information	Remarks and references to Appendices
YPRES I.8.c.35.25 (Sheet 28)	8/4/17		Between 11.0 a.m. and 9.0 p.m. enemy shelled RAILWAY WOOD & WEST LANE cross continuously. During the latter two or three days the enemy has given less attention to the back area and has turned his attention to the works ached to us but with great accuracy. HELL FIRE CORNER shelled with 77 mm shells about 9.30 pm. Numerous aeroplane were seen owing to the dull weather. 6534 PTE. F. BAGNALL who was tried by F.G.C.M. on the 13th inst. and sentenced to 6 months I.H.L. was handed over to A.P.M. today to be committed to prison. 1 O.R. to Sanitation School, inspection Ad.	
	9/4/17		The Company was relieved in the line on the night of 9th/10th July by the 4th M.G. Coy., 25th Divn. Relief complete at 5.0 a.m. 1 O.R. killed. 1 O.R. to School of Sanitation, 1 O.R. from leave. 1 O.R. to Hospital A.J.	APPENDIX III Relief Orders
DOMINION CAMP. G.24 c.3.6. (Ref. Sheet 28)	10/4/17		Upon relief the Company moved to the transport lines at DOMINION CAMP. 2 O.R. wounded. 1 O.R. to Brig-under-age. 1 O.R. leave to U.K. 1 O.R. to Hospital. Company morning took to TOURNEHEM AREA. Transport left DOMINION CAMP at 11.30 a.m. and moved by road south west of Brigade Transport to WEMAERS-CAPPEL (HAZEBROUCK AREA) where the night of 10th/11th was spent. A.J.	

Army Form C. 2118.

WAR DIARY
or
INTELLIGENCE SUMMARY.
(Erase heading not required.)

Instructions regarding War Diaries and Intelligence Summaries are contained in F.S. Regs., Part II. and the Staff Manual respectively. Title pages will be prepared in manuscript.

Place	Date	Hour	Summary of Events and Information	Remarks and references to Appendices
DOMINION CAMP G.24.C.95. (Ref. Zillebeke 28) and AUDENFORT (Ref. CALAIS 13).	11/9/17		The Company less transport left DOMINION CAMP at 12:30 pm and marched to OUDERDOM railhead G.30.C.0.1. (Ref. Zillebeke 28) and entrained with the battalion R.M. T.M. Battery at 2:30 pm (Ref. HAZEBROUCK MAP) Detrained at AUDRUICQ at 7:15 pm and marched to AUDENFORT (Ref. CALAIS 13) arriving at 11:10 pm. Transport moved from WEMAERS-CAPPEL to AUDENFORT, arriving at 5:30 pm. LIEUT. F.P. SPOONER joined from BASE.	
AUDENFORT	12/9/17		Cleaning and overhauling guns and equipment. A1.	
	13/9/17		Company marched to GOENY (Ref. HAZEBROUCK 1:100,000) to attend a lecture on Regimental fighting by Col. Campbell. Lecture from 9:30 – 10:30. Men marched back to billets and carried on training up to 9:0 pm. Buses were arranged and they furnished lecture up position. 4 O.R. from leave to U.K. 2 O.R. from leave 1 O.R. from hospital A1.	
	14/9/17		Parades :- 6:45-7:45 overhauling guns etc. 9:0 to 10:45, 11:0 to 12:30 and 2:0 pm to 3:30 pm training under Battery Commanders. A1.	
	15/9/17		Sunday - retraining. 1 M.R. from School of Sanitation.	
	16/9/17		Training with Brigade on TOURNEHEM training area. Company paraded at 6:30 am and returned to billets at 4:30 pm. A1. 17908 Pte R. FULTON tried by F.G.C.M. 1 O.R. furnished.	

Army Form C. 2118.

WAR DIARY
or
INTELLIGENCE SUMMARY

(Erase heading not required.)

Instructions regarding War Diaries and Intelligence Summaries are contained in F.S. Regs., Part II. and the Staff Manual respectively. Title pages will be prepared in manuscript.

Place	Date	Hour	Summary of Events and Information	Remarks and references to Appendices
AUDENFORT (Ref. CALAIS 13)	17/7/17		Training around AUDENFORT. Parades as follows :- 7.0 to 7.30; 9.0 to 11.15; 11.30 to 12.30; 2.0 to 3.0 p.m. 1 O.R. evacuated. AJ	
	18/7/17		Training around AUDENFORT. Parades as on 17/7/17. "B" Battery fired on 30" range. 6 O.R. Leave to U.K. 1 O.R. to hospital. 1 reinforcement - a saddler. AJ	
	19/7/17		Training around AUDENFORT. Parades as on 17/7/17. Both Batteries on the range in the morning. In the afternoon Coy. started at 3.30 pm. moved off from AUDENFORT and took up billets in TOURNEHEM, arriving at 5.30 pm. 2 O.R. to hospital. 1 O.R. from leave. AJ	
AUDENFORT and TOURNEHEM (Ref. CALAIS 13)				
TOURNEHEM	20/7/17		Coy. started well out of the Brigade, leaving billets at 8.0 am and returning at 7.30 pm. Cleaning guns etc. in afternoon. AJ	
	21/7/17		1 O.R. from hospital. 1 O.R. from C.C.S. 1 O.R. transferred to Coy from 2/Rifle Brigade. AJ Coy. again turned out rest of Brigade, leaving billets at 7.30 am and returning at 7.30 pm. 1 O.R. to hospital. AJ	
	22/7/17		Training under Section Officers from 9.0 am to 12.30 pm and from 2.0 - 5.0. All gun equipment etc. packed in readiness for transport moving first thing in the morning. AJ	
	23/7/17		No training. Rest day by Bde. Order. Transport moved off under orders of	

WAR DIARY or INTELLIGENCE SUMMARY

(Erase heading not required.)

Army Form C. 2118.

Place	Date	Hour	Summary of Events and Information	Remarks and references to Appendices
TOURNEHEM (Ref HAZEBROUCK 1/100,000)	23/4/17		Brigade Transport Officer at 5:30 a.m. and will spend the night at NOORDPEENE (Ref HAZEBROUCK 1/100,000). 1 O.R. to hospital. 2 O.R's evacuated. A.J.	
RENINGHELST G.36.d.7.3 (Ref 28 NW)	24/4/17		Company paraded at 5.15 a.m. and moved off from TOURNEHEM at 5.50 a.m. Marched to AUDRUICQ Station, where breakfast was served. Coy. entrained and left AUDRUICQ at 7.0 a.m., arriving at HOPOUTRE siding near POPERINGHE (Ref Sheet 28) at 11.20 p.m. Marched to RENINGHELST "Staging O" arriving at 6.30 p.m. A.J. Sur. Off. & 51 O.R. of 2nd E. LANCS reported for duty as Cinema O.J. Overhauled guns etc. In the afternoon the Company marched to see the Cinema model of the enemy country over which it is proposed to attack. 1 O.R. rejoined from Base. 1 M.R. from C.C.S. A O.R. leave to U.K. 3 O.R. evacuated A.J.	
	25/4/17		Guns cleaned & kits filled. Half an hour devoted to gas drill. Company marched to the 2/Brigade parade ground where the Brigadier addressed the Company. 2 O.R. from leave. A.J.	
	26/4/17		Half an hour on gas drill again in view of the prevalence of gas shelling on the line. Practise in fulfilling and writing leads which carried on throughout operation. 2 O.R. from leave. 1 Off. & 1 O.R. from M.G. 1 O.R. attached from 8th DIV. TRAIN returned to M. TRAIN A.J.	

Army Form C. 2118.

WAR DIARY
or
INTELLIGENCE SUMMARY.
(Erase heading not required.)

Instructions regarding War Diaries and Intelligence Summaries are contained in F.S. Regs., Part II. and the Staff Manual respectively. Title pages will be prepared in manuscript.

Place	Date	Hour	Summary of Events and Information	Remarks and references to Appendices
RENINGHELST (C.32 d 7.3) Ref Sheet 28 and "DOMINION AREA" G.17.d.8.4.	28/9/14		Company paraded from 9.0 am to 12.0 noon. Gun drill was carried out. At 10.25 pm Company moved off and marched in rear of rear of Brigade to a camp at G.17.d.7.4. in the DOMINION area arriving about 12 midnight. 2 O.R. from M.G. School a.d.	
HALIFAX Area (G.4.c.6.5.9.5) Ref Sheet 28	29/9/14		Company paraded in the morning and prepared limbers etc. for moving with divisibly position at night. About mid-day pioneers entered our ration wagons for its Coy. It moved to HALIFAX area tonight and into the line tomorrow night. Coy paraded that moved off from camp in Dominion Area at 8.35 pm. Reached camp in HALIFAX area at 9.45 pm. 1 O.R. from C.C.S. a.d.	
	30/9/14		Prepared guns etc. for line during the morning. The Company paraded at 4.25 pm and left HALIFAX CAMP for the line at 4.30 pm. The moves were not complete until after midnight. a.d. 2 O.R. from leave a.d.	

A Summers Capt
Commanding 25th M.G. Coy.

Secret.

APPENDIX I

COPY. No. 7

25 Machine Gun Company

RELIEF ORDER No. 2

Ref. Zillebeke Trench Map 1/10,000
      Sheet 28 N.W.   1/20,000

1. On the night of the 2nd/3rd. July two sections of the 218th Machine Gun Company will be relieved by Nos. 1 & 2 Sections of the 25th M.G. Coy. in the line held by the 24th Infantry Brigade.

2. The guns are situated as follows

	Front Line	I 17 b 0 5
	Leinster Trench	I 17 d 1505
Right	China Wall	I 16 d 70
Sector.	Gordon House	I 16 b 43
	A.A.	I 17 c 55
	A.A.	I 17 c 96

Left ~~Section~~ Sector   Two A.A. guns near Beek Trench
         These guns are under the control of a Section Officer
         of the 24th M.G. Coy.

3. No. 1 Section will take over China Wall, Gordon House, and the first two A.A. positions.
   No. 2 Section will take over the front line and Leinster Trench positions and provide the guns for the left Sector

4. On completion of relief the two sections of the 25th M.G. Coy. in the line will come under the orders of the G.O.C. 24th Inf. Bde., Lt. Goodeve will be in charge of the guns of the 25th M.G. Coy. in the right sector and will be responsible to the O.C. 24th M.G. Coy.

5. Two guides will be provided by the 24th M.G. Coy. to Guide Sections to Gordon House and Sections will Halifax Camp at 9.0 pm
   One guide from each gun position will be at Gordon House at 11.0 pm

6. Belt Boxes will be taken over, but no other mobilization stores. A list showing number of belt boxes taken over will be forwarded to Coy. H.Q. on night of 3rd July.

7. Completion of relief will be wired direct to:-
   1. 24th Inf. Brigade.
   2. 24th M.G. Coy.
   3. 25th Inf. Brigade.
   4. 25th M.G. Coy.

~~The code word STUCK will be used~~

The code word " STUCK " will be used

2.7.17   Capt,
                                           Comndg. 25 M.G. Coy.

Copy. No.1 Lt. E.N. Goodeve
     No.2 Lt. F.C. Ashworth
     No.3 Lt. R.E. Norris
     No.4 25th Inf. Bde.
     No.5 218th M.G. Coy.
     No.6 24th M.G. Coy.
  ✓ No.7   War Diary
     No.8   Retained.

APPENDIX I – RELIEF ORDERS.

SECRET.   25th Infantry Brigade No. G.1/11.

    25th Machine Gun Company.
    218th Machine Gun Company.)
    24th Infantry Brigade.   ) for information.
    Divnl. Machine Gun Officer.)

---

1. On the night July 2nd/3rd two Sections 25th Machine Gun Coy. will relieve two Sections 218th Machine Gun Coy., in the Right sector of the 24th Infantry Brigade Front.

2. Relieving Sections will leave HALIFAX Camp at 8 p.m. on July 2nd. Guides have been left by 24th Machine Gun Coy. at HALIFAX Camp; these guides will take the relieving Sections from HALIFAX Camp up to their positions in the line to be taken over from 218th Machine Gun Coy.

3. On completion of relief two Sections 25th Machine Gun Coy., in the line will come under the orders of the G.O.C., 24th Infantry Brigade.

4. Senior Section Officer will be in charge of the two Sections 25th Machine Gun Coy in the line. He will report completion of relief direct to 24th Infantry Brigade by the Code Word "STUCK", repeating the wire to this Office.

5. O.C., 25th Machine Gun Coy., will also arrange to relieve one Subsection 218th Machine Gun Coy employed on the Anti-Aircraft Defence of ammunition dumps. Relief to be complete by 6 a.m. July 2nd. All arrangements for this relief will be made direct with O.C., 218th Machine Gun Coy., whose Headquarters are about G.22.b.7.6.

6. Please acknowledge.

                                                    Captain,
                                                    Brigade Major,
30th June, 1917.   25th Inf. Bde.

SECRET.

APPENDIX IX

Copy No. 10

8TH DIVISION ORDER No.241.

21st November, 1917.

1. 23rd Inf. Bde. will relieve 24th Inf. Bde. in the line on November 23rd and night November 23rd/24th.

2. On relief, the 24th Inf. Bde. will become the Brigade in Support and will be accommodated in the camps vacated by the 23rd Inf. Bde.

3. All details of relief will be arranged direct between Brigadiers concerned.

4. Trench Stores, Aeroplane Photographs and Intelligence details will be handed over.

5. Machine Gun Companies will be relieved under arrangements to be made direct by Company Commanders concerned as follows:-

   25th M.G. Coy. in barrage positions by 23rd M.G. Coy. on November 23rd and night November 23rd/24th.

   218th M.G. Coy. in forward positions by 24th M.G. Coy. on night November 24th/25th.

   Movements of M.G. Cos. will be made by lorry under arrangements to be made direct between D.M.G.O. and "Q". Relieved Cos. will occupy billets vacated by relieving Cos.

6. ACKNOWLEDGE.

E Beddington
Lieut.-Colonel,
General Staff.

Issued at 8 a.m.

Copies to:-

No.1	Div. Commdr.		No.20	1st Divn. *
2	23rd Inf. Bde.		21	VIII Corps "G" *
3	24th Inf. Bde.		22	VIII Corps "Q" *
4	25th Inf. Bde.		23	War Diary.
5	G.O.C., R.A., 14th Div.		24	8th Div. File.
6	" " 8th Div.			
7	22nd D.L.I.			
8	23rd M.G. Coy.		* For information.
9	24th M.G. Coy.			
10	25th M.G. Coy.			
11	218th M.G. Coy.			
12	O.C., Signals.			
13	C.R.E.			
14	D.M.G.O.			
15	"Q".			
16	A.D.M.S.			
17	A.P.M.			
18	82nd H.A.G. *			
19	33rd Division. *			

APPENDIX II   RELIEF ORDERS.

SECRET   35 Machine Gun Company   Copy. No. 6.

Relief Order. No. 4.

Ref. Sheet 28 N.E. 1/20,000   6th July 1917

1. On the night of 6th/7th July Nos.3 and 4 Sections of the 35th
   M.G. Company will relieve two sections of the 34th M.G. Company
   in the left subsector of the line, and upon completion of relief
   the command of the machine guns in both subsectors will pass to
   O.C. 35th M.G. Company

2. No.3 Section will relieve the following guns:-
   South of WHITE POST PT.   I 11 d 10.45
   Birr Cross Roads   I 17 b 05.80
   Rifle Farm   I 11 c 1.5
   Hell Fire Corner   I 10 d 15.60

   No.4 Section will relieve:-
   "I.11.3" Railway Wood   I 11 b 65.45
   "I.11.8"   "   I 11 b 75.45
   Junction of Cambridge   I 11 b 5. 5
   Trench and West Lane
   Mud Lane   I 11 d 75.60   A.A.

   O.C. No.4 Section will also be responsible for the two guns of
   No.3 Section in Bock Trench at I 11 c 80.80

3. Sections will leave Halifax Camp at 8.30 pm and proceed to
   Gordon House.

4. One Guide from each Gun position will be at Gordon House at 21.0 pm

5. Belt boxes will be taken over but no other mobilization stores.
   The number of belt boxes taken over at each gun position will be
   reported to Coy. H.Q. by 12.0 noon 7th July.

6. A list of trench stores taken over at each Gun position will also
   be forwarded to Coy. H.Q. by 12.0 noon 7th July.

7. Completion of relief will be reported to Coy.H.Q. using the
   Code Word "LANDED"

8. Coy. H.Q. will move from Halifax Camp to the present H.Q. //////
   ///////////. of 34th M.G. Coy. at I 8 c 38.95 The transport will
   remain at HALIFAX CAMP.

                                        A.Simmonds Capt.
6.7.17   Comdg. 35 M.G. Company

Copy.No.1 O.C. No.3 Section
     2 O.C. No.4   "
     3 Lieut. R.W. Goodeve
     4 34th M.G. Coy.
     5 35th Inf. Bde.
     6.War Diary
     7 Retained

SECRET   **APPENDIX III**   Copy... 8 ...
25 Machine Gun Company

Relief Orders No.5

Ref. Sheet 28 N.W. 1/20000.   8th July 1917

1. The 7th M.G. Company will relieve the 25th Company in the line on the night of the 9th/10th July.

2.
RAILWAY WOOD.	I 11b 65.45	
" "	I 11b 75.45	
Junction of CAMBRIDGE TRENCH and WEST LANE	I 11b 3.3	Will be relieved by No.4 Section of 7th M.G. Coy.
MUD LANE.	I 11d 75.60	
South of WITTE POORT FM.	I 11d 10.45	
BIRR CROSS ROADS	I 17b 05.80	Will be relieved by No.2
RIFLE FM.	I 11c 1.5	
HELL FIRE CORNER.	I 10d 15.80	
GORDON HOUSE.	I 16b 85.85	
CHINA WALL.	I 16d 6.9.	Will be relieved by No.3
LEINSTER TRENCH	I 17d 1.8	
Front Line.	I 17b 8.3	

7. No.4 Section will relieve the 4 A.A. guns

3. Four guides from Coy. H.Q. will report at H.Q. 7th M.G. Coy. HALIFAX CAMP at 8.0 pm. to guide the sections to GORDON HOUSE. One guide from each gun will be at GORDON HOUSE at 10.45pm

4. Belt boxes will be handed over and receipts obtained, no other mobilization stores will be handed over

5. All trench stores will be handed over and receipts obtained.

6. Completion of relief will be wired to Coy. H.Q. using the code word " PEACE "

7. The Company upon relief will move to DOMINION CAMP.

8. Please acknowledge.

8/7/17   A. Simmonds Capt.
Commdg. 25 M.G. Coy.

Copy No. 1. O.C. No.1 Section
       2.   "   No.2   "
       3.   "   No.3   "
       4.   "   No.4   "
       5. Lieut. R.E. Norris
       6. 7th M.G. Coy.
       7. 25th Inf. Bde.
       8. War Diary
       9. Retained.

Army Form C. 2118.

WAR DIARY
or
~~INTELLIGENCE SUMMARY.~~

(Erase heading not required.)

25th M.G. COMPANY

31/7/17 to 31/8/17

Vol 20

Instructions regarding War Diaries and Intelligence Summaries are contained in F. S. Regs., Part II. and the Staff Manual respectively. Title pages will be prepared in manuscript.

Place	Date	Hour	Summary of Events and Information	Remarks and references to Appendices
Before YPRES	31/7/17		By 1 a.m. the Company was assembled with the other units ready for the attack on the swing road north of YPRES. Our dispositions were as following:— 16 guns organised in two batteries of eight guns assembled in ZOUAVE TRENCH between its junctions with UNION STREET and REGENT STREET (I.17.d. – I.11.c.28)	APPENDIX I OPERATION ORDERS
			Coy H.Q. at 1.0 a.m. was in RITZ STREET dugout about I.17.C.36 and we joined with the 24th Inf. Bde. H.Q. at HALFWAY HOUSE. The transport lines were at BELGIAN CHATEAU in H.23.a. Guns were at 3.50 a.m. An account of the action is attached together with operation Orders.	APPENDIX II ACCOUNT OF OPERATION
			4 O.R. from leave, 2 officers & 35 O.R. battle casualties. 24 O.R. of Carrying Party battle casualties. AJ	
In the line before YPRES.	1/8/17		Company came out of action and went back to VANCOUVER CAMP. Transport also there. AJ	
Bivouacs at VANCOUVER CAMP				
H.14.a.70.	2/8/17		Cleaning guns, gun equipment and clothing. Inventory taken of deficiencies in Mobilization stores. Men bathed.	
			1 off. & 1 S.O.R. leave to U.K. 1 off. & 27 O.R. of East Surreys rejoined their unit. AJ	

Army Form C. 2118

WAR DIARY
or
INTELLIGENCE SUMMARY.
(Erase heading not required.)

25th M.G. COMPANY.

Instructions regarding War Diaries and Intelligence Summaries are contained in F.S. Regs., Part II. and the Staff Manual respectively. Title pages will be prepared in manuscript.

Place	Date	Hour	Summary of Events and Information	Remarks and references to Appendices
VANCOUVER CAMP	3/8/17		Carried on with cleaning of guns & equipment.	
H.M.Q.T.O. (Sheet 28)			4 O.R. sent to Base Depôt. Authority D.A.G. – C.R. No. 18.30/713/A. 2 O.R. to FIFTH ARMY Rest Camp. 2 O.R. to hospital. 2 O.R. reinforcements from C.C.S. AJ	
	4/8/17		Cleaning equipment. Inspection by II CORPS COMMANDER.	
			1 O.R. Prescott reported missing, reported AJ	
Moved to	5/8/17		Company moved to STEENVOORDE. Transport was brigaded and moved off at 10.15 am. Remainder of Company entrained on the VLAMERTINGHE – OUDERDOM road at 2.0 pm, moved off at 2.30 pm and arrived in billets at STEENVOORDE at 4.15 pm. Men billeted in school.	
STEENVOORDE (HAZEBROUCK MAP)			Transport is billeted on the POPERINGHE road. HQ just off the EECKE road on outskirts of town. 1 O.R. from leave. 1 O.R. previously reported wounded now reported died of wounds AJ	
STEENVOORDE	6/8/17		Company paraded during morning and cleaned guns & fighting equipment. 1 O.R. from C.C.S. AJ	
	7/8/17		Cleaning limbers and fighting equipment. 2 O.R. from leave AJ	
STEENVOORDE	8/8/17		C10 & 5 O.R. proceeded on leave to U.K. parades under Section ♯/No. 5½.	
	9/8/17		Company parade. 1 O.R. from C.C.S.	

Army Form C. 2118

WAR DIARY
INTELLIGENCE SUMMARY.
(Erase heading not required.)

252 h/Coy.

Place	Date	Hour	Summary of Events and Information	Remarks and references to Appendices
STEENVOORDE	10/8/17		Packed Adjustment of equipment. Packing Limbers	
YPRES		7.30 pm	Coy moved by bus & route march to the SERAPHIM HALFWAY HOUSE YPRES halting at the transport lines at BELGIAN CHATEAU for tea	
HALIFAX HOUSE	11/8/17		Withdrew to HALIFAX CAMP	
	12/8/17		Moved to ESPLANADE, YPRES	
YPRES	13/8/17		All available men of the Coy carried ammunition from BIRR XROADS & created a dump on near the Bauer features as fuel under LIEUT SPOONER - Gas shells in YPRES	
	14/8/17		All available men again carried for the whole night. They were subjected to be casualties by a carrying party which was not of ennui use. SGT CORBETT was killed 1 OR admitted to hospital. Wis-gunner GWILLIAM missing	
	15/8/17		Killed 1st lelts. 2/LT LOCKHART & 5 OR proceeded on leave to U.K. 3 OR returned from leave. 1 OR from C.C.S. Coy moved up to Bauer features in the night. 1 no. gunnel personnel went astray in the dark (See narrative)	

Army Form C. 2118.

WAR DIARY
or
INTELLIGENCE SUMMARY.
(Erase heading not required.)

Place	Date	Hour	Summary of Events and Information	Remarks and references to Appendices
YPRES	16/8/17		Attack on GREEN LINE. ZERO hour 4.45 a.m. (See Narrative attached) The attack was foredoomed to failure owing to the weakness of the attacking troops and the fact that supports were, to all intents & purposes a minus quantity. The GREEN LINE was reached in places but such troops as did reach it had to come back to form a line just this side of the HANBEEK owing to their finding themselves up in the air. The Infantry suffered very heavy losses the 1/R.Irish being practically wiped out. At about 9 a.m. the enemy counter attacked heavily from POLYGON WOOD and from the HANBEEK RIDGE. Our artillery barrage was not put down until 15 mins after the counter attack began, the only explanation being that there were not sufficient S.O.S. rockets and that the pigeons did not get back. The division on our right fell back, leaving our right flank in the air. The Infantry fell back to the BLACK LINE and formed a defensive flank on the right.	APPENDIX II Account of Operation

WAR DIARY
or
INTELLIGENCE SUMMARY.
(Erase heading not required.)

Army Form C. 21

Place	Date	Hour	Summary of Events and Information	Remarks and references to Appendices
YPRES	16/8/17	about	At about 8 p.m. – The Brigadier came up to the BLACK LINE (his second visit) and instructed Coy Commanders about relief. The M.G. Coy continued to occupy defensive positions on the WEST HOEK RIDGE.	
	17/8/17		15th – the exception of No.1 Section under Lt GOODEVE the Coy Withdrew to positions in JACOB TRENCH and then H.Q. became ZIEV HOUSE – Coy H.Q. remained with No.1 Section in a fairly decent dug out. This dug out was at first quite dry and there to no apparent reason became flooded – there was no rain – then suddenly began to drain off. No.1 Section remained in very good spirits, having found a dump of extra special rations, spent part of the day eating and the rest sleeping. Every now and then whizz bangs lit senty at the entrance, & on the top of the dug out but disturbed no one, however constant drifting were seen concrete and everyone was glad to hear that the Coy was to be	
	18/8/17			

Army Form C. 2118.

WAR DIARY
or
INTELLIGENCE SUMMARY.
(Erase heading not required.)

Instructions regarding War Diaries and Intelligence Summaries are contained in F. S. Regs., Part II. and the Staff Manual respectively. Title pages will be prepared in manuscript.

Place	Date	Hour	Summary of Events and Information	Remarks and references to Appendices
YPRES	18/8/17		Relieved – Stretcher & Guides guided the Coy in and the relief was very smoothly carried out. Each team made for BIRR X ROADS as soon as it ends & as soon as it was relieved – the Coy rendezvoused at the HALIFAX CAMP and very glad to be there. Casualties – during the operations Lt ASHWORTH H. Sgt CORBETT. Sgt ROGERS. & 5 OR's Killed. Sgt KILFORD, L.Sgt ROBINSON, L.Cpl CHISHOLME & 16 OR's wounded. 2 OR's missing.	
HALIFAX CAMP	19/8/17		Not fit for the wicked. At 6 a.m. motor lorries arrived that the Coy would move by bus to the CAESTRE area. Duly entrained at 2.30 p.m. and arrived at BORRE at 6 p.m. the Coy billeted at PRADELLES E of BORRE. 2-Lt. J.M. HOOD joined Coy from 2nd Bedf & 13 OR.	
	20/8/17		Cleaned limbers – C.O. & 2 I/C returned from leave.	
PRADELLES to	21/8/17		Finished cleaning limbers. Inspection by O.in C. 30 OR's Reinforcement joined at about 11 a.m.	
	22/8/17		Highly geared thoroughly overhauled prior to moving and deficiencies noted. All inspection in the afternoon. AJ	

Army Form C. 2118

WAR DIARY
or
INTELLIGENCE SUMMARY.
(Erase heading not required.)

Instructions regarding War Diaries and Intelligence Summaries are contained in F. S. Regs., Part II. and the Staff Manual respectively. Title pages will be prepared in manuscript.

Place	Date	Hour	Summary of Events and Information	Remarks and references to Appendices
PRADELLES Sheet 27 - N.21.	23/8/17		Parade as follows. 7.0 - 9.45 Coy Drill. 9.0 - 10.15 - Drill with residence. Inspection of Arms & Gas Mouth, Phot. td. (the is every officer that during last ten days each Company has been apotted with revolver). 10.30 - 12.30 Lecture under Section Officers.	
			2-LT D.C. PRITCHARD joined Coy from base. 1.O.R. frontline. AS	
	24/8/17		7.0 - 9.45 Coy Drill. 10.30 am. Brigade Church service followed by inspection of the GOC. II ANZAC CORPS.	
			1.O.R. to hospital. AS	
	25/8/17		Company talked during morning. Inspection of gas appliances by Div. Gas N.C.O. AS	
	26/8/17		Sunday. R.C. voluntary Church Parade. Company Drill from 7.0am - 10.00am. 1.O.R. evacuated.	
			42491 PTE W. DAWKINS & 38053 PTE H.W. HICK killed by H.O.C.M. 10.R. evacuated.	
			1 LCST. MACNAMARA and 5 OR - Leave to U.K. AS	
GREENJACKETS CAMP Sheet 36 B.28.39	27/8/17		Brigade moved to the STEENWOECK area - Battalion Reserve for the new front north of ARMENTIERES. Company marched in reverse of Bn. HQ. to present the elasticty front in BORDEAUX at 6.2 am. Route - STRAZELE and BAILLUIL. Arrived GREENJACKETS CAMP at 10.0 am.	
			2-LT. LOCKHART from base. AS	

Army Form C. 2118

WAR DIARY
or
INTELLIGENCE SUMMARY.
(Erase heading not required.)

Instructions regarding War Diaries and Intelligence Summaries are contained in F.S. Regs, Part II. and the Staff Manual respectively. Title pages will be prepared in manuscript.

Place	Date	Hour	Summary of Events and Information	Remarks and references to Appendices
GREENJACKETS CAMP near STEENBECK Dist 28 B.E.F.	28/8/17		Parades 7.0-7.45 & 9.0-12.30. Training under Section Officers a.b. recognised their Keams.	
			1 O.R. to 2 Army Gas School. 1 O.R. found safe at Pandel.	
	29/8/17		Parades: 7.0-7.45 Close Order Drill. 9.15-12.30. Training under Section Officers	
			1 O.R. to Div. Rest Station. 3 O.R. from leave. 1 O.R. evacuated to	
	30/8/17	7.0-12.30	Training under Section Officers. On night of 30/31st August the four guns	APPENDIX IV. Relief Orders
			of "C" Section relieved 4 guns of 36th M.G. Coy in U.22 & U.16 (Sheet 28) the four	
			guns of "D" Section relieved 4 guns of 216th M.G. Coy in U.22 c. (Sheet 29).	
			Two guns of "B" Coy were under Orders of G.O.C. 22nd Inf. Bde. Remainder under G.O.C. 25th I.B.	
			1 O.R. from leave. Ret.	
	31/8/17		A & "C" Sections trained under section officers. 1 O.R. from leave.	
				Adamsons Capt
				Commanding 25th M.G. Coy

APPENDIX II
The Attack before YPRES.
31/7/17.

(1) Assembly

Both batteries and the Carrying Party got into their assembly position in ZOUAVE TRENCH between its junctions with UNION STREET and REGENT STREET by 1.0 am. on zero day 31/7/17 with only two casualties.

(2) Barrage Work

They left the assembly trench about 4.20 a.m. (zero + 20 mins.) and crossing the MENIN road just east of the CULVERT made straight for the first battery positions in CHATEAU WOOD. Two teams of "D" battery sustained casualties on the way up and one gun was put out of action, but the time chosen for the journey seemed to be quite suitable, for the shelling was not excessive and both batteries were in position and ready to fire five minutes before zero + 1 hr. 15 minutes when the first barrage was to be put down.

Both barrages were fired although the Carrying Party did not arrive.

Upon completion of the second barrage the teams packed up and moved to the slope of BELLEWARDE Ridge about J.7.c.4.5. where they sat down and waited for the pack animals to come up in order that everyone might know where the S.A.A. dump was. The pack animals arrived about 6.20 a.m., i.e. zero + 2½ hours and dumped the ammunition at the corner of the wood at J.13 a 55.70.

In the meantime the battery commanders had gone forward and upon the arrival of the pack animals the batteries moved on toward their second position viz. ZIEL HOUSE. On the way down from ZIEL HOUSE considerable shelling was encountered and some time was lost because it was necessary for the battery commanders to ascertain the tactical situation which was obviously different from what was expected. However "E" battery got into its second battery position about 9.0 a.m., i.e. zero + 5 hrs. 10 mins. and shortly afterwards a barrage was put down on ANZAC in accordance with orders received from

The Attack before YPRES on 31/7/17 con.

the D.M.C.O. This left the guns with rather less than their S.O.S. reserve, and as so far no ammunition had been brought up by the Carrying Party no further barrage was put down.

(3) <u>Consolidation</u>

At zero + 5hrs. when "D" battery came under the orders of the G.O.C. 25th Inf. Bde. for consolidation it had lost three guns, and three were therefore borrowed from "E" battery. About this time LIEUT. WALDIE became a casualty and 2nd LT. LOCKHART therefore took charge of the four guns on the right whilst a N.C.O. took over the two centre battalion guns. 2nd LT. WESTON took forward two guns on the left. These guns eventually consolidated the front held by the 25th Inf. Bde. along the WESTHOEK ridge and were undoubtedly largely responsible for breaking up the counter attacks which were launched by the enemy during the afternoon.

The five remaining guns of "E" battery took up defensive positions between KIT AND KAT and WESTHOEK and also did good work in wiping out or dispersing parties of the enemy who from time to time tried to approach our line.

(4) <u>Relief</u>

On the night of the 31st July / 1st Aug. four guns were relieved by the 28th M.G. Coy. Four were withdrawn about mid-day on 1st Aug., and the remainder withdrew at 10.0 p.m. on 1st Aug. after the line had been taken over by the 25th Division.

(5) <u>Pack Animals</u>

After the first journey the pack animals came up with a second load of SAA. and finally at zero + 11 hours returned with a third load consisting of ammunition and rations. The transport did excellent work and kept to their timetable in spite of fairly heavy shelling and the extremely boggy ground near BELLEWAARDE LAKE.

The Attack before YPRES on 31/7/17 con-

(6) The Carrying Party of 1 Off and 32 O.R. from the infantry was a complete failure. They did not arrive at the front battery position at all and less than half a dozen reached the second. They apparently lost touch in all directions and ceased to be a party from the moment they left the assembly trench. Had I not personally collected a number of them and conducted them to and from the S.A.A. dump they would never have brought up any ammunition at all. The behaviour of this party was in exact accord with my previous experience of <u>temporarily</u> attached men. I am of the opinion machine gunners will never be sure of their ammunition supply until either the establishment of M.G. Corps is sufficiently increased to allow of the gunners carrying all their equipment or until a party of say 48 men are <u>permanently</u> attached to each Company.

(7) <u>Losses in Men & Material.</u>

Officers — LIEUT. J.G. WALDIE — killed.
LIEUT. C.H. ASBURY, M.C. wounded.

O.R. — Machine Gunners.
  Killed 10
  Wounded 23
  Missing <u>2</u>
  Total <u>35</u>

O.R. — Carrying Party attached from 2nd Bn. East Yorks.
  Killed 3
  Wounded 6
  Missing <u>15</u>
  Total <u>24</u>

Material
  3 guns & 4 mountings
  154 belts & beltboxes

Animals
  6 pack animals.

A. Simmonds Capt.
Commanding 25th M.G. Coy.

SECRET.   APPENDIX I   Copy No. 10

25th. MACHINE GUN COMPANY - OPERATION ORDER No. 6.

Ref.Map; (1) 28 N.E. 1/20,000
         (2) 28 N.W. 1/20,000
         (3) Skeleton Map attached.

(1)   The 8th. Division on the left of the II Corps will attack the enemy E. and N.E. of YPRES on a date to be notified later.

(2) (a) The objective of the 8th. Division will be to capture, consolidate and hold the GREEN Line. If the tactical situation is favourable a further advance will be made on Z day to the RED Line.
    (b) The advance to the GREEN Line will be made on Z day in three stages, each one simultaneously with the Divisions on our Right and Left.
        (1) Advance to the BLUE Line at zero.
        (2) Advance to the BLACK Line at zero plus 1 hour 15 minutes.
        (3) Advance to the GREEN Line at zero plus 6 hours 20 minutes.
    The further advance to the Red Line will depend on the amount of opposition encountered.

(3)   The attack will be carried out as follows :-
    (a) (1) On BLUE Line by 23rd. and 24th. Infantry Brigades.
        (2) " BLACK Line   ditto.
        (3) " GREEN Line by 25th. Infantry Brigade.
        (4) " RED Line by reserve Battalion of 25th. Infantry Brigade but when captured the ground will be taken over by the 23rd. Infantry Brigade.
    (b) The 25th. Infantry Brigade will attack for the GREEN Line on a three Battalion Front. Each battalion will attack in two waves, each Company having two platoons in the front wave and one platoon in the second, with the fourth platoon carrying. The fourth Company of each battalion will provide Moppers-up.

(4)   The 2nd. Lincoln Regt. will attack on the Right of the Brigade Front, 1st. Royal Irish Rifles in the Centre, and the 2nd. Rifle Brigade on the Left.
    The 2nd. Royal Berks Regt. will be in Brigade Reserve.
    At zero plus 8 hours 40 minutes fighting patrols of the 2nd. Royal Berks Regt. accompanied by a squadron of cavalry and four tanks will pass through the GREEN Line, and if the resistance met with is small they will seize the ground as far as the RED Line. This ground will be taken over from the 2nd. Royal Berks Regt. by the 23rd. Infantry Brigade.

ACTION OF MACHINE GUNS.

(1)   The attack on the first Objective will be assisted by barrage fire provided by the Machine Guns of the 25th. Division firing from our present trench system. During the remainder of the operation, a series of barrages will be put down by the Machine Guns of the 8th. Division which will be organised in six batteries lettered from "A" to "F".

(2)   The 25th. Machine Gun Company will provide two batteries of eight guns, to be known as "D" and "E" Batteries.

"D" Battery, under Lieut.J.G.Waldie
 { 4 guns of No.3 Section under 2nd.Lieut.K.V.Weston.
 { 4 guns of No.4 Section, under 2nd.Lieut.F.R.Lockhart.

"E" Battery, under Lieut.C.H.Asbury,MC.
 { 4 guns of No.1 Section, under Lieut.R.N.Goodeve.
 { 4 guns of No.2 Section, under 2nd.Lieut.F.G.Ashworth.

The detail of the movement of these batteries is given in APPENDIX I. Orders for assembly will be issued later. The detail for the barrages is given in APPENDICES II and III.

(3) About zero plus 5 hours the 8 guns of "D" Battery will be relieved in "D2" position by the 218th. Machine Gun Company and the guns of "D" Battery will then come under the orders of the G.O.C. 25th. Infantry Brigade and will assist in the consolidation of the GREEN Line.
   The action to be taken by these guns is detailed in 25th. Infantry Brigade Instruction No.8, issued to all concerned.

(4) The 8 guns of "E" Battery will come under the orders of the G.O.C. 25th. Infantry Brigade at Zero plus 9 hours 50 minutes after completing their 7th. barrage.

23rd. July 1917.

Capt.
Commdg. 25 M.G.Coy.

COPIES TO :-
- No.1. O.C. "D" Battery
- 2. O.C. "E" Battery
- 3. Lieut. Goodeve
- 4. 2/Lt. Weston
- 5. 2/Lt. Lockhart
- 6. 2/Lt. Ashworth
- 7. Lieut. Norris
- 8. 25th. Inf. Bde.
- 9. 8th. Div. M.G.O.
- 10. War Diary
- 11-14. Retained.

SECRET   25TH. MACHINE GUN COMPANY.   APPENDIX I #. OPERATION ORDER No.6.

Battery	Battery Position	Target	Timetable for Firing	Duration of Barrage.	Rate of Fire per gun per minute.	Further Action.
"D"	"D1" I.12.d.28.15 to E.18.b.28.26.	J.1.d.95.75. to J.2.c.30.45.	0 plus 1 hr. 15 mins. to 0 plus 1 hr. 31 mins.	16 mins.	60	
	- do.-	J.2.a.8.7. to J.2.a.9.3.	0 plus 1 hr. 31 mins to 0 plus 1 hr. 51 mins.	20 mins.	60	Move to "D2" position
	"D2" J.7.b.3.9. to J.7.b.3.7.	D.26.d.29 to J.2.b.9.4.	0 plus 4 hrs. to about 0 plus 5 hrs.	S.O.S. call only		As soon as relieved by "C" Battery, 218th.M.G.Coy.,reverts to orders of G.O.C. 25 Inf.Bde. for consolidation.
"E"	"E1" J.13.a.10.85.to J.13.a.10.60.	J.2.c.3.4. to J.2.c.65.00.	0 plus 1 hr. 15 mins. to 0 plus 1 hr. 31 mins.	16 mins.	60	
	- do.-	J.2.a.99.20. to J.2.d.40.65.	0 plus 1 hr. 31 mins. to 0 plus 1 hr. 51 mins.	20 mins.	60	Move to "E2" position.
	"E2" J.7.b.45.70. to J.7.b.45.50.	D.26.d.2.9. to J.2.b.9.4.	0 plus 4 hrs. to 0 plus 6 hrs. 20 mins.	S.O.S. call only		
	- do.-	J.3.a.20.10. to J.3.c.45.50.	0 plus 6 hrs. 20 mins. to 0 plus 6 hrs. 36 mins.	16 mins.	60	
	- do.-	J.3.b.55.95. to J.3.b.80.43.	0 plus 6 hrs. 36 mins. to 0 plus 7.hrs.28 mins.	52 mins.	60	Move to "E3" position.
	"E3" J.5.c.9.6. to J.3.c.9.8.	D.22.c.75.45 to D.28.b.5.8.	0 plus 8 hrs. 40 mins to 0 plus 8 hrs. 50 mins.	10 mins.	60	
	- do.-	D.22.b.25.65. to D.23.c.5.9.	0 plus 8 hrs. 50 mins to 0 plus 9 hrs. 50 mins.	60 mins.	60	Remain on barrage position under orders of G.O.C. 25 Inf.Bde.

SECRET.

25th Infantry Brigade No. F/26.

25th INFANTRY BRIGADE INSTRUCTIONS No. 8.

Reference 8th Division Instructions No.22:-

1. From about ZERO plus 5 hours, 8 guns of the 25th Machine Gun Coy. are to come under the orders of the 25th Infantry Brigade.

2. These guns will move forward with the attacking Battalions during the advance to the GREEN LINE. They will move 300 yards in rear of the second wave and will be distributed as follows:-
   - 2nd Lincoln Regt.   One Section.
   - 1st R.Irish Rifles.   One Sub-section.
   - 2nd Rifle Brigade.   One Sub-section.

   They must be ready to deal with any hostile counter-attack and help forward our troops with covering fire where necessary.

3. On arrival at the GREEN LINE these guns will be disposed as follows:-
   - 4 guns on the spur about J 3 c 3.7. to cover the spur and to deal with counter-attacks from the high ground on the right.
   - 2 guns in front of the GREEN LINE about J 3 a 1.9. to flank the front of the GREEN line to the North and to the South.
   - 2 guns about D 26 d 6.8. to fire up the valley towards ALBANIA in case of the enemy collecting in this valley.

4. The actual sites for the position of these guns will be chosen by the Machine Gun Officers in consultation with the Infantry Company Commander on the spot.

5. Please acknowledge.

                                         Captain,
                                         Brigade Major,
                                         25th Inf. Bde.

22nd July 1917.

Copies to:-   2nd Lincoln Regt.   (5 copies)
              2nd R.Berks Regt.   do
              1st R.Irish Rifles.   do
              2nd Rifle Brigade.   do
              25th Machine Gun Coy.   do
              25th Trench Mortar Bty (1 copy)
              "A" Bn. H.B.M.G.C.   (5 copies)
              2nd Bde. H.B.M.G.C.
              45th Infantry Brigade.
              53rd Infantry Brigade.
              23rd Infantry Brigade.
              24th Infantry Brigade.
              1/1 Yorkshire dragoons.
              8th Division (3 copies)

APPENDIX IV.

To 25th. Machine Gun Coy. Operation Order No. 6.

Ammunition Supply.

(1)   In order to assist in maintaining the ammunition supply one Carrier will be permanently attached to each team and the remainder of the carriers will work as a party.

(2)   Each team will take with it to the first battery position 12 belt boxes (3000 rounds). The carrying party will follow as rapidly as possible with a further 3000 rounds per gun.

(3)   At O plus 2 hours 30 mins. twenty pack animals will bring up from assembly position west of Wall of China to the first battery position 48,000 rounds of S.A.A. and 32 petrol tins of water. About this time the batteries will be moving forward and if the situation is favourable the pack animals will follow 300 yards in rear of the gunners to the second battery position. If this is not possible the S.A.A. and water will be dumped at the first battery position and man-handled up to the second position.

(4)   On a second journey the pack animals will bring 60,000 rounds from the BIRR CROSS ROADS Dump to the second battery position arriving about O plus 6 hrs. 30 mins.

(5)   When "E" Battery moves to its 3rd. position it will be assisted by 32 carriers who will convey ammunition from "E2" to "E3" positions.

(6)   The pack animals will make a third journey with rations and 18,000 rounds of S.A.A. to the 2nd. Battery position which will be the ration dump for all sections.
    The rations will be drawn from the Divisional Dump at Gordon House and the S.A.A. from the BIRR CROSS ROADS Dump.
    The pack animals should arrive at "E2" position about O plus 11 hours.

25/7/17.   Capt.
                                                Commdg. 25 M.G.Coy.

Issued to recipients of O.O. No.6.

APPENDIX II

Account of Operations at YPRES on 15/16 1917.
by 25th. M.G. Company

Owing to the weakness of the Coy. only 12 guns could be manned. On the night 13/14 a convoy of 25 mules conveyed ammunition to the neighbourhood of IDIOT TRENCH and all the available men of the Coy. (30) went to BIRR X Roads and dug out the ammunition which the Coy. had previously dumped there and which had been buried – The original intention was to carry this ammunition right up to to the barrage positions on WESTHOEK RIDGE on pack animals, however what with the darkness and difficult going it was impossible to get it further than the dump near IDIOT TRENCH.

On the night of the 14/15 all available men again went up to BIRR X ROADS where they were to be joined by a carrying party of 50 at 8.45 pm. This carrying party turned up 2 hrs. late in an exhausted condition, having had a long march carrying full packs and rifles. Their condition necessiated very slow going and the ammunition was only got as far as JACOB TRENCH where the carrying party had to leave it in order to be in position in RAILWAY WOOD by 5.30 am. On the afternoon of the 15th a carrying party of 80 men reported tp an officer of the Coy. at BIRR X Roads. This party had marched from STEENVOORDE the previous day and carried ammunition all the previous night until 7.0.am. and were very exhausted- Progress was slow and made under heavy shell fire and by 10.0 pm. only 40 boxes had been carried. It was then too late to make another journey, even if the men had been in a fit condition to do so, which they were not.

<u>Night of 15/16.</u> At this time 6 guns were in position on the WESTHOEK RIDGE holding the line – Two guns were now attached to the 1/R.I.Rifles and two to the 2/Royal Berks and marched with these battalions from YPRES. The remainder of the Coy. with the remaining two guns moved up to BIRR X ROADS where they expected to find a carrying party of 50- This party failed to turn up so after waiting some time, the Coy. moved off, carrying as much as they could (20 belts in boxes). The guides lost their way in the dark and at ZERO hour they had only reached IDIOT LANE where they remained until the intensity of the enemy's barrage appeared somewhat less when the two officers went forward. Six guns were in the Barrage positions at ZERO hour and fired the two barrages, but owing to the lack of ammunition the rate of fire had to be modified to 30 rounds per minute.

At about ZERO x 2 hrs. all eight guns moved to the forward slope of the WESTHOEK RIDGE behind the BLACK LINE in order to deal with an enemy counter attack.

The four guns with the assulting troops suffered very heavy gas casualties including the officer and both sergeants and having exhausted their ammunition were brought back with great difficulty (the two corporals who took command of the respective Sub-sections have been recommended)-

Had the two guns been fully manned and the carrying parties a success better work could have been done- As it was the personnel of the Coy. worked continuously for three days and two nights before ZERO day and with one exception could not have behaved better during the action.

It is essential that a carrying party be attached to the Coy. for at least a week before an action of this kind-

21.8.17

Lieut.
O.C. 25th M.G. Coy. during the operations

Secret   APPENDIX IV   Copy No.

25 Machine Gun Company

Relief Order No.6.

Ref.Map 28 S W & S E (parts of) $\frac{1}{20,000}$

: : 36 N W $\frac{1}{20000}$ 30th August 1917

(1) The following reliefs will take place on the night of 30th/31st August.

    (a) The four guns of "B" Section will relieve four guns of the 24th M.G. Company in positions
        about U 22 a 70.05
              U 22 a 9.2.
              U 22 a 25.95.
              U 16 c 22.15

    (b) The four guns of "D" Section will relieve four guns of the 218th M.G. Coy. in positions
        about U 22 a 13.37
              U 22 a 45.60
              U 22 a 45.70
              U 22 a 45.75

(2) The two guns at U 16 c 22.15 and U 22 a 25.95 come under the orders of G.O.C. 24th.Infantry Brigade. The remainder come under the orders of G.O.C. 23rd.Infantry Brigade.

(3) One guide from each gun of the 24th M.G.Coy. will be at CAMPAC DUMP at 9.30. pm.
One guide from each gun of the 218th M.G. Coy. will be at PROWSE POINT at 9.30 pm.

(4) A list of Trench Stores taken over will be forwarded to Coy H.Q. by 2.0pm on 31st August.
No mobilisation Stores will be taken over.

(5) Completion of relief will be reported to Coy.H.Q. by runner.

(6) Company H.Q. will remain for the present at GREENJACKETS CAMP (B 8 c 38)

                                    A. Summers, Capt.
30/8/17   Commdg. 25 M.G. Coy.

Copy. No.1. O.C. "B" Section
         2. O.C. "D" Section
         3. Transport Officer
         4. 25th Infantry Brigade
         5. D.M.G.O.
         6. 24th M.G. Company
         7. 218th M.G. Company
         8. War Diary
         9. Retained.

Army Form C. 2118.

WAR DIARY
25th MACHINE GUN COMPANY
INTELLIGENCE SUMMARY

from 1st SEPT. 1917 to 30th SEPT. 1917.

Vol 21

Place	Date	Hour	Summary of Events and Information	Remarks and references to Appendices
GREENJACKETS CAMP Dist 36 B.R.C. 38.	1/9/17		Training under officers in m.g. required cover. 1 O.R. wounded. 1 O.R. to Hosp.	
			Nth Lulu Crns. 7 O.R. joined Coy from Base Depot. At	
	2/9/17		As on 1st. 1 O.R. to hospital. 1 O.R. to Base Rest Station. 2nd LIEUT. OMEARA & S. O.R. joined	
			N.W.R. 2nd LIEUT. HARRIS from base N.W.R. At	
	3/9/17		"B" & "C" Subsecs. training under section officers. Last night the guns on the line fired	
			on the following targets :— SPINNING HOUSE & enemy tracks in U.I9, tracks leading to L9 Farm	
			& tracks on U.24.a.1. and the Junction near WIGHT FARM. Between friendly mortar areas. (Ref	
			FLEEGSTEERT 70/10). 1 O.R. wounded. At	
	4/9/17		Section out of line — Clean and refit — Battalion relieved 9.0 – 11.0 am. Enemy	
			made action offensive 11.0 – 11.30 p.m. During the day 2550 rounds were fired at E.A.	
			During the night 1000 rounds fire fired on the the enemy tracks at U.18.d.65.25.	
			1 O.R. evacuated out & 2 O.R. to Hospital At	
	5/9/17		During the morning "C" Section prepared guns for the line and at night relieved "D" Section	APPENDIX I Relief Orders
			which relieved to GREENJACKETS CAMP. "A" Section transferred from 9.0 – 12.30 p.m. At	
	6/9/17		"A" Section trained from 9.0 – 12.30. "D" Section killed & spent ammunition of units	
			cleaning guns & harassed systems. 2 O.R. to hospital. 1 O.R. to Base. 1 O.R. to prisoner. At	

Army Form C. 2118.

WAR DIARY
or
INTELLIGENCE SUMMARY.
(Erase heading not required.)

Instructions regarding War Diaries and Intelligence Summaries are contained in F.S. Regs., Part II. and the Staff Manual respectively. Title pages will be prepared in manuscript.

Place	Date	Hour	Summary of Events and Information	Remarks and references to Appendices
GREENJACKETS CAMP B.E.F. 38	7/9/17	7.0 – 7.45	Close Order Drill. 9.0 – 12.30 Training under Platoon Officers. 2.0 – 3.0 "A" Lecture Jews aeroplanes. Last night 2000 rounds were fired safely into street of WARNETON and 1800 rounds were fired sweeping the back of the RIVER LYS south of WARNETON. Lamp shelled in retaliation.	
	8/9/17	7.0 – 7.45	Close Order Drill. 9.0 – 12.30 Training under Platoon Officers. 2.0 – 3.0 P. Lecture – Revolver Practice. Between 9.0 p.m. and 12.0 mid. 1000 rounds were fired at tracks leading to Telephone Exchanges V24d. During the day 300 rounds were fired at E.A. 1 O.R., from leave + 1 O.R. from P.T. Course Att.	
	9/9/17	7.0 – 7.45	Rapid March discipline. Voluntary Services. 2.0 – 2.30 A. Lecture on Revolver Range. 8.30 – 9.15, 400 rounds were fired at Cross track V18 c 6335. Between 9.30 pm + 1.0 am 900 rounds were fired at tracks leading to Telephone Exchange V24 c 60 25. Between 12.0 mn. + 2am 1000 rounds were fired on to the main street of WARNETON + the road south of the village. 1 O.R. evacuated 1 O.R. from hospital. LIEUT. LARKNORTHY + 3 O.R. leave to U.K. 2nd LT. LOCKHART + 3 O.R. to Course on A.A. duties Att.	
	10/9/17		Company attended demonstration at Div. Gas School during the morning.	

Army Form C. 2118.

WAR DIARY
or
~~INTELLIGENCE SUMMARY~~
(Erase heading not required.)

Instructions regarding War Diaries and Intelligence Summaries are contained in F. S. Regs., Part II. and the Staff Manual respectively. Title pages will be prepared in manuscript.

Place	Date	Hour	Summary of Events and Information	Remarks and references to Appendices
GREENJACKETS CAMP B8 c 3.8. Sheet 36 and Env. near PLOEGSTEERT	10/9/17		Between 9.30 pm to 1.0 am 750 rounds were fired on to neighbourhood of SPINNING MILL in U18 d. Between 3.45 am & 5.10 am 750 rounds were fired on tracks leading to Telephone Exchange on U24 c. 2950 rounds were fired during the night on to main street of WARNETON & rear bank north of village.	
			SERGT. MEREDITH & CORPL. KING awarded D.C.M. 1 OR. from Wels Fusilier Casual. A1.	APPENDIX II Movement Order
Sheet 28. T27 a 55	11/9/17		Portion of Coy. out of line moved to camp in KORTEPYP road where unlimbered 27th Coy. Move complete at 10.10 am. 500 rounds were fired at E.A. met between 5.0 am & 5.10 am. 500 rounds were fired on tracks leading to Telephone Exchange. 1 OR. to hospital. 10R. from hospital. 10R. to Base. 32 OR. attached from the Infantry. ad.	
	12/9/17		4.0 - 4.45 Dublin & Alger batteries on a barrel drill. 9.0-12.30 Lectures limbering under dation officer. "D Section & reconnaissance from 2.0 - 3.0. 1200 rounds were fired on E.A. 2050 rounds were fired during the night on main street of WARNETON & neighbourhood north of village. Rat on U17 & U18 a = 1000 rounds. 1 OR. to hospital & 1 OR. from hospital. 1 OR. Leave to U.K. ad.	

WAR DIARY or INTELLIGENCE SUMMARY

Army Form C. 2118.

(Erase heading not required.)

Place	Date	Hour	Summary of Events and Information	Remarks and references to Appendices
Area 28 I.2 & S.5	13/9/17	9.0 – 7.45	Inspection on fatigues. Musketry practice on Anna Doll. 9.0-12.30. Training under Section Off.	
			"D" Section Rhodes Range 2.0-5.0.	
			800 rounds were fired at E.A. during the day and between 8.0 p.m. & 2.0 a.m. 3500 rounds were fired into WARNETON & the Centre of the L.Y.S. south of it.	
			4 O.R. from leave. 1 O.R. to leave. AS	
	14/9/17	9.0 – 7.45	Route March Discipline. 9.0-12.30 Training under Section Off. D Section on Rhodes Range from 2.0-3.0 pm.	
			During the evening 450 rounds were fired at E.A. Between 8.0 pm & 2.0 am 3000 rounds were fired against the ground around the SPINNING MILL, WARNETON main street & the WARNETON L.Y.S. south of WARNETON.	
			Lt. GOODEVE & 3 O.R. from leave. 1 O.R. from hospital. AS	
	15/9/17	9.0 – 7.45	Close Order Drill. Training under Section officers 9.0 – 12.30. "A" Section on miniature range from 2.0-3.30 pm.	APPENDIX III Orders for movement of
			On the night of 15/9/16 a Harassment programme of the enemy line commenced. A total of our guns exchanged 3000 rounds during the night in accordance with the programme.	
			1 O.R. to hospital. 1 O.R. to hospital. 1 O.R. to P. Course. 1 O.R. from leave. AS	

WAR DIARY
or
INTELLIGENCE SUMMARY.

(Erase heading not required.)

Army Form C. 2118.

Place	Date	Hour	Summary of Events and Information	Remarks and references to Appendices
Sheet 28 T.27 a 5.5	16/9/17		Sunday - Church Parade for all not on duty.	
			During the night two guns his road just 200 yards to our rear but with no casualties or damage. Lt Bingeman.	
			LIEUT. SPOONER & 1 O.R. leave to U.K. 2nd LT LOCKHART & 2 O.R. from A.T. Course. 1 O.R. from C.C.S. 1 O.R. to hospital at	
	17/9/17	9.10 - 9.45	Enemy aeroplane over lines. 9.0 - 12.30 Enemy aeroplane bombing Ypres. Perhaps a rookie aircraft.	
			During afternoon. Enemy aeroplane over lines and bombing. Two fire as usual. At 6.0 P.M. at Ok 10 R. from hospital at	APPENDIX IV. Orders in connection with the raid.
	18/9/17		At 4.10 am a raid was carried out by the 2nd Lancashire Regt. over the 2nd Royal Berks on a strong point in U10 g on the enemy front line in U.18 a (sheet 28). The four guns of "C" Battery assisted in the raid. They were grouped into a battery and put a barrage on the enemy front line in U.18 c from Zero to Zero + 30 with a view to preventing the enemy from bringing enfilade fire to bear on the raiding party.	
			At 6.0 am About half the machine guns on the line put down a barrage to facilitate	APPENDIX V. Barrage Planning Orders.

WAR DIARY or INTELLIGENCE SUMMARY

Army Form C. 2118.

Place	Date	Hour	Summary of Events and Information	Remarks and references to Appendices
Sheet 28 7.27 a 5.5	18/9/17		During the afternoon all the artillery (the four guns of "B" division had for a specially chosen battery position) were come south of MARRIERES on 2.16 a 7.6 and 2.13.c. As the battery horses could not be made to advance over by the enemy of the increased movement the guns remained there throughout the day and were drawn to positions during the night (these took longer than it was expected would have been the case as were engaged.	
Moving to B.13 c 8.39 Sheet 36 "MOERLAND CAMP"			Coy H.Q. & the Transport Lines were made during the day at MOERLAND CAMP. B.13 c 8.39 – Sheet 36. Where available at 12.30pm. As the camp was in a very bad state of repair the men available on the camp for the rest of the day. 2 O.R. from Base.	APPENDIX VI Movement Order
	19/9/17		The two sections out prepared for the line but the proposed relic railed did not take place owing to a new of infantry being put in to the line. In the afternoon they marched out the lats putting in hats. On the night of 19 - 7/20 the reinforcements for the two received was by seven guns.	

WAR DIARY
or
INTELLIGENCE SUMMARY.

(Erase heading not required.)

Army Form C.2118.

Instructions regarding War Diaries and Intelligence Summaries are contained in F. S. Regs., Part II. and the Staff Manual respectively. Title pages will be prepared in manuscript.

Place	Date	Hour	Summary of Events and Information	Remarks and references to Appendices
WOODLAND CAMP (G.13.b.3.5.) and line attacks WARNETON (Sheet 28)	19/9/19		1 C.O.R. from line O.I.	
	20/9/19		In conjunction with the artillery attempt a practice S.O.S. barrage at dawn. Guns came at 5.40 am, and by 6 am shot from O.P.s at 6.40. Five guns were fit for action to be taken as enemy and if no answer fire to be carried on by the hour of observer to clear the presence of hostile S.A. in camp of peacetime charge of hostile an area of participating charge of hostile. At night 4 guns commenced harry fire C.O.R. relieved 10 C.O.R. from line O.I. Scheme on of line prepared for relief.	APPENDIX VIII Practice Barrage Orders
	21/9/19		During night of 21/2/22 A Sub made with 2 guns of 216th Coy x 2 guns of 226th Coy on left 15th Divn. "D" sub also taken over 3 guns of 226th Coy on left. 15th Divn and augments movements for the 6th gun to take up position in the front line on right of 226th Coy thus 16 guns were in the line Harry fire was commenced by ABC sub-divns during the night. 1 O.R. from line O.I.	APPENDIX IX Relief Orders
	22/9/19		On the night of 22/23 Sept. 4 guns the Right Hah Sub-divn were relieved by 216th Coy and the remainder withdrawn. The left 2 guns in the line will be	

WAR DIARY or INTELLIGENCE SUMMARY

Army Form C. 2118.

(Erase heading not required.)

Instructions regarding War Diaries and Intelligence Summaries are contained in F. S. Regs., Part II. and the Staff Manual respectively. Title pages will be prepared in manuscript.

Place	Date	Hour	Summary of Events and Information	Remarks and references to Appendices
WASSRAND	22/9/17		Heavy fire on communication T.L. Sector during the night.	
Sub Hdqrs (A12 B 20)	23/9/17		2 O.R. joined Bn. at. "B" x C. Section stanay gun + personal equipment. Whole of Coy out of line bathed. Two guns of "A" Section fired 2500 rounds searching the tracks today from the SPINNING MILL and WEARY FARM Lines. 9. Coy. B.H.Q. Orm. 5 O.R. from base. 10 O.R. joined Coy from Base. I attended O.R. to hospital. A.I.	
	24/9/17		Section having another Lewis Gun Officer till 12.30 pm. Enemy unusually quiet. Between 9.0 + 6.0 am 2000 rounds searched as last night. A.I.	
	25/9/17		Section opened indirect Lewis gun fire at 12.30 pm. Between 9 + 9.20 pm. 25 t rounds were fired on a bridge over U.A. Douve at U.12.B.1565. At 9.0 pm a message was received from the C.O. 2nd Bn. R.B. North office that the unusual quietness by H.A. during the day night mean a raid. Guns therefore ceased fire + held in S.O.S. kine ready to give immediate response to S.O.S. call. S.O.R. from base + from Inspect Bpt.	
	26/9/17		Section training under section officers till 12.30 pm. Between 9.0 pm + 4.0 am 2000 rounds were fired by this "A" Section guns on the Road function at U.12 B.4580.	

G. O.R. Capt. O. R. A.I.

Army Form C.2118.

WAR DIARY
or
INTELLIGENCE SUMMARY.

(Erase heading not required.)

Instructions regarding War Diaries and Intelligence Summaries are contained in F. S. Regs., Part II. and the Staff Manual respectively. Title pages will be prepared in manuscript.

Place	Date	Hour	Summary of Events and Information	Remarks and references to Appendices
WACLAW CAMP B13.d.9.7 (Sheet 36) and Line opposite WARNETON (Sheet 28)	27/9/17		Actions out of line. Training under Section Officers.	
		4.0 pm	Between 4.0 pm & 4.0 am 2000 rounds rapid fire on no mans land at intervals.	
			3 O.R. to hospital. Lieuts MACNAMARA & SPOONER & 3 O.R. from leave.	
			10.R. rejoined from C.C.S. 1 O.R. rejoined from R.O. detail a.s.	
	28/9/17		Actions out of line. Transport under Section Officers up to 12.30 pm.	
			During the night 300 rounds were fired on to the following targets - Trench Tramway Junction at U12.b.3838, Bridge over River LYS at U12.d.5523, and road between U12.b.42.22 & U12.b.70.32.	
			8 O.R. from leave. a.s.	
	29/9/17		"D" Section prepared for the line, and moved off at 5.45 pm. to relieve "B" Section. Relief was complete at 11.0 pm.	APPENDIX X Relief Order
			"B" Section arrived in camp improvements.	
			Between 2.0 pm & 3.30 am firing was carried on last night, 3500 rounds being fired. During the day between 9.0 pm 1500 rounds were fired at E.A.	
			10 O.R. to hospital & 1 O.R. from leave. a.s.	
	30/9/17		Voluntary Church Services. Officers - "B" & "D" Sections bathed.	

Army Form C. 2118.

WAR DIARY
or
INTELLIGENCE SUMMARY.
(Erase heading not required.)

Instructions regarding War Diaries and Intelligence Summaries are contained in F. S. Regs., Part II. and the Staff Manual respectively. Title pages will be prepared in manuscript.

Place	Date	Hour	Summary of Events and Information	Remarks and references to Appendices
WACKLAND CAMP B.13 c 3.9 (Sheet 36) and Gun Flash HARNETON (Sheet 28)	30/9/17		Two guns each fired 2000 rounds between 9.0pm & 7.30am. Truck tramway junction at V.12.c.3.8.3.8 and Road junction at V.12.c.6.4.3. Another gun fired 500 rounds at 9.0pm & 500 at 7.30am. harassing the road & truck Railway between V.6.d.0.5.0.0 & V.6.b.5.7.4.0. 1 O.R. 16 G.M.G. S.A. Sect. 1 O.R. transferred to 244th S. Coy. 1 O.R. transferred A.I. 1 O.R. to Base. 2 O.R. to hospital.	

A. Annesley Capt.
Commanding 25th M.G. Coy.

Secret

APPENDIX I

Copy No. 6

25 Machine Gun Company

Relief Order No. 7

Ref. PLOEGSTEERT Map $\frac{1}{10,000}$

5/9/17

(1) "C" Section will relieve "D" Section in the line on the night of 5/6th. September.

(2) The positions are as follows

U 22 a 15 57
U 22 a 45 60
U 22 a 45 70
U 22 a 45 75

(3) One guide from each of "D" Section's guns will be at CAMPAC DUMP at 9.15 pm.

(4) "C" Section will leave GREENJACKETS CAMP at 8.0 pm. and will move via RED LODGE and HYDE PARK CORNER.

(5) Belts, Belt boxes and A.A. Sights will be handed over but no other mobilisation stores.

(6) LIEUT. SPOONER will remain in the line until 11.0 am 6th September.

(7) Details of barrage arrangements etc. will be carefully handed over

(8) Completion of relief will be reported to Coy. H.Q.

(9) Please acknowledge.

A Simmonds Capt.
Commdg. 25 M.G. Coy.

5/9/17

Copy. NO. 1. O.C. "C" Section
2.   :   "D"   :
3.   :   "B"   :
4. 23rd. Inf. Bde.
5. D.M.G.O.
6. War Diary
7. Retained.

APPENDIX II

8th Division No.1/52/A.

25th Inf. Bde.

25th Machine Gun Company (GREENJACKET Camp, B.8.c.1.8.) and 218th Machine Gun Company (KORTEPYP Road, T.27.a.5.5.) will exchange camps and horse lines.

Move to be completed by 12 noon 11th September, 1917.

(Sd) H.RAMSBOTHAM, Captain,
D.A.A.G., 8th Division.

9th September, 1917.

--2.--

25th Inf. Bde. No. A/10/6.

25th Machine Gun Coy.
Brigade Signal Officer (for information).

For information and necessary action. All details connected with the move to be arranged by you direct with O.C. 218th M. G. Coy.

Completion of move to be notified to this office.

ACKNOWLEDGE.

Captain,
Staff Captain,
25th Inf. Bde.

9/9/17.

APPENDIX III

Secret

Reference Attached from 8th Division No. G 96/28.

(1) "B" Section will fire on the Bridges over the LYS referred to in para. (6).

"C" Section will fire on the other two targets given in para. (6)

(2) "B" Section will fire on the first target in para.7.
"C" Section will use two guns on the second target in para.7.

(3) In firing on the bridges over the LYS great care must be taken to avoid firing on the quiet area north of the river.
The quiet areas are not to be fired on until "C" day.

(4) For the purpose of carrying out the practice barrages and the harassing fire LIEUT. GOODEVE will act as battery commander and control the eight guns. He will be responsible that the firing is carried out in accordance with the orders laid down, and he will render ~~twice daily~~ reports twice daily to Coy. H.Q.
Section Officers will continue to be responsible for the close defence of the line and the general conduct of their sections.

            A. Simmons Capt
15/9/17   Commdg. 25 M.G. Coy.

Copies to:-

 O.C. "B" Section
   "C" Section
   Lieut. Goodeve
   War Diary
   Retained.

SECRET   Copy No.

Extract from 8th Division No. G 25/26.
                                                                14/9/17
Ref. GLOUCESTERT 1/10,000
       Sheet 28 N.W. and S.E. parts of 1/20,000

(1) Harrassing fire will be undertaken by Machine Guns in conjunction
    with artillery.

(2) Code letters have been given to the days of the month as follows:-

              Sept.11 - V   Sept. 21 - F
                   12 - W   22 - G
                   13 - X   23 - H
                   14 - Y   24 - I
                   15 - Z   25 - J
                   16 - A   26 - K
                   17 - B   27 - L
                   18 - C   28 - M
                   19 - D   29 - N
                   20 - E   30 - O

(3) Firing will commence on the night of Y/Z.

(4) 316th M.G. Coy. will etc.
(5) 24th M.G. Coy. will etc.
(6) 25th M.G. Coy. will engage targets nightly as follows:-
       The Bridges on the River LYS betwwen U 18 a 7.3. and
             V 7 c 4.7. with 2 guns

       U 13 c 30.15. to U 14 d 5.8. with 1 gun.

       WIGARF FARM and U 18 c 7.3. with 1 gun.

(7) On C/D night the following lines will be fired on:-

       316th M.G. Coy. -------
       24th M.G. Coy. -------
       25th M.G. Coy.   V 13 c 25.90. to V 13 c 4.0. by 1 gun.
                         U 18 b 4.1.   to U 18 d 5.4. by 2 guns.

(8) On the nights following C/D Night the lines indicated in para.7.
    will be fired on by Companies together with those indicated in
    paras. 4.5.6.

(9) Guns will engage these targets from positions fairly close to
    their normal positions and arrangements should be made each night
    so that the guns could be switched on to their S O S lines in
    case of need.
    Each gun will fire 3,000 rounds a night.

                                        (Signed) H. HEDDINGTON.
                                                 Lieut-Colonel.
   8th Division   General Staff.
   14th September 1917

APPENDIX IV

SECRET

To Lieut. K.V. WESTON.

Ref. Attached Copy of
25th Infantry Brigade Raid Orders
----

(1) The four guns which are not carrying out the practice barrage laid down in 8th Division G 96/30 dated 15/9/17 will fire on UNCUT TRENCH in connection with this raid with a view to preventing the enemy from ~~firing~~ *bringing* enfilade fire to bear on the raiding troops.

(2) The four guns will be grouped into a battery for ease of control.
    The position *which* you were instructed to reconnoitre for to-day will do provided that it gives the requisite clearance as laid down in the Machine Gunner's Pocket Book, Section 10.

(3) Upon the completion of the firing the guns will return to their normal positions which they should reach before day break.
    You will retain control of them until "STAND DOWN" on the evening of the 18th as laid down in my G 96/30 of to-day's date.

(4)

No. of guns	Target	Time of firing	Rate of fire
1 Gun	U 18 c 4.0. to U 18 c 47.17	Zero to Zero plus 30 mins.	60 rounds per gun per minute.
1 Gun	U 18 c 47.17 to U 18 c 61.35	ditto	ditto
1 Gun	U 18 c 61.35 to U 18 c 63.52	ditto	ditto
1 Gun	U 18 c 63.52 to U 18 c 65.70	ditto	ditto

(5) Clearances will be calculated for each gun position and all safety precautions taken.

(6) Please acknowledge.

16/9/17

A. Simmonds, Capt.
Commdg. 25 M.G. Coy.

SECRET.

25th INFANTRY BRIGADE RAID ORDERS.

16th September, 1917.

Map. Ref. Sheet 28 S.W. 1/10,000

1. (a) On the night of September 17th/18th two small raids will be carried out simultaneously by the 2nd. Lincolnshire Regt. and the 2nd. Royal Berkshire Regt.

   (b) The object of the raids is to capture prisoners for purposes of obtaining identifications and to kill as many of the enemy as do not surrender as possible.

2. OBJECTIVES.

   (a) 2nd. LINCOLNSHIRE REGT.

   Strong point and enemy machine gun position at U.11.d.92.38.

   (b) 2nd. ROYAL BERKSHIRE REGT.

   Suspected enemy dump at U.18.a.45.42. including enemy front line from about U.18.a.36.33. to U.18.a.39.38.

3. ZERO Hour will be 4 a.m., September, 18th.

4. (a) Barrages, according to attached table, will fall at ZERO and both raiding parties will, at the same moment, enter the enemy's positions, having previously formed up as close to the enemy's position as possible.

   (b) Raiding parties will withdraw at ZERO plus 15 minutes and barrages will die down, finally ceasing at ZERO plus 30 minutes.

   (c) Strength of each raiding party will be one Platoon, about 30 all ranks.

5. All papers, badges, and identifications will be taken from raiding parties before operations commence.

6. Prisoners will be sent back to Divisional Headquarters via Brigade Headquarters.

7. Watches will be synchronised by an Officer from Brigade H.Qrs. who will visit Battalion Headquarters concerned during the afternoon of the 17th.

8. Please acknowledge.

E.H.Richards

Major,
A/Brigade Major,
25th Infantry Brigade.

Copies to :-

Copy No. 1 G.O.C.
"   2 Bde. Major.
"   3 Staff Captain.
"   4 2/Lincoln. Regt.
"   5 2/R.Berks. Regt.
"   6 119th F.A. Group.
"   7 25th Machine Gun Coy.

No. 8 41st Inf. Bde.
"   9 23rd Inf. Bde.
" 10 C.R.E. 8th Divn.
" 11 8th Division.
" 12 8th Division.
" 13 War Diary.
" 14 Office.

Copy No. 15. "Heavies". (99th H.A. Group).

S E C R E T.

25th Infantry Brigade No.294/G/14.

O/C, 25th Machine Gun Coy.
~~8th Division.~~ ~~(For information)~~
23rd Infantry Bde.   "   "
2nd Lincoln Regt.   "   "
~~2nd R. Berks Regt.~~ "   "

----

1.   Reference this Brigade Raid Orders of 15/9/17.

2. (a). You will arrange for the following Machine Gun Barrage to be laid at ZERO hour, and to cease at ZERO plus 30 mins. From WICART FARM to U.18.c.69.71.

    (b) If you cannot site your guns to fire on WICART FARM without endangering our troops you will lay barrage on UNCUT TRENCH as close to WICART FARM as possible.

    (c) The four guns used for practice barrages are not to be used for this barrage.

                                           Major,
                                   A/Brigade Major.
16th Septr 1917.   25th Inf. Bde.

APPENDIX V

Copy No. 4

Instructions in Connection with
8th Division   No. G 96/30 dated 16/9/17

(1)   "D" Section will supply the guns from the two night positions at U 22 a 79.05 and U 22 a 6.3.

"C" Section will supply the guns from the two night positions at U 22 a 45.00 and U 22 a 65.70

(2)   LT. WESTON will give all assistance possible in the preparations but the actual firing will be carried out by LT. GOODEVE and 2nd.LT.PRITCHARD.

From Zero until "Stand Down" on evening of the 18th when the guns return to their normal positions Lieut. WESTON will assume command of the 4 guns left behind.

(3)   8 additional belt boxes per section are being sent up to-night

(4)   Each gun will use its spare barrel.

(5)   Please acknowledge

16/9/17

A. Simmonds Capt.
Comdg. 25 M.G. Coy.

N.B. There will be no practice barrage on the 17th as laid down in 25th Infantry Brigade G 1/44 dated 15/9/17 but it is possible that firing will be carried out in connection with the 25th Infantry Brigade Raid on the morning of 18th.Sept.

No. 25
MACHINE GUN
COMPANY.
No. G 96/30
Date 16/9/17

SECRET.   8th Div. No. G.96/30.

23rd Inf. Bde.,
25th Inf. Bde.,
218th Machine Gun Co.,
24th Machine Gun Co.,
25th Machine Gun Co.,
8th Div. R.A.,
----

1. In co-operation with the Artillery a machine gun barrage will be fired as shewn in the attached Tables on 18th September at 6 a.m..

2. 24th, 25th and 218th M.G. Companies will employ four guns each.

3. All guns in barrage positions will have their Zero lines laid on their proper S.O.S. defence lines.

4. Barrage positions will be dug, occupied and furnished with requisite water and lubricating oil, 3 boxes S.A.A. per gun and 14 full belt boxes, by dawn 18th September.
Belt-filling arrangements must be made at positions.

5. Positions must be carefully concealed especially from aircraft, and no movement permitted about them by day.

6. Safety Precautions:-
(a). Allowances must be made in accordance with the "Meteor" report of the day.
(b). New barrels will be used.
(c). Clearances will be calculated for each gun in each battery position.
(d). Depression stops will be used.
(e). Gun platforms must be rendered stable.
(f). Guns will be checked during fire by an officer, with a clinometer; - a form of searching aiming post might very well be employed.

7. Guns will return to their normal positions after dusk on the 18th September.

/2......

- 2 -

8. Watches will be synchronised by the D.M.G.O. at Adv. Coy. H.Q. of 218th M.G. Coy. at U.15.c. Central, at 11 a.m., 17th September.

9. ACKNOWLEDGE.

8th Division,
15th September, 1917.

EBeddington
Lieut.-Colonel,
General Staff.

Copies to:-
VIII Corps.
14th Division.
57th Division.

BARRAGE TABLE FOR 25TH MACHINE GUN COMPANY, BATTERY 'C'.

No. of Guns.	Approximate Location.	Targets.	Time of opening fire.	Ceasing fire.	Rate of fire per Gun per minute.	Further action.
4.	U.16.b.4.8.	U.12.c.99.00. to U.18.b.13.65.	Zero.	Z plus 9	60	Increase range.
		U.12.d.60.00. to U.18.b.60.65.	Z plus 10	Z plus 17	"	"
		V.7.c.00.00. to V.13.a.00.65.	Z plus 18	Z plus 30	"	"
		V.7.c.40.00. to V.13.a.40.65.	Z plus 31	Z plus 42	"	Cease fire.

APPENDIX VI

S E C R E T.

25th Infantry Brigade No. A 1918.

~~2ND Lincoln Regt.~~
2nd R.Berks Regt.
1st R.Irish Rifles.
~~2nd Rifle Brigade.~~
25th M.G.Coy.
~~25th T.M.Bty.~~

For information.

1. The 1st R.Irish Rifles will move their Transport Lines from their present position at T.27.b.3.7. to ANTRIM LINES (T.27.b.6.3.) vacated by 2nd Northants. Transport, on 18th inst. They will not move before 11 a.m. and will be clear of present standings by 12 noon.

2. The 25th Machine Gun Coy. will move from their present position at T.27.a.5.5. to WACKLAND LINES (B.13.b.3.9.) on 18th instant. They will not move before 11 a.m. and will be clear of present billets by 12 noon. Route - T.27.b.4.8. - B.4.a.6.0 - B.8.b.05.45. - B.8.a.7.6.

3. Officers Commanding will ensure that the instructions contained in the attached 8th Division letter No.1/66/A are carried out.

Rogan Gay
Captain,
Staff Captain,
25th Inf. Bde.

16th Septr 1917.

SECRET   APPENDIX VII   Copy No. 4

INSTRUCTIONS REGARDING PRACTICE BARRAGE

referred to in 8th Div. G.96/57 dated 17/9/17

1. There will be no relief to-night as the proposed change in Sectors will probably take place to-morrow night (night of 20/21 Sept.)

2. Zero day is to-morrow 20th Sept.

3. Zero hour is not yet known but will be notified as soon as received. As however the 14th Division are going to make a raid zero will probably be during the early morning, either before or at dawn.

4. The period of fire is not yet known but will be notified as soon as received.

5. Officers will synchronise their watches with that of the bearer of this message.

6. LIEUT. GOODEVE will choose battery positions, make requisite calculations and all necessary arrangements. The battery positions used for the practice Barrage on the 18th will probably be found suitable. In the case of "B" Section however their present practice barrage position will give comparatively small clearance over our own troops and therefore special attention must be paid to Depression Stops and Allowances for the Error of the Day.

7. Harrassing fire should be commenced early to-night so as to allow for teams being in their practice barrage positions as soon after midnight as possible.
   If the positions are such that after firing the barrage the teams cannot leave without being seen by the enemy arrangements will be made for the teams to remain in their practice barrage positions until "Stand Down" on the evening of the 20th.

8. Lieut. GOODEVE will render a report as soon as the operation is concluded.

                                        A Simmonds Capt.
19/9/17   Commdg. 25 M.G. Coy.

Copy. No. 1 Lieut. GOODEVE.
       2. O.C. "B" Setion
       3. O.C. "C" Section
       4. War Diary.
       5. Retained.

SECRET   Copy. No. 4

Ref. 8th Div. G 26/37 dated 17/9/17

(1) Zero is at 5.40 am. on 20th Sept.

(2) Time of firing is Zero plus 5 minutes to Zero plus 40 minutes.

(3) For the purposes of this practice <u>all barrage lines will be laid down 100 yards further east</u> as the clearance allowed in the actual S.O.S. is so small.

(4) Please acknowledge.

                                                    A. Simmonds Capt.
                                                    Comdg. 25 M.G. Coy.

19/9/17

Copy No. 1   Lieut. Goodeve.
        2   O.C. "B" Section
        3   "   "C" Section
        4   War Diary
        5   Retained.

S E C R E T.　　　　　　　　　　　　　　8th Div. No. G.96/37.

23rd Inf. Bde., (2),
24th Inf. Bde., (2),　　7th M.M.G.Bty.,
25th Inf. Bde., (2),　　218th M.G. Coy..
G.O.C., R.A.,
C.R.E.,
D.M.G.O.

1. In accordance with 8th Division Order No. 229, para. 2 (b), all machine guns which have S.O.S. lines on to the WARNETON Barrage will fire on these lines, except that/four guns of "C" Battery, 218th Machine Gun Co. will be moved to a position about U.10.d.4.3, and barrage an area U.6.c.37.60. - U.6.b.0.2. - U.6.d.25.80. - U.6.c.6.3.

2. The two guns of the 7th M.M.G. Battery will fire on their S.O.S. lines on the SPINNING MILL.

3. The machine guns of 24th Machine Gun Co. which enfilade the new German front line trench West of WARNETON, will also fire.

4. Rate of fire for all guns will be 120 rounds per gun per minute.

5. Company Commanders will make the necessary arrangements and observe all safety precautions. No gun, however, will fire from its battle position, but will be moved well away into shell hole positions.

6. Zero day and hour, period of fire, and arrangements for synchronisation of watches will be issued to Os. C. Machine Gun Companies and 7th M.M.G. Battery by the 8th Div. Machine Gun Officer later.

Copies to:-
VIII Corps,
14th Divn.,
38th Divn..

8th Division,　　　　　　　　　　　　　　　　Lieut.-Colonel,
17th September, 1917.　　　　　　　　　　　　General Staff.

APPENDIX IX

SECRET　　　　　　　　　　　　　　　　　　　　　　　Copy No. 8

26th M.G. Coy. Relief Order No.7

Ref. FLORBECQUE 1/20000.　　　　　　　　　　　　　　21st September 1917.

(1) The following reliefs will take place on the nights of 21/22 September.

    (a) 2 guns of "A" Section will relieve 2 guns of 24th M.G.Coy at U 16 a 65.38 and U 16 a 75.70.

    (b) 2 guns of "A" Section will relieve 2 guns of 213th. M.G.Coy. about U 15 d 3.5.

    (c) 3 guns of "D" Section will relieve 3 guns of 24th.M.G.Coy. at U 17 d 80.35, U 16 d 56.95, and U 16 d 59.60.

    (d) Instead of occupying the position at U 16 d 65.38 the relieving gun will be placed in position at U 17 c 2.1.

    (e) O.C. "D" Section will arrange to put his fourth gun in the front line about U 23 b 3.3.

(2) Guides from the 24th and 213th M.G.Coys. for the guns mentioned in 1 (a) and 1 (b) will be at the Advanced H.Q. of the 24th M.G.Coy. at 5.0 p.m.

(3) Guides from the 24th.M.G.Coy. for the guns mentioned in 1(c) will be at the advanced H.Q. of the 24th.M.G.Coy. at 7.30 p.m.

(4) 8 belts and beltboxes per gun will be taken over but no other Mobilisation Stores.

(5) Section Officers will forward to Coy.H.Q. not later than the evening of the 22nd.September a list of all Trench Stores taken over.

(6) Section Officers will impress upon their Gun Team Commanders the importance of obtaining the fullest information from the out-going teams.
    Gun Team Commanders will take over Range Cards, "Sentry's Order Boards" and "Sentry's Information Boards".

(7) Completion of relief will be reported to Coy.H.Q. by runner.

                                                    A. Simmonds, Capt.
                                                  Commdg. 26 M.G. Coy.

21/9/17

Copy No. 1. O.C."A" Section
       2. O.C."D" Section
       3. Lieut. GOODMAN for information
       4. 24th M.G. Coy.
       5. 213th M.G. Coy.
       6. 26th Inf. Bde.
       7. D.M.G.O.
       8. War Diary.
       9. Retained.

Copy No. 2

25 M.G. Coy. Relief Order No. 5.

(1) On the night of 29/30 September the 218th M.G. Coy. will relieve

    (a) Two guns of "B" Section at U 22 a 70.05 and U 16 c55.15

    (b) Two guns of "C" Section at U 22 a 15.37 & U 22 a 45.70

(2) Upon completion of these reliefs O's. Commanding "B" & "C" Sections will each withdraw their other two guns.

(3) Upon the completion of the reliefs and withdrawals "B" & "C" Sections will proceed to WACKLAND CAMP.

(4) A guide from each gun which is being relieved will be at CAMPAC DUMP at 4.0 PM.
    Limbers to convey the guns to WACKLAND CAMP will be at CAMPAC DUMP at 5.30 PM.

(5) (a) 5 belts and belt boxes will be handed over to each relieving team.
    No other Mobilisation Stores will be handed over.

    (b) Receipts will be obtained for all Trench Stores handed over.

A. Simmonds Capt.
Commdg. 25 M.G. Coy.

21/9/17

Copy No. 1 O.C. "B" Section
      2 O.C. "C" Section
      3 218th M.G. Coy.
      4 25th Inf. Bde.
      5 D.M.G.O.
      6 War Diary
      7 Retained.

S E C R E T.
                                        8th Division No.G.96/44.

                                        25th Inf Bde no 42/13

    23rd Inf. Bde. (2)
    24th Inf. Bde. (2)
    25th Inf. Bde. (2)
    218th M.G. Coy.
    7th M.M.G. Battery.
    G.O.C., R.A.
    C.R.E.
    "Q".
    O.C., Signals.
    D.M.G.O..

1. With a view to arranging that normally each Machine Gun Company in the Division has only 8 guns and the 7th Motor Machine Gun Battery 4 guns in the line, Machine Gun Positions on the Divisional front will be re-adjusted in accordance with the attached Table 'A'. Details of reliefs to be arranged direct between Machine Gun Company and Battery Commanders.

2. On completion of the moves on night 22nd/23rd September, S.O.S. Barrage lines will be altered as follows:-

   (a) WARNETON Barrage.

Company.	No. of guns.	Position.	Frontage of Barrage.
218th M.G.Co.	2.	U.22.a.13.37. U.22.a.70.05.	U.18.a.78.48. - U.18.a.65.80.
218th " "	2.	U.16.c.6.1. U.22.a.45.70.	U.18.a.65.80. - U.12.c.49.14.
25th " "	2.	U.16.a.63.32. U.16.a.75.70.	U.12.c.49.14. - U.12.c.35.45.
28th M.G. Co.	2.	About U.15.d.8.5.	U.12.c.35.45. - U.12.c.20.75.
24th " "	2.	About U.10.c.1.4.	U.12.c.20.75. - U.12.a.06.06.

   (b) DEULEMONT Barrage.

   218th M.G. Coy. will employ the 4 guns at U.22.a.70.05., U.22.a.13.37., U.16.c.55.15., U.22.a.45.70. on Secondary S.O.S. lines between U.30.a.82.69. and U.24.c.58.50.

   (c) PONT ROUGE Barrage.

   218th M.G. Coy. will employ the 4 guns at U.28.a.15.25., U.28.a.14.30., U.28.b.38.80., U.22.d.45.40., to fire on Primary S.O.S. lines between U.30.a.0.0. and U.29. Central. The gun at U.22.d.45.40. will not traverse East of U.29.b.5.0.

3. Close defence areas of fire will be arranged in accordance with Map which is being issued very shortly.

4. Defence Schemes, Range Cards, Local Defence Orders for each gun etc., will be taken over.

                                                    /5. ...

5.   Completion of reliefs will be reported by the relieving M.G. Coy. to Brigade in whose Sector the relief takes place and to Div. H.Q.

6.   Div. M.G. Officer will ensure that all arrangements for taking over, and duties in new positions are thoroughly understood by Machine Gun Unit Commanders concerned.

7.   ACKNOWLEDGE.   Done HM.

8th Division,
20th September, 1917.

E Beddington
Lieut.-Colonel,
General Staff.

TABLE "A". ISSUED WITH 9TH DIVISION No.G.96/44.

1. Serial number	2. Night	3. UNIT	4. ACTION.
1.	Sept.21/22nd	25th M.G. Coy.	Relieves 5 guns 24th M.G. Coy. at U.17.d.50.82., U.16.d.85.95., U.16.d.83.68., U.16.a.63.32., U.16.a.75.70. Instead of occupying the gun position at U.16.d.83.68., the relieving gun will be placed in action at TROIS TILLEULS FARM.
2.	- do -	- do -	Places in action 2 guns at U.15.d.8.5. in relief of 6 guns 218th M.G. Coy.
3.	- do -	- do -	Place 1 gun in action about U.17.d.4.1.
4.	- do -	24th M.G. Co.	Relieve 1 gun 218th M.G. Coy. at U.10.a.8.7.
5.	- do -	- do -	Places 2 guns in action about U.5.c.65.40. and withdraws 1 gun from U.16.b.25.80
6.	- do -	- do -	On completion of reliefs ordered in Serial No.1 withdraws relieved guns.
7.	- do -	218th M.G. Co.	On completion of reliefs ordered in Serial Nos.2 & 4, withdraws relieved guns and also gun at U.15.b.7.0.
8.	Sept.22/23rd	- do -	Relieves 4 guns 25th M.G. Coy. at U.22.a.70.05., U.22.a.13.37., U.16.c.55.15., U.22.a.45.70.
9.	- do -	- do -	Relieves 4 guns 7th M.M.G. Battery at U.28.a.15.25., U.28.a.14.30., U.28.b.38.80., U.22.d.45.40. Instead of occupying the gun position at U.28.b.38.80., the relieving gun will be placed in action at U.28.b.05.16.
10.	- do -	25th M.G. Co.	Withdraws relieved guns on completion of relief ordered in Serial No.9 and also withdraws 4 guns at U.22.a.8.3., U.22.a.35.95., U.22.a.45.60., U.22.a.45.75.
11.	- do -	7th M.M.G.Bty.	Withdraws relieved guns on completion of relief.
12.	Sept.26/27th	- do -	Relieves 4 guns 23rd M.G. Coy. at C.10.a.3.3., C.4.a.42.42., C.4.a.05.45., U.28.d.1.8.

SECRET   APPENDIX X   Copy. No. 4.

25 M.G. Company Relief Order No. 2.

Ref. PLOEGSTEERT 1/10,000   29/9/17

(1) "C" Section will relieve "D" Section in the following positions in the line to-night (night of 29/30 Sept.)

       U 23 b 25.60
       U 17 d 50.75
       U 17 c 25.20
       U 16 d 85.90

One guide from "D" Section will be at Advanced H.Q. at ST. IVES at 7.30 p.m.

(2) One guide from each gun will be at the Iron Gate in ULTIMO AVENUE at 8.0 p.m.

(3) Belts and belt boxes will be handed over but no other Mobilisation Stores.

(4) All Trench Stores will be carefully handed over and receipts rendered to the Orderly Room by O.C. "D" Section.

(5) "Sentries Order Boards" and "Sentry's Information Boards" will be carefully handed over.
     O.C. "C" Section will impress upon his gun Team Commanders the necessity for obtaining full information from the out-going teams.

(6) Completion of relief will be reported by O.C. "D" Section on arrival at Coy. H.Q.

29/9/17

                                           A. Simmonds, Capt.
                                           Comdg. 25 M.G. Coy.

Copy No. 1   O.C. "D" Section
         2   O.C. "C" Section
         3   Lieut. GOODEVE
         4   War Diary
         5   Retained.

Army Form C. 2118.

WAR DIARY
of 25 MACHINE or GUN COMPANY
INTELLIGENCE SUMMARY
(Erase heading not required.)

from 1st OCT. 1917

Vol 22

Place	Date	Hour	Summary of Events and Information	Remarks and references to Appendices
MACKLAND CAMP B.13 c.4.5.9 (Sheet 36) and Bois opposite WARNETON (Sheet 28)	1/10/17		"D" Section trained under Section Officer till 12.30 p.m. Afternoon - Camp Improvement.	APPENDIX I Relief Orders
			"B" Section prepared for the line entrained off at 3.30 p.m. to relieve "C" Section.	
			Relief complete at 7.30 p.m. "C" Section commenced to WARNLAND CAMP.	
			3 O.R. from leave. LIEUT. R.N. GOODEVE attached to artillery for instruction. A.J.	
	2/10/17		"A" Section spent day cleaning guns, equipment, clothing ets. "D" Section trained under Section Officer. 1000 rounds machine gun fired during the night exploiting the man about of WARNETON.	
			LIEUT. K.V. WESTON unrivalled. 1 O.R. & 1 attached O.R. from hospital. 1 attached O.R. to hospital. 2 O.R. from leave. A.J.	
	3/10/17		"A" & "D" Sections training under Section Officers. During the night two guns fired 1500 rounds each. Targets - 3 PANNING M144 to V18C & Enemy front line about V12C81. 1 O.R. to hospital. A.J.	
	4/10/17		"A" & "D" Sections worked on camp improvements until 10.15. Company Parade for fall at 10.30. Again marched on camp in afternoon. During the night two guns each fired 1500 rounds covering the tracks in V18C & the river border in V18a. 3 O.R. to hospital. A.J.	
	5/10/17		"A" & "D" Sections training under Section Officers until 12.30 p.m. Camp improvements in the afternoon. 1 O.R. attached from Invalid hospital type.	
			Firing was carried out as last night. 1 O.R. from hospital. A.J.	

2 O.R. L.D.R. & London, W.C. Sch. 52a. Forms/C/2118/4

WAR DIARY
or
INTELLIGENCE SUMMARY

Army Form C. 2118.

Place	Date	Hour	Summary of Events and Information	Remarks and references to Appendices
MACKLAND CAMP B.13 & 3.9 (Sheet 36) and Line opposite	6/10/17		"A" & "B" Sections training under Section Officers until 12.30 p.m. Confinement in afternoon. 800 rounds each fired at E.A. during the day. During the night two guns each fired 1500 rounds - Targets - Road tracks in V.18.a and X roads at V.18.d.75.25.	
WARNETON (Sheet 28)			2nd Lt. R.C. HALL joined Company. 10.R. from hospital. a.d.	
	7/10/17		Sunday - voluntary church parade. 550 rounds each fired at E.A. During the day. During the night two guns each enfiladed WARNETON cross roads, firing 3000 rounds. 10.R. from C.C.S. 6.O.R. from lines. a.d.	
	8/10/17		Relieve Company from the line. "B" Section moved off from the Camp about 3.0 p.m. to relieve "B" Section and "A" Section moved off about 4.30 p.m. to relieve "C" Section. No night firing in view of relief and the relatively wet night. 10.R. from hospital & LIEUT. K.P. WESTON from hospital. a.d.	APPENDIX II Relief Orders.
	9/10/17		Section which was out of line cleaned guns & equipment, turned gunpost etc. Kit inspection in afternoon. Baths. Between 6.10 p.m. and 7.30 a.m. each gun each fired 1500 rounds on to T.M. emplacement at V.12.c.66.85. 2 O.R. from & 1 O.R. to hospital. a.d.	

Army Form C. 2118.

WAR DIARY
or
INTELLIGENCE SUMMARY.
(Erase heading not required.)

Instructions regarding War Diaries and Intelligence Summaries are contained in F.S. Regs., Part II. and the Staff Manual respectively. Title pages will be prepared in manuscript.

Place	Date	Hour	Summary of Events and Information	Remarks and references to Appendices
WACKLAND CAMP B13 & 58 (Sheet 36) and line opposite WARNETON (Sheet 28)	10/10/17		Sections out of line cleaning up and preparing belt of ofference in gun experience. During the night & between 6.30pm & 12.30am 1000 rounds were fired on to each of two bridges over the LYS at V12d 62 & V2 & 7.5. 2 O.R. leave to U.K. & 1 O.R. from hospital.	
	11/10/17		"C" Section building range dummy & "B" section training back in camp. Movement in afternoon. Between 6.35 pm & 12.15 am 2000 rounds were fired amongst the trucks leading to the SPINNING MILL at V18c. 1 O.R. from hospital & 1 O.R. from leave. LIEUT. MACNAMARA to artillery course.	
	12/10/17		Nos. 1 overhauling guns etc. N.C.O's attending lectures on Map Reading & Fire Direction. All in camp improvement in afternoon. Remainder building range. Between 6.10 & 12.15 2000 rounds were fired unloading the SERVICE road in WARNETON.	
	13/10/17		No. 1 overhauling guns etc. Attended men training under Supt. Morrow. N.C.O. attended lectures on Map Reading & Fire Direction. Remainder on fatigues in camp. All in camp improvement in afternoon. On the night of 13/14 the 25th Inf Bde relieved the 20th Bde on its line. In areas	

Army Form C. 2118.

WAR DIARY
or
INTELLIGENCE SUMMARY.
(Erase heading not required.)

Instructions regarding War Diaries and Intelligence Summaries are contained in F. S. Regs., Part II. and the Staff Manual respectively. Title pages will be prepared in manuscript.

Place	Date	Hour	Summary of Events and Information	Remarks and references to Appendices
WACKLAND CAMP B 13 & 3.9 (Sheet 36) and from WARNETON (Sheet 28)			of the relief our guns did not fire. 1 O.R. from F 10CR. to hospital. 1 O.R. from detach of Ordnry Corses. at	
	14/10/17		Sunday. Voluntary Church Parades. inclust. About dusk fires were opened on a suspected M.G. about 1168 2590. Movement has been observed there every night at dusk & no engagement was made from the front line. Unfortunately front to be found on whilst an officer observed from the front line. Tracks leading to the SPINNIN & MILL necessitated this could be obtained. Considerable foot in them thus the night. 1 O.R. from down & 1 O.R. from P.T. Corses. at	
	15/10/17		Company fatigues as on Saturday except that an officer was detailed to supervise the work of 10 men on a watering trough. Watering was quite on our positions. 1 O.R. from C.L. at	
	16/10/17		"B" - "C" Section practical form line & then went to Baths together with the Transport Personal. An officer & 10 men are now detailed daily for work on the watering trough. On the Evening of 16/10/17 "B" & "C" Section relieved "A" & "D" in the line. At the event line an adjustment of guns took place. Four of the old positions were given up and	APPENDIX III Relief Orders

WAR DIARY
~~INTELLIGENCE SUMMARY~~

Army Form C. 2118.

(Erase heading not required.)

Place	Date	Hour	Summary of Events and Information	Remarks and references to Appendices
WACKLAND CAMP B13 & 5, 9 (Huts 3(a) and Line) afterwards WARNETON (Hut 28)	16/10/17 am		Four new ones arrived. Relief & adjustment complete at 8.0 pm. 2 O.R. to M.B. Base Depot. 1 O.R. to hospital. LIEUT. MACNAMARA & 1 O.R. from Artillery Annex. LIEUT. SPOONER & 1 O.R. to Artillery Annex. 2nd Lt. PRITCHARD & 1 O.R. to F. A.A. Course. A.I.	
	17/10/17		"A" & "D" Sections setting guns & group emplacement. Clearing clothes, Belts & kits inspection in afternoon. During the day 12·0 enemy aero fired at E.A. During the night 1750 rounds were fired on H.E. tracks in V.18 & the neighbourhood of the SPINNING MILL in V.18d. 2 O.R. leave to U.K. 2 O.R. from leave. A.I.	
	18/10/17		No. 1 overhauled sparepacts. N.C.O.'s attended lecture from 10·0 – 11·0 & 11·30–12·30. on mapreading & fire direction. Usual fatigue party on water through Reserve on fatigue. Gun refreshment in afternoon. During the night 2900 rounds were fired on H.E. tracks. LIEUT. MACNAMARA to M.G. TRAINING CENTRE, GRANTHAM. 1 O.R. to hospital. 1 O.R. to C.C.S. A.I.	

WAR DIARY
or
INTELLIGENCE SUMMARY.

(Erase heading not required.)

Army Form C. 2118.

Place	Date	Hour	Summary of Events and Information	Remarks and references to Appendices
WAERLAND CAMP B.13.d.3.9 (Sheet 36) and huts opposite	19/10/17		Clear. Colder. Dull at 7.0 a.m. After inspection morning spent in cleaning up "A" & "D" Sections paraded at 12.30 to march to a Ribbon Distribution Parade to be held by the Divisional Commander at ROMARIN at 2.0 p.m. Parade consisted of J.R. Lieut Ryffer and 22 O.R. Drawbourne in addition to number. 7 O.R. of this unit were present to receive decoration – 1 D.C.M. and 6 M.M.'s. Usual fatigue party on water troughs. During the day 6.00 rounds were fired at E.A. During the night 5000 rounds were fired on to registration about V.12.d.50.70 and 1500 rounds on to trench near the SPINNING MILL. During the last two nights the enemy's fire positions have been [enforced] with a number having them ready to give immediate support with [ ] fire to any infantry [ ]. Our position were made at O.16.a.72.40 and V.16.a.70.48. 4 O.R. Leave to U.K. 1 O.R. to hospital. 1 O.R. from hospital. Q.S.	
	20/10/17		Noise : 1 enemy gun. N.C.O. attending lectures -10.0 – 11.0 & 11.30 – 12.30. Usual events	

Army Form C. 2118.

WAR DIARY
or
INTELLIGENCE SUMMARY.

(Erase heading not required.)

Instructions regarding War Diaries and Intelligence Summaries are contained in F. S. Regs., Part II. and the Staff Manual respectively. Title pages will be prepared in manuscript.

Place	Date	Hour	Summary of Events and Information	Remarks and references to Appendices
WACKLAND CAMP (Sht 36) and thine opposite	20/10/17		Troops fatigue. Remainder on fatigue in the Camp. All on employment in the afternoon.	
WARNETON (Sht 28)			No firing was done until the early morning of 21/10/17. a.s.	
			LIEUT. SPOONER from artillery courses.	
	21/10/17		Sunday. Voluntary Service. Various working parties fatigues.	
			A raid was carried out by the infantry at 3.55 a.m. Artillery & machine guns cooperated. Two of our guns took up a position on the front line to engage any hostile M.G. which might open fire & to keep down rifle fire. The targets presented themselves. Two other guns put down an indirect fire barrage on the flank of the road. There guns fired 5000 rounds. The raiding party entered the hostile front then the scheduled time but found no enemy. The raiding party suffered no casualties.	APPENDIX IV Operation Orders for Raid.
			During the day 600 rounds were fired at E.A. During the night 1500 rounds were fired on the E. Forks behind Telephone House V24 & 1095. at 25 NRH & 10 R. to artillery course. a.s.	
	22/10/17		Relieve out of line. Training made Lectin officers. Lectures for N.C.O.s	

Army Form C. 2118.

WAR DIARY
or
INTELLIGENCE SUMMARY.
(Erase heading not required.)

Instructions regarding War Diaries and Intelligence Summaries are contained in F. S. Regs., Part II. and the Staff Manual respectively. Title pages will be prepared in manuscript.

Place	Date	Hour	Summary of Events and Information	Remarks and references to Appendices
WACKLAND CAMP B.13-6-59 (Sheet 31) and Home approach	22/10/17 6am.		1500 rounds were fired at E.A during the day and during the night 500 rounds were fired on both communications at U.18.a.75.55 harassing trucks moved between U.18.a.75.55 & U.18.a.65.40.	
WARNETON (Sheet 28)			1 O.R. to hospital & 2 O.R. from leave. A.D.	
	23/10/17		Harassing & tasks. Between 8.0 p.m. & midnight 1500 rounds were fired on the Roulers trunk & E. approach line at U.18.a	
	24/10/17		2nd Lt. PRITCHARD from A.D. Cannes. 10 O.R. to Div. Gas School. A.D. A.P.O. Saulsou proceeded from the line. The whole of the attached were fired in range & more fastest by aviations.	APPENDIX V. Relief Orders
			Relief in the evening. 2 O.R. to Div Signal School. & 1 O.R. from hospital A.D.	
	25/10/17		Cleaning guns, clothing equipments. Kit inspection. Baths. During the night 1500 rounds were fired on the E. Trunks in V.24.a. 1 O.R. from hospital. 20 O.R. from leave.	
	26/10/17		Training. Tuition for N.C.O's.	

WAR DIARY or INTELLIGENCE SUMMARY.

Army Form C. 2118.

Instructions regarding War Diaries and Intelligence Summaries are contained in F. S. Regs., Part II. and the Staff Manual respectively. Title pages will be prepared in manuscript.

(Erase heading not required.)

Place	Date	Hour	Summary of Events and Information	Remarks and references to Appendices
WACKLAND CAMP D73 & 74 (Hut 36) and shed Oxfords WARNEFORD (Hut 28)	26/10/17		1000 Recruits arrived during the night to road between U12d 01.49 - U12d 26.60.	
			1 O.R. Sian to U.K. 2=Lt. HALL & 5 O.R. to A.A. Course. Lt. WESTON & 1 N.R. to Artillery Course. 1 O.R. from Anti-Gas School. 2 O.R. to hospital. Lt. MORRIS proceeded to Rec H.D. to take up duties of Rec Transport Officer. 2=Lt PRITCHARD assumes duties of Cp. T.O. A.S.	
	27/10/17		Training under Section officers. Lt. GOODEVE taking charge of "C" section in absence of Lt. WESTON. NCO's - duties. Men unrivaled in use of Field glasses. During the night 1000 recruits were found on the road went on V12c and 1000 recruits reported on to Road at U12d 31.20 & proceed between that & the riv--	
	28/10/17		Sunday. Gas Drill between 9.0 & 9.20 a.m. Voluntary Services. At 9.0 p.m. a raid was carried out by the infantry on enemy trench about U11d 92. In car--- No prisoners were taken as enemy were found. The bodies promised themselves 750 recruits were found during the stay at E.A. 2 O.R. from Rec'd. 1 O.R. from GDS School & 1 O.R. attached from 2/R. Barta to Refr. were accepted. A.S.	APPENDIX VI Raid Orders
	29/10/17		Route March 9.15 - 11.15. Interior Organization of I.B. officers - NCO's - Letters	

Army Form C. 2118.

WAR DIARY
or
INTELLIGENCE SUMMARY.
(Erase heading not required.)

Instructions regarding War Diaries and Intelligence Summaries are contained in F. S. Regs., Part II, and the Staff Manual respectively. Title pages will be prepared in manuscript.

Place	Date	Hour	Summary of Events and Information	Remarks and references to Appendices
WACKLAND CAMP B.13 & 3.9 (Sheet 36) and sheet opposite WARNETON (Sheet 28)	28/10/17		750 rounds fired at E.A. during day. 1250 rounds fired during night at trenches in V.18.d. & V.24.b. a.d.	
	29/10/17		Training under Section Officers. Lectures to officers by M.O. in afternoon. 250 rounds were fired during day at E.A., and 1250 rounds were fired at night on to road & light railway in V.12.b. & V.16.c.	
			4 O.R. from leave a.d.	
	30/10/17		Barrage Drill & Range in morning. Lectures to N.C.O's and reading in afternoon. During the night 1250 rounds were fired on to light railway in V.12.b. 1 O.R. leave to U.K. a.d.	

A Drummond Capt
Commanding 25th M.G. Coy.

APPENDIX I

SECRET   Copy No. 6

36 Machine Gun Company. Relief Order No.10

Ref. PLOEGSTEERT 10,000   1st October 1917

(1) "B" Section will relieve "A" Section in the line to-night.

(2) O.C. "B" Section will not take over the H.Q. of "A" Section at ST. IVES but will establish his H.Q. in the concrete dug-out about U 18 a 4.2

(3) One guide from each of "A" Section's Guns will be at HYDE PARK CORNER at 4.30 pm.

(4) Belt boxes, clinometers and A.A. Sights will be handed over but no other mobilisation stores.

(5) All trench stores will be handed over and receipts rendered to Orderly Room by O.C. "A" Section.

(6) "O.C." B Section will impress upon his Gun Team Commanders the necessity for obtaining the fullest information from the outgoing teams. The No.1 of the Thatched Cottage Gun will remain in the line until one hour after evening stand-down in order to ensure that this position is properly handed over.
All "Sentry's Information Boards" and "Sentry's Order Boards" will be handed over and O.C. "B" Section will arrange to revise them as soon as possible.

(7) Completion of relief will be reported to Company H.Q. by O.C. "A" Section on his arrival at WACKLAND CAMP.

1/10/17   A. Simmons Capt.
                                                                  Comm'g. 36 M.G. Coy.

Copy No. 1 O.C. "B" Section
         2 2nd. Lt. PRITCHARD.
         3 O.C. "A" Section
         4 LIEUT. MACNAMARA   for information
         5 Lieut. Weston   "   "
         6 War Diary
         7 Retained.

SECRET APPENDIX II Copy No...9..

25 Machine Gun Company, Relief Order No.11

Reference PLOEGSTEERT 1/10,000   7th. October 1917

(1) The following reliefs will take place on the night of 8/9th. October.
      (a) "A"Section will relieve "C"Section
      (b) "D"Section will relieve "B"Section

(2) One guide from each of "B"Section's teams will be at HYDE PARK CORNER at 4.30 pm.
    One guide from each of "C"Section's teams will be at the IRON GATE in ULTIMO AVENUE at 7.0 pm.

(3) Belt boxes, clinometers and A.A.Sights will be handed over but no other mobilisation stores.

(4) All trench stores will be handed over and receipts rendered to the Orderly Room by O's.C. out-going sections.

(5) O's.C. in-going sections will impress upon their Gun Team Commanders the necessity for obtaining the fullest information from the out-going teams. The No.1 of the Thatched Cottage Gun will remain in the line until one hour after evening stand-down in order to ensure that this position is properly handed over.
    All "Sentry's Information Boards" and "Sentry's Order Boards," will be handed over and O's C. in-going sections will arrange to revise them as soon as possible.

(6) Completion of relief will be reported to Coy.H.Q. by O's.C. out-going sections.

(7) Please acknowledge.

7/10/17
                                    Capt.
                         Commdg. 25 M.G. Coy.

Copy No. 1. O.C."A"Section.
        2. O.C."B"Section.
        3. O.C."C"Section.
        4. O.C."D"Section.
        5. Lieut.Macnamara.
        6. Lieut.Goodeve.
        7. 24th.Infantry Brigade.
        8. D.M.G.O.
        9. War Diary.
      10. Retained.

APPENDIX III

SECRET   Copy.No. 6

25th Machine Gun Company Relief Order No.15

Reference PLOEGSTEERT 1/10,000   16th October 1917

(1) The reliefs and adjustments shown in attached table will take place to-night.

(2) As soon as in-coming Section Officers have all their guns in position they will report the fact to the out-going Section Officer concerned who will then evacuate the positions which are not being taken over.

(3) Guides for "B" Section's teams will be at the IRON GATE at 5.15 pm.
Guides for "C" Section will be at "D" Sections H.Q. at 5.15.pm.

(4) Limbers will reach HYDE PARK CORNER at 3.45 pm.

(5) Belt boxes will be handed over by the teams which are being relieved. O's.Commanding in-going Sections will arrange to draw 12 belt boxes for each new position from out-going sections. The teams which are withdrawing will not hand over more than 6 beltboxes until all the new positions are occupied.
A.A.Sights and Clinometers will be handed over but no mobilisation stores other than those mentioned.

(6) All Trench Stores will be handed over and receipts rendered to Company Orderly Room by O.'s.C. out-going sections.

(7) Completion of relief will be reported by O's.C. out-going sections on their arrival at Company H.Q.

(8) Please acknowledge to Advanced H.Q.

16/10/17   Capt.
                                                              Commdg. 25 M.G. Coy.

Copy No.1 O.C."A"Section
       2 O.C."B"Section
       3 O.C."C"Section
       4 O.C."D"Section
       5 Lieut.Goodeve
       6 War Diary
       7 Retained

SECRET.

TABLE ISSUED WITH 23rd M. G. COY. RELIEF ORDER NO. 15

PRESENT POSITIONS		HELD BY	RELIEF OR EVACUATION	NEW POSITIONS		HELD BY
CRATER	U 15 d 92·62	"D" SECTION	EVACUATED			
O.G. LINE	U 15 b 97·04	"	"			
ULTIMO AVENUE	U 16 a 70·34	"	RELIEVED	No. 19 ULTIMO AVENUE	U 16 a 70·34	"C" SECTION
THATCHED COT	U 16 a 82·99	"	EVACUATED		U	
MOULIN CARLIN	U 17 d 58·78	"A"	RELIEVED	No. 17 MOULIN CARLIN	U 17 d 58·78	"B" "
VOID POST	U 23 b 36·88	"	EVACUATED		U	
TROIS TILLEULS	U 17 c 05·20	"	RELIEVED	No. 14 TROIS TILLEULS	U 17 c 05·20	"C" "
ALDERSHOT TRENCH	U 16 d 98·90	"	"	No. 18 ALDERSHOT TRENCH	U 16 d 78·90	"B" "
				No. 15 VANCOUVER	U 16 d 70·10	"C" "
				No. 21 LONG RUNY	U 15 b 85·95	"C" "
				No. 20 RIGHT SUPPORT	U 17 a 30·54	"B" "
				No. 23 LEFT "	U 17 a 30·73	"B" "

SECRET.   8th Division No.G.06/87.

23rd Inf. Bde. (2)
24th Inf. Bde. (2)   G5/19
25th Inf. Bde. (2)
218th M.G. Coy.

1. In order to improve the Machine Gun Defence of the Sector, the existing Dispositions will be modified in accordance with the attached Tables.

2. The necessary construction of new emplacements and shelters will be commenced forthwith. All work will be sufficiently well in hand to render the new posts tenable by dawn 17th instant. A daily progress report will be forwarded with Fire Report, to D.M.G.O.

3. The position at U.28.b.1.1. at present held by 218th M.G. Company, will be taken over by the 23rd M.G. Company, on night 15th/16th.

4. Company Commanders will ensure the exact siting of the guns to give the required battle arcs and will resect the new positions. Diagrams showing visibility will be forwarded to D.M.G.O. when positions are occupied.

5. Maps showing the M.G. Defence will be issued to-morrow.

(6. ACKNOWLEDGE.)

8th Division,
13th October, 1917.

E Beddington
Lieut.-Colonel,
General Staff.

Copies to:-
    G.O.C., R.A.
    C. R. E.
    C. M. G. O.
    D. M. G. O.

8th Div. No.G.96/87.

TABLE 'g'.   25th M.G. Company.

Gun No.	Gun Position.	Battle Arc.	Indirect S.O.S. Barrage (if any).	Remarks.
13.	U.16.d.5.1.	25° - 50° Grid	-	Concrete shelter; emplacement to be built.
14.	U.17.c.10.15.	30° - 60° "	-	Occupied now.
17.	U.17.d.65.75.	50° - 70° "	-	- do -
18.	U.16.d.8.9.	65° - 90° "	-	- do -
19.	U.16.a.8.3.	40° - 70° "	U.12.c.5.2. - U.12.c.3.8.	- do -
20.	U.17.a.3.5.	45° - 60° "	-	Position to be dug and shelter constructed.
23.	U.17.a.40.75.	95° - 115° "	-	- do -
21.	U.15.c.8.9.	65° - 105° "	U.12.c.6.2. - U.12.c.3.8.	Old position to be re-occupied.

APPENDIX IV

~~SECRET~~   Copy.No. 4.

33 Machine Gun Company No.M.5.

Reference PLOEGSTEERT 1/10,000.   18th October 1917
            Reference 9th Division No.G.o/1/1
                        dated 17/10/17

(1)   Guns 31 and 19 will form "D" Battery. Lieut.K.V.Weston will act as Battery Commander. He will make all necessary arrangements and forward copy of his calculations to Coy. H.Q. by night of 19/10/17.

(2)   Lieut.H.J.Larkworthy will be in charge of the two guns about U.17.d.6.7. He will arrange to use Nos. 17 and 18 guns.

(3)   In the absence of further orders all guns should be moved into position at dusk on night of 20th October.

(4)   Officers concerned will arrange to synchronise their watches with that of the D.M.G.O. at Advanced Coy.H.Q. at ST.YVES at 3.0 p.m. on 20th October. Para 6. of 88th Inf. Bde.Order No.245 is cancelled so far as it affects this Company.

(5)   Guns will be packed up and moved back to their normal positions at Zero plus 40.

(6)   A full report will be forwarded to Advanced Coy.H.Q. as soon as possible after completion of the operations.

(7)   Please acknowledge.

18/10/17   A Simmonds   Capt.
                                              Comndg. 33 M.G. Coy.

Copy No. 1 Lt.K.V.Weston.
        2.Lt.H.J.Larkworthy.
        3.Lt.R.H.Goodeve.
        4.War Diary.
        5.Retained.

Copy No. 4

Extract from TABLE "A"
issued with 8th Division O. 9/1/17

UNIT	BATTERY	NO. OF GUNS	LOCATION	TASK
25th M.G. Coy	"D"	2	U16 a 8.3	To barrage road junction in DEN ROOSTER CABARET (U12 C)
do	—	2	U17 d 6.7	Two guns to await direct targets in U18 c, to engage any hostile M.G. opening fire during the operations and to keep down rifle fire from right flank.

SECRET.

Copy No. 9.

25th INFANTRY BRIGADE ORDER No. 245.

18th October 1917.

Reference Map, Sheet 28 S.W.4, 1/10,000.

1. 2nd Royal Berks Regt. will carry out a raid on the enemy's trenches on the night 20/21st October 1917, at an hour ZERO to be notified later. The strength of the raid will be approximately one Platoon.

2. The object of the raid is to capture prisoners and to kill as many of the enemy as possible should they not surrender.

3. ZERO hour will be that at which the barrage is put down.

4. Orders for Machine Gun and Trench Mortar co-operation and maps showing the Artillery, Machine Gun and Trench Mortar Barrages are being issued separately.

5. The enemy's trenches will be entered close behind the Artillery barrage, which lifts from the point of entry at U.11.d.9.7. at ZERO plus 4.

6. Opposite the point of entry, a gap of 20 yards is being cut in the enemy's wire. From this point the raiding party will proceed in three directions as follows:- 40 yards Northwards and 40 yards Southwards along Front Line, and 40 yards down Communication Trench running Eastwards from the Front Line – withdrawing at ZERO plus 20.

7. The barrage will begin to die down at ZERO plus 30 and will cease at ZERO plus 35.

8. A watch with correct time will be sent to 2nd Royal Berks Regt, 25th Machine Gun Coy and 25th Trench Mortar Bty. by 3 p.m. on October 20th.

9. Prisoners will be sent to RED LODGE.

10. All papers, badges and identifications will be taken from Raiding Party before operation commences.

11. Acknowledge.

W.F. Somervail
Captain,
A/Brigade Major,
25th Inf. Bde.

Issued at 12 noon.

Issued to :-

Copy No. 1. G.O.C.
" 2. Brigade Major,
" 3. Staff Captain.
" 4. Signal Officer.
" 5. 2nd Lincoln Regt.
" 6. 2nd R.Berks Regt.
" 7. 1st R.Irish Rifles.
" 8. 2nd Rifle Brigade.
" 9. 25th M.G.Coy.
" 10. 25th T.M.Bty.
Copy No. 11. 8th Division.
" 12. 8th Div.Arty.
" 13. 23rd Inf. Bde.
" 14. 24th Inf. Bde.
" 15. 100th Inf. Bde.
" 16. Left Group R.A.
" 17. Right Group R.A.
" 18. War Diary.
" 19. Office.

HEADING FOR BROADCAST No.248   Copy No......

                                                 14th October 1917.
Reference map Sheet 28.N.W. 1/5000.

1. 2nd Royal Berks R. will carry out a raid on the enemy's
   trench ——— on operation no/list catalog PIT, at an hour to be
   notified later. The duration of the raid will be
   approximately one hour.

2. The object of the raid is to obtain prisoners and to kill
   as many of the enemy as possible should they not surrender.

3. Zero hour will be that at which the barrage is put down.

4. Orders for Machine Gun and Trench Mortar co-operation and
   mapsmsohowing the Artillery, Machine Gun and Trench Mortar Barrages
   are being issued separately.

5. The enemy's trenches will be entered close behind the
   Artillery barrage, which lifts from the point of entry at
   L/L/A.W. at ZERO plus 4'.

6. Opposite the point of entry, a cov of 80 yards is being cut
   in the enemy's wire. From this point the raiding party will
   proceed in three directions as follows:- 40 yards northwards
   and 40 yards Southwards along enemy line, and 40 yards down
   communication trench running Easterly from the front line -
   finishing at ZERO plus 30'.

7. Two barrage will begin to lift down at ZERO plus 15 and will
   end at ZERO plus 30.

8. At such time as possible will be sent to 2nd Royal Berks
   Regt. H.Q. detailing the Coy and exam trench Mortar Bty. by 2 p.m.
   on October 16th.

9. Prisoners will be sent to BDE HDQRS.

10. All papers, badges and identifications will be taken from
    Bridge Party before operation commences.

11. Acknowledge.

                                         (sgd)........
                                         A/Lieut/Colonel,
                                         Comdg. 2nd Royal Berks.

Issued : 12 noon.

Issued to :-

   1. G.O.C. B.G.C.   Copy No.12. 7th Division.
   2. G1 Headquarters.   "   "   13. 8th Div. Arty.
   3. G1 of F Section.   "   "   14. 25th Inf. Bde.
   4. Gen'l O/Sean.   "   "   15. 23th Inf. Bde.
   5. 2nd Lincoln Regt.   "   "   16. Scots Inf. Regt.
   6. 2nd R.Berks Regt.   "   "   17. Left Group Hav.
   7. 1/4 R. Irish Rifles.   "   "   18. Right Group Hav.
   8. 2 Rifle Brigade.   "   "   19. Gas Offr.
   9. 25 M.G. Coy.   "   "   20. Orders.
  10.
  11. Signals.

S E C R E T.

25th Infantry Brigade No.294/G/33.

25th Machine Gun Coy.

    Reference 25th Inf. Bde. Order No.245.

    Instructions for co-operation of 25th Machine Gun Coy. are issued herewith.

Captain,
A/Brigade Major,
25th Inf. Bde.

18th October 1917.

SECRET.   8th Division No.G.9/1/19.

        23rd Inf. Bde. (2)
        24th Inf. Bde. (2)
        25th Inf. Bde. (3)
        218th M.G. Coy.
        D.M.G.O.

---

1.   Reference 8th Division Order No.232 of 17th October, Machine Gun Companies of the Division will co-operate in a raid being carried out by 25th Inf. Bde. against the enemy's trenches at U.11.d.91.70. on night October 20th/21st, in accordance with attached Table 'A'.

2.(a)   All guns except those of 25th M.G. Company at U.17.d. 6.7. will open fire at Zero hour which will be notified later.

  (b)   Rate of fire for all guns except those of 25th M.G. Coy. at U.17.d.6.7. will be:-

        Zero - Zero plus 30   60 rounds per gun per minute.

        Zero + 30 - Zero + 35   120 rounds per gun per minute.

  (c)   Guns of 25th M.G. Coy. at U.17.d.6.7. will fire at maximum rate on any target disclosed.

3.   New barrels only, will be used. Particular attention will be paid to direction. Depression stops will be fitted.

4.   Machine Gun Company Commanders will work out their own clearances and will ensure that an officer is present with each battery during the operation. An Officer will also be present with the 2 guns 25th M.G. Coy. at U.17.d.6.7.

5.(a)   Watches of Machine Gun Companies will be synchronised by the D.M.G.O. at 24th and 25th M.G. Cos.' Adv. H.Q. ST. YVES, at 3 p.m. on October 20th.

  (b)   A watch with correct time will be sent to 25th Inf. Bde. H.Q. before 1 p.m. on October 20th.

6.   ACKNOWLEDGE.

                                              E. Bedd[ing]t[o]n.

8th Division,   Lieut.-Colonel,
17th October, 1917.   General Staff.

        Copy to:-
                VIII Corps.
                VIII Corps M.G.O.
                "L" Special Co. R.E.
                G.O.C., R.A.
                C.R.E.
                O.C., Signals.

TABLE 'A'.

UNIT.	Battery.	No. of Guns.	Location.	Task.
23rd M.G. Coy.	'A'	6	U.28. Central.	To enfilade German front line from U.18.c.4.0. - U.18.c.75.70. to keep down enemy fire from this trench and from WIGART FARM.
218th M.G. Coy.	'B'	2	U.22.d.4.5.	To enfilade German line in front of SPINNING MILL U.18.c.75.70. - U.18.a.95.00.
- do -	'C'	2	U.22.a.8.2.	To barrage Road Junction in DEN ROOSTER CABARET (U.12.d.)
25th M.G. Coy.	'D'	2	U.16.a.8.3.	- do -
- do -	-	2	U.17.d.6.7.	Two guns to await direct targets in U.18.c., to engage any hostile M.G. opening fire during the operations and to keep down rifle fire from Right flank.
24th M.G. Coy.	'E'	2	U.16.b.7.7.	To barrage road U.12.c.9.4. - U.12.d.3.6.
- do -	'F'	2	U.4.d.6.6.	To provide flanking fire on Left flank from U.12.a.2.0. - U.12.c.5.8.

257 M.G.Coy.

SECRET.

25th Infantry Brigade No.294/G/48.

Reference 25th Infantry Brigade Order No.245:-

ZERO will be at **3.55** a.m. 21st/10/17.

Acknowledge.

                          Captain,
                         A/Brigade Major,
19th October 1917.   25th Inf. Bde.
Issued at 8.30 p.m.

Issued to all recipients of 25th Inf. Bde. Order No.245.

SECRET   APPENDIX V.   Copy No. 6

25th M.G. Company Relief Order No. 16.

Ref. PLOEGSTEERT 1/10,000.   23rd October 1917.

(1). The following reliefs will take place on the 24th October
    "A" Section will relieve "C" Section.
    "D" Section will relieve "B" Section.

(2) One guide from each of "C" Sections guns will be at HYDE PARK CORNER at 3.45 p.m.
    One guide from each of "B" Sections guns will be at the Iron Gate at 5.15. p.m.

(3). Belt boxes, clinometers & A.A. sights will be handed over but no other mobilisation stores.

(4). All trench stores will be handed over and receipts rendered to Coy. H.Q. by O's C. out-going sections.

(5). Handing over will be done very carefully and gun team commanders of in-going sections will see that they thoroughly understand their position before allowing the out-going teams to leave.

(6). Upon relief "B" & "C" sections will march to WACKLAND CAMP.

(7). Officers will see that strict march discipline is maintained marching to and from the line.

(8) Completion of relief will be reported to Advanced H.Q. & to Coy. H.Q. by out-going section Officers.

(9) Please acknowledge

23-10-17.   A. Simmonds Capt.
                                          Commdg. 25. M.G. Coy.

Copy No 1.   O.C. "A" Section.
     2.   O.C. "B" Section.
     3.   O.C. "C" Section.
     4.   O.C. "D" Section.
     5.   Lieut. SPOONER.
     6.   War Diary
     7.   Retained

SECRET   APPENDIX VI   COPY No. 5

25th M.G. COMPANY No. X.6.

Ref. PLOEGSTEERT 1/10,000   27th Oct. 1917.

(1) Herewith copies of 8th Div. G.7/1/25 dated 26/10/17 and 25th Infantry Brigade Order No. 248 dated 26/10/17.

(2) Guns No. 17 and 20 will form "D" Battery about U17 d 6.7 and will be under the charge of LIEUT. F.P. SPOONER. He will arrange for these guns to move into position, control them during the operation, and see that they return to their normal positions afterwards.

(3) Gun No. 23 will form "E" Battery about U17 b 8.3. 2nd LT. F.R. LOCKHART will remain with this gun throughout the operation and arrange for it to return to its normal position afterwards.

(4) Both officers will make a reconnaissance tonight and decide on the exact positions which they will occupy. A report on the reconnaissance will be forwarded to Coy. H.Q.

(5) All guns will be in position half an hour before ZERO and will commence to pack up to move back at ZERO + 40.

(6) LIEUT. F.P. SPOONER will arrange for one of his guns to be laid in the direction of the suspected M.G. at U18c 15.30.

(7) 2nd LT. F.R. LOCKHART will take care that his gun does not fire north of the line drawn on a bearing of 30° G from U17 b 8.3.

(8) Both officers will synchronise their watches with that of the D.M.G.O. at Forward Coy. H.Q., ST. YVES at 3.0 pm. on 28th Oct.

(9) A full report of the operation will be forwarded as soon as possible after its completion to Advanced Coy. H.Q.

(10) Please acknowledge.

A. Simmonds Capt
Commanding 25th M.G. Coy.

Copy No. 1   LIEUT. F.P. SPOONER
       2   2nd LT. F.R. LOCKHART
       3   O.C. "A" Section — for information
       4   D.M.G.O
       5   WAR DIARY
       6   RETAINED

SECRET

Copy No. ..9..

25th INFANTRY BRIGADE ORDER No. 248.

Ref. Map Sheet 28 S.W. 1/10,000

26th October, 1917.

1. 2nd. Rifle Brigade will carry out a raid on the enemy's trenches about U.11.d.9.2. on the night 28th/29th October, 1917, at an hour ZERO to be notified later. The strength of the raid will be approximately one Platoon.

2. The raid will be carried out under cover of an artillery, trench mortar and machine gun barrage, details of which are being issued separately.

3. ZERO hour will be that at which the barrage is put down.

4. The barrage will begin to die down at ZERO plus 30 minutes and will cease at ZERO plus 35 minutes.

5. The enemy's trenches will be entered close behind the barrage which lifts from the point of entry at ZERO plus 4 minutes.

6. A watch with the correct time will be sent to 2/Rifle Brigade and 25th Trench Mortar Battery by 3 p.m. on the 28th instant.

7. Prisoners will be sent to RED LODGE.

8. ACKNOWLEDGE.

Captain,
A/Brigade Major,
25th Inf. Bde.

Issued at 9 p.m.
Issued to :-

Copy No.		Copy No.	
1	G.O.C.	11	8th Division.
2	Brigade Major.	12	8th Div. Arty.
3	Staff Captain.	13	23rd Inf. Bde.
4	Signal Officer.	14	24th Inf. Bde.
5	2/Lincoln. Regt.	15	98th Inf. Bde.
6	2/R.Berks. Regt.	16	"L" Special Co. R.E.
7	1/R.Irish Rifles.	17	Left Group R.A.
8	2/Rifle Brigade.	18	Right Group. R.A.
9	25/M.G. Coy.	19	War Diary.
10	25/T.M. Bty.	20	Office.

SECRET.
25th Machine Gun Coy. 25th Infantry Brigade No.294/G/15.

Forwarded for action.

Captain,
A/Brigade Major,
25th Inf. Bde.

26th October, 1917.

SECRET.

8th Division No. G.9/1/25.

23rd Inf. Bde. (2)
24th Inf. Bde. (2)
25th Inf. Bde. (3)
218th M.G. Coy.
D.M.G.O.

1. Reference 8th Division Order No.235 of the 26th October, Machine Gun Companies will co-operate in a raid to be carried out by 25th Inf. Bde. against the enemy Trenches at U.11.d.9..2. on the night of October 28th/29th, in accordance with attached Table 'A'.

2. All guns will open fire at Zero hour, except the guns of 25th Machine Gun Company. at about U.17.d.6.7. and U.17.b.8.4., and will fire at the following rates:-

    Zero to Zero plus 30 mins. - 60 rounds per gun per min.

    Zero plus 30 to Zero plus 35 mins - 120 " " " " "

3. The guns of 25th Machine Gun Company will fire at a maximum rate on any targets which may appear South of the road LA BASSEVILLE - WARNETON
    O.C., 25th Machine Gun Company will detail one of the guns at U.17.d.6.7. especially to counter enemy machine gun at U.18.c.15.30.

4. New barrels and depression stops will be used.

5. Machine Gun Company Commanders will work out the clearances and forward copy of calculations to D.M.G.O. They will ensure that an Officer is present with each battery during the operation. O.C., 25th M.G. Coy. will detail an officer to the 2 guns at U.17.d.6.7. and one to U.17.b.8.4.

6. Watches will be synchronised by D.M.G.O. at 25th M.G. Co's. Adv. H.Q., ST YVES, at 3 p.m. on October 28th.

7. ACKNOWLEDGE.

8th Division,
26th October, 1917.

E Beddington.
Lieut.-Colonel,
General Staff.

Copy to:- VIII Corps.
VIII Corps M.G.O.
"L" Special Co. R.E.
G.O.C., R.A.
C.R.E.
O.C., Signals.

8th Div. No.G.9/1/25.

TABLE 'A'
=*=*=*=

UNIT.	Battery.	No. of Guns.	Approximate Location.	Task.
23rd M.G. Coy.	'A'	5	U.28. Central	To enfilade German front line from U.18.c.4.0. - U.18.c.75.70.
218th M.G. Coy.	'B'	3	U.22.d.4.5.	To enfilade German front line from U.18.c.75.70. - U.18.b.2.1.
- do -	'C'	2	U.22.a.8.2.	Barrage WARNETON HIGH STREET at U.12.c.6.2.
25th M.G. Coy.	'D'	2	U.17.d.6.7.	Direct fire on any targets which appear between Grid bearings 40° & 150°
- do -	'E'	1	U.17.b.8.3.	Direct fire on any targets which appear between Grid Bearings 30° & 110°
24th M.G. Coy.	'F'	4	U.10.d.4.9.	Barrage on WARNETON from U.12.c.9.4. to U.12.a.9.1.
- do -	'G'	2	U.4.d.2.9.	Flank barrage from U.11.b.80.25. to U.12.c.25.90.

S E C R E T.

25th Infantry Brigade No. 294/G/19.

Brigade Major.
2/Lincoln. Regt.
2/R.Berks. Regt.
1/R.Irish Rifles.
2/Rifle Brigade.
25/M. G. Coy.
25/T. M. Bty.
Left Group, R.A.

Reference 25th Infantry Brigade Order No. 248.

1. ZERO will be at 9 p.m. on the 28th October, 1917.

2. Acknowledge by wire.

Captain,
A/Brigade Major,
25th Inf. Bde.

27th October, 1917.

Army Form C. 2118.

WAR DIARY
or
INTELLIGENCE SUMMARY.
(Erase heading not required.)

Vol 23

Instructions regarding War Diaries and Intelligence Summaries are contained in F. S. Regs., Part II. and the Staff Manual respectively. Title pages will be prepared in manuscript.

Place	Date	Hour	Summary of Events and Information	Remarks and references to Appendices
WACKLAND CAMP B.15.b.3-9 and area opposite WARNETON (Sheet 28)	1/11/17		"B" & "C" Sections bathed & prepared for the line. The relief of "A" & "D" sections by "B" "C" sections took place in the evening. 1 O.R. from hospital. ad.	APPENDIX I Relief Orders
	2/11/17		"A" & "D" Sections Lewis gun cls; clothes & equipment. Kit inspection & baths in afternoon. During the night "B" Section fired 1500 rounds on the Cross Roads at V.18.d.65.25. The enemy on the line are & will be very busy each night constructing alternative positions in addition to the works on esking trenches etc. 30.O.R. to hospital. 1st Lt. HALL & 4 OR from A.A. Camp. ad	
	3/11/17		Close Order Drill Gunlimber & gun equipment. Lectures. N.C.O's on Fire Direction & Map Reading. During the night "B" Section fired 1500 rounds searching the tracks behind the Lilleforge exchanges on V.24.a. 3 O.R. to hospital ad	
	4/11/17		Sunday Parade. C of E service at 10.15. Other ranks voluntary. During the night "B" Section fired 1500 rounds searching the neighbourhood of the 3 O.R. to hospital. ap ad 3 enemy MG in V.18.c.	

WAR DIARY or INTELLIGENCE SUMMARY

Army Form C. 2118.

(Erase heading not required.)

Place	Date	Hour	Summary of Events and Information	Remarks and references to Appendices
WACKLAND CAMP B.13.d.5.9 and land opposite WARMINTON (Sheet 28)	5/11/17		Close Order Drill. Gas Drill. Barrage Work Lecture. Barrage Drill.	
			NCO's lecture in Lewis Drill or Lewis Gunners dug and buried of ammunition on A.A. work.	
			Officers attended a lecture on the Lewis Gun in the afternoon.	
			During the day "B" Section fired 250 rounds at E.R. and during the night 1500 rounds were fired on to the tracks	
			1 O.R. to hospital. 1 O.R. from hospital. 1 O.R. evacuated. A/S	
	6/11/17		Close Order Drill followed by a 2 hour route march.	
			A Lewis Match at WIGANS FARM has been going considerable trouble and we ordered never seems to 2/8" + 25" Coy. to fire on the flare at night returning at the time where transport is normally heard that the transport convoys nightly & probably large ammunition.	APPENDIX II Operation Orders.
			During the night four of our guns fired T 19,750 rounds were used.	
			2 O.R. from hospital A/S	
	7/11/17		Close Order Drill followed by 2 hour routemarch.	
			During the night "B" Section fired 3000 rounds on to WIGART FARM.	
			2nd LT. HOOD leave to U.K. 1 O.R. to 24th M.G. Coy. LIEUT S POONER 2.2. Ott to Course at G.H.Q. S.A. School. A/S	

Army Form C. 2118.

WAR DIARY
or
INTELLIGENCE SUMMARY.
(Erase heading not required.)

Instructions regarding War Diaries and Intelligence Summaries are contained in F. S. Regs., Part II. and the Staff Manual respectively. Title pages will be prepared in manuscript.

Place	Date	Hour	Summary of Events and Information	Remarks and references to Appendices
WACKLAND CAMP (Hut 36 and hut opposite)	8/11/17		Close order drill followed by Mechanism of Lewis gun Action.	
			"B" Section again fired on WRART Pit. during the night scoring 25.00 rounds	
			1 O.R. attached from 2/B Hampshire and 1 O.R. from hospital. O.d.	
WARNETON (Hut 28)	9/11/17		"A" & "B" Section bathed in the morning. Cleaning Lewis Guns in the afternoon.	
			During the night "B" Section again fired on WRART MARM using 2800 rounds	
	10/11/17		1 O.R. sent to U.K. 2 O.R.s joined the Company 2 O.R.s to hospital. 1 O.R. from hospital O.d.	
			Close order drill followed by a lecture to the Company by O.C. on Lessons learnt from recent fighting.	
			Remainder of morning was occupied in making of preparations for the move. In the afternoon made further preparations for the move.	
			On the night of the 10/11 the Company was relieved in the line by the 24th Company.	APPENDIX III Relief & Return
			At the same time the 218th Coy was relieved by the 23rd Coy. this left 24th & 23rd Coys. holding the whole divisional front.	
			1 O.R. to hospital. 1 O.R. from hospital. 2 O.R. evacuated O.d.	
	11/11/17		Sunday. C of E Service for "A" & "D" Sections. Transport 1 H.Q. & "B" Section left Remainder of Coys stood in Lawag Camp & Transport for move.	

Army Form C. 2118.

WAR DIARY
or
INTELLIGENCE SUMMARY.
(Erase heading not required.)

Instructions regarding War Diaries and Intelligence Summaries are contained in F. S. Regs., Part II. and the Staff Manual respectively. Title pages will be prepared in manuscript.

Place	Date	Hour	Summary of Events and Information	Remarks and references to Appendices
MOORLAND CAMP B13 d.z.9. (Sheet 36.)	11/11/17		Tomorrow.	
			3 O.R. to hospital. 2 O.R. from Divisional School. 2 O.R. from hospital. 1 O.R. from Base Bn.	
LA MOTTE D.30 central (Sheet 36 a)	12/11/17		25th Bde. moved to the LAMOTTE area near HAZEBROUCK. The Company marched with the rest of the Brigade. Dinner camp at 9.2 am. Transport came + Brigaded.	APPENDIX IV Movement Order.
			Company arrived in billets at LAMOTTE about 2.0 p.m.	
			1 O.R. from hospital.	
	13/10/17		Portsmouth Aingtha + overhaul of officer + engine equipment.	
			3 O.R. to hospital. 1 - 2 O.R. reinstated.	
	14/11/17		Training under Section Officers. "C" Section sent to MERVILLE for baths.	
			3 O.R. to hospital. 5 O.R. reinstated. 1 O.R. joined by. LIEUT. W.K. RENNIE joined	
			Cy. from 98th Cy. on appointment as 2nd i/c. adj.	
	15/11/17		Company practised recall sound drill. The sound gong, gong signals + whistles.	
			1 O.R. home to U.K.	
	16/11/17		Company marched out of LA MOTTE at 5.30 a.m. and bivouaced with the rest of the Brigade for YPRES. YPRES was reached in the early afternoon and Company Hdqrs. marched Mont Couten.	APPENDIX V
			at CAESTRE	

Army Form C. 2118.

WAR DIARY
or
INTELLIGENCE SUMMARY.
(Erase heading not required.)

Instructions regarding War Diaries and Intelligence Summaries are contained in F. S. Regs., Part II. and the Staff Manual respectively. Title pages will be prepared in manuscript.

Place	Date	Hour	Summary of Events and Information	Remarks and references to Appendices
SAINT JEAN C 26 d 8.4 (Sheet 28).	16/11/17		In a camp on the SAINT JEAN road, about C 26 d 8.4. (Sheet 28). 1 O.R. Sent to U.K. a.I.	
PASSCHENDAELE Coy. H.Q. at D 13 d 8.2 (sheet 28).	17/11/17		On the 17th & night of 17th/18th Nov. the 8th Canadian Division relieved the 3rd Canadian Division in the PASSCHENDAELE sector. The Divisional Front was held by one Brigade. The Bde. M. Gs. in use the 25th Inf. Bde. in relief of the 7th Canadian Inf. Bde. There were two Canadian M.G. Coys in the line. Orders were received for the 218th M.G. Coy. to relieve a group of barrage guns on the 17th and for the 25th Coy. to relieve the close defence guns on the 18th. As the 218th Coy did not arrive in the YPRES area in sufficient time to go into the line on the morning of the 17th Nov. arrangements were made mutually for the 25th Coy. to go in on the morning of the 17th and take over the barrage guns, and for the 218th Coy to take over the close defence guns on the 18th Nov. This was done. Upon completion of relief Coy. H.Q. was at Bde. H.Q., CAPITOL (D 13 d 8.2); 16 guns were in barrage positions between D 50.5.2 and D 5 c 3.5 ; the Armament were at C 26 d 8.4. 1 O.R. to Base Depot to proceed to U.K. for special courses. 1 O.R. evacuated a.I.	APPENDIX II Relief Orders
	18/11/17		No firing called for. Reconnoitred for a H.Q. nearer guns and selected an pillbox at	APPENDIX III Relief Orders

WAR DIARY or INTELLIGENCE SUMMARY

Army Form C. 2118.

(Erase heading not required.)

Place	Date	Hour	Summary of Events and Information	Remarks and references to Appendices
Line by PASSCHENDAELE Coy. H.Q.			LAAMKEEK - D 10 b central. A.d.	
LAAMKEEK D10 b central (Sheet 28)	19/10/17		The firing called for. Moved my H.Q. to LAAMKEEK. 25th Bde relieved at night by 24th Bde. 3 O.R. wounded + 2 wounded - graced. A.d.	
	20/10/17		At 4:10 p.m. "S.O.S." was sent up and all guns opened fire until 4:25 p.m. when all were quiet. 3 O.R. to hospital A.d.	
	21/10/17		Firing was carried out in accordance with Divisional Harassing Fire Programme. 1 O.R. evacuated. A.d. 2 O.R. wounded - graced. 1 O.R. to hospital.	APPENDIX VIII
	22/10/17		Firing in accordance with programme. Reconnoitred for a battery position between MEETCHEELE and GRAF and surveyed a church of S.A.A. for it about D 5 d 4.7. 2nd Lt. HODD from leave. 1 O.R. evacuated. A.d.	
BRANDHOEK D5c5.4 (Sheet 28)	23/10/17		Battery relieved on the line on the morning of 23rd by 23rd Coy., and moved back to BRANDHOEK. Orders were received regarding the defence policy for the high ground N. of PASSCHENDAELE and the M.O. Defence was allotted. In consideration of the probable enemy movements in the event of his outstanding it	APPENDIX IX APPENDIX X

Army Form C. 2118.

WAR DIARY or INTELLIGENCE SUMMARY

Army Form C. 2118.

(Erase heading not required.)

Place	Date	Hour	Summary of Events and Information	Remarks and references to Appendices
	23/10/17		attack a new Harrassing Fire Programme was carried by Divisions	APPENDIX XI
BRANDHOEK 25c 54 (Sheet 28)	24/10/17		9 O.R. joined Coy. 1 O.R. to hospital. A.S. Cleaning guns, gun equipment, limbers etc. 1 O.R. from leave A.S.	
ST JEAN I.3.c.05.95 (Sheet 28)	25/10/17		Baths in the morning. Company paraded at 2.0 p.m. and moved back to the ST. JEAN area. This move was made in view of a forthcoming operation and the necessity for getting S.A.A. up to the line. Conditions at ST JEAN were very poor for rest. Tents. Transport lines in a sea of mud. On the night of the 24/25th the Divisional Front was moved slightly to the right. Tomorrow night the M.G. disposition will be altered accordingly. 1 O.R. to hospital & 2 O.R. to hospital A.S.	APPENDIX XII
	26/10/17		Cleaning guns etc and attempting to dry kit. Transport bathed. 3 O.R. to hospital - sick - general, & 3 to hospital sick. 6 O.R. joined from 215th Coy. A.S.	APPENDIX XIII
	27/10/17		Cleaning gun equipment. Making 7 spare a/s in preparation for forthcoming operation. 2 O.R. to hospital - sick - general. 2 O.R. to hospital sick. 3 O.R. leave to U.K. A.S.	

Army Form C. 2118.

WAR DIARY
or
~~INTELLIGENCE SUMMARY~~
(Erase heading not required.)

Instructions regarding War Diaries and Intelligence Summaries are contained in F. S. Regs., Part II. and the Staff Manual respectively. Title pages will be prepared in manuscript.

Place	Date	Hour	Summary of Events and Information	Remarks and references to Appendices
ST. JEAN I.3.c.05.95 (Sheet 28)	28/10/17		Orders received last night for operations to take place on or about 1st Dec. Reconnoitred and chose battery position near CREST FARM. In the afternoon moved 100,000 rounds of S.A.A. up to battery position. This operation was very arduous from the mud and being transported to carry. The total including NCO's was 108 only, in spite of there being 22 infantrymen attached to the Company. The number of men in hospital, or excused duty is very large indeed. 1 O.R. from hospital. 5 O.R. evacuated. A.J.	
	29/10/17		Company turned out again in afternoon and carried up another 100,000 rounds to battery position. A.J.	
	30/10/17		In the evening the Company moved up to the battery position having to be taken forward of the 16 guns and one 7 furrows forwards trifoul. Each team dug a position for teamage, made an emplacement, established the position with 10,000 rounds of S.A.A. & 10 belt boxes, and camouflaged the whole. The battery of 16 guns made its position on the line D.11.d.85.90 — D.5.d.75.10. It is now known that the operations will take place tomorrow night. A.J.	

1 O.R. returned to hospital to 2 O.R. to hospital. A.J.

A Ammunition Capt
Commanding 25th M.G. Coy.

SECRET.   **APPENDIX I**

                                                    Copy No. 7

                    25 M.G. Company Relief Order No. C.

PLOEGSTEERT 1/10000   31st October 1917.

(1). The following reliefs will take place on the 1st November
    "B" Section will relieve "A" Section.
    "C" Section will relieve "D" Section.

(2). One guide from each of "A" Section Guns will be at HYDE
    PARK CORNER at 3.45. p.m.
    One guide from each of "D" Section Guns will be at the Iron
    Gate at 5.15. p.m.

(3). Belt boxes, chronometers, A.A. sights & belt filling machines will
    be handed over but no other mobilization stores.

(4). All trench stores will be handed over and receipts rendered
    to Coy. H.Q. by O's C. out-going sections.

(5). Handing over will be done very carefully and Gun team
    commanders of in-going sections will see that they thoroughly
    understand their position before allowing the out-going
    teams to leave.

(6). After relief "A" & "D" Sections will march to WACKLAND
    CAMP

(7). Officers will see that strict march discipline is maintained
    marching to and from the line.

(8). Completion of relief will be reported to Advanced H.Q.
    and to Coy. H.Q. by out going Section Officers

(9). Please acknowledge.

    31. 10. 17.   A. Simmonds Capt.
                                            Commdg 25. M.G.Co.

Copy No 1. O.C. "A" Section
        2. O.C. "B" Section
        3. O.C. "C" Section
        4. O.C. "D" Section
        5. Adjt Command
        6. War Diary
        7. Retained.

SECRET.   8th Division No.G.96/103.

APPENDIX II

23rd Inf. Bde.   (2)
24th Inf. Bde.   (3)
25th Inf. Bde.   (2)
218th M.G.Coy.   (1)
D.M.G.O.   (1)

1. Harrassing fire by Machine Guns will be undertaken on night of 6th November, as shewn in the attached table.

2. This is in order to engage carrying parties which, it is reported, bring up T.M. ammunition to WICART FARM.

3. On nights of 7th, 8th and 9th inst, 25th M.G.Coy and 218th M.G.Coy will fire one gun each at intervals onto the area U.24.a.5.8. - U.18.c.5.0. - U.18.d.1.0. - U.24.b.1.8. firing to be especially heavy between 8 p.m. and 9 p.m.

4. Watches will be synchronised by arrangement between M.G.Coy. Commanders concerned.

8th Division.
5th November 1917.

E.V. Riddell
Lieut.-Colonel,
General Staff.

To 25th M.G. Coy

Passed for necessary action

B. Greening Capt
a/Bde Major 25th Inf Bde

8th Division No.G.96/103.

HARRASSING FIRE TABLE.

UNIT.	No. of GUNS.	APPROXIMATE LOCATION.	TASK.	NATURE OF FIRE.	TIME OF FIRE.
25th M.G.Co.	1	THATCHED COTTAGE.	Traverse road from U.18.c.7.4. to U.24.a.57.85.	Intermittent.	Dusk to 8 p.m.
25th M.G.Co.	4	- do -	Barrage track from U.18.d.10.65. to U.13.c.8.1.	Heavy.	8 p.m. - 8.5 p.m. 8.10 p.m. - 8.15 p.m.
213th M.G.Co.	1	LOOPHOLE FARM.	Traverse road from U.24.a.20.95. to U.24.a.57.85.	Intermittent.	Dusk to 8 p.m.
213th M.G.Co.	4	LOOPHOLE FARM U.22.central BURNTOUT FARM	Barrage track from U.18.c.8.1. to U.24.a.8.8.	Heavy.	8 p.m. to 8.5 p.m. 8.10 p.m. to 8.15 p.m
25th M.G.Co.	1	THATCHED COTTAGE.	Fire on area U.24.a.5.8. - U.18.c.5.0. - U.18.d.1.0. - U.24.b.1.8.	Intermittent.	8.15 p.m. till dawn.
213th M.G.Co.	1	U.22.central.	- do -	- do -	- do -

SECRET   COPY NO. 3

25th M.G. COMPANY X·12

Ref. PLOEGSTEERT 1/10,000   6 Nov. 1917

(1) In continuation of the scheme set forth in my X·9 of today's date, O.C. "B" section will arrange to fire in conjunction with the 218th M.G. Coy. on the nights 7th, 8th and 9th inst.

No. of Guns	Approximate Location	Task	Nature of Fire	Time of Firing
1	Thatched Cot.	Fire at intervals on to areas — U 24 a 5.8 — U 18 c 5.0 — U 18 d 1.0 — U 24 b 1.8	Intermittent but especially heavy between 8.0 p.m. and 9.0 p.m.	Dusk to Dawn

(2) LIEUT. GOODEVE will send in fire report to Bde. at usual time but will forward a report on the night's firing to Coy. HQ each morning.

                                             A. Simmonds Capt.
                                    Commanding 25th M.G. Coy.

Copy No. 1 — O.C. "B" Section
         2 — LIEUT. GOODEVE
         3 — War Diary
         4 — Retained

SECRET

APPENDIX III

G.331/

24th M.G.Coy.
25th M.G.Coy.

     The attached, 8th Division letter No.G.96/107, is forwarded for your information and necessary action.

7th November, 1917.

                                        Captain,
                Brigade Major, 24th Inf. Brigade.

8th Division No.G.96/107.

S E C R E T.

23rd Inf. Bde. (3)
24th Inf. Bde. (3)
25th Inf. Bde.
G.O.C., R.A.
D.M.G.O.
218th M.G.Co.

---

1. On November 10th and night November 10/11th, 218th and 25th M.G.Cos. will be relieved in the line by 23rd and 24th M.G.Cos.

2. (a) 23rd M.G.Co. will take over all gun positions of 218th M.G.Co. and one gun position of 25th M.G.Co. at U.16.a.8.3.
(b) 24th M.G.Co. will take over all gun positions of 25th M.G.Co. with the exception of that mentioned in para. 2 (a).

3. Acknowledge.

8th Division.
6th November 1917.

Lieut.-Colonel,
General Staff.

Copies to :-
VIII Corps.
3rd Australian Division.

S E C R E T.

8th Division No.G.96/10.

    23rd Inf. Bde. (3)
    24th Inf. Bde. (3)
    25th Inf. Bde.
    G.O.C., R.A.
    D.M.G.O.
    218th M.G. Coy.
----

1.   Reference 8th Division No.G.96/107 dated 6th November, 1917, para. 2(a) and (b).

    24th M.G. Company will take over the gun at U.16.a.8.3. from 25th M.G. Company.

    23rd M.G. Company will take over one gun of 25th M.G. Company at U.16.d.60.10.

2.   Acknowledge.

8th Division,
8th November, 1917.

Lieut.-Colonel,
General Staff.

Copies to:- VIII Corps.
          3rd Australian Division.

Secret.   Copy No. 7

25. M.G. Co. Relief Order No. 18.

Ref. PLOEGSTEERT 1/10,000.

(1). The Company will be relieved in the line by the 23rd & 24th Co's. on the night of 10/11th.

(2). The 23rd Co. will relieve No. 13. Gun.
    The 24th Co. will relieve Nos. 17. 20. 23. 14. 19. & 21. guns.

(3). Each gun will supply one guide. Guides will assemble as follows:-
    (a). Guide from No. 13 gun will be at M.G.12. (U.22.a.50.10) at 6.0.pm. to guide incoming team of 28th Co.
    (b). Guides from Nos. 17. 14. & 8. guns will be at KHOHBATA at 5.0.pm.
    (c). Guides from Nos. 20. 23. 19 & 21. will be at Advanced Co. H.Q. at 4.30.pm.

4. 8. belt-boxes per gun will be handed over (and receipts obtained) but no other unliquidable stores.

5. All trench stores will be handed over and receipts obtained.

6. Section Officers will give the fullest information to incoming officers and will instruct their gun team commanders to hand over carefully.

7. Section Officers will report to Adv. Co. H.Q. when their relief is complete. LIEUT. GOODEVE will report completion of relief to Co. H.Q. by wire using the code word "MUDDLE".

8. One limber per section will be at the Y.M.C.A. at 6.30 pm.

9. 11. 17.   A. Simmonds. Capt.
                                                    Commdg. 25. M.G. Co.

Copy. No. 1. O.C. "B" Section.
      2. O.C. "C" Section.
      3. LIEUT. GOODEVE
      4. O.C. 23rd. M.G. Co.
      5. O.C. 24th. M.G. Co.
      6. D.M.G.O.
      7. War Diary
      8. Retained.

APPENDIX IV

SECRET.   Copy No. 10

25th INFANTRY BRIGADE ORDER No. 249.

Ref. Sheet 36 A, 1/40,000
     Sheet 36, 1/40,000

10th November, 1917.

1. The 8th Division (less Artillery) will be relieved in the Right Sector, VIII Corps Front, on the 12th, 13th, 14th and 15th November, by the 3rd Australian Division (less Artillery).

2. The 10th Australian Brigade will relieve the 25th Infantry Brigade in the Reserve Brigade Area on November 12th and 2 Battalions of the 9th Australian Brigade will relieve 2 Battalions 23rd Infantry Brigade in the Right Subsector.

3. (a) The 25th Infantry Brigade will move to LA MOTTE Area by road as detailed in attached Table "A".
   The 2 Battalions, 23rd Infantry Brigade will move to the BERQUIN Area by road as detailed in attached Table "B".

   (b) Instructions as to billetting in LA MOTTE Area will be issued by Staff Captain, 25th Infantry Brigade and in BERQUIN Area by Staff Captain, 23rd Infantry Brigade.

4. (a) Travelling Kitchens, Water Carts and Mess Carts will travel with units immediately behind the rear Company. Remainder of 1st Line Transport, 25th Brigade, will move brigaded under Brigade Transport Officer.

   (b) 2nd Line Transport will move under O.C., No. 4 Company, Divisional Train.

   (c) The Transport of 2 Battalions, 23rd Infantry Brigade will move with units.

5. (a) The following distances will be maintained between units on the march :-

   Companies.   100 yards.
   Battalions.   500 yards.
   Unit and its transport.   100 yards. (applies
                               to 2 Battalions 23rd Inf. Bde. only.)
   Between Battalion Transports. 100 yards.

   (b) On roads where vehicular traffic is heavy, Infantry will march in file.

6. Area Stores, all 1/10,000 Trench Maps, Defence Schemes, Air Photographs, Log Books, Intelligence Notes, Work in hand and proposed, etc. will be handed over to relieving units and receipts taken.

7. (a) Rear Parties will be detailed by units as under to bring on any men who have fallen out on the march :-

   Each Battalion.   1 Officer and 1 Section.
   M.G.Coys.   1 N.C.O. and 4 men.
   T.M.Bty.   1 N.C.O. and 3 men.

   These parties will march under the Senior Officer. In the case of the 25th Infantry Brigade they will march in rear of the Brigade Transport.

7. (b)

- 2 -

7. (b) O.C., 25th Field Ambulance will detail 1 Ambulance to move some distance behind these parties to carry any men who cannot possible walk.

   (c) Parties of the 2nd Devon Regt. and 2nd Middlesex Regt. will move in rear of the 2nd Middlesex Regt.

   (d) O.C., 26th Field Ambulance will detail 1 Ambulance to be at B.8.b.2.6. at 2.30 p.m. to follow these parties.

8. No man other than the driver will ride on any transport vehicle.

9. Each Battalion, M.G.Coy. and T.M.Bty. will arrange for one cyclist orderly to be at S.E. corner, STEENWERCH, A.17.c.3.3., at 12 noon, 12th instant, to act as guides to units of 3rd Australian Division. 23rd Infantry Brigade guides to meet 9th Australian Brigade units, 25th Infantry Brigade guides, 10th Australian Brigade units.

   Guides will receive orders from units of Australian Division as to appointed billets, and guide them accordingly.

10. Completion of moves will be reported to Brigade Headquarters.

11. 25th Infantry Brigade Headquarters close at 8.30 a.m. on November 12th and will reopen on arrival at E.22.b.5.5.

12. All camps and billets must be left scrupulously clean.

13. ACKNOWLEDGE.

L.S.Greening
Captain,
Brigade Major,
25th Inf. Bde.

Issued at :- 9 p.m.
Issued to :-

Copy No.				
1	G.O.C.	20	24th Inf. Bde.
2	Bde. Major.	21	9th Aus. Brigade.
3	Staff Captain.	22	10th Aus. Brigade.
4	Bde. Signal Offr.	23	2/Devon. Regt.
5	Bde. Transport Offr.	24	2/Middlesex Regt.
6	2/Lincoln. Regt.	25	Q.M.2/Devon. Regt.
7	2/R.Berks. Regt.	26	Q.M.2/Middlesex Regt.
8	1/R.Irish Rifles.	27	Supply Offr. 23rd Inf. Bde.
9	2/Rifle Brigade.	28	No. 2 Coy. A.S.C.
10	25/M.G.Coy.	29	26th Fld. Ambce.
11	25/T.M.Bty.	30	218th M.G.Coy.
12	QrMr 2/Lincoln R.	31	Area Commandant, STEENWERCK Area.
13	" 2/R.Berks R.		
14	" 1/R.Ir. Rifles.	32	8th Division, "G"
15	" 2/Rifle Bde.	33	8th Division, "Q".
16	25/Fld. Ambce.	34	A.D.M.S.
17	No. 4 Coy. Train.	35	A.P.M., 8th Division.
18	Bde. Supply Offr.	36	War Diary.
19	23rd Inf.Bde.	37	Office.
		38	C.R.E.

March Table "A" to accompany 25th Infantry Brigade Order No. 249.

Serial No.	Date.	Unit.	From.	To.	Starting Point.	Time.	Route.	Remarks.
1	Nov. 12	Bde. H.Q.	STEENWERCK, A.17.a.00.15.	LA RUE DU BOIS E.22.b.5.5.	STEENWERCK, Road Junction, A.17.c.20.15.	9 a.m.	PONT WEMEAU – F.23.c. – F.21. – F.14.c. –	Halts will be made 10 minutes before every clock hour. All units except Brigade Headquarters and 2/Rifle Bde. will move to Starting Point via A.23.b. A.17.c.90.25.
2	do.	2/R.Berks. R.	MENEGATE Camp.	K.16.b.2.9.		9.2 a.m.		
3	do.	2/Lincoln. R	HOLLEBEKE Camp.	E.13.c.2.8.		9.14 a.m.		
4	do.	1/R.I.Rifles.	WATERLANDS Camp.	E.28.d.		9.27 a.m.		
5	do.	2/Rifle Bde.	LE BULLE Camp.	E.22.a.		9.39 a.m.		
6	do.	25/M.G.Coy.	A.3.b.2.8.	LA MOTTE E.8.c.3.2.		9.52 a.m.		
7	do.	25/T.M.Bty.	A.18.c.7.2.	E.19.b.9.5.		9.55 a.m.		
8	do.	218/M.G.Coy.	B.8.c.10.80.	E.12.c.5.9.		9.57 a.m.		
9	do.	25/Fld Amce.	F.8.b.1.5.	SWARTENBROUCK E.14.c.		10 a.m.		
10	do.	No. 4 Coy. Train.	B.9.c.5.6.	K.5.d.4.5.		as below.		

1st Line Transport of all units will move in above order under Brigade Transport Officer, leading unit to pass Starting Point at 10.4 a.m.

2nd Line Transport under O.C., No. 4 Coy., A.S.C. to pass Starting Point at 10.20 a.m.

Rear of column must be clear of Starting Point by 10.30 a.m.

APPENDIX V

Copy No. 10

15th November, 1917.

25th INFANTRY BRIGADE ORDER No. 250.

Ref Maps 36 A.) 1/40,000.
       27.)
       28 N.W. 1/20,000.
       HAZEBROUCK 5 A.

1. (a). 8th Division (less Artillery) will relieve the 3rd Canadian Division (less Artillery) in the left sector of the Canadian Corps Front.
    Relief of the front line will take place during the night 17th/18th November.

   (b). After relief, the 4th Canadian Division will be on our right but will be relieved by 33rd Division (VIII Corps) on the night 18th/19th November. The 1st Division, II Corps, will be on our left.

2. Reliefs and moves for personnel and transport will be carried out in accordance with attached Tables "A", "B" and "C".

3. The following distances will be maintained between units on the march :-
   (a). Companies.   100 yards.
       Unit and its transport.   100 yards.
       Battalions.   500 Yards.
       When transport is Brigaded)
          between each Battalion) 100 yards.
          transport.)

   (b). In new area, 500 yards will be maintained between Companies forward of YPRES Station.

   (c). On roads where vehicular traffic is heavy, Infantry will march in file.

4. Brigade Group will be constituted as follows :-
      25th Infantry Brigade.
      218th Machine Gun Coy.
      2nd Field Coy. R.E.
      25th Field Ambulance.
      No.4 Coy. Train.

5. Staff Captain will issue the necessary Administrative Instructions for the relief, details of accommodation in new area and of lorries for blankets, etc.

6. All dumps, special Maps of the area, Defence Schemes (if any) aeroplane photos and Intelligence notes will be taken over.

7. (a) 2nd Lincoln Regt. will detail a Captain to act as Entraining Officer. He will report to R.T.O. CAESTRE by 7.15 a.m. November 16th and will know the strength of all units (this will be sent him by Staff Captain). He will be responsible for allotting of trucks etc and travel to YPRES by the last train. Name to be sent to this Office November 15th.

   (b). 1st R.Irish Rifles will detail a Captain to act as Detraining Officer. He will proceed to YPRES by lorry leaving Brigade Headquarters 5 a.m. November 16th and will report to R.T.O. YPRES on arrival. Name to be sent to this Office November 15th.

/8...

-2-

8. (a). Billeting parties of 2nd R.Berks Regt, 1st R.Irish Rifles, 218th Machine Gun Coy, 2nd Field Coy, R.E. and 25th Field Ambce. will proceed by first train and will be at CAESTRE Station by 8.30 a.m.
(b). Billeting parties of Brigade Headquarters, 2nd Lincoln Regt. 2d Rifle Brigade, 25th Machine Gun Coy and 25th Trench Mortar Bty. will proceed by lorry leaving Brigade Headquarters 5 a.m.

9. Command of the Left Sector of the Canadian Corps Front will pass to G.O.C., 8th Division at 10 a.m. on November 18th.
Command of front line will pass to G.O.C., 25th Infantry Brigade on completion of relief.

10. 25th Infantry Brigade Headquarters will close at RUE DE BOIS at 7 a.m. November 16th and open on arrival at WIELTJE, C.28.b.6.8.

11. ACKNOWLEDGE.

S.S. Greening
Captain,
A/Brigade Major,
25th Inf. Bde.

Issued at :- 9 p.m.

Issued to :-

Copy No.1. G.O.C.	No.21. 4th Canadian Divn.
2. Bde. Major.	22. 33rd Division.
3. Staff Captain.	23. 1st Division.
4. Bde. Signal Officer.	24. No.2 Coy. A.S.C.
5. Bde. Transport Offr.	25. 26th Field Ambce.
6. 2/Lincoln Regt.	26. 218th M.G.Coy.
7. 2/R.Berks Regt.	27. 8th Division "G".
8. 1/R.Irish Rifles.	28. 8th Division "Q".
9. 2/Rifle Brigade.	29. 3rd Canadian Divn. (3)
10. 25/M.G.Coy.	30. A.D.M.S.
11. 25/T.M.Bty.	31. A.P.M. 8th Divn.
12. QrMr. 2/Lincoln R.	32. C.R.E. 8th Divn.
13. " 2/R.Berks R.	33. War Diary.
14. " 1/R.Irish R.	34. Office.
15. " 2/Rifle Bde.	35. No.2 Field Coy, R.E.
16. 25/Field Ambce.	
17. No.4 Coy. Train.	
18. Bde. Supply Officer.	
19. 23rd Inf. Bde.	
20. 24th Inf. Bde.	

TABLE "A". (PERSONNEL)

Serial No.	Date.	Unit.	From.	To.	Route.	Remarks.
1.	16th Novr.	H.Q. 25th Inf. Bde.	Billets.	AELUE Dug-outs C.28.b.6.8.	March to CAESTRE and thence by rail. March from YPRES. See Table "B".	Train Leaves CAESTRE 9.35 a.m.
2.	do.	2nd Lincoln Regt.	do.	"A" CAMP, C.23.c.3.8. H.W., Pill-box, C.23.c.1.9.	ditto.	ditto.
3.	do.	2nd Rifle Brigade.	do.	"C" CAMP. C.29.a.central.	ditto.	ditto.
4.	do.	25th M. G. Coy.	do.	CAMP at C.27.c.3.5.	ditto.	ditto.
5.	do.	25th T. M. Bty.	do.	CAMP at C.29.a.central.	ditto.	ditto.
6.	do.	2nd R.Berks Regt.	do.	"B" CAMP, C.28.a.4.8. H.Q. JASPER FARM C.29.b.3.7.	ditto.	Train leaves CAESTRE 2.55 p.m.

TABLE "A" (continued)

Serial No.	Date.	Unit.	From.	To.	Route.	Remarks.
7.	18th Novr.	1st R.Irish Rifles.	Billets.	"D" CAMP, C.27.c.8.5.	March to CAESTRE and thence by rail. March from YPRES. (see Table "B").	Train leaves CAESTRE 2.55 p.m.
8.	do.	218th M.G.Coy.	Billets.	"E" CAMP, C.27.a.8.2.	ditto.	ditto.
9.	do.	2nd Field Coy, R.E.	do.	CAMP at I.8.a.4.4.	ditto.	ditto.
10.	do.	25th Field Ambce.	do.	VIETJE, C.28.b.5.5.	ditto.	ditto.

TABLE "B" (PERSONNEL).

Serial No.	Date.	Unit.	From.	To.	Starting Point.	Time.	Route.	Remarks.
11.	15th Novr.	H.Q. 25th Inf. Bde.	Billets.	CAESTRE Station.	STRAZEELE	7 a.m.		Train leaves CAESTRE Station 9.35 a.m.
12.	do.	2nd Lincoln Regt.	do.	do.		7.3 a.m.		
13.	do.	2nd Rifle Brigade.	do.	do.		7.15 a.m.		
14.	do.	25th M.G. Coy.	do.	do.		7.28 a.m.		
15.	do.	25th T.M. Bty.	do.	do.		7.30 a.m.	1.6.	Steel helmets will be worn.
16.	do.	2nd R. Berks Regt.	do.	do.		1 p.m.		
17.	do.	1st R. Irish Rifles.	do.	do.		1.14 p.m.		Train leaves CAESTRE Station 2.55 p.m.
18.	do.	218th M.G. Coy.	do.	do.		1.27 p.m.		
19.	do.	2nd Field Coy. R.E.	do.	do.		1.29 p.m.		
20.	do.	25th Field Ambce.	do.	do.		1.31 p.m.		

TABLE "C"

Serial No.	Date.	Unit.	From.	To.	Starting Point.	Time.	Route.	Remarks.
21.	16th Novr.	Brigade H.Q.	Present Lines.	GOLDFISH CHATEAU, H.11.b.	Road junction VIEUX DEMUIN,	9 a.m.	OUTTERSTEENE - BAILLEUL - LOCRE - RENINGHELST - VLAMERTINGHE.	Baggage and supply wagons will travel loaded with units.
22.	do.	2nd Rifle Bde.	do.	do.		9.1 a.m.		O/C, No.4Coy A.S.C. will issue instructions that the 22 wagons of No.1 Coy, A.S.C. follow the same route as shown on this table and report to Units with supplies on 17th inst.
23.	do.	2nd Lincoln R.	do.	do.		9.4 a.m.		
24.	do.	1st R.Irish R.	do.	do.		9.7 a.m.		
25.	do.	2nd R.Berks R.	do.	do.		9.10 a.m.		
26.	do.	25th M.G.Coy.	do.	C.27.c.1.7.		9.13 a.m.		
27.	do.	218th M.G.Coy.	do.	do.		9.16 a.m.		Lorries and Motor Ambulances will travel under orders issued by G.O.C. 23rd Inf. Bde. and O/C, 25th Field Ambulance respectively. Route shown on this table must be followed.
28.	do.	2nd Field Coy. R.E.	do.	Hop Factory VLAMERTINGHE H.8.a.5.8.		9.19 a.m.		
29.	do.	25th Field Amb.	do.	RED FARM, G.5.d.7.3.		9.22 a.m.		
30.	do.	No.4 Coy.	do.	G.5.a.6.6.		9.25 a.m.		Steel helmets will be worn.

25th Infantry Brigade No.282/G/17.

2nd Lincoln Regt.
2nd R.Berks Regt.
1st R.Irish Rifles.
2nd Rifle Brigade.
25th M.G.Coy.
25th T.M.Bty.
218th M.G.Coy.
2nd Field Coy, R.E.
25th Field Ambce.

Small parties of units proceeding by first train may be left behind to load lorries and will report to nearest unit by 10 a.m. to proceed by second train.

B. Greening

Captain,
A/Brigade Major,
25th Inf. Bde.

16/11/17.

<u>25th Infantry Brigade No.292/G/18.</u>

2nd Lincoln Regt.
2nd R.Berks Regt.
1st R.Irish Rifles.
2nd Rifle Brigade.
25th M.G.Coy.
25th T.M.Bty.
218th M.G.Coy.
2nd Field Coy, R.E.
25th Field Ambce.

    Reference train journey tomorrow, all ranks will be warned to put on equipment when the train passes RENINGHELST and will on arrival at YPRES detrain quickly. If YPRES station is being shelled, train will probably stay outside. All ranks will immediately detrain.

                                                Captain,
                                      A/Brigade Major,
16/11/17.   25th Inf. Bde.

SECRET.   Copy No. 10

APPENDIX VI

16th November 1917.

25th INFANTRY BRIGADE ORDER No. 251.

Reference maps:-
    Sheet
    " 28. 1/40,000.
    PASSCHENDAELE, 1/10,000.

1. The 25th Infantry Brigade will relieve the 7th Canadian Infantry Brigade in the trenches on the 17th and night 17th/18th November 1917.

2. Reliefs will be carried out as follows:-

   (a). 2nd LINCOLN REGT. will relieve the R.C.R. in the front line. Right Sub-section.

   (b). 2nd RIFLE BRIGADE will relieve the 42nd Battalion in the front line, Left Sub-section.

   (c). 2nd ROYAL BERKS REGT. will relieve the P.P.C.L.I. which has two Companies in Support Right Sub-section, and two Companies on BELLEVUE SPUR.

   (d). 1st ROYAL IRISH RIFLES will relieve the 116th Battalion in Reserve in CAPRICORN Area.

   (e). 25th TRENCH MORTAR BTY. will remain in its present position.

   (f). 25th and 218th MACHINE GUN COYS. will move into the line on the 18th. Details will be issued later.

3. Headquarters on completion of relief will be as follows:-

BRIGADE H.Q.	THE CAPITOL.
2nd LINCOLN REGT.	MEETCHEELE.
2nd R.BERKS REGT.	BELLEVUE SPUR.
1st R.IRISH RIFLES.	CAPRICORN KEEP.
2nd RIFLE BRIGADE.	MEETCHEELE.

4. Guides from Battalions in the line on the scale of 2 per platoon will meet ingoing Battalions at WATERLOO. 2nd Lieut. A.G.C.RICE, 2nd R.Berks Regt. will be at WATERLOO and will ensure that all guides are correctly distributed.

5. Battalions will pass GRAVENSTAFEL CROSS ROADS, D.9.c.8.3. as follows:-
2nd LINCOLN REGT.	4.45 p.m. 17th instant.
2nd RIFLE BRIGADE.	5.45 p.m. " "
2nd R.BERKS REGT.	6.45 p.m. " "

6. Relief of Reserve Battalion to be complete by 3 p.m. 17th instant.

7. Brigade Headquarters will close at its present position at 3 p.m. on the 17th and will open at the CAPITOL on arrival.

8. Completion of relief will be reported by the code word "SNAG"

9. Further details of relief will be arranged between Commanding Officers concerned.

10. All trench stores, aeroplane photographs and Defence Schemes will be taken over.

11. ACKNOWLEDGE.

Issued at 5 p.m.

Captain,
A/Brigade Major,
25th Inf. Bde.

/P.T.O.

Issued to:-
Copy No. 1. G.O.C.
2. Brigade Major.
3. Staff Captain.
4. Brigade Signal Officer.
5. Brigade Transport Officer.
6. 2nd Lincoln Regt.
7. 2nd R.Berks Regt.
8. 1st R.Irish Rifles.
9. 2nd Rifle Brigade.
10. 25th Machine Gun Coy.
11. 25th Trench Mortar Bty.
12. QrMr. 2nd Lincoln Regt.
13. " 2nd R.Berks Regt.
14. " 1st R.Irish Rifles.
15. " 2nd Rifle Brigade.
16. 25th Field Ambulance.
17. No.4 Coy. Train.
18. Brigade Supply Officer.
19. 23rd Inf. Bde.
20. 24th Inf. Bde.
21. 3rd Canadian Div.
22. 4th Canadian Div.
23. 7th Canadian Inf. Bde.
24. 8th Division.
25. C.R.A. 8th Division.
26. C.R.E. 8th Division.
27. 218th Machine Gun Coy.
28. No.2 Field Coy, R.E.
29. Lieut. RICE.
30. Camp Comt. WIELTJE Area.
31. 33rd Division.
32. 1st Division.
33. No.4 Coy. Train.
34. War Diary.
35. Office.

SECRET.

APPENDIX VII

Copy No 6

17/11/17

Ref. Passchendaele Map.

25th M.G. Company Relief Order No. 19.

(1) The Company will relieve the 7th Canadian M.G. Coy. in Barrage Positions between D.5.c.5.2. and D.5.c.3.5. on the 17th Nov. 1917.

(2) "A" + "B" Sections, forming No. 1 Battery, will relieve the eight right hand guns. As "B" Section has only three guns in action the right hand gun will not be relieved.
   LIEUT. N.J. LARKWORTHY will command No. 1 Battery.
   "C" + "D" Sections, forming No. 2 Battery, will relieve the eight left hand guns. LIEUT. K.V. WESTON will command No. 2 Battery.

(3) One guide for each pair of guns will be at the Transport Lines at 7.30 a.m.
   Sections will leave the Transport Lines as follows:—
   "B" – 7.30 a.m.; "A" – 7.40 a.m.; "C" – 7.50 a.m.; "D" – 8.0 a.m.
   From the point where it becomes necessary to man-handle guns, teams will move in pairs at 5 minutes interval.

(4) Each team will take over 10 belt-boxes from the 7th Company and will not take any in. Each team will take in its gun, tripod, 1st aid case (not spare parts box) condenser etc. and one tin of water. Guns + tripods will be carried on pack mules as far as GRAVENSTAFEL, and then manhandled.

(5) Section Officers will carefully check all stores handed over to them + forward a list to Coy. H.Q. as soon as possible.

(6) LIEUT GOODEVE will relieve LIEUT NEATBY at the forward report centre at KOREK (D.9.c)

(7) All reports, including report of completion of relief will be forwarded to KOREK.
   LIEUT GOODEVE will forward them to O.C. Coy at CAPITOL (D.13.d)

(8) Coy H.Q. will close at present position at 8.0 a.m. + reopen at CAPITOL about 10.0 a.m. Transport lines will remain unchanged.

Copy No 1   O.C. A Section
      2   "   B
      3   "   C
      4   "   D
      5   LIEUT GOODEVE
      6   WAR DIARY

A. Simmonds Capt.
Commanding 25th M.G. Coy.

SECRET

Copy No.......

7TH. CANADIAN MACHINE GUN COMPANY
OPERATION ORDER No. 34

November 16. 1917

1. In accordance with D.M.G.C.-3rd.Cdn.Divn.O.O.53, the 25th. Machine Gun Company will relieve the 7th. Canadian Machine Gun Company in barrage positions at D.5.c.5.2. to D.5.c.3.5.

2. Lieut. Weston with 7 guns will relieve Lieut. Coyne of the 7th.Cdn.M.G.Coy. at battery position No.5.
Lieut. Larkworthy with 8 guns will relieve Lieuts. Fair and Parkins in battery positions No.6,

3. Guides will be supplied from the 7th.Cdn.M.G.Coy transport lines and will pick up crews of the 25th.M.G.Coy. at their Transport Lines at 7.30.a.m. 2 Guides per Section.

4. Lieut. Goodeve will relieve Lieut. Neatby at KOREK. Guide to be supplied from 7th.Cdn.M.G.Coy,Rear and ready at 25th.M.G.Coy's Rear H.Q. at 7.30.a.m.

5. Capt. Simmonds to relieve Major Weir at CAPITOL . Pte. Morris to be at their Lines at 7.30.a.m. to act as guide.

6. 10 belt boxes per gun to be handed over but no tripods.

7. 12 pack animals from 7th.Cdn.M.G.Coy. to be on PLANK ROAD opposite KANSAS HOUSE at 11.00.a.m. to carry out guns and tripods.

8. Acknowledge relief complete by code word "BRONCHO"

9. Acknowledge.

F.W.Burnham Lieut.
Major.
O.C.7th.Canadian Machine Gun Company.

APPENDIX VIII

SECRET.   8th Division No.G.97/18.

NIGHT HARASSING FIRE.

1. Night harassing fire of Divisional Artillery and Machine Guns will be co-ordinated as outlined herewith.

   (a) Sketch "A" attached divides the Divisional frontage into 6 lanes. The Western harassing fire boundaries for all arms will be their S.O.S. lines and the Eastern boundary for the present for the Divisional Artillery and M.G's. will be a line running 500 yards from and parallel to the S.O.S. line.

   (b) Table "B" attached shows six columns of letters from "A" to "F" inclusive each representing a period of two hours, and allots harassing fire areas to respective arms for each period of two hours.

   (c) Table "C" attached gives the date and time to which the different periods refer.

   Brigades in the line will be responsible for harassing the enemy West of the Divisional Artillery S.O.S. lines.

   List of targets in each lane is attached.

                                              E Beddington
                                              Lieut.-Colonel,
8th Division,   General Staff.
19th November, 1917.

   Distribution:-

G.O.C., R.A.	45 copies.
D.M.G.O.	12 "
62nd H.A. Group	1 copy for information.
23rd Inf. Bde.	8 copies.
24th Inf. Bde.	8 "
25th Inf. Bde.	8 "
33rd Division	1 copy.
1st Division	1 "
VIII Corps	2 copies.
A.D.C. for G.O.C.	1 copy.
14th Division	1 "

SKETCH "A"
8TH DIVISION.
HARASSING FIRE NOV 20TH 1917.

Lane 1
Lane 2
Lane 3
Lane 4
Lane 5
Lane 6
SOS
Front Line
Approximate 30'

Reference Sheet
Paschendaele 1/10,000.

8th Division No.G.97/18.

TABLE "B".

HARASSING FIRE.

To accompany 8th Division No.G.97/18 dated 19th November, 1917.

Area	A	B	C	D	E	F
1	Div. Arty.	M.G's.	Div. Arty.	Div. Arty.	Div. Arty.	Div. Arty.
2	M.G's.	Div. Arty	Div. Arty.	M.G's.	Div. Arty.	Div. Arty.
3	Div. Arty.	Div. Arty	M.G's.	Div. Arty.	M.G's.	M.G's.
4	Div. Arty.	M.G's.	Div. Arty.	Div. Arty.	Div. Arty.	M.G's.
5	Div. Arty.	Div. Arty	M.G's.	M.G's.	Div. Arty.	Div. Arty.
6	M.G's.	Div. Arty	Div. Arty.	Div. Arty.	M.G's.	Div. Arty.

TABLE "C".

Showing date and time to which periods refer.

Date night.	6 p.m. to 8 p.m.	8 p.m. to 10 pm	10 p.m. to 12 m.n.	12 m.n. to 2 a.m.	2 a.m. to 4 a.m.	4 a.m. to 6 a.m.
Novr.						
20/21	A	B	C	D	E	F
21/22	B	C	D	E	F	A
22/23	C	D	E	F	A	B
23/24	D	E	F	A	B	C
24/25	E	F	A	B	C	D
25/26	F	A	B	C	D	E
26/27	A	B	C	D	E	F
27/28	B	C	D	E	F	A
28/29	C	D	E	F	A	B
29/30	D	E	F	A	B	C
30/1	E	F	A	B	C	D
Decr.						
1/2	F	A	B	C	D	E
2/3	A	B	C	D	E	F
3/4	B	C	D	E	F	A
4/5	C	D	E	F	A	B

8th Div. No.G.97/16.

LIST OF TARGETS - HARASSING FIRE.

LANE 1.

    (W.25.c.35.50. Redoubt and trenches around.)

1.   W.25.c.70.95.)
        to   ) Infantry track.
    W.25.c.50.70.)

2.   W.25.c.60.65.)
        to   ) Track.
    W.25.d.35.70.)

3.   W.25.d.00.95.   D.O.

4.   W.25.d.45.95.   Group of D.O's.

5.   W.25.d.55.75.   D.O.

6.   W.25.d.65.78.   D.O.

7.   W.25.d.00.77.)
        to   ) Infantry track.
    W.25.b.50.38.)

8.   W.25.c.72.91.   Occupied shell hole.

LANE 2.

1.   W.25.a.75.20.(approx.) Redoubt and WRATH FME.

2.   W.25.a.96.23.   D.O.

3.   W.25.a.80.60.)
) Infantry track.
4.   W.25.c.75.98.)

5.   W.25.a.55.35.)
        to   ) Infantry track.
    W.25.a.60.20.)

LANE 3.

1.   W.25.a.51.35.)
        to   ) Infantry track.
    W.25.a.25.83.)

2.   W.25.a.25.83.)
        to   ) Infantry track.
3.   W.19.c.70.28.)

4.   W.19.c.70.28.)
        to   ) Infantry track.
    W.25.a.82.00.)

5.   W.25.a.90.90.   WRAP COTT and "T" Road Junction.

6.   W.19.c.70.22.   H.Q. and "T" Road Junction.

7.   W.19.c.83.35.   D.O.

/LANE 4.

LANE 4.

1. V.30.b.75.75.   VENISON TRENCH REDOUBT.
2. W.25.a.21.99.   D.O.
3. W.19.c.48.15.   DUMP.
4. W.19.c.25.55.   D.O.
5. W.19.c.42.16.   D.O.

LANE 5.

1. V.24.d.67.10.   D.O.
2. V.24.d.20.55.   D.O.
3. V.24.d.70.45.)
   to   ) Infantry track.
   W.19.c.15.52.)
4. W.19.c.09.50.   D.O.
5. V.24.d.56.70.   D.O.
6. V.24.d.57.87.   D.O.
7. V.24.d.80.90.   H.Q.
8. V.24.d.25.95.   VENISON.FARM.
9. V.24.d.70.75.   D.O.
10. W.19.c.15.70. WRANGLE FARM.

LANE 6.

1. V.24.c.40.33.   D.O.
2. V.24.c.40.30.   D.O.
3. V.24.c.12.78.   D.O.
4. V.24.c.25.80.   M.G.
5. V.24.c.80.25.   D.O.
6. V.24.c.62.50.   Occupied shell holes.
7. V.24.c.72.58.   "   "   "
8. V.24.c.79.21.   "   "   "
9. V.24.c.48.70.   "   "   "

MESSAGE FORM.

To :—   No.

1. I am at........................ (Note:—Either give Map Reference or mark your position by a 'X' on the Map on back.)

2. I have reached limits of my Objective.

3. My Platoon / Company is at.............................. and is consolidating.

4. My Platoon / Company is at.............................. and has consolidated.

5. Am held up by (a) M.G. / (b) Wire at...................... (Place where you are).

6. Enemy holding strong point ....

7. I am in touch with................on Right / Left at............

8. I am not in touch with ....on Right / Left.

9. Am shelled from.....................

10. Am in need of :—

11. Counter Attack forming at ....

12. Hostile (a) Battery / (b) Machine Gun / (c) Trench Mortar active at ....

13. Reinforcements wanted at

14. I estimate my present strength at .... rifles.

15. Add any other useful information here :—

Name.................................

Platoon.............................

Time .... m.   Company............................

Date .... 1917.   Battalion...........................

(A). Carry no maps or papers which may be of value to the Enemy.

(B). Give no information if captured, except the following, which you are bound to give :—

    Name and Rank.

(C). Collect all captured maps and papers and send them in at once.

SECRET   COPY NO.

25th M.G. COY. RELIEF ORDER No. 21

REF. MAPS 28. N.E. 1/20,000
            28 N.W. 1/20,000   22 Nov. 1917

(1) The Company will be relieved in the line tomorrow morning, 23/11/17, by the 23rd M.G. Coy.

(2) LIEUT. RENNIE will arrange for 8 guides to be at WIELTJE (road junction at C.28.b.25.55) at 5.0 a.m. Each guide will be required to guide two teams to the battery positions.

(3) O's. C. "A", "C" & "D" Sections will hand over 6 beltboxes per gun.
"B" Section will be relieved by 4 guns & O.C. "B" Section will arrange to hand over 20 belts & beltboxes to the relieving section. Receipts will be obtained.
No other mobilisation stores will be handed over.
The relieving sections will have a carrying party of 2 men per gun to bring in beltboxes. Arrangements have been made for these men to carry out two beltboxes per gun for us, and O's. C. Sections will see that this is done.

(4) All trench stores, (except as many petrol tins as can be carried out) will be handed over and receipts obtained.
O's. C. Sections will see that no N.C.O. or man leaves the battery position without a load.

(5) LIEUT. RENNIE will arrange for 16 pack mules to reach GRAVENSTAFEL in batches of 4 at five minute intervals commencing at 8.30 a.m. Each mule will be loaded with a gun and tripod and will be taken back to the transport lines. Nos. 1 will go with their guns to the transport lines where they will report to the C.S.M. on arrival.

(6) LIEUT. RENNIE will arrange for a limber to be at the Dressing Station on the BANK ROAD about D13 c 8.6 at 9.0 a.m. to collect billboxes, petrol tins, etc which cannot be put on the mules. O's C. Sections will arrange for all billboxes, petrol tins, etc to be carried to this limber. The last officer to leave the battery position will be responsible for telling the driver of this limber when he may return to the transport lines.

(7) Sections will rendezvous at WEILTJE Dugout (Bn. HQ.) and will be conveyed to the BRANDHOEK area by lorries. Lorries will be at WEILTJE about 11.0 a.m.
Guides will return to the transport lines & report to the C.S.M. on arrival there.
Carrying parties of the 23rd Coy. will also proceed to the transport lines.

(8) LIEUT. RENNIE will arrange for a guide to be at the cross roads SAINT JEAN at 5.0 a.m. to guide the transport of the 23rd Coy to the transport lines.
The transport may be late & in any case will not be the full transport.

(9) Please acknowledge.

A Simmonds Capt.
Commanding 25th M.G. Coy

Copy No. 1 O.C. No 1 Battery
 "   " 2 "   " 2   "
 "   " 3 LIEUT. RENNIE
 "   " 4   "   GOODEVE
 "   " 5 23rd M.G. Coy
 "   " 6 24th Inf Bde
 "   " 7 War Diary
 "   " 8 Retained

APPENDIX X

DEFENCE POLICY for HIGH GROUND N. of PASSCHENDAELE and REORGANISATION of the M.G. DEFENCE.

SECRET

DEFENCE POLICY FOR SECTOR AT PRESENT HELD BY 8th DIVISION.

1. It is of the utmost importance that no part of the high ground North of PASSCHENDAELE now held by us, be lost.

    In consequence of the confined nature of the only approach to this high ground the BELLEVUE - HOSSELMARKT SPUR, it will be extremely difficult to send forward troops from the rear in case of a serious enemy attack. On this account, the two Battalions and the Machine Gun Company holding the Line must fight it out on the ground they hold.

2. Should an enemy attack penetrate our front, the Support Companies of the two Battalions holding the Line must be used for immediate counter-attack, on the initiative of the Commander on the spot.

3. If, however, it be found impossible to hold the high ground North of PASSCHENDAELE, the BELLEVUE - HOSSELMARKT SPUR must be held at all costs.
    With this object in view, the Battalion in Support at BELLEVUE will, in case of attack, move forward to a position East of the "Pill Boxes" about D.5.b.6.6.

4. In case of attack, the Battalion in Reserve will at once move up to BELLEVUE.

5. Battalion Commanders will ensure that all Officers under their command are thoroughly acquainted with the high ground on the ridge and know all the routes up to it.

6. It has been arranged that the G.O.C., F.A., will put down a barrage, if required, on the line D.6.a.8.3. - V.30.c.1.2. so as to cover the Battalion holding the BELLEVUE SPUR as detailed in para 3 above, O.C. 62nd H.A.G. will put down East of this Line. These barrages will not be put down without the sanction of the G.O.C. Brigade in the Line. (a barrage)

7. The D.M.G.O. will arrange to cover the Battalion referred to in para 3. by Machine Guns. Machine Gun positions will be notified when known.

8. Battalion Commanders will notify Brigade when instructions contained in para. 5 have been complied with, and give the routes chosen.

9. Previous instructions on this subject are now cancelled.

10. <u>ACKNOWLEDGE.</u>

                                                    Captain,
                                    Brigade Major, 24th Inf. Brigade.

23rd November, 1917.

Copies to :-   1/Worc.R.   2nd Inf. Bde.
               2/E.Lancs.R.   93th Inf. Bde.
               1/S.Foresters.   Left Group F.A.
               2/North'n.R.   Right Group F.A.
               24th M.G.Coy.   Group H.A.
               24th T.M.B.   25th M.G.Coy.
               8th Division "G"   218th M.G.Coy.
               8th Divn. Art.   War Diary.
               23rd Inf. Bde.   File.
               25th Inf. Bde.

SECRET.   8th Division No.G.22/16/35.

   23rd Inf. Bde.
   24th Inf. Bde.
   25th Inf. Bde.
   23rd M.G. Coy.
   24th M.G. Coy.
   25th M.G. Coy.
   218th M.G. Coy.
   D. M. G. O.

1.   The dispositions of the machine guns in close defence of the 8th Divisional Forward Area will be reorganised at once in accordance with the Table attached.

2.   The general action of each Group will be defined by the M.G. Company Commander in accordance with the instructions of the Brigadier, and the tactical handling of these guns will lie with the officers mentioned in the "Command" column of the Table.

   The action of the VENTURE FARM GUN will be directed by the Infantry Company Commander on the spot, on a plan previously arranged upon between him and the M.G. Company Commander.

3.   Reports will be sent by the M.G. Company Commander concerned to the G.O.C. the Brigade in the line and to the D.M.G.O. when the reorganisation has been completed.

8th Division
23rd November, 1917.

    E. Beddington.
    Lieut.-Colonel,
    General Staff.

  Copy to:- 8th Div. Arty.
     C. R. E.
     62nd H.A.G.
     VIII Corps
     VIII Corps M.G.O.
     1st Division.
     23rd Division.

8th Division No.G.??/16/35.

MACHINE GUN DISPOSITION TABLE.

No. of Guns.	Letter of Group.	Location.	Command.	TACTICAL DUTY	
				Attack from North.	Attack from East.
2.	"A"	Concrete Dugout at D.6.b.4.9.	1 Sect: Officer.	Open fire on direct targets.	Open fire on direct targets.
2.	"B"	Concrete Dugout V.30.c.5.25.	1 Sect: Officer.	Cover "C" Gun and fire on direct targets.	Cover "A" Group and fire on direct targets.
1.	"C"	VENTURE FARM.	Infantry Coy. Commdr. on the spot.	Fire on direct targets.	Fire on direct targets.
5.	"D"	MEETCHEELE	1 Sect: Officer.	Cover Division on our Left and VENTURE FARM, with all or a portion of the guns.	With all or a portion of guns on over North or South or both sides of the MEETCHEELE MOSSELMARKT Road and "A" and "B" Groups.

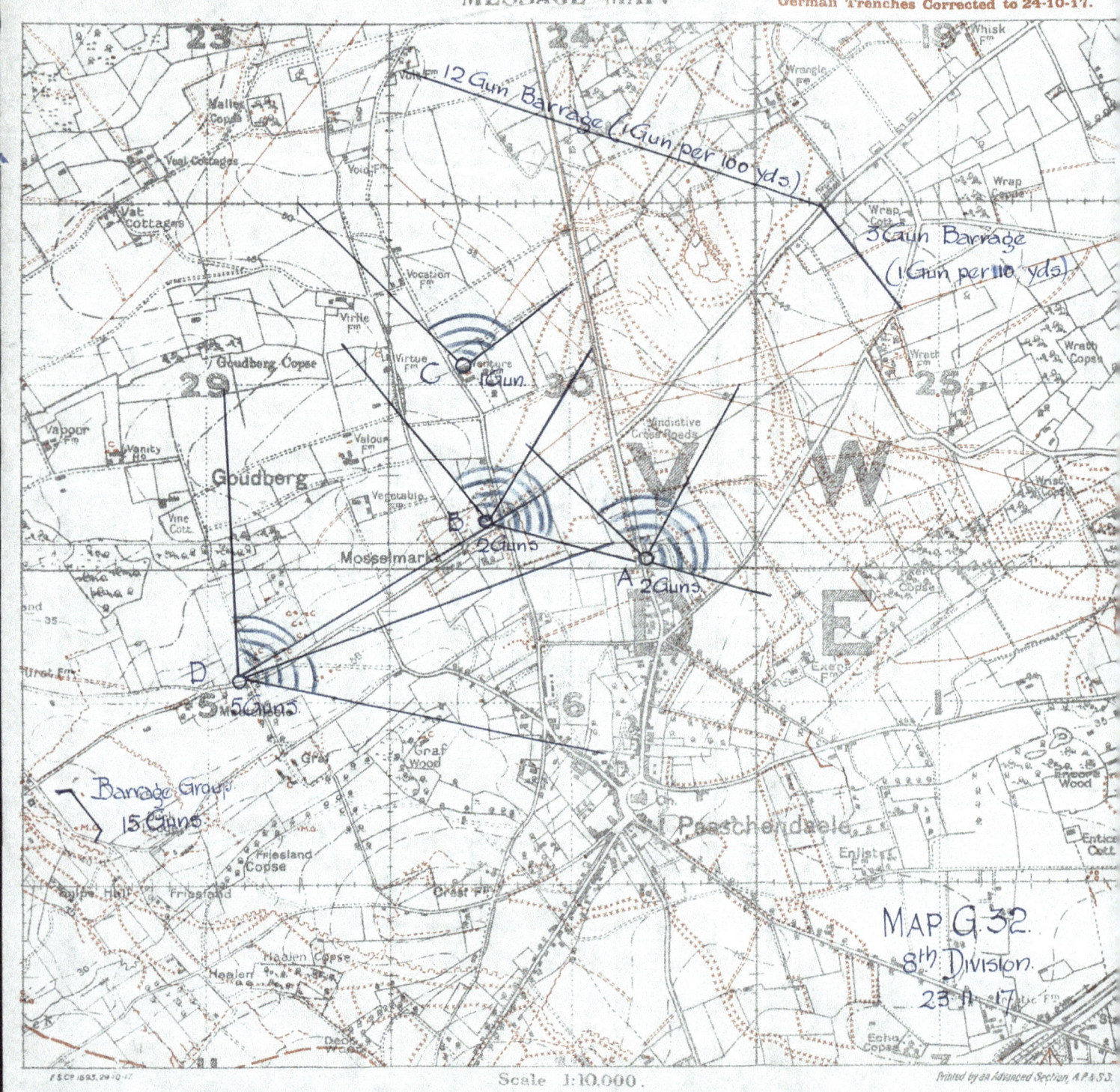

MESSAGE FORM.

To:—   No.

1. I am at.......................... (Note:—Either give Map Reference or mark your position by a 'X' on the Map on back.

2. I have reached limits of my Objective.

3. My Platoon / Company is at.............................. and is consolidating.

4. My Platoon / Company is at.............................. and has consolidated.

5. Am held up by (a) M.G. (b) Wire at..................(Place where you are).

6. Enemy holding strong point ....

7. I am in touch with..................on Right / Left. at............

8. I am not in touch with ....on Right / Left.

9. Am shelled from.....................

10. Am in need of :—

11. Counter Attack forming at................

12. Hostile (a) Battery
           (b) Machine Gun   active at.....................
           (c) Trench Mortar

13. Reinforcements wanted at

14. I estimate my present strength at .... rifles.

15. Add any other useful information here :—

Name..........................

Platoon........................

Time .... m.   Company.......................

Date .... 1917.   Battalion......................

(A). Carry no maps or papers which may be of value to the Enemy.

(B). Give no information if captured, except the following, which you are bound to give :—

    Name and Rank.

(C). Collect all captured maps and papers and send them in at once.

APPENDIX XI

ANTI-COUNTER ATTACK HARASSING FIRE PROGRAMME

SECRET.

25th Infantry Brigade No.G.2/70.

~~2nd Lincoln Regt.~~
2nd R.Berks Regt.
1st R.Irish Rifles.
~~3rd Rifle Brigade.~~
25th M.G.Coy.
~~25th T.M.Battery.~~

1. It has been pointed out at a recent Army Conference that information obtained from various sources indicates the probability of the enemy attempting to recapture PASSCHENDAELE RIDGE, a late afternoon attack being considered likely.

2. Provided that ample warning of such an attempt is given to our Artillery, the great concentration of guns now available combined with rifle and machine gun fire should defeat any such intention.

3. It is essential that there should be special vigilance on the part of troops in the front line, particular attention being paid to the plateau west of VENISON TRENCHES.

4. While bearing in mind the necessity of not using the S.O.S. Signal without cause, at the same time care must be exercised that there is an ample supply of these, and that subordinate commanders have them close at hand. A chain of stations to repeat these must be arranged.

5. Arrangements are being made for the shelling at dawn and dusk of all areas suitable for the massing of hostile troops. Air reconnaissances will also be made over these localities with a view to dispersing any assembly of troops by bombs.

22nd November, 1917.

Captain,
A/Brigade Major,
25th Inf. Bde.

SECRET.   8th Division No.G.97/27.

NIGHT HARASSING FIRE.

1. Instructions for night harassing fire issued under 8th Division No.G.97/16 dated 19th November is cancelled from noon 23rd November, and the following substituted.

2. With a view to breaking up any hostile troops which may be forming up for counter-attack on our front, the following action will be carried out daily at about dawn and dusk, varying in intensity according to the areas from which attack is most likely to develop.

3. The measures to be taken will consist of searching fire and concentrations by M.G's., Field and Heavy Artillery.

4. The lanes to be swept by M.G's.& Field Artillery respectively, are shown on the attached Diagram 'A'. Map 'B' sent to VIII Corps, 8Div.R.A. and 62nd H.A.G., only shows areas from which attack is most likely to be expected, coloured RED and possible lines of approach BLUE. Areas of responsibility for M.G's., Field Artillery and H.A. are also shown.

5. Tables "B" and "C", give the areas to be searched by M.G's.& Field Arty., and the arrangements for harassing fire during the night.

6. The H.A. are arranging to cover the lanes traversing the "RED" Areas during the periods 3 p.m. to 6 p.m. and 3.30 a.m. to 6.30 a.m., firing a minimum of 50% of the total daily allotment of ammunition during these periods.

C Beddington

Lieut.-Colonel,
General Staff.

8th Division,
22nd November, 1917.

G.O.C., R.A., 8th Div.	(45)	Copies
D. M. G. O.	12	"
62nd H. A. Group	1	copy for information.
23rd Inf. Bde.	8	Copies.
24th Inf. Bde.	8	"
25th Inf. Bde.	8	"
33rd Division	1	Copy.
1st Division	1	"
VIII Corps	2	Copies.
14th Division	1	Copy.
A.D.C. for G.O.C.	1	"

COUNTER OFFENSIVE MEASURES
AND NIGHT HARASSING FIRE.

TABLE "B".

AREA	A	B	C	D	E	F	G
1.	D.A.	D.A.	M.G	D.A.	D.A.	D.A.	-
2.	D.A.	D.A.	D.A.	M.G.	-	-	D.A.
3.	D.A.	D.A.	-	D.A.	-	D.A.	-
4.	D.A.) M.G.)	D.A.	D.A.	-	D.A.	M.G.	-
5.	D.A.	D.A.) M.G.)	-	D.A.	D.A.	-	D.A.
6.	D.A.) M.G.)	D.A.) M.G.)	D.A.	D.A.	D.A.	M.G.	D.A.

TABLE "C".

		P.M.					A.M.				
Date.	3-4	4-0 to 4.30	4.30 to 5.0	5-0 to 7-0	7-0 to 9-0	9-0 to 11.0	11-0 to 1.0	1-0 to 3-0	3-0 to 4-0	4-0 to 5-0	5-0 to 5.30	5.30 to 6.30
Nov. 23/24	E	A	B	D	E		G	C	E	D	B	A
24/25	A	D	B	G	F	E	C		D	A	C	B
25/26	B	A	C	F	G	D		E	G	B	A	C
26/27	E	B	A	C	D	G		D	F	A	E	G
27/28	A	D	B	G	F		C	G	D	A	C	B
28/29	B	A	C	F	G		F	E	G	B	A	C
29/30	E	B	A	C	D	G	C		F	A	E	G

First 3 and last 3 periods (4½ hours) to fire 50% of total harassing rounds fired in the 24 hours.

Total rounds per 18-pdr. battery in action for harassing fire 100 and for 4.5" How: 50.

Fire during periods laid down will consist of one or two bursts at 1 round per gun per minute. Targets should be varied at each burst within the limits of the allotted lanes.

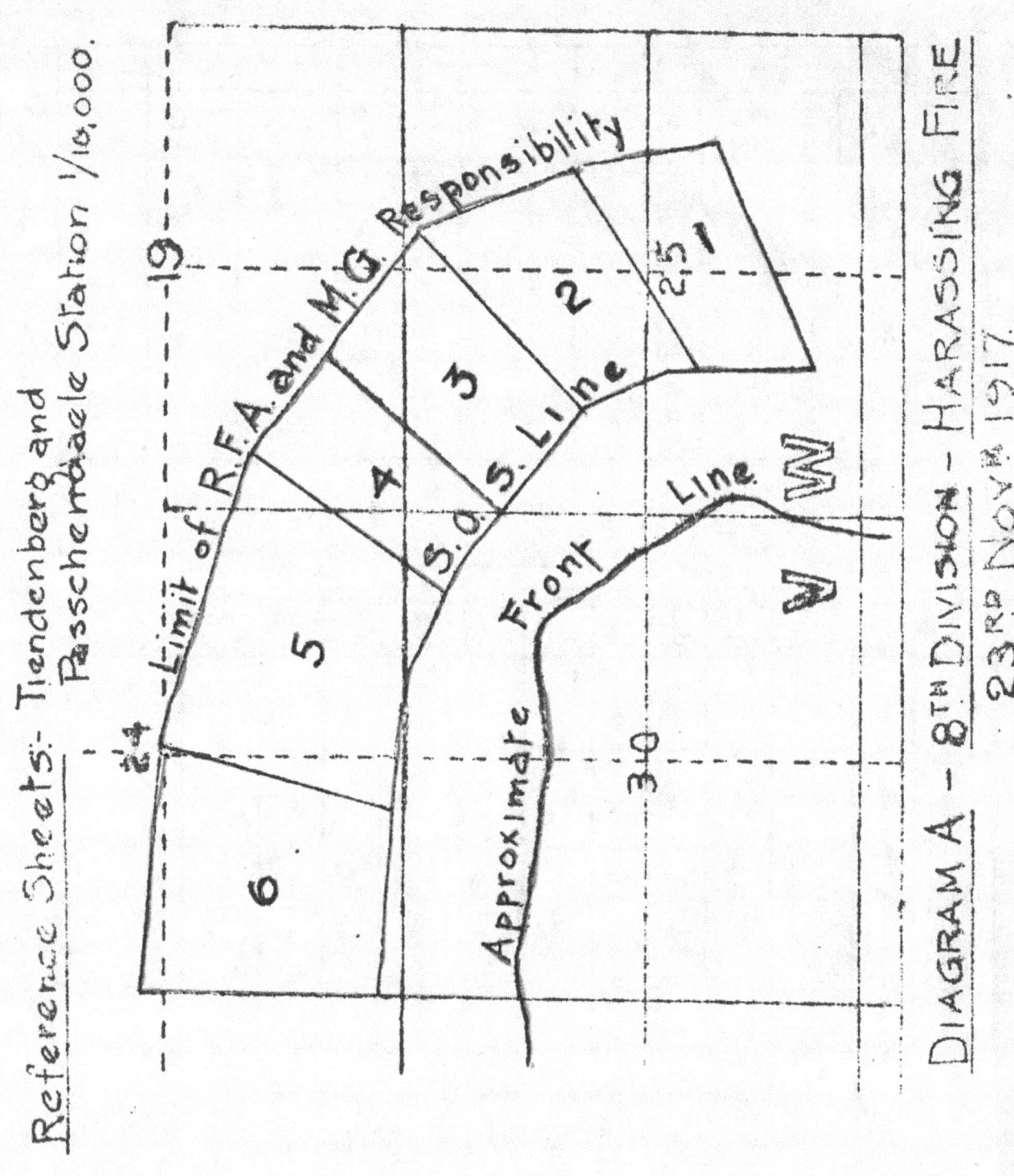

No. 27.

MESSAGE MAP.

German Trenches Corrected to 24-10-17.

Scale 1:10,000.

MESSAGE FORM.

To :— No.

1. I am at.................... (Note:—Either give Map Reference or mark your position by a 'X' on the Map on back.

2. I have reached limits of my Objective.

3. My Platoon / Company is at........................ and is consolidating.

4. My Platoon / Company is at........................ and has consolidated.

5. Am held up by (a) M.G. (b) Wire at................ (Place where you are).

6. Enemy holding strong point ....

7. I am in touch with................on Right / Left at............

8. I am not in touch with ....on Right / Left.

9. Am shelled from......................

10. Am in need of :—

11. Counter Attack forming at ....

12. Hostile (a) Battery
    (b) Machine Gun   active at ....
    (c) Trench Mortar

13. Reinforcements wanted at

14. I estimate my present strength at .... rifles.

15. Add any other useful information here :—

Name...........................

Platoon........................

Time............m. Company........................

Date.........1917. Battalion......................

(A). Carry no maps or papers which may be of value to the Enemy.

(B). Give no information if captured, except the following, which you are bound to give :—

    Name and Rank.

(C). Collect all captured maps and papers and send them in at once.

APPENDIX XII

SECRET.   Copy No....

8TH DIVISION ORDER No.243.

24th November, 1917.

1.   25th and 218th Machine Gun Companies will move to the
ST. JEAN Area on November 25th.
     Route - VLAMERTINGHE Road juno. I.2.c.3.3.

2.   218th Machine Gun Company will be clear of VLAMERTINGHE
by 2.30 p.m. 25th Machine Gun Company will not enter it
before that hour.

3.   Accommodation will be as follows:-
     25th M.G. Coy. ... Camp, I.2.d.7.6.
     218th M.G. Coy. .. I.3.a.1.9.
     Transport of both Cos. ... C.26.d.8.3.

4.   Billeting parties will report to the Area Commandant,
ST. JEAN, at C.27.d.1.1., at 12 Noon 25th November.

5.   ACKNOWLEDGE.

                                                         Lieut.-Colonel,
                                                         General Staff.

Issued at 10.30 p.m.

     Copies to:- No.1 23rd Inf. Bde.
                   2   24th Inf. Bde.
                   3   25th Inf. Bde.
                   4   218th M.G. Coy.
                   5   25th M.G. Coy.
                   6   "Q".
                   7   Area Commandant, ST. JEAN.
                   8   A.P.M.
                   9   War Diary.
                  10   File.

APPENDIX XIII

ORDERS relating to the MOVING to the RIGHT of the DIVISIONAL FRONT and the consequent adjustment of M.G's.

SECRET.   Copy No. 10

8TH DIVISION ORDER No.242.

Ref: Map G.31 issued   23rd November, 1917.
     with 8th Div.
     instructions No.1
     of Nov. 22nd, 1917.

1. (a)   On night 24th/25th November, the 97th Inf. Bde. (32nd Divn.) will relieve the 23rd Inf. Bde. from the present Left boundary of the Divisional Sector to as far East as TEAL COTTAGES inclusive to 8th Division.

   (b)   On night 24th/25th November, the 23rd Inf. Bde. will relieve the 98th Inf. Bde. (33rd Divn.) from the present Right boundary of the Divisional Sector to as far South as the road from D.6.b. central - E.1.c.4.8. inclusive to 8th Division.

   (c)   All arrangements for the reliefs will be made direct between Brigadiers.

2.   Reliefs of machine guns will take place in both cases on night 25th/26th November, under arrangements to be made by D.M.G. Officers concerned.

3. (a)   Command of the new Sectors will pass to the relieving Inf. Brigadiers on completion of reliefs.

   (b)   Command of the new Sectors will pass to Divisional Commanders at same hour.

4.   Aeroplane photos, all Intelligence details, and trench stores will be handed over.

5.   Completion of reliefs will be reported to Divisional Headquarters.

6. (a)   The boundary between 8th and 33rd Divisions will be that shown on Map G.31 issued with 8th Division Instructions No.1 of November 22nd. The following accommodation in 32nd Divisional Area will be retained by 8th Division:-

   Bn. H.Q.   ...   BELLEVUE.
   One of the 2 Bn. H.Q. at MEETCHEELE.
   Advanced Bn. H.Q. and Aid Post, MOSSELMARKT.

   The 8th Division will have exclusive rights of traffic on the extensions of No.5 Track S. of the BELLEVUE - VINDICTIVE CROSS ROADS Road. 8th Division may use the last mentioned road for pack transport except when otherwise ordered from Div. H.Q. These occasions will be rare, and ample notice will be given.

   (b)   It is hoped to obtain accommodation for two Companies just S. of BELLEVUE. 23rd Inf. Bde. will be notified as early as possible.

7.   ACKNOWLEDGE.

                                                        Lieut.-Colonel,
                                                        General Staff.

Issued at 8.30 p.m.
                                                                P.T.O.

Copies to:-
- No.1 23rd Inf. Bde.
- 2 24th Inf. Bde.
- 3 25th Inf. Bde.
- 4 G.O.C., R.A.
- 5 C.R.E.
- 6 22nd D.L.I.
- 7 D.M.G.O.
- 8 23rd M.G. Coy.
- 9 24th M.G. Coy.
- 10 25th M.G. Co.
- 11 218th M.G. Coy.
- 12 O.C., Signals.
- 13 "Q".
- 14 A.D.M.S.
- 15 VIII Corps "G".)
- 16 VIII Corps "Q".)
- 17 62nd H.A.G.   ) For information.
- 18 32nd Division.   )
- 19 33rd Division.   )
- 20 War Diary.
- 21 File.

SECRET.   8th Division No.G.97/38.

23rd Inf. Bde.
24th Inf. Bde.
25th Inf. Bde.
23rd M.G. Coy.
24th M.G. Coy.
25th M.G. Coy.
218th M.G. Coy.
D. M. G. O.

---

1. The following reliefs will take place among the Machine Guns of the 32nd, 8th and 33rd Divisions on the night of 25th/26th November, 1917:-

2. 5 guns 92nd Machine Gun Coy. will relieve 5 guns 24th Machine Gun Coy. at 'D' Group (BEETCHESLE).

3. 1 gun 92nd Machine Gun Coy. will relieve 1 gun 24th M.G. Coy. at VENTURE FARM.

4. O.C., 24th M.G. Coy. will arrange to have guides at Bde. H.Q., WIELTJE DUGOUTS at 3 p.m. 25th November to lead the incoming teams to Advanced Coy. H.Q.

5. 1 Gun 24th M.G. Coy. will relieve 1 gun of the 100th M.G. Coy. at D.6.b.78.24. This gun will then come under the command of 'A' Group Section Officer.

6. Two guns 24th M.G. Coy. will relieve 2 guns 100th M.G. Coy. at D.6.a.91.03. and D.6.a.88.15.
These guns will then form a Group lettered 'E', under the command of a Section Officer with Headquarters at the Concrete Pill-Box at D.6.d.05.03.

7. Details of these reliefs will be arranged between Company Commanders.

8. Barrage lines for the 23rd M.G. Coy. will be altered to a line from V.24.d.65.30. to W.19.c.44.10. to W.25.d.25.55. at 8 a.m. 26th November.

9. From the morning of the 26th November, Machine Gun Dispositions will be as shown on the attached map.

8th Division,
24th November, 1917.

Lieut.-Colonel,
General Staff.

Copies to:-
VIII Corps.
VIII Corps M.G.O.
33rd Division.
32nd Division.
14th Division.

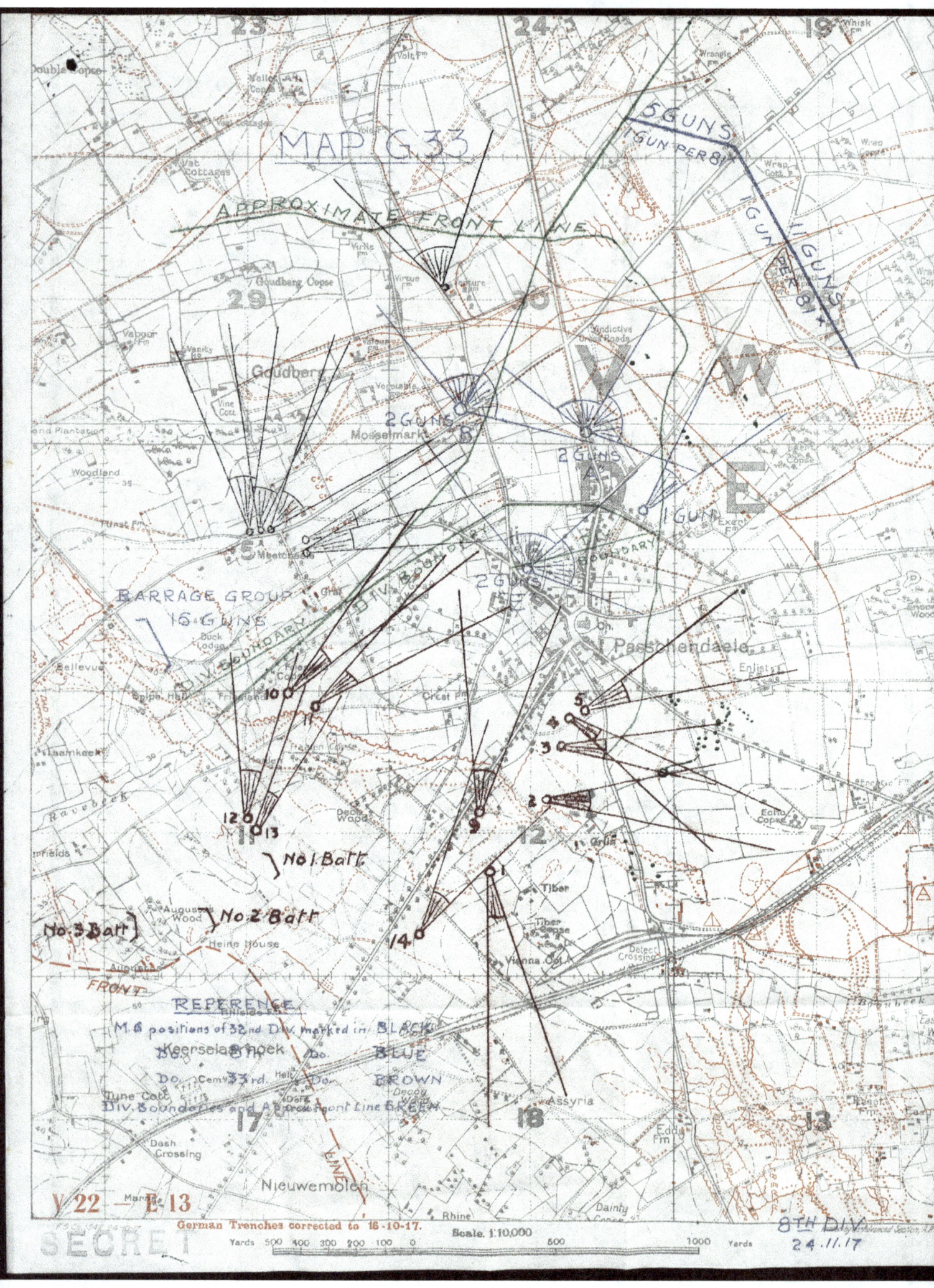

Army Form C. 2118.

25 M.G. Coy
Vol 24

WAR DIARY
or
INTELLIGENCE SUMMARY.
(Erase heading not required.)

Place	Date	Hour	Summary of Events and Information	Remarks and references to Appendices
LINE near PASSCHENDAELE	1/12/17		On the night of the 1st/2nd the 25th Inf. Bde took over the 8th Division front and	APPENDIX I Orders for the assembly & attack of the Bde.
FRANKFORT LINES ST. JEAN (Sheet 28)			were allotted for an attack in conjunction with the Corps to our left.	APPENDIX II Orders for the Company
			The Company co-operated by forming a battery of 16 guns for barrage.	APPENDIX III Action of Coy in the attack.
	2/12/17		In the attack on the enemy of the 1st Div. at [illegible] the attack at 1.55 a.m. In advance of the action of the Company is attached.	
			Among the Casualties & attack the following communities occurred. LIEUT. R.N. CROODIE wounded, [illegible]; 2nd LT R. CHALK wounded; 1 2nd Lt killed; 10 OR wounded. [illegible] 1 OR in hospital. A.S.	
	3/12/17		On the night of the 2nd/3rd the 25th Inf Bde were relieved in the line by the 21st Bde of manner back to the WYTLJE area. The whole Division was now moving back having been relieved by the 14th Div. During the 2nd Bde moved the 25th & 21st M.G. Companies into and relieved with the 13th in the line but were relieved tonight. Relief of Company by the 41st & 42nd Companies were complete at 9.00 pm & the Company moved back to M. Transport lines ST JEAN A.S.	APPENDIX IV Orders for relief & broken manner of Rels. APPENDIX V Relief Orders

WAR DIARY
or
INTELLIGENCE SUMMARY.
(Erase heading not required.)

Army Form C. 2118.

Place	Date	Hour	Summary of Events and Information	Remarks and references to Appendices
SAINT JEAN road back to VLAMERTINGHE Area	4/12/17		Transport left SAINT JEAN about 12.30 p.m. VLAMERTINGHE Station and rest of Company followed in lorries at 1 p.m. Whole Company entrained and left VLAMERTINGHE about 4 o'c.p.m., reaching WIZERNE (Sht. 36 D) about 9 o'c.p.m. Then detrained and marched to WESTBECOURT (Sheet 27 A — V 14) and were in the Car at "BOIS RIDOULT". Battalion will probably rest for 3 weeks. 2 O.R. from hospital.	APPENDIX VI Movement Order
WEST BECOURT V 14 (Sheet 27 a)	5/12/17	11.0 a.m.	Reveille. Remainder of day spent in cleaning clothes & personal equipment. 2 O.R. rejoined Coy.	at 2.30 a.m. 5/12/17 Battalion woke
	6/12/17		Cleaning guns & fighting equipments in the morning. Line of difference inspected. Inspection of kit in afternoon at 3 O.R. to hospital. 1 Lieut. F.R. SPOONER & 2 O.R. from M.G. School. 10 O.R. joined Coy.	
	7/12/17		Morning devoted to Drill, P.T., and cleaning harness. 2 Lt. PRITCHARD & 2 O.R. leave to U.K. 1 O.R. to M.G. School at Morning devoted to Drill, P.T., and overhauling of kit, etc. at	
	8/12/17			

Army Form C. 2118.

WAR DIARY
or
INTELLIGENCE SUMMARY.
(Erase heading not required.)

Instructions regarding War Diaries and Intelligence Summaries are contained in F. S. Regs., Part II. and the Staff Manual respectively. Title pages will be prepared in manuscript.

Place	Date	Hour	Summary of Events and Information	Remarks and references to Appendices
WEST DE OOYCK V.14. (Sheet 27A).	9/2/17		Sunday. Refer Church in morning. Parade for Church Union at 5.30pm.	
	10/2/17		1 O.R. from hospital & 1 O.R. joined Coy. Col. Training during day in accordance with Training Programme attached.	APPENDIX VII Training Programme
			Started to Reorganise except for special parades.	Afternoon.
	11/2/17		Training as on 10/2/17.	
			1 O.R. joined Coy. 1 O.R. to hospital & 1 O.R. from hospital Col.	
	12/2/17		Training in accordance with programme. Col.	
	13/2/17		Training in accordance with programme. 1 O.R. to Conv. of Instruction (Colt Story)	
			Lieut STOCKLEY R.L. joined Coy. H.P.R.	
	14/2/17		2 O.R. evacuated 1 O.R. To Hospital W.T.R.	
			Training in accordance with programme. Capt Simmonds & 3 O.R. proceeded on leave to U.K.	
	15/2/17		Training in accordance with programme. 3 O.R. Returned from Leave 1 O.R. to Hospital W.T.R.	APPENDIX VIII Training Programme
	16/2/17		C of E Service in A Section Billet at 6.30pm. 2 O.R. to Hospital. 2 O.R. to Hospital. H.P.R.	
	17/2/17		Training in accordance with programme. Team of 10 Men from the Coy finished second in Batt Cross-country run.	
			1 O.R. from hospital. 1 O.R. joined Coy. W.T.R.	

Army Form C. 2118.

WAR DIARY
or
INTELLIGENCE SUMMARY.
(Erase heading not required.)

Instructions regarding War Diaries and Intelligence Summaries are contained in F. S. Regs., Part II. and the Staff Manual respectively. Title pages will be prepared in manuscript.

Place	Date	Hour	Summary of Events and Information	Remarks and references to Appendices
WESTBECOURT V.14. (Sheet 27A)	18/12/17		Training in accordance with Programme. Coy paraded for Baths at ACQUIN at 2.30pm	A.K.R.
	19/12/17		Training as on 18/12/17. LIEUT. P.H. STOCKLEY off to Coy appointed 2nd i/c 89th M.E. Coy	A.K.R.
	20/12/17		Training in accordance with Programme	A.K.R.
	21/12/17		Training in accordance with Programme. 3 O.R. have to U.K. Hosp.	A.K.R.
	22/12/17		Training as on 21st	A.K.R.
	23/12/17		Coy had divine Xmas Service. 2/Lieut Partlow returned from leave, also 2 O.R. 1 O.R. to Hospital.	A.K.R.
	24/12/17		Day spent in charging ammunition in Belts & packing limbers.	A.K.R.
	25/12/17		Transport less Coy moved off at 6 o.m. for the Proused area. There billets for first night were in the ZERMEZEELE area. Sections spent the day in charging Metta etc.	APPENDIX IX Movement Orders A.K.R.
	26/12/17		Coy moved off at 5.15 a.m. for WIZERNE where they entrained at 9.o.am Train moved off at 10.o am & arrived VLAMERTINGHE at 1.45 p.m. where Coy detrained and marched to Camp situated at H.7.a.2.9. Transport arrived in the Camp at 11.30 p.m. 1 O.R. to Hospital. LIEUT. E.A. CUFFE-ADAMS joined Coy from Base.	A.K.R.
SHEET 28 N.W.	27/12/17		Transport moved off at 10.45 am for YPRES, Standings situated at I.8.a.8.9. Coy moved at 12 o noon for Camp situated at C.27.c.7.5. Owing to the Coy being in support the few fighting limbers were taken up to C.27.c.7.5 as the the guns Centre. He moved up immediately orders were received. 2 O.R. to Hospital.	A.K.R.
	28/12/17		Section Inspection 9 o am. remainder of day spent in Cleaning Guns & Gun Equipment. 2 O.R. to Hospital. 1 O.R. from Prison	

Army Form C. 2118.

WAR DIARY
or
INTELLIGENCE SUMMARY.
(Erase heading not required.)

Place	Date	Hour	Summary of Events and Information	Remarks and references to Appendices
SHEET 28 N.W. C.27.C.7.5.	28/2/17		1 Saddler transferred to 214th M.G. Coy authority A.G. Office Base. 2 O.R. transferred to 212th M.G. Coy authority Base Adm. M.K.R.	
	29/2/17		Coy moved to new position at I.26.C.5.5 Capt Simmonds rejoined Unit from leave to UK. 3 OR to Hospital MR	
	30/2/17		Morning spent in cleaning guns etc & improving Camps Lieut Adams & 3 OR left for Mons Corner AA. 1 OR to Hospital MRR	
	3/12/17		Coy relieved 244th M.G Coy in the line 14 guns being in leaving position & 1 gun at WURST FARM. 2 guns of the 21st ? ? at KOREK. 3 O.R. from leave to UK. 1 OR to Hospital MRR	APPENDIX X RELIEF ORDERS

A Simmonds Capt
Commanding 25th M.G. Coy.

APPENDIX No. I

ORDERS & INSTRUCTIONS relating to the ASSEMBLY FOR and CONDUCT OF the 25th INF. BDE. ATTACK on 1st Dec. 1917.

SECRET.

25th Infantry Brigade No. G.1/8.

25th INFANTRY BRIGADE INSTRUCTIONS No.1.

1. The offensive will be resumed by the VIII and II Corps at a date which will be communicated separately, to those whom it directly concerns.

2. The operation will be carried out by the 25th Infantry Brigade in co-operation with the 32nd Division (II Corps) on the Left.

3. The 25th Infantry Brigade will attack with three Battalions disposed from Right to Left as follows:-
        2nd ROYAL BERKSHIRE REGT.
        2nd LINCOLNSHIRE REGT.
        2nd RIFLE BRIGADE.
The 1st ROYAL IRISH RIFLES will be in Brigade Reserve.

4. The objective probable Inter-Battalion, Northern Divisional and approximate Southern Divisional Boundaries are shewn on the attached Map "G.2". The 25th Infantry Brigade Boundaries coincide with the Divisional Boundaries.

5. The Northern Divisional Boundary Lines allot tactical responsibility for the BELLEVUE SPUR to the 32nd Division. It is understood, however, that the following sites for H.Q. and lines of approach within the 32nd Divisional Area will be allotted to the 8th Division.
(a) HEADQUARTERS.
        BELLEVUE.
        MEETCHEELE.
        MOSSELMARKT.
(b) Lines of Approach.
    The 25th Infantry Brigade to have:-
  (i) Exclusive right to the two duckboard tracks running South of the BELLEVUE - MEETCHEELE Road.
  (ii) Use of Main Road as far as BELLEVUE.
  (iii) Except on night of assembly from dusk to ZERO the right of pack traffic only on BELLEVUE - MEETCHEELE Road.

6. It is hoped that by the 26th November our line will have been extended on the Right to run from D.6.b.9.2. through W.25.c.3.0. to W.25.c.1.7. One the Left TEALL COTTAGE is already in our hands.

7. ACKNOWLEDGE.

                                    Captain,
                                 A/Brigade Major,
23rd November, 1917.   25th Inf. Bde.

Issued to:-
G. O. C.	25th T.M.Bty.
Brigade Major.	23rd Inf. Bde.
Staff Captain.	24th Inf. Bde.
2nd Lincoln Regt.	8th Division.
2nd R.Berks Regt.	War Diary.
1st R.Irish Rifles.	Office.
2nd Rifle Brigade.	
25th M.G.Coy.	

No map issued
with this copy

SECRET.

25th Infantry Brigade No.G.1/9.

25th INFANTRY BRIGADE INSTRUCTIONS No.2.

1. ~~25th Infantry Brigade will relieve the Brigade holding the Divisional front during the early part of Y/Z night. Each Battalion will relieve the troops holding the front within the boundaries between which it is going to attack.~~ *Cancelled*

2. Companies detailed to hold the line will move forward in advance. Guides will be provided by the Brigade in the line.

3. The leading wave of attacking Companies will form up on a tape running from E.1.a.1.4. to V.30.b.15.55. Direction tapes will be laid along the forming up tape every 50 yards. These tapes will be 50 yards long and will lead out along the line of advance towards the objective.

4. The tapes will be laid by the Brigade Intelligence Officer and a party of R.E. Instructions for the laying of the tapes are being issued separately to those whom it concerns.

5. ~~The second and third waves of attacking Companies will form up in columns of sections on a tape laid 25 yards in rear of and parallel to the leading wave.~~ *Cancelled*

6. 2nd ROYAL BERKSHIRE REGT. will form a defensive flank on the Right of the attack, and will have one Company in Battalion Reserve in D.6.b.

7. 2nd LINCOLNSHIRE REGT. will arrange to fill the gap caused by their left Boundary being askew.

8. 2nd RIFLE BRIGADE will make special arrangements to ensure that touch is maintained throughout the operation with the 32nd Division on their Left; particular attention being paid to joining hands at V.30.b.40.95. and V.24.d.60.15. This duty will be performed by an Officer.

9. Map "G" 5.attached shows the forming up tapes and the direction of the advance in each case.

10. ACKNOWLEDGE.

Captain,
A/Brigade Major,
25th Inf. Bde.

24th November, 1917.
Issued at 6.30 a.m.

Issued to:-
G.O.C.   25th M.G.Coy.
Brigade Major.   25th T.M.Bty.
Staff Captain.   23rd Inf. Bde.
2nd Lincoln Regt.   24th Inf. Bde.
2nd R.Berks Regt.   8th Division.
1st R.Irish Rifles.   War Diary.
2nd Rifle Brigade.   Office.

25th M.G.Coy

S E C R E T.

25th Infantry Brigade No.G.1/13.

Reference 25th Infantry Brigade No.G.1/10:-

For W.25.c.48.70. read W.25.c.43.83. (reading from the bottom grid).

25th November, 1917.
   Issued at 6.30 a.m.

                                          Captain,
                                 A/Brigade Major,
                                  25th Inf. Bde.

Issued to all recipients of 25th Inf. Bde. No.G.1/10.

SECRET.

25th Infantry Brigade No.G.1/19.

AMENDMENT No.1 to Maps "G.2" and "G.3" issued
with 25th Infantry Brigade Instructions No.1
and No.2 respectively.

The Boundary between the Right and Centre Battalions is amended to run as follows:-

    V.30.d.70.48. (Reading from bottom grid) - W.25.c.48.70.

Please make the necessary alteration to Maps "G.2" and "G.3".

                                                Captain,
                                      A/Brigade Major,
                                        25th Inf. Bde.

24th November, 1917.
Issued at 12 noon.

        Issued to:-   G. O. C.
                           Brigade Major.
                           Staff Captain.
                           2nd Lincoln Regt.
                           2nd R.Berks Regt.
                           1st R.Irish Rifles.
                           2nd Rifle Brigade.
                           25th M.G.Coy.
                           25th T.M.Bty.
                           23rd Inf. Bde.
                           24th Inf. Bde.
                           8th Division.
                           War Diary.
                           Office.

SECRET.

25th Infantry Brigade No.G.1/24.

25th INFANTRY BRIGADE INSTRUCTIONS No.3.

25th Inf. Bde. No.G.1/11 is cancelled and the following will be substituted:-

EQUIPMENT and AMMUNITION to be carried by attacking troops.

1. **1st and 2nd LINES.**
   (a) <u>Riflemen.</u> Rifle and bayonet. Bayonets to be blacked.
   170 rounds S.A.A.
   1 shovel.
   Valise.
   Iron Ration.
   Rations for day of attack.
   Water bottle full.
   2 Sandbags.
   2 Ground Flares.
   Small Box Respirator.
   Leather jerkin.
   Ground Sheet.
   1 Watson Fan per Section.

   (b) <u>Bombers.</u> As for (a) except:-
   120 rounds S.A.A. only.
   5 Mills Grenades.

   (c) <u>Rifle Bombers.</u> As for (a) except:-
   50 rounds S.A.A. only.
   8 Rifle Grenades.
   16 Cartridges for same.

   (d) <u>Lewis Gunners.</u> As for (a) except:-
   Nos. 1 & 2 carry no rifle or bayonet.
   50 rounds S.A.A. only.
   20 drums S.A.A. per Gun.
   Only 2 shovels per Gun.

2. **3rd WAVE**
   As for 1, except the following will be carried in addition:
   <u>Riflemen.</u> 100 rounds S.A.A. (i.e. 270 in all)

   <u>Bombers.</u> 2 Men 16 L.G. drums.
   Remainder 100 rounds S.A.A. (i.e. 270 in all)

   <u>Rifle Grenadiers.</u> 100 rounds S.A.A. (i.e. 270 in all)

   <u>Lewis Gunners.</u> 10 extra drums (i.e. 30 in all) S.A.A. per Gun.

3. 10 S.O.S. Grenades per Company, divided between Company H.Q., Platoon Commanders and Sergeants.

   1 box "Very" Lights divided between Companies.

Captain,
A/Brigade Major,
25th Inf. Bde.

27th November, 1917.
Issued at 7.30 p.m.

Issued to:- G.O.C.
Brigade Major.   25th M.G.Coy.
Staff Captain.   25th T.M.Bty.
2nd Lincoln Regt.   23rd Inf. Bde.
2nd R.Berks Regt.   24th Inf. Bde.
1st R.Irish Rifles.   8th Division.
2nd Rifle Brigade.   War Diary.
Office.

SECRET.

25th Infantry Brigade No. G.1/12.

25th INFANTRY BRIGADE INSTRUCTIONS No.4.

ASSEMBLY.

ROUTES FORWARD.

1. The two duckboard tracks mentioned in 25th Infantry Brigade Instructions No.1, para.5 (b) (1) will run as shown on the attached map No.G.4.

2. Pending further instructions, they will be known as "No.5 North" and "No.5 South" respectively.

3. Routes forward are allotted to Battalions as follows:-
    2nd Rifle Brigade.
        By road to WATERLOO, thence Track No.5 North.
    2nd Lincoln Regt.
        Track No.5 - Track No.5 South.
    2nd R.Berks Regt.
        Attacking Companies - Track No.5 - Track No.5 South.
        Support Company - By Road to WATERLOO, thence Track No.5 North.

4. GUIDES.
    Battalions will find their own guides for the attacking troops as far as the head of the duckboards.
    For this purpose, 2nd Lincoln Regt., 2nd R.Berks Regt. and 2nd Rifle Brigade will each send 1 Officer and 10 O.R. 24 hours in advance to reconnoitre the route to be followed by their Battalion. These parties will be found from those left out of the battle, and will return to their Camps immediately their guiding duty has been completed.

5. Guides on the scale of 1 per Company will be distributed by the Brigade Intelligence Officer at a point on the duckboards due South of BELLEVUE. These guides will lead Companies on to the tape at the Right of their respective Battalion boundaries.

6. It is possible that the tapes may not be laid or may be destroyed by shell fire and guides may fail to meet their Companies. Every Officer and Platoon Commander must know:-
    (a) The magnetic bearing of the forming up line -
        ($166°$ with Standard Compass)
    (b) The magnetic bearing of their advance -
        (2nd R.Berks Regt. and 2nd Lincoln Regt,
            $76°$ with Standard Compass.
        2nd Rifle Bde. $51\frac{1}{2}°$ "   "   "   )
    (c) The distance of the point on a road at which the forming up line crosses the road from any well defined object, e.g.:-
        2nd Rifle Brigade and 2nd Lincoln Regt.-
            170 yards from VINDICTIVE Cross Roads.
        2nd R.Berks Regt. - 300 yards from the Cross Roads in D.6.b.

7. ACKNOWLEDGE.

                                          Captain,
                                          A/Brigade Major,
                                          25th Inf. Bde.

25th November, 1917.
Issued at 6.30 a.m.
    Issued to:- G. O. C.   25th M.G.Coy.
                 Brigade Major.   25th T.M.Bty.
                 Staff Captain.   23rd Inf. Bde.
                 2nd Lincoln R.   24th Inf. Bde.
                 2nd R.Berks R.   8th Division.
                 1st R.Ir.Rifles.   War Diary.
                 2nd Rifle Bde.   Office.

SECRET.
Copy No...

25th INFANTRY BRIGADE ORDER No.259.

29th November, 1917.

1. (a) The VIII Corps is to assume the offensive at a date which will be communicated to all concerned.

   (b) The 32nd Division (II Corps) will attack on the Left of and simultaneously with the 8th Division. The 33rd Division on the Right will not be attacking.

2. (a) The attack of the 8th Division will be carried out by the 25th Infantry Brigade, H.Q., BELLEVUE.

   (b) Battalions of the 25th Infantry Brigade will attack as follows:-

       2nd R.Berks Regt. - On the Right.
         H.Q., V.30.d.4.2.

       2nd Lincoln Regt. - In the Centre.
         H.Q., MOSSELMARKT.

       2nd Rifle Brigade. - On the Left.
         H.Q., MEETCHEELE.

   (c) 1st.R.Irish Rifles will be in Support in D.6.a.
         H.Q., Not yet selected.

   (d) Details of the co-operation by 25th Trench Mortar Bty. will be notified later.

   (e) The objective of the Brigade, its boundaries and inter-Battalion boundaries are shown on Map "G.3" issued with 25th Inf. Bde. Instructions No.2, and amended in 25th Inf. Bde. No.G.1/10.

   (f) The attack will take place at an hour ZERO, which will be notified later.

   (g) At ZERO hour the Infantry will advance to the assault.

3. The approximate front line to be consolidated will be the objective line; old enemy trenches will, so far as possible, be avoided, but consolidation must be in depth.

4. Details of the Artillery co-operation will be notified later.

5. (a) A Machine Gun Barrage will be placed from ZERO plus 8 min. to ZERO plus 9 min. on the line W.25.d.1.5. - W.24.d.8.9. and on the line W.25.d.45.60. - W.19.a.1.3. from ZERO plus 9 mins. to ZERO plus 25 min. when fire will die down, ceasing at ZERO plus 6 hours 10 min. and reopening from 3 p.m. till 6 p.m. Avenues of approach will be searched approximately between the same hours.

   (b) 7 Machine Guns of the 24th Machine Gun Coy. will be employed for the close defence of the captured ground.

   (c) Machine Gun Companies of the Divisions on our Right and Left will be prolonging the second barrage line and will be searching all enemy approaches.

6. All Battalions and 25th Trench Mortar Bty. will be in their allotted positions for the attack by ZERO minus 2 hours.

7. (a) A contact aeroplane will fly over the area of the attack at 7.30 a.m. or as soon as the weather is sufficiently clear, and will call for flares by sounding its KLAXON Horn and by firing VERY Lights.

/(b)....

-2-

    (b) The Aeroplane will have the following distinguishing marks:-
      (i) A black plaque extending behind the lower planes.
     (ii) A dumbbell painted on the fuselage.
        (An illustration of these markings has been sent to all concerned).

    (c) As soon as an aeroplane with these markings gives the above signals, but not before, the most advanced Infantry will light GREEN flares and wave WATSON FANS.

    (d) A counter-attack patrol will be in the air during the morning following the attack for the special purpose of locating and notifying by wireless any enemy counter-attack.

8.   Watches will be synchronised as follows:-

    (a) 2nd Lincoln Regt. and 2nd Rifle Brigade will each send a representative to WIELTJE DUGOUTS at 2 p.m. to synchronise watches with an Officer of the Divisional Staff.

    (b) A representative of the Brigade Staff will synchronise watches at Battalion Headquarters at BELLEVUE and MEETCHEELE between the hours of 4 and 5 p.m.

    (c) The telephone will not be used for synchronisation of watches.

10. (a) 25th Inf. Bde. Instructions Nos. 1 - 4 as already issued and amended are hereby confirmed and rendered operative as Orders.

    (b) 8th Division Instructions Nos.1 - 6 are confirmed and will be complied with and treated as Orders in so far as they refer to Units.

11.   ACKNOWLEDGE.

                                                                 Captain,
                                            A/Brigade Major,
Issued at 8 p.m.   25th Inf. Bde.

Issued to:-

Copy No.1. G.O.C.   Copy No. 15. 25th Field Amb.
     2. Brigade Major.   16. 8th Division "G".
     3. Staff Captain.   17. 8th Division "Q".
     4. Bde. Signals.   18. C.R.E. 8th Div.
     5. 2nd Lincoln Regt.   20. C.R.A.   "   "
     6. 2nd R.Berks Regt.   21. A.D.M.S.
     7. 1st R.Irish Rifles.   22. 32nd Division.
     8. 2nd Rifle Brigade.   23. 33rd Division.
     9. 25th M.G.Coy.   24. 41st Inf. Bde.
   10. 25th T.M.Bty.   25. 97th Inf. Bde.
11, 24th M.G.Coy.   26. War Diary.
   12. 218th M.G.Coy.   27. Office.
   13. 23rd Inf. Bde.
   14. 24th Inf. Bde.

Secret.

ADDENDUM No.1 to 25th INFANTRY BRIGADE
Order No.259.
----

1. The following contains the details of the 25th Trench Mortar co-operation referred to in para. 2(b) of 25th Infantry Brigade Order No.259.

2. 2 Guns will be established in previously prepared Emplacements about V.30.b.5.0. with at least 100 rounds of ammunition at the position.

3. The guns will only fire as the tactical situation demands and must be prepared to open fire on any Strong Point which may offer resistance to the attacking troops. Requests for Trench Mortar fire should be sent direct by the Officer requiring support to the Officer i/c of the Guns at the emplacements.

4. When the attacking troops are considered to have reached their objective, one gun will be pushed forward in close support to the most advanced troops, to a point on the road running N.E. through VINDICTIVE CROSS ROADS.

5. As much ammunition as possible, up to half the remaining rounds will be carried to the Forward position and fire will be opened on any counter attacks which may threaten our front.

Captain,
A/Brigade Major,
25th Inf. Bde.

29th November, 1917.

Issued at 11.30 p.m.

Issued to all recipients of 25th Infantry
Brigade Order No.259.

SECRET.

Copy No. 11.

25th INFANTRY BRIGADE ORDER No.255.

27th November 1917.

1. 25th Infantry Brigade (less 25th Machine Gun Coy.) will relieve the 24th Infantry Brigade in Support on November 29th and will move to ST. JEAN Area.

2. Movements and locations will be in accordance with Table "A".

3. No unit will pass Road Junction, I.2.c.2.3. before 2.30 p.m.

4. 2nd Lincoln Regt. will ensure that 2nd Royal Berks. Regt. and 2nd Rifle Brigade are clear before moving onto Main POPERINGHE - VLAMERTINGHE Road. Similarly 2nd Rifle Brigade will ensure that 2nd R.Berks Regt. are clear before moving on to this road.

5. Distances as laid down under Traffic Regulations in Corps Routine Order will be maintained.

6. Brigade Headquarters will close at present position at 12.30 p.m. and on completion of march will open at WILTJE DUGOUTS.

7. Completion of move will be reported to Brigade Headquarters.

8. ACKNOWLEDGE. ✓

Captain.
A/Brigade Major,
25th Inf. Bde.

Issued at 4 p.m.

Issued to:- Copy No. 1. G.O.C.
2. Brigade Major.
3. Staff Captain.
4. Bde. Signals.
5. Bde. Supply Officer.
6. Bde. Transport Officer.
7. 2nd Lincoln Regt.
8. 2nd R.Berks Regt.
9. 1st R.Irish Rifles.
10. 2nd Rifle Brigade.
11. 25th M.G.Coy.
12. 25th T.M.Bty.
13. Q.Mr. 2nd Lincoln R.
14. " 2nd R.Berks R.
15. " 1st R.Ir. Rifles.
16. " 2nd Rifle Bde.
17. 218th M.G.Coy.
18. 2nd Field Coy. R.E.
19. 23rd Inf. Bde.
20. 24th Inf. Bde.
21. 25th Field Ambce.
22. 32nd Division.
23. 33rd Division.
24. 8th Division "G".
25. 8th Division "Q".
26. C.R.E 8th Division.
27. C.R.A. " "
28. Left Group R.A.
29. Right " F.A.
30. No.4 Coy. Train.
31. A.D.M.S.
32. Area Commdt. ST. JEAN.
33. " " WILTJE.
34. War Diary.
35. Office.

TABLE "A".   Attached to 25th Infantry Brigade Order No.255.

Serial No.	Date.	Unit.	From.	To.	Route.	To pass VLAMERTINGHE Road junction, H.3.c.2.1.
1.	29th Novr.	Brigade Headquarters	RIDGE CAMP.	MENIN DUGOUTS, C.28.b.6.8.	VLAMERTINGHE. Road junction I.2.c.3.3.	1.25 p.m.
2.	do.	2nd LINCOLN REGT.	RED ROSE CAMP.	M.G.CAMP, C.27.a.3.0.		2.15 p.m.
3.	do.	2nd R.BERKS REGT.	RIDGE CAMP.	"B" CAMP, C.27.d.1.6.		1.45 p.m.
4.	do.	1st R.IRISH RIFLES.	VLAMERTINGHE	HASLER CAMP, C.27.d.5.2.		1.30 p.m.
5.	do.	2nd RIFLE BRIGADE.	"B" CAMP.	"F" CAMP, C.27.c.9.7.		2.0 p.m.
5.	do.	2 Sections 25th TRENCH MORTAR BATTERY.	"B" CAMP.	"E" CAMP.		2.30 p.m.

SECRET.

Copy No. 11

25th INFANTRY BRIGADE ORDER No.257.

29th November, 1917.

1. The following reliefs will take place on December 1st and night 1st/2nd December.
    (a) 1 Coy. 2nd Rifle Brigade relieves part of 1st R.Irish Rifles in the front line on frontage of attack of 2nd Rifle Brigade.
    (b) 1 Coy. 2nd Lincoln Regt. relieves part of 1st R.Irish Rifles in the front line on frontage of attack of 2nd Lincoln Regt.
    (c) 2nd R.Berks Regt. extends to the left in relief of part of 1st R.Irish Rifles as far as left boundary of attack frontage of the 2nd R.Berks Regt.
    (d) 1st R.Irish Rifles will relieve 2 Rear platoon Posts occupied by 2nd R.Berks Regt.

2. Command of the left and centre subsectors will pass to the C/O's. of 2nd Rifle Brigade and 2nd Lincoln Regt. respectively on the arrival at Battalion H.Q. of their Headquarter party.

3. On completion of relief:-
    (a) 1st R.Irish Rifles, less platoons holding the rear line of Supporting Posts, will move to D.6.a. where they will dig in.
    (b) 2nd R.Berks Regt. will move into " " positions " " " " as for "Z" day.

4. The above reliefs will be carried out as soon after dark as possible.

5. All details and provision of guides will be arranged between Commanding Officers concerned.

6. Routes forward are allotted as follows:-
    2nd Rifle Brigade.   Road and Track No.5 North.
    2nd Lincoln Regt.   Track No.5 and Track No.5 South.

7. An interval of 200 yards will be maintained between platoons during daylight.

8. The Companies 2nd Rifle Brigade and 2nd Lincoln Regt. will pass BELLEVUE at 5 p.m.

9. Completion of relief will be reported by 1st R.Irish Rifles by the Code word "FIXED".

10. ACKNOWLEDGE.

Captain,
A/Brigade Major,
25th Inf. Bde.

Issued at 12 noon.

Issued to:- Copy No. 1. G. O. C.   Copy No.15. QrMr, 1st R.Ir.Rif.
                    2. Brigade Major.   16. "   2nd Rifle Bde.
                    3. Staff Captain.   17. 218th M.G.Coy.
                    4. Bde. Signals.   18. 23rd Inf. Bde.
                    5. Bde. Supply Officer.   19. 24th Inf. Bde.
                    6. Bde. Transport Offr.   20. 25th Field Amb.
                    7. 2nd Lincoln Regt.   21. 8th Div. "G".
                    8. 2nd R.Berks Regt.   22. 8th Div. "Q".
                    9. 1st R.Irish Rifles.   23. C.R.E. 8th Div.
                   10. 2nd Rifle Brigade.   24. C.R.A.   "   "
                   11. 25th M.G.Coy.   25. A.D.M.S.
                   12. 25th T.M.Bty.   26. 41st Inf. Bde.
                   13. QrMr, 2nd Lincoln R.   27. War Diary.
                   14.   "   2nd R.Berks R.   28. Office.

SECRET.

Copy No... 11

25th INFANTRY BRIGADE ORDER No.258.

29th November, 1917.

1. On the night of the forthcoming operation, the date of which is being notified separately to those whom it concerns, the 25th Infantry Brigade will assemble for the attack. The frontages for attacking Battalions will be as described on Map G.3. already issued and amended.

2. Orders for the assemble of 2nd R.Berks Regt. 2nd Rifle Brigade and 25th Trench Mortar Bty. have already been issued. 25th Machine Gun Coy. will move under orders from Division H.Q.

3. The move forward of the 2nd Lincoln Regt. and 2nd Rifle Brigade will be carried out as follows:-

Unit.	From.	Route.	Move Commences at
2nd Lincoln Regt.	"A" CAMP.	Track No.5 and Track No.5 South.	4.30 p.m.
2nd Rifle Brigade.	CAPRICORN.	WIELTJE-BELLEVUE Road, Track No.5 North.	5 p.m.

4. Completion of forming up will be reported to Brigade H.Q. by the Code words "RELIEF COMPLETE".

5. ACKNOWLEDGE.

Captain,
A/Brigade Major,
25th Inf. Bde.

Issued at 12.30 p.m.

Issued to:-
- Copy No.1. G. O. C.
- 2. Brigade Major.
- 3. Staff Captain.
- 4. Bde. Signals.
- 5. Bde. Supply Officer.
- 6. Bde. Transport Offr.
- 7. 2nd Lincoln Regt.
- 8. 2nd R.Berks Regt.
- 9. 1st R.Irish Rifles.
- 10. 2nd Rifle Brigade.
- 11. 25th M.G.Coy.
- 12. 25th T.M.Bty.
- 13. QrMr, 2nd Lincoln R.
- 14. " 2nd R.Berks R.
- 15. " 1st R.Ir. Rifles.
- 16. " 2nd Rifle Bde.
- Copy No.17. 218th M.G.Coy.
- 18. 23rd Inf. Bde.
- 19. 24th Inf. Bde.
- 20. 25th Field Amb.
- 21. 8th Div. "G".
- 22. 8th Div. "Q".
- 23. C.R.E. 8th Div.
- 24. C.R.A. " "
- 25. A.D.M.S.
- 26. 41st Inf. Bde.
- 27. 97th Inf. Bde.
- 28. War Diary.
- 29. Office.

25th M.G.Coy

SECRET.

25th Infantry Brigade No.G.1/18.

2nd Field Coy., R.E.
Bde. Intelligence Officer.

LAYING OF TAPES.

1. The attached Map shows the tapes required to be laid for the forthcoming operation.

2. The forming up tape will be laid on iron pickets bearing white distinguishing marks as follows:-

   2nd R.Berks Regt. □

   2nd Lincoln Regt. ○

   2nd Rifle Brigade. △

3. Inter-Battalion boundaries will be marked by 2 pickets, about 18 inches apart, the right-hand picket bearing the distinguishing mark of the Battalion whose left boundary it denotes, and the left-hand picket bearing the distinguishing mark of the Battalion whose right boundary it denotes.

4. The second tape will be laid on wooden pickets painted white.

5. The direction tapes will connect with the forming up tape and the second tape.

6. Tapes and iron pickets are being provided by 2nd Field Coy. R.E. The wooden pickets will be delivered to 2nd Field Coy. R.E. by 25th Infantry Brigade.

7. The Brigade Intelligence Officer and a party of 6 men will live with the 2nd Field Coy. R.E. from the morning of "X" day.

8. The ground will be reconnoitred on the night X/Y when some important points will be marked. The tapes will be laid as early as possible on night Y/Z.

GUIDES.

9. Three guides for each of the 2nd Lincoln Regt. and the 2nd Rifle Brigade, and two for the 2nd R.Berks Regt. are required to guide Companies to the Right Boundary of their Battalion forming up tape.

10. These guides will be familiar with the position of the tapes and should lay guide tapes to guide them to their Battalion Boundaries if this is considered necessary.

11. Companies to be guided to the forming up tapes will come along the two duck board tracks South of the WESTHOEK - BELLEVUE ROAD, as follows:-

Unit.	Route.	Time at head of duckboards.
2nd R.Berks Regt. -	No.5 South.	8 p.m.
2nd Lincoln Regt. -	No.5 South.	9 p.m.
2nd Rifle Brigade. -	No.5 North.	9 p.m.

/12....

-2-

12. Guides will meet their Battalions on these Tracks near the head of the duckboards at these times.

13. All arrangements for the laying of the tapes and the provision of guides will be co-ordinated by the Brigade Intelligence Officer in consultation with O/C, 2nd Field Coy, R.E.

29th November, 1917.

Captain,
A/Brigade Major,
25th Inf. Bde.

Copies to :- 2nd Lincoln Regt.
2nd R.Berks Regt.
1st R.Irish Rifles.
2nd Rifle Brigade.
25th M.G.Coy.
25th T.M.Bty.

MAP. No. G.6

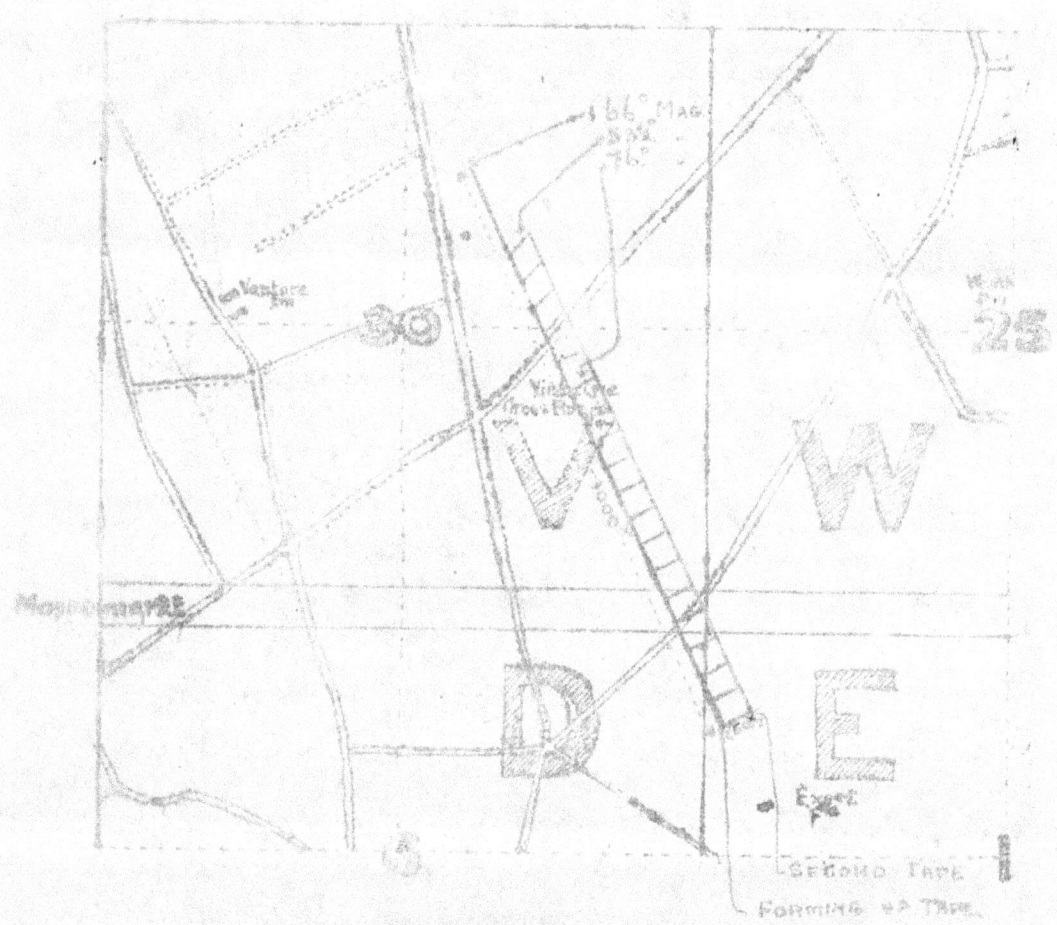

APPENDIX II

ORDERS for the COOPERATION of M.G's in the ATTACK on 1 Dec. 1917

SECRET   Copy No. 10

25th M.G. Company Operation Order No.

Ref. PASSCHENDALE $\frac{1}{10,000}$ 30th November 1917

      TIENDENBERG $\frac{1}{10,000}$

(1) On the night of the 1st./2nd. December the 8th Division will attack in conjunction with the 2nd. Corps on the left. The attack on the 8th Division front will be carried out by the 25th. Inf. Bde.

(2) Zero hour will be notified later.

(3) The Jumping Off Line and the Objective of the 8th. Division are shown on the attached map.

(4) The action of the Machine Guns of the Division will be as follows:-
    (1) 8 guns of the 24th Company will remain in their normal close defence positions.
        The remaining 8 guns will form a battery situated about D.5 d 85.15. This battery will be known as No.3.
    (2) The 23rd Company will form No.5 Battery, composed of 16 guns and situated about D 5 d 3.9.
    (3) The 218th Company will form Batteries 1 & 2, each composed of 6 guns and situated about D 5 b 95.40.
    (4) The 25th Company will form No.4 Battery, composed of 16 guns and situated about D 5 d 80.00.

(5) No.4 Battery will be divided into two halves.
    Right Half Battery - Guns 1 to 8 - Commanded by
                                       Lieut. R.N. GOODEVE.
    Left Half Battery - Guns 9 to 16 Commanded by
                                       LIEUT. K.V. WESTON.

(6) The battery will move up to the previously prepared position on the night of 1st./2nd December.
    (a) Sections will move off with pack mules from the camp as follows:-
            "A" Section   4.30 pm.
            "C" Section   4.40 pm
            "B" Section   4.50 pm.
            "D" Section   5.0 pm.
    (b) Route:-
            via WELTJE - KANSAS CROSS - D 4 d 5.0. road thence due south to No.5 Track Southern Extension.
        The leading Section will not pass SOMME Dressing Station before 5.45 pm.
    (c) Mules will off load on KANSAS CROSS - BELLEVUE road at D 10 b 2.8. and West of where Northern extension of No.5 Track crosses the road.
    (d) Sections will move with the Section Sergt. leading and the Officer in rear. The importance of keeping closed up and of not losing touch will be impressed upon all N.C.O's & men.

(7) It is hoped to acquire the dugout at GRAF as a Battery H.Q. Officers commanding Half Batteries will report to Battery H.Q. when all preparations are complete.

(8) Firing will commence at Zero plus 8 minutes as laid down in attached Table "A", and will continue in accordance with Tables "B" and "C".

(9) One of the primary duties of the battery is to respond to the S.O.S. call and that will have precedence over all other firing.

(10) Officers will impress upon everyone the importance of avoiding
all unnecessary movement by day in order to prevent the location
of the Battery by E.A..
O.C. Right Half Battery will arrange for an A.A. position about
200 yds. from the Battery. This will be manned during the hours
of daylight and fire will be opened with a view to preventing E.A.
from flying low over the Battery position.

(11) The Company will probably withdraw from the Battery position on
the night of 2nd./3rd. December.
Orders on this subject will be issued later.

A. Simmonds, Capt.
Commdg. 25 M.G. Company.

Copy No. 1. - O.C. Right Half Battery
       2. - O.C. Left Half Battery.
       3. - O.C. "A" Section.
       4. - O.C. "B" Section.
       5. - O.C. "C" Section.
       6. - O.C. "D" Section.
       7. - 2nd. 1/c.
       8. - D.M.G.O.
       9. - 25th. INF. Bde.
    10. - War Diary.
    11. - Retained.

TABLE "A"

RIGHT HALF BATTERY

GUNS 1 to 8 inclusive

Nº OF GUN	LOCATION	TARGET	DIRECTION	TRAVERSE	ELEVATION	TIME OF FIRING	Nº OF ROUNDS PER GUN PER MINUTE	REMARKS
1	D11.b.85.78	W.25a.44.69				ZERO +8 TO ZERO +9	12.5	LIFT ON TO "S.O.S." LINE AND FIRE AT 60 ROUNDS PER GUN PER MINUTE UNTIL ZERO + 25'.
2	D11.b.80.20	W.25a.36.83				"	"	
3	D11.b.83.86	W.25a.28.99				"	"	
4	D11.b.82.88	W.19c.20.13	LINE "A"			"	"	
5	D11.b.80.90	W.19c.14.26				"	"	
6	D11.b.80.93	W.19c.06.41				"	"	
7	D11.b.79.94	V.24D.97.57				"	"	
8	D11.b.78.96	V.24D.90.70				"	"	

LEFT HALF BATTERY

TABLE "A"

No OF GUN	LOCATION	TARGET	DIRECTION	TRAVERSE	ELEVATION	TIME OF FIRING	No OF ROUNDS PER GUN PER MINUTE	REMARKS
9	D11.d.77.97	W.25.d.04.42				Zero + 2	125	Shift on to "S.O.S." LINE
10	D11.d.77.99	W.25.c.97.57				"	"	own fire at 60 seconds per gun per minute until Zero + 25.
11	D5.d.76.00	W.25.c.88.73				"	"	
12	D5.d.76.63	W.25.c.87.87				Zero + 9	"	
13	D5.d.75.04	" W.25.a.75.14				"	"	
14	D5.d.74.06	LINE W.25.a.66.28				"	"	
15	D5.d.73.08	W.25.a.58.42				"	"	
16	D5.d.72.10	W.25.a.50.57				"	"	

TABLE "B"

RIGHT HALF BATTERY
Guns 1 to 8 inclusive.

No of Gun	Location	Target	Direction	Traverse	Elevation	Time of Firing	No of Rounds per Gun per Minute	Remarks
1	D.11.b.85.78	W.19.c.75.07				ZERO + 9 & ZERO + 25	60	Cross fire at zero + 25
2	D.11.b.85.82	W.19.c.67.24				4 m	"	and prepare to open fire
3	D.11.b.83.86	W.19.c.58.41				4 m	"	again at zero + 37 m
4	D.11.b.82.88	W.19.c.50.58 "S.O.S" LINE				4 m	"	in accordance with Table "C".
5	D.11.b.80.90	W.19.c.42.74					"	
6	D.11.b.80.93	W.19.c.33.89					"	
7	D.11.b.79.94	W.19.a.25.05					"	
8	D.11.b.78.96	W.19.a.16.22					"	

All "S.O.S." calls will be answered. Fire will be opened from time 1st "S.O.S." rocket is seen till 10 min from the time the last rocket is displayed.
Rate of fire per gun per minute for "S.O.S." — 125 rounds.

TABLE "B"

LEFT HALF BATTERY

Guns 9 to 16 inclusive

Nº OF GUN	LOCATION	TARGET	DIRECTION	TRAVERSE	ELEVATION	TIME OF FIRING	Nº OF ROUNDS PER GUN PER MINUTE	REMARKS
9	D.11.77.97	W25D 41.67				Zero + 9 to Zero + 25	60	Cease fire at Zero + 25
10	D.11.77.99	W25D 33.82				"	"	and prepare to open fire
11	D.5.D.76.00	W.25.b.25.12 S.N.17				"	"	again at Zero + 37 m
12	D.5.D 76.03	W.25.b.17.29 05				"	"	Accordance with Table "C"
13	D.5.D 75.04	W.25.b.07.45				"	"	
14	D.5.D 74.06	W.25.a.60.99				"	"	
15	D.5.D.73.08	W.25.a.92.77				"	"	
16	D.5.D 72.10	W.25.a.80.93				"	"	

All "S.O.S." calls will be answered. Fire will be opened from the time the 1st "S.O.S." Rocket is seen till 10 mins. after the last rocket is displayed. Rate of fire per gun ten minutes for "S.O.S." = 125 rounds.

TABLE "C"

Nº OF SERIES	Nº OF GUN	TARGET	TIME OF FIRING		Nº OF ROUNDS PER GUN PER MIN.	REMARKS
1	ALL GUNS	S.O.S. LINE	0+37 - 0+40	am to am	60	S.O.S. CALLS HAVE PRECEDENCE OVER THIS FIRING.
2			0+70 - 0+73	am to am	"	
5			0+105 - 0+108	am to am	"	
7			0+145 - 0+148	am to am	"	
9			0+195 - 0+198	am to am	"	
11			0+240 - 0+243	am to am	"	
13			0+295 - 0+298	am to am	"	
15			0+345 - 0+348	am to am	"	
1	ALL GUNS	"S.O.S." LINE		3.37 pm to 3.40 pm	60	S.O.S. CALLS HAVE PRECEDENCE OVER THIS FIRING.
2				4.10 pm to 4.13 pm	"	
5				4.45 pm to 4.48 pm	"	
7				5.25 pm to 5.28 pm	"	
9				6.15 pm to 6.18 pm	"	
11				7.0 pm to 7.3 pm	"	
13				7.25 pm to 7.28 pm	"	
15				8.5 pm to 8.8 pm	"	
Nº OF SERIES	Nº OF GUN	TARGET	TIME OF FIRING		Nº OF ROUNDS PER GUN PER MIN.	REMARKS

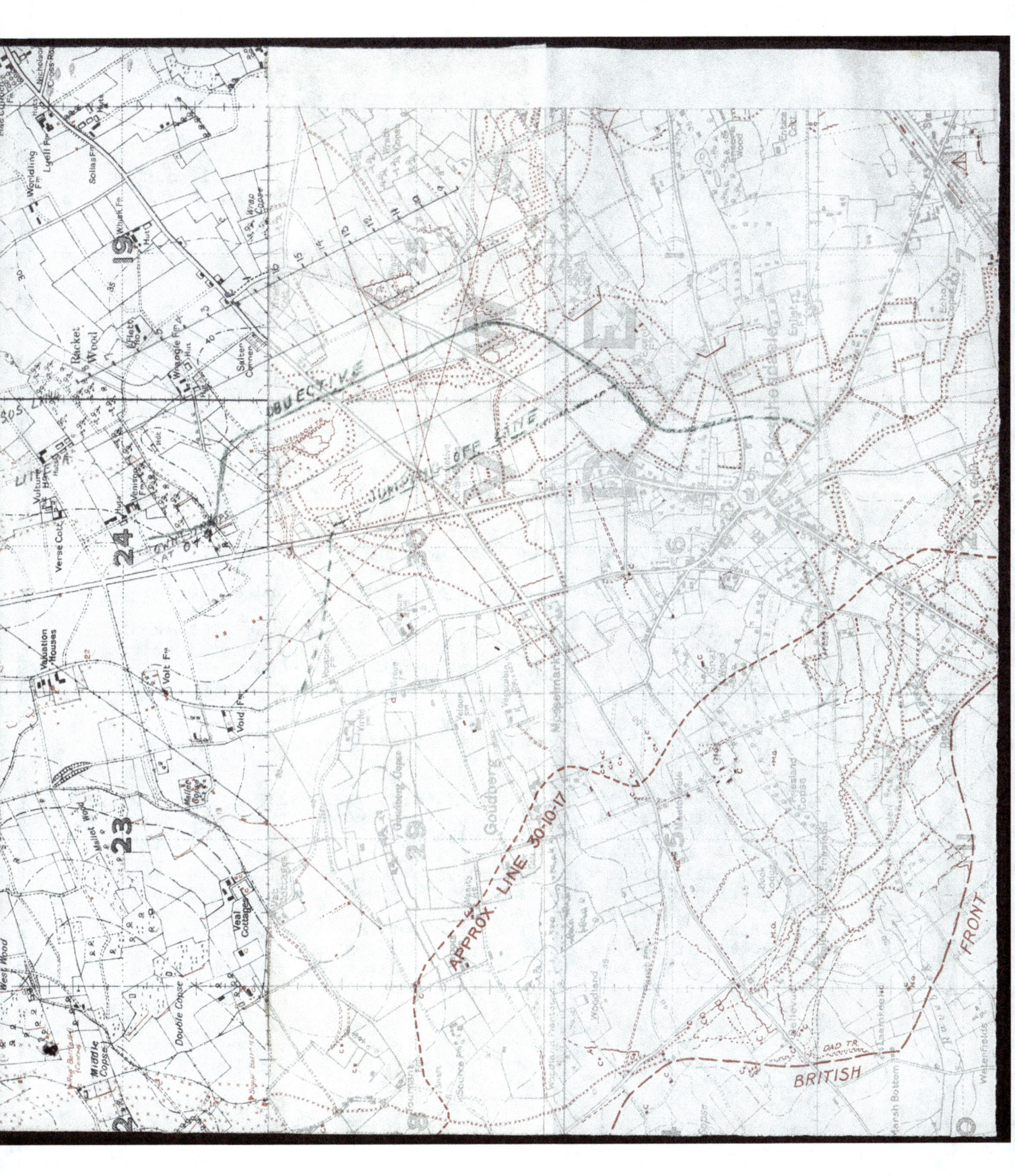

SECRET. 8th Division No.G.97/1/12.

Copy No. 15

8TH DIVISION INSTRUCTIONS No.4.

1. Machine Gun Companies of the 8th Division will occupy positions for barrage and harassing fire as shown on Table 'A'.

2. Company Commanders will arrange to have at least 15,000 rounds per gun concealed at their positions.

3. The positions will be constructed on a night to be notified by the D.M.G.O. to Company Commanders. All aiming posts will be put out on that night.

4. Company Commanders will ensure that the following precautions are adopted:-

   (a) Wooden tripod stands made use of.
   (b) New barrels used.
   (c) Depression stops made use of.
   (d) Calculations made for the error of the day according to "Meteor's" reports.

5. Fire action of the machine guns of 8th Division (less 7 guns of 24th Inf. Bde. in close defence positions) is shown on the attached Tables 'A', 'B', 'C' and Map G.34.

6. The close defence guns of 24th Inf. Bde. will be under the orders of G.O.C., 25th Inf. Bde. to whom an officer of 24th M.G. Coy. will report when 25th Inf. Bde. take over the line.

7. The S.O.S. Machine Gun Barrage of 8th Division is being prolonged to the South by the 33rd Division and to the N.W. by the 32nd Division as shown on the attached map G.34.

8. The 32nd and 33rd Div. Machine Guns will be carrying out harassing fire on their respective fronts on the same lines as the machine guns of 8th Division.

9. All machine gun Companies of 8th Division (less the 7 machine guns of 24th Inf. Bde. employed on close defence) will be under the orders of the Div. M.G.O. who will be at 25th Inf. Bde. H.Q., BELLEVUE, and who will be under the orders of G.O.C., 25th Inf. Bde.

10. S.O.S. Calls have precedence over all tasks allotted in the attached Tables 'A', 'B' and 'C'.

11. ACKNOWLEDGE.

Beddington.
Lieut.-Colonel,
General Staff.

27th November, 1917.

For distribution P.T.O.

Copies to :-

No. 1. Divisional Commander.
2. 23rd Inf. Bde.
3. 24th Inf. Bde.
4-9. 25th Inf. Bde.
10. 8th Div. Artillery.
11. C. R. E.
12. D. M. G. O.
13. 23rd. M.G.Coy.
14. 24th M. G. Coy.
15. 25th M. G. Coy.
16. 218th M. G. Coy.
17. O.C., Signals.
18. "Q"
19. A. D. M. S.
20. A. P. M.
21. VIII Corps.
22. VIII Corps R.A.
23. VIII Corps M.G.O.
24. 14th Division.
25-27. 33rd Division.
28-29. 32nd Division.
30. 62nd H.A.G.
31. 21st Squadron, R.F.C.
32. War Diary.
33. File.

TABLE 'A' ATTACHED TO 8TH DIVISION INSTRUCTIONS NO.4.

1	2	3	4	5	6	7	8
Serial No.	Coy.	No. of Guns.	No. of Battery.	Approximate Location.	Task.	Time of fire	Rate of fire per gun per min.
1.	218th	6	2	D.5.b.95.30.	Harassing fire in accordance with Table 'B'.		60.
2.	218th	6	3	D.5.b.90.45.	Harassing fire in accordance with Table 'B'.		60
3.	24th	8	1	D.5.c.20.25.	Harassing fire in accordance with Table 'B'.		60
4.	25th	16	4	D.5.d.9.3.	S.O.S. Barrage Lines from W.25.d.45.60. to W.19.a.1.3. and in accordance with Table 'C'.	From time of 1st S.O.S. rocket seen till 10 mins. from time of last S.O.S. rocket displayed.	125.
5.	23rd	16	5	D.F.d.3.9.	- ditto -	-ditto -	125.

NOTE: Batteries Nos.4 and 5 will fire from Zero plus 8' till Zero plus 9' on 'A' Line shown on attached Map at the rate of 125 rounds a minute, and will then lift on to the S.O.S. Barrage Line, on which they will fire at the rate of 60 rounds a minute till Zero plus 25' when they cease fire.

TABLE 'B' ATTACHED TO 8TH DIVISION INSTRUCTIONS NO.4.

Battery.	Task.	Series.1.	Series 2.	Series 3.	Series 4.	Series 5.	Series 6.	Series 7.
Battery No.1.	Task A	0 plus 37'– 0 plus 40'	0+1 hr.7'– 0+1 hr.10'	0+1 hr.25'– 0+1 hr.28'	0+2 hr.7'– 0+2 hr.10'	0+2 hr.25'– 0+2 hr.28'	0+3 hr.7'– 0+3 hr.10'	0+3 hrs.25'– 0+3 hrs.28'
	Task B	0 plus 25'– 0 plus 28'	0+1 hr.1'– 0+1 hr.4'	0+1 hr.31'– 0+1 hr.34'	0+1 hr.55'– 0+1 hr.58'	0+2 hr.31'– 0+2 hr.34'	0+3 hr.55'– 0+3 hr.58'	0+3 hrs.31'– 0+3 hrs.34'
	Task C	0 plus 31'– 0 plus 34'	0+ 55'– 0+ 58'	0+1 hr.37'– 0+1 hr.40'	0+2 hr.1'– 0+2 hr.4'	0+2 hr.37'– 0+2 hr.40'	0+3 hr.1'– 0+3 hr.4'	0+3 hrs.37'– 0+3 hrs.40'
Battery No.2.	Task D	0 plus 27'– 0 plus 30'	0+ 57'– 0+ 1 hr.	0+1hr.15'– 0+1hr.18'	0+1hr.57'– 0+2 hrs.	0+2 hr.15'– 0+2hr.18'	0+2 hr.57'– 0+3 hrs.	0+3 hrs.15'– 0+3 hrs.18'
	Task E	0 plus 15'– 0 plus 18'	0+ 51'– 0+ 54'	0+1hr.27'– 0+1hr.30'	0+1hr.45'– 0+1hr.48'	0+2hr.27'– 0+2hr.30'	0+2hr.45'– 0+2hr.48'	0+3 hrs.27'– 0+3 hrs.30'
	Task F	0 plus 21'– 0 plus 24'	0+ 45'– 0+ 48'	0+1hr.21'– 0+1hr.24'	0+1hr.51'– 0+1hr.54'	0+2hr.21'– 0+2hr.24'	0+2hr.51'– 0+2hr.54'	0+3 hrs.21'– 0+3 hrs.24'
Battery No.3.	Task G	0 plus 47'– 0 plus 50'	0+1hr.17'– 0+1hr.20'	0+1hr.35'– 0+1hr.38'	0+2hr.17'– 0+2hr.20'	0+2hr.35'– 0+2hr.38'	0+3hr.17'– 0+3hr.20'	0+3 hrs.35'– 0+3 hrs.38'
	Task H	0+ 55'– 0+ 58'	0+1hr.11'– 0+1hr.14'	0+1hr.41'– 0+1hr.44'	0+2 hr.5'– 0+2 hr.8'	0+2hr.41'– 0+2hr.44'	0+3 hr.5'– 0+3 hr.8'	0+3 hrs.41'– 0+3 hrs.44'
	Task J	0+ 41'– 0+ 44'	0+1hr.5'– 0+1hr.8'	0+1hr.47'– 0+1hr.50'	0+2hr.11'– 0+2hr.14'	0+2hr.47'– 0+2hr.50'	0+3hr.11'– 0+3hr.14'	0+3hrs.47'– 0+3hrs.50'

Battery.	Task.	Series 8.	Series 9.	Series 10.	Series 11.	Series 12.
Battery No.1.	Task A	0+4 hrs.7'– 0+4 hrs.10'	0+4 hrs.25'– 0+4 hrs.28'	0+5 hrs.7'– 0+5 hrs.10'	0+5 hrs.25'– 0+5 hrs.28'	0+6 hrs.7'– 0+6 hrs.10'
	Task B	0+3 hrs.55'– 0+3 hrs.58'	0+4 hrs.31'– 0+4 hrs.34'	0+4 hrs.55'– 0+4 hrs.58'	0+5 hrs.31'– 0+5 hrs.34'	0+5 hrs.55'– 0+5 hrs.58'
	Task C	0+4 hrs.1'– 0+4 hrs.4'	0+4 hrs.37'– 0+4 hrs.40'	0+5 hrs.1'– 0+5 hrs.4'	0+5 hrs.37'– 0+5 hrs.40'	0+6 hrs.1'– 0+6 hrs.4'

TABLE 'B' ATTACHED TO 8TH DIVISION INSTRUCTIONS No.1. (Continued)

Battery.	Task.	Series 8.	Series 9.	Series 10.	Series 11.	Series 12.
Battery No.2.	Task D.	0+3 hrs.57'- 0+4 hrs.	0+4 hrs.15'- 0+4 hrs.18'.	0+4 hrs.57'- 0+5 hrs.	0+5 hrs.15'- 0+5 hrs.18'.	0+5 hrs.57'- 0+6 hrs.
	Task E	0+3 hrs.45'- 0+3 hrs.48'	0+4 hrs.27'- 0+4 hrs.30'.	0+4 hrs.45'- 0+4 hrs.48'.	0+5 hrs.27'- 0+5 hrs.30'.	0+5 hrs.45'- 0+5 hrs.48'.
	Task F	0+3 hrs.51'- 0+3 hrs.54'	0+4 hrs.21'- 0+4 hrs.24'.	0+4hrs.51'- 0+4hrs.54'.	0+5 hrs.21'- 0+5 hrs.24'.	0+5 hrs.51'- 0+5 hrs.54'.
Battery No.3	Task G	0+4 hrs.17'- 0+4 hrs.20'.	0+4 hrs.35'- 0+4 hrs.38'.	0+5hrs.17'- 0+5hrs.20'.	0+5 hrs.35'- 0+5 hrs.38'.	0+6 hrs.17'- 0+6 hrs.20.
	Task H	0+4 hrs.5'- 0+4 hrs.8'.	0+4 hrs.41'- 0+4 hrs.44'.	0+5 hrs.5'- 0+5 hrs.8'.	0+5 hrs.41'- 0+5 hrs.44'.	0+6 hrs.5'- 0+6 hrs.8'.
	Task J	0+4 hrs.11'- 0+4 hrs.14'.	0+4 hrs.47'- 0+4 hrs.50'.	0+5 hrs.11'- 0+5 hrs.14'.	0+5 hrs.47'- 0+5 hrs.50'.	0+6 hrs.11'- 0+6 hrs.14'.

NOTES:
1. Series 1 - 6 inclusive will be fired again in the afternoon taking 3 p.m. as Zero hour.

2. Rate of fire for all the above, 60 rounds a minute.

3. For S.O.S. Calls, Series No.1 will be fired immediately by all guns and continued for 10 minutes after last S.O.S. Signal has been displayed. Rate of fire, 60 rounds a minute.

TABLE "C" ATTACHED TO 8TH DIVISION INSTRUCTIONS No.4.

Battery.	Target.	Series No. 1.	Series No. 2.	Series No. 5.	Series No. 7.
Battery No. 4.	S.O.S. Barrage Line.	0+37 - 0+40.	0+1hr.10 - 0+1hr.13	0+1hr.45-1hr.+48	0+2hrs.25 - 0+2hrs.28
Battery	Target.	Series No. 2.	Series No. 4.	Series No. 6.	Series No. 8.
Battery No.5.	S.O.S. Barrage Line.	0+57 - 0+1 hr.	0+1hr.32-0+1hr.35	0+2hrs.10-0+2hrs.13.	0+2 hrs.50 - 0+2 hrs. 53.
Battery	Target.	Series No. 9.	Series No.11.	Series No.13.	Series No.15.
Battery No.4.	S.O.S. Barrage Line.	0+3hrs.15 - 0+3hrs 18.	0+4 hrs. - 0+4 hrs. 3.	0+4 hrs. 55 - 0+4 hrs. 58.	0+5 hrs.45 - 0+5 hrs. 48.
Battery	Target.	Series No.10.	Series No.12.	Series No.14.	Series No.16.
Battery No.5.	S.O.S. Barrage Line.	0+3 hrs. 37 - 0+3 hrs. 40.	0+4 hrs. 27 - 0+4 hrs. 30.	0+5 hrs.20 - 0+5 hrs. 23.	0+6 hrs. 7 - 0+6 hrs. 10.

NOTES.
1. Series 1 - 9 will be fired again in the afternoon, taking 3 p.m. as Zero hour.
2. Rate of fire 60 rounds per gun per minute.

SECRET.   8th Division No.G.97/1/18.

                                                              Copy No....

            8TH DIVISION INSTRUCTIONS No. 6.
        ════════════════════════════════════

1.   MOVING UP.

        On the night of the attack, the 25th Inf. Bde. will have
to move up two battalions from CAPRICORN and 'A' Camp respectively.

2.   The routes available are:-

    (i)   WIELTJE - BELLEVUE Road and the Northern extension of
    No.5 Track.

    (ii)   No.5 Track and its Southern extension.

3.   In no case will any unit of 8th Division make use of No.6
Track or of BELLEVUE - VINDICTIVE CROSS ROADS Road between
points D.4.d.5.0. and V.30.c.7.3. both exclusive to 8th Divn.

4.(a)   No unit of 8th Division will pass a North and South line
through WIELTJE Cross Roads before 4.30 p.m., nor will any
unit East of that line move before that hour.

 (b)   The battalion at CAPRICORN will all be South of No.6
Track by 4.45 p.m.

5.   Machine Gun Companies will move up as follows:-

        25th M.G. Coy. via WIELTJE - KANSAS CROSS - D.4.d.5.0. road
                thence due S. to No.5 Track Southern Extension
                and thence to its position. Not to pass SOMME
                DRESSING STATION before 5.15 p.m. (5.45)

        218th M.G. Coy. via WIELTJE - KANSAS CROSS - D.4.d.5.0. road
                thence by No.5 Track Northern Extension to its
                position. Not to pass SOMME DRESSING STATION
                before 5.30 p.m.
                          6.0

        Mules of 25th and 218th M.G. Cos. will off load on
KANSAS CROSS - BELLEVUE Road at D.10.b.2.8., and West of where
Northern extension of No.5 Track crosses that road.

6.(a)   A.P.M., 8th Division will place experienced Traffic
Control Posts at the following places:-

    (i)   At the bifurcation of No.5 Track at D.9.d.8.5.
    to direct troops along the Northern or Southern Tracks
    according to the orders they have received from 25th
    Inf. Bde., who will send a copy of their orders on this
    subject to A.P.M.

    (ii)   At D.10.a.15.65. to see that all units of 8th
    Division arriving at that point proceed East by the
    Northern extension of No.5 Track and not North to PETER
    PAN.

    (iii)   At D.4.d.5.0. on the BELLEVUE - GRAVENSTAFEL Road
    to see that all units of 8th Division arriving at that
    point, proceed East by the Northern Extension of No.5
    Track and not by the BELLEVUE - MEETCHEELE Road.

 (b)   32nd Division are placing a Traffic Control Post at D.4.d.
5.0. on the BELLEVUE - GRAVENSTAFEL Road to see that all their
traffic moves by the duckboard track from PETER PAN to D.4.d.5.1.
                                                        /and ....

2.

and thence by the BELLEVUE - MEETCHEELE Road.

7. C.R.E. will erect additional notice boards as follows:-

(a) At D.9.d.8.5. (i)

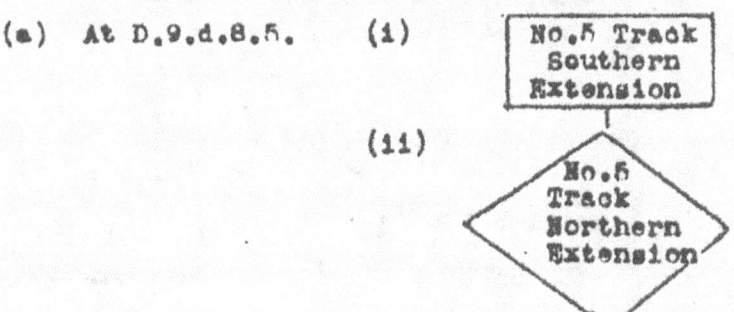

(b) At D.10.a.15.65. notice board referred to in para.(a) (ii) will be erected and a direction post placed on the track running North as follows:-

To PETER PAN

(c) At D.4.d.5.0. notice board referred to in para. (a) (ii) will be erected.

(d) Notice boards as described in para. (a) (i) and (ii) will be erected at such other places as the C.R.E. considers necessary.

8. A.P.M. will arrange direct with C.R.E. for such notice boards as are required for marking the route to Divisional Cage, and to the locality where 25th Inf. Bde. hand over their prisoners to 23rd Inf. Bde.

9. Track Maps revised up to date will be issued tomorrow.

10.(a) G.O.C., 25th Inf. Bde. will arrange that all routes from the end of the duckboard tracks forward to the forming up places, are carefully reconnoitred and marked with WHITE Posts. C.R.E. has arranged for a party of 2nd Field Co. R.E. to assist in this.

(b) Wherever forming up will take place within 150 yards of our present advanced line of posts, posts will be pushed out to cover it. This will be done nightly till the assault.

11. COMMUNICATIONS.

D.M.G.O. will arrange, in conjunction with O.C., Signals, for communication with all Machine Gun Cos. by runners and visual signalling.

12. ANTI-AIRCRAFT.

(a) G.O.C., 25th Inf. Bde. will arrange that heavy rifle and Lewis Gun fire is brought to bear on all hostile low flying aeroplanes. It is of the utmost importance that they should be brought down or driven off at once, as accurate and heavy hostile shelling of our positions is sure to follow a successful reconnaissance at a low height.

(b) D.M.G.O. will arrange that one Machine Gun per Coy. is equipped for Anti-Aircraft Duties during the hours of daylight, and that it is freely used against low flying hostile aircraft.

/13. .....

13. REPORTS.

  (a)   The following reports will be rendered:-

    (i)   That FORMING UP is completed by the Code Words "RELIEF COMPLETE".

    (ii)   Situation reports at Zero plus 45 minutes and every half hour afterwards till Zero plus 6 hrs. 45 mins.

  (b)   G.O.C., 25th Inf. Bde. will impress on the troops the importance of frequent reports giving full information in writing or on Situation Maps.

14.   ACKNOWLEDGE.

E. Boddington.
Lieut.-Colonel,
General Staff.

28th November, 1917.

Copies to:-
```
            No. 1   Div. Commdr.
                2   23rd Inf. Bde.
                3   24th Inf. Bde.
              4-9   25th Inf. Bde.
               10   8th Div. Arty.
               11   C. R. E.
               12   D. M. G. O.
               13   23rd M.G. Coy.
               13   24th M.G. Coy.
               15   25th M.G. Coy.
               16   218th M.G. Coy.
               17   O.C., Signals.
               18   "Q".
               19   A. D. M. S.
               20   A. P. M.
               21   VIII Corps.
               22   VIII Corps R.A.
               23   VIII Corps M.G.O.
               24   14th Division.
               25   33rd Division.
            26-27   32nd Division.
               28   62nd H.A.G.
               29   21st Squadron, R.F.C.
               30   War Diary.
               31   File.
```

SECRET.   8th Division No.G.97/1/22.

23rd M.G. Coy.
24th M.G. Coy.
25th M.G. Coy.
218th M.G. Coy.
D. M. G. O.

1.   In accordance with 8th Division No.G.97/1/18 of 28th November, the signalling communications for the Machine Gun Barrage Batteries will be as follows:-

2.   218th and 23rd M.G. Cos. will detail 2 runners each to remain at the Advanced Brigade Signalling Station at MEETCHEELE. Their communications will be by runner from Battery positions to MEETCHEELE and/then through Divisional Signals to Advanced Brigade H.Q.

3.   (a) 24th M.G. Coy. will establish a Lamp Signalling Station at a convenient position for both 24th and 25th Battery positions
        (b) 25th M.G. Coy. will establish another station at the present Company H.Q., D.10.b.53.55. to communicate with the 1st Station. Here, a runner from each of 24th and 25th M.G. Cos. will maintain communication with Advanced Brigade H.Q. at D.4.d.6.4.

    Station referred to in para 3(a) above At D10 b.53.55

4.   218th and 23rd M.G. Cos. will provide one runner each for the D.M.G.O.; to report to Brigade Headquarters, D.4.d.6.4. at an hour to be notified later.

                                                          [signature]

8th Division,   Lieut.-Colonel,
28th November, 1917.   General Staff.

    Copies to:- 25th Inf. Bde.
                O.C., Signals.

S E C R E T.   8th Division No.G.97/1/33.

        25th Inf. Bde.
        23rd M.G. Coy.
        24th M.G. Coy.
        25th M.G. Coy.
        218th M.G. Coy.
        G.O.C., R.A., 8th Div.
        C. R. E.
        D.M.G.O.
        62nd H.A.G.

---

1.   Reference 8th Division Order No.247 dated 28th November, para 2 (c), Zero Hour will be at *1.55.A.M.* on *2*nd December, 1917.

2.   *Acknowledge by wire*

8th Division,
30th November, 1917.

                                              Lieut.-Colonel,
                                              General Staff.

        Copies to:- VIII Corps.
                        32nd Division.
                        33rd Division.

SECRET.   8th Div. No. G.97/1/25.

                                      Copy No........7....

1.   The operations referred to in 8th Division Instructions Nos. 1 - 6 and in 8th Division Order No. 247, will take place on the night December 1st/2nd.   Zero hour will be notified later.

2.   The night of assembly will be the night December 1st/2nd.

3.   Watches will be synchronised as detailed in para. 8 of 8th Division Order No. 247 on December 1st.

4.   ACKNOWLEDGE BY WIRE. ✓

                                              E. Bedington
                                              Lieut.-Colonel,
8th Division,   General Staff.
29th November, 1917.

          Copies to :-
             1.   25th Inf. Bde.,
             2.   8th Div. R.A.,
             3.   C.R.E.,
             4.   D.M.G.O.,
             5.   23rd M.G. Company,
             6.   24th M.G. Company,
             7.   25th M.G. Company,
             8.   218th M.G. Company,
             9.   O.C., Signals,
            10.   22nd D. L. I.,
            11.   A. D. M. S.,
            12.   A. P. M.,
            13.   "Q",
            14.   VIII Corps,   )
            15.   32nd Division,   )
            16.   33rd Division,   )For
            17.   14th Division,   )information.
            18.   62nd H. A. G.,   )
            19.   21st Squadron, R.F.C.,)
            20.   War Diary,
            21.   File.

25th M.G. COMPANY.

APP III

Action of the Company in the Attack on night 1/2nd Dec.

(1) Orders Received.

It was laid down that the 16 guns would be grouped to form "No. 4 Battery," and would be situated about D 5 d 9.3.

The action of the battery was to be as follows:—

(1) To put down a barrage from 0+8 to 0+9 on a "Line A" about 400ˣ in front of the line on which the troops would be at that time.

(2) To lift at 0+9 on to the "S.O.S." Line about 450ˣ in front of the objective and to maintain fire on that line until 0+25.

(3) To fire a series of eight 3 mins. bursts at stated times on to the "S.O.S." Line between 0+37 and 0+5 hrs 43.

(4) To fire a series of five 3 min. bursts on to the S.O.S. at stated times between 3.37 pm and 6.18 pm on Dec. 2nd.

(5) To give immediate response to "S.O.S." calls; this duty to have precedence over all others.

(2) Preparations

(a) Site of Battery.

Orders were received on the night of 27th Nov. On the morning of the 28th Nov. I reconnoitred the ground and chose the battery position. The line decided on, D 11 b 85.80 — D 5 d 75.10, on the W. slope from CREST FARM, was selected because it was comparatively lightly shelled and was quite dry, thus allowing of digging.

(b) S.A.A Supply.

On the afternoons of the 28th and 29th Nov. the whole Company was turned out to carry up ammunition to the battery position. The ammunition was drawn at SPREE FM. Dump and conveyed by transport to the place where No. 5 track crossed the BELLEVUE — WATERLOO road. Thence it was man handled to the dump about D 5 d 35.20. In all 200,000 rounds were carried up.

On the night of 30th/1st tin belt-boxes per gun were

carried up and put in the gun pits.

(c) **Digging Positions**
On the night of the 30th Nov/1st Dec. beltboxes were carried up as stated above and also T frames for tripods. Each team then dug its position, made an emplacement, camouflaged the whole, and returned to camp as on the two previous nights.

(3) **Assembly.**
The Company moved up to its positions on the night of 1st Dec. in accordance with orders issued by Division. Assembly was complete about 9.0 p.m.
Just before off loading the mules "D" Section sustained 6 casualties, losing one entire team. Apart from this everything worked smoothly and the arrangements made seemed to be quite satisfactory.

(4) **H.Q. and Communications**
Headquarters were formed at GRAF and communication was established by lamp with the D.M.O.O. who was with Bde. HQ. at BELLEVUE, an intermediate station being made at D 10 b 5.2.

(5) **Firing**
Fire was opened according to programme both during the operation and on the afternoon of 2nd Dec. About 4.0 p.m. however the "S.O.S." signal was displayed. Fire was immediately opened and maintained for 45 mins. The normal programme was then resumed until 6.18 p.m. when firing ceased.
No further firing occurred before the Company was relieved.

(6) **Change of Position.**
After completing their firing programme about 6.18 p.m. 2nd Dec. the 24th Coy. on our left evacuated their barrage position in accordance with orders previously issued. Two guns on the left of the Battery moved down a few yards and occupied two of the evacuated positions. This was done in view of the fact that their own gun positions lay in the direct line of fire of an enemy gun — the cone of which crossed the battery at right angles.

(7) **Relief.**
On the afternoon of the 3rd Dec. the 4 guns on the right were relieved by the 41st M.G. Coy. and the remainder by the 42nd Coy. Relief was complete at 5.0 p.m.

(1) <u>Casualties</u>:
    2 Off. wounded
    4 O.R. killed and 10 wounded.

Six of the O.R. casualties occurred on the way up to the positions. The battery came in for a good deal of the general shelling, which occurred on the morning and evening of 2nd Dec. but none of the shelling seemed to have the Battery as its target.

(2) <u>Losses in Material</u>

One gun and two mountings, together with a small amount of equipment was destroyed by shell fire.

6/12/17

A Simmonds Capt
Commanding 25th M.G. Coy.

APPENDIX No IV

SECRET.
Copy No. 11

25th INFANTRY BRIGADE GROUP ORDER No.260.

Reference Maps:-
    Sheets 28 N.W. 1/20,000.
    HAZEBROUCK, 5A.

1. 25th Infantry Brigade group Order No.256 and the attached Table "A" to 25th Infantry Brigade Group Order No.256 dated 28th Novr. 1917 are cancelled and the following substituted.

2. The 25th Infantry Brigade will relieve the 23rd Infantry Bde. in the line on November 30th and on the night of Novr 30th/Dec.1st. All details later.

3. The 8th Division (less Artillery) will be relieved by the 14th Division in the Left Sector of the VIII Corps Front commencing 30th November 1917.

4. The 25th Inf. Bde. will be relieved in the line by the 41st Inf. Bde. on the night 2nd/3rd December and withdraw to WIELTJE Area. All details later.

5. On December 3rd the 25th Inf. Bde. Group, composed as under, will move from WIELTJE to BOISDINGHEM Area by train, with the exception of the Transport, which will go by road.

6. 25th Inf. Bde. Group consists of:-
    25th Inf. Bde. (less 25th M.G.Coy).
    23rd Machine Gun Coy.
    24th Machine Gun Coy.
    25th Field Ambulance.
    No. 4 Company Train.

7. Train arrangements and moves to and from detraining and entraining Stations, will be notified by the Staff Captain.

8. Transport will march to the BOISDINGHEM Area in accordance with the attached Table "A".

9. Advanced parties for the Transport will report to the Area Commandant, WINNIZEELE for billets in the STEENVOORDE Artillery Area (OUDERZEELE) before noon on the day of arrival.

10. The Transport of the Brigade Group will be under the command of the Brigade Transport Officer, 25th Infantry Brigade.

11. Motor Ambulance Cars will move under orders to be issued by O/C, 25th Field Ambulance. Route shown on attached Table to be followed and all cars to be clear of Cross Roads G.4.d.4.4. by 8.45 a.m.

12. ACKNOWLEDGE. ✓

                                      Captain,
                                    A/Brigade Major,
                                    25th Inf. Bde.

ISSUED at 8.30 a.m.
Issued to:- Copy No. 1. G.O.C.
              2. Bde. Major.
              3. Staff Captain.   No.15. QRMR, 2nd Lincoln R.
              4. Bde. Signals.   16. "   2nd R.Berks R.
              5. Bde. Supply Officer.17. "   1st R.Ir.Rifles.
              6. Bde. Transport Offr.18. "   2nd Rifle Bde.
              7. 2nd Lincoln Regt.   19. 23rd Inf. Bde.
26. A.D.M.S. 8th Div. 8. 2nd R.Berks Regt.   20. 24th Inf. Bde.
27. No. 4 Coy Train.   9. 1st R.Irish Rifles. 21. 41st Inf. Bde.
28. Area Commdt.   10. 2nd Rifle Brigade. 22. 8th Div. "G".
    WINNIZEELE.   11. 25th M.G. Coy.   23. 8th Div. "Q".
29. " " WIELTJE.   12. 25th T.M. Bty.   24. C.R.A. 8th Div.
30. War Diary.   13. 23rd M.G.Coy.   25. C.R.E. 8th Div.
31. Office.   14. 24th M.G.Coy.

P.T.O

TABLE "A" to accompany 25th Infantry Brigade Group Order No.260.

T R A N S P O R T.

Serial No.	Date.	Unit.	Starting point.	Time.	Destination.	Route.	Remarks.
1.	2nd Decr.	Brigade H.Q.		8.7 a.m.	OUDEZEELE AREA.	POPERINGHE - CASSEL - ARQUES - BOISDINGHEM AREA.	
2.	do.	2nd R.Berks Regt.		8.8 a.m.			All Transport to be clear of
3.	do.	2nd Rifle Bde.		8.11 a.m.			
4.	do.	2nd Lincoln Regt.	G.3.c.8.6.	8.14 a.m.			Cross Roads, G.4.d.4.4. by
5.	do.	1st R.Ir. Rifles.		8.17 a.m.			
6.	do.	23rd M.G. Coy.		8.20 a.m.			8.45 a.m.
7.	do.	24th M.G. Coy.		8.23 a.m.			
8.	do.	25th Field Amb.		8.26 a.m.			
9.	do.	No.4 Coy. Train.		8.30 a.m.			
10.	3rd Decr.	25th Inf. Bde. Group Transport.	--	--	BOISDINGHEM AREA.		To follow transport of 23rd Inf. Bde. All times and details to be arranged by Brigade Transport Officer, so that the Brigade Group will be clear of CASSEL by 9 a.m.

N.B. One hundred yards interval must be maintained between each Group of 6 vehicles.

APPENDIX NO. V

SECRET.

Copy No. 32

ADDENDUM No.1 to 8TH DIVISION ORDER No.246.

1. The 25th and 218th M.G. Cos. will remain in the line, when the 25th Inf. Bde. is relieved, until the night of the 3rd/4th December, when they will be relieved by two Machine Gun Companies of 14th Division under arrangements made between D.M.G.O's. 8th and 14th Divisions.

2. When the 25th Inf. Bde. is relieved, 25th and 218th M.G. Companies will come under orders of G.O.C., 41st Inf. Bde.

3. The transport of 25th and 218th M.G. Companies will not now form part of 25th Inf. Bde. Group: it will be available to assist in the withdrawal of 23rd and 24th M.G. Cos. from the line on the night of 2nd/3rd December, under arrangements to be made by D.M.G.O.

4. On night 2nd/3rd December, 218th M.G. Coy. will take over the close defence guns from 24th M.G. Coy. under orders of G.O.C., 25th Inf. Bde. 25th M.G. Coy. will be responsible for whole of the M.G. barrage on Div. front when the 23rd M.G. Coy. is withdrawn.

5. D.M.G.O. will remain with G.O.C., 41st Inf. Bde. until 25th and 218th M.G. Cos. are relieved.

6. Separate orders will be issued for the move of 25th and 218th M.G. Companies to the WIZERNES Area.

7. 25th & 218th M.G. Cos. to acknowledge.

8th Division,
29th November, 1917.

Lieut.-Colonel,
General Staff.

Copies to:-
No. 1 23rd Inf. Bde.
2 24th Inf. Bde.
3 25th Inf. Bde.
4 G.O.C., R.A.
5 C.R.E.
6 22nd D.L.I.
7 D.M.G.O.
8 218th M.G. Coy.
9 O.C., Signals.
10-12 "Q".
13 A.D.M.S.
14 A.P.M.
15 D.A.D.O.S.
17 S.S.O.
18 8th Div. Supply Col.
19 41st Inf. Bde.
20 VIII Corps "G" *
21 VIII Corps "Q" *
31 D.A.D.V.S.
32 25 M.G.C.

No. 22-23 14th Div. *
24 32nd Divn. *
25 33rd Divn. *
26 War Diary.
27 File.
28 15th M.V.S.
29 O.C. Div. Train.
30 Area Commdt.
   WINNIZEELE.

* For information.

Secret   Copy No 7

25th M. G. Company
Relief Order No 25

Ref. 28 N.E. 1/20,000
28 N.W 1/20,000   2. Dec. 1917
PASSCHENDAELE 1/10,000

(1) The Company will be relieved in the line on the evening of the 3rd Dec. 1917.
   The 4 guns of A Section will be relieved by 4 guns of the 41st M.G. Coy.
   B, C & D Sections will be relieved by 12 guns of the 42nd M.G. Coy.

(2) Guides. Lieut Rennie will arrange to supply one guide per two guns & one guide for Coy. H.Q. from the personnel at the Transport Lines. These guides will parade at follows:—
   Guides for 41st Coy — WELTJE X roads at 1.45 p.m.
   "   "   42nd " — ST. JEAN X roads at 1.15 p.m.

(3) 10 belt boxes per gun will be handed over and receipts obtained, but no other mobilisation stores.
   All trench stores will be handed over & receipts obtained.
   Officers will hand over barrage maps and full particulars of the "S.O.S." barrage.

(4) One limber for A & B Sections will be at the point where the road leaves the plank track at 6.0 p.m. and one for C & D Sections at 6.15 p.m.

(5) Officers will report completion of relief to an orderly who will be stationed at the late 23rd Coy. H.Q. at LAANKEEK.

(6) On completion of relief the command of the battery will pass to O.C. 42nd Company.

(7) Acknowledge.

                                         A Simmonds Capt
                                         Commanding 25th M.G. Coy
Copies to all Officers
41st & 42nd M.G. Coys.
Wandering
Retained

APPENDIX NO. VII

SECRET.   Copy No.... 1

ADDENDUM No.2 to 8TH DIVISION ORDER No.246.

1.   25th and 218th Machine Gun Companies will proceed to WIZERNES Area by train from VLAMERTINGHE Station on December 4th complete with Transport, under orders to be issued by 8th Division "Q".

2.   25th and 218th Machine Gun Coys. will acknowledge.

                                            E. Beddington.
                                            Lieut.-Colonel,
                                            General Staff.

1st December, 1917.

Copies to:-
   No.1   25th M.G. Coy.
     2   218th M.G. Coy.
   3-6   "Q".
     7   25th Inf. Bde.   )
     8   D.H.G.O.   )
     9   A.D.M.S.   )
    10   O.C., Signals.   ) For information.
    11   14th Division.   )
    12   VIII Corps "G".)
    13   VIII Corps "Q".)
    14   War Diary.
    15. File.

8th Division No.C/275/11/Q.

A.D.C. to G.O.C.
"G"
25th Infantry Brigade
25th M.G.Coy
218th M.G.Coy
D.M.G.O.
A.P.M.
8th Div.Signal Coy R.E.
H.Q. 14th Division.

Reference addendum No. 2 to 8th Divl Order No. 246.

1. 25th and 218th Machine Gun Companies will entrain complete with transport on the 4th December, on train which leaves VLAMERTINGHE Station at 4 p.m.
This train will arrive detraining station WIZERNES at approximately 7 p.m.

2. Transport with a loading party of 1 officer and 30 men per Company will arrive at VLAMERTINGHE three hours before the train is due to leave, remaining personnel arriving one hour before departure.

3. The 25th Machine Gun Company will detail an Officer to superintend entraining, and the 218th M.G.Coy will detail an Officer to superintend detraining.
Entraining officer should report to R.T.O. VLAMERTINGHE at 1.30 p.m. 4th December.

4. 10 lorries (5 for each M.G.Coy) will report Area Commandant's office, ST JEAN at 12 noon, to convey personnel blankets and kit to VLAMERTINGHE Station.
Guides will report Area Commandant, ST JEAN, in time to meet lorries.

5. Arrangements are being made for lorries to meet the train at WIZERNES to convey blankets and kit to billots.

Feilding
Lieut-Colonel,
2nd December 1917.   A.A. & Q.M.G., 8th Division.

1 Lorry to stop at Div. to pick up D.M.G.O. kit & Servant.

APPENDIX VII

Training Programme

25th M.G. Company

Training Programme
for the week 9th/15th Dec 1917

DAY	HOUR	PARADES
Sunday 9/12/17		Church Services & Recreation
Mon 10/12/17	8.45 a.m.	Company Parade. Inspection by O.C.
	9.0 to 9.30 am	Infantry Drill
	9.30 to 9.45 am	Physical Training
	10.0 to 10.45 am	Mechanism
	10.45 to 11.15 am	Gun Drill
	11.30 to 12.15 am	Immediate Action
	12.15 to 12.45 pm	Care and cleaning
Tues 11/12/17	8.45 am to 11.30 am	As above
	11.30 to 12.15 pm	Repairs and adjustments
	12.15 pm to 12.45 pm	Care and cleaning
Wed 12/12/17	8.45 to 9.45	As on Monday
	10.0 am to 12.45pm	A & B Sections on Range. Before going on to range Officers will devote 30 mins to Sights before, during, and after firing.
		C & D Sections
	10.0 to 10.30 am	Mechanism
	10.30 to 11.15 am	Gun Drill
	11.15 to 11.45 am	I.A.
	11.45 to 12.15 pm	Revolver exercises
	12.15 to 12.45 pm	Sights before, during, and after firing
Thursday 13/12/17	8.45 am to 12.45 pm	As on Wednesday but with Sections reversed
Friday 14/12/17	8.45 to 9.45 am	As on Monday
	10.0 to 12.45pm	A & B Sections on range
		C & D Sections
	10.0 to 10.15 am	T.S.O.T.
	10.15 am to 11.45am	Gun Drill including handling the guns whilst wearing S.B.R.
	11.45am to 12.15pm	Revolver exercises
	12.15 pm to 12.45pm	Care and cleaning
Saturday 15/12/17	8.45 am to 12.45 pm	As on Friday, but with Sections reversed

Training Programme
for the week 9th/15th Dec 1918

Special Parades

N.C.O's

(a) Map Reading — Monday 2·30 to 3·30
                    10/12/18
                  — Wednesday 2·30 to 3·30
                    12/12/18

(b) Fire Direction — Tuesday 5·30 to 6·30
                     11/12/18
                   — Thursday 5·30 to 6·30
                     13/12/18

Backward Men

(a) Gun Drill — Monday 2·30 to 3·30
                10/12/18
                Thursday   do
                13/12/18

(b) Mechanism — Tuesday 2·30 to 3·30
                11/12/18
                Friday   do
                14/12/18

(c) Immediate Action — Wednesday 2·30 to 3·30
                       12/12/18
                       Saturday   do
                       15/12/18

Signalling

The signallers will attend Belt Course. Remainder will man a Dummy Station and will be given instructional work by practice managers.

Range Taking

Lectures on Monday, Wednesday and Friday from 2·30 pm to 3·30 pm
Practical work every morning from 11 a.m. to 12·45 a.m. except when their section is on the range on a day members work.

Scouts (Runners)

Parades — Tuesday — 5·30 pm to 6·30 pm
          11/12/18
          Thursday — 2·30 pm to 3·30 pm
          13/12/18
          Saturday   do

APPENDIX. VIII

25th M.G. Coy

Training Programme

for the week 16th/22nd Dec. 1917

DAY	HOUR	PARADES
SUNDAY 16/12/17		Church Services Recreation
MON. 17/12/17	8.45am	Coy Parade Inspection by O.C.
	9.0 to 9.20am	Infantry Drill
	9.30 to 9.45am	Physical Training
	10.0 to 12.45am	A & B Sections on Range (aiming off for wind etc.)
		C & D Sections
	10.0 to 10.45am	Mechanism
	10.45 to 11.15	Gun Drill including handling the guns whilst wearing S.B.R.
	11.30 to 12.15	Immediate action
	12.15 to 12.45	Care & cleaning
Tues 18/12/17	8.45am to 12.45pm	As on Monday but with Sections reversed.
Wed 19/12/17	8.45am to 9.45	As on Monday
	10.0am to 12.45pm	A & B Sections on Range Firing whilst wearing S.B.R.
		C & D Sections
	10.0am to 10.30am	I A whilst wearing S.B.R.
	10.30 to 11.30	Barrage Drill
	11.45 to 12.15	Revolver practice on Range
	12.30 to 12.45pm	Cleaning guns
Thur 20/12/17	8.45am to 12.45pm	As on Wednesday but with Sections reversed.
Friday 21/12/17	8.45am to 9.45am	As on Monday
	10.0am to 12.45pm	A & B Sections on Range Firing with & without S.B.R.
		C & D Sections
	10.0am to 11.0am	Revolver practice on range
	11.15 to 12.0	Barrage Drill
	12.0 to 12.30	I A
	12.30 to 12.45pm	Cleaning Guns
Saturday 22/12/17	8.45 to 12.45pm	As on Friday but with Sections reversed.

Training Programme
for the week 16th/22nd Dec. 1917

Special Parades.

N.C.Os

(a) Map reading — Monday 17/12/17   2.30 to 3.30.

                — Wednesday 19/12/17   2.30 to 3.30

(B) Fire Direction — Tuesday 18/12/17   5.30 to 6.30

                — Thursday 20/12/17   5.30 to 6.30

Backward Men

(a) Gun Drill — Monday 17/12/17   2.30 to 3.30.

           — Thursday 20/12/17   2.30 to 3.30.

(B) Mechanism — Tuesday 18/12/17   2.30 to 3.30.

             — Friday 20/12/17   2.30 to 3.30.

(C) Immediate Action — Wednesday 19/12/17   2.30 to 3.30

                      — Saturday 22/12/17   2.30 to 3.30.

Scouts. (Runners)

PARADES. — Tuesday 18/12/17 — 5.30 p.m. to 6.30 p.m.

             — Thursday 20/12/17 — 2.30 to 3.30

Range Takers

Lectures on Monday & Wednesday from 2.30 p.m. to 3.30 p.m.
Practical work every morning except when their Sections are on the range or doing revolver practice.

25th Infantry Brigade No.Q/6/32.

~~2nd Lincoln Regt.~~
~~2nd R.Berks Regt.~~
1st R.Irish Rifles.
2nd Rifle Brigade.
~~23rd M.G.Coy.~~
25th M.G.Coy.
~~25th T.M.Bty.~~
~~25th Field Ambce.~~
----

1. Reference para.3 of 25th Inf. Bde. Order No.262 dated 24/12/17, the following is the detail of lorries for conveyance of blankets, kits etc, from VLAMERTINGHE to billets in the new Area.

2. Only 14 lorries are available and they are allotted as follows:-

2nd Lincoln Regt.	3 lorries.
2nd R.Berks Regt.	3 lorries.
1st R.Irish Rifles.	3 lorries.
2nd Rifle Brigade.	3 lorries.
23rd M.G.Coy.)	
25th T.M.Bty.)	2 lorries.
25th Inf. Bde. H.Q.)	

3. No lorries will be available for the 25th M.G.Coy. and 25th Field Ambulance. As these units will be billeted near VLAMERTINGHE they will collect their blankets and kits from the Station with their own transport.

4. The lorries will be available only for a single journey, and will be handed over to units of the 24th Inf. Bde. on arrival in the Camps in the new Area.

Roger Grey
Captain,
Staff Captain,
25th Inf. Bde.

25th December, 1917.

25th Inf. Bde. No.Q/6/32.

2nd. ~~Lincoln. Regt.~~
2nd. R.Berks. Regt.
1st. R.Irish Rifles.
2nd. ~~Rifle Brigade.~~
25th M. G. Coy.
~~23rd M. G. Coy.~~
25th T. M. Bty.
~~25th Field Ambulance.~~

----

1. Reference para. 3 of 25th Infantry Brigade Order No. 262 dated 24/12/1917. The following is the detail of lorries for the conveyance of blankets and kits to WIZERNES Station on the 26th instant :-

2/Lincoln. Regt.	3 Lorries.
2/R.Berks. Regt.	3 Lorries.
1/R.Irish Rifles.	3 Lorries.
2/Rifle Brigade.	3 Lorries.
25/M. G. Coy.) 23/M. G. Coy.)	1 Lorry.
25/T. M. Bty.	1 Lorry.
25/Field Ambulance.	1 Lorry.

2. These lorries will report to units on the evening of the 25th instant, and will remain with units overnight. Only 1 Lorry will report to 2/Rifle Brigade on the 25th instant; 2 Lorries allotted to 1/R.Irish Rifles will proceed direct from WIZERNES after dumping blankets to ACQUIN. On morning of 26th instant O.C. 1/R.Irish Rifles will ensure that these two lorries leave WIZERNES in sufficient time to reach ACQUIN by 6 a.m.

3. Lorries should leave units' Headquarters on morning of 26th instant so as to arrive at WIZERNES not later than 8 a.m.

Logan Grey
Captain,
Staff Captain,
25th Inf. Bde.

24th December, 1917.

Dear Rennie,

I am returning to Div H.Q. to-day. You will be taking on support company duties from the 41st M.G. Coy who are at C27c 8.5. There are certain orders concerning running guns up to a Div reserve defence line in case of necessity. Your transport & sufficient [a pocket] thinking for the purpose will have to be always in a constant state of readiness. Work out a scheme. See that your orderly officer inspects every detail each day.

Your camp is ~~H7a~~ H7a.2.9 on 26th Dec with all transport & on 27th Dec you move to I2c 2.1 & be clear of H7a 2.9 by 12 noon 27th Dec.

John Ward

SECRET.
Copy No. 13.

25th INFANTRY BRIGADE ORDER No.261.

Reference Sheet 27A. S.E. 1/20,000.
HAZEBROUCK 5A. 1/100,000.

1. (a) The 8th Division (less Artillery) is going to relieve the 14th Division (less Artillery) in the line between 25th and 27th Decr.

   (b) A map showing Divisional boundaries, dispositions of Brigades holding the line, and details of Switch lines, is being issued separately.

2. For purposes of the move, the 25th Brigade Group will be constituted as follows:-
   - 25th Infantry Brigade.
   - 25th Machine Gun Coy.
   - 23rd Machine Gun Coy.
   - 25th Field Ambulance.
   - No.4 Coy, Div. Train.

3. The personnel of the 25th Brigade Group will proceed by rail to the WIELTJE Area on December 26th. Transport of the Brigade Group will proceed by road on December 25th and December 26th under the orders of O.C., No.4 Coy. Div. Train, in accordance with attached March Table.

4. (a) On arrival in the WIELTJE Area the 25th Infantry Brigade will become Brigade in Support and will come under the orders of G.O.C. 14th Division until 12 noon December 27th.

   (b) Relief of Machine Gun Coys. will take place under arrangements to be made by the D.M.G.O.

5. Detailed orders as to entrainment and the allotment of Camps in the new Area will be issued separately.

6. The following distances will be maintained on the march:-
   - Between Companies.   100 yards.
   - Between Battalions.   500 "
   - When Transport is Brigaded,)
     between each Battn Transport) 100 "

7. Brigade Headquarters will close at BOISDINGHEM on December 26th and will reopen at WIELTJE on completion of the move.

8. ACKNOWLEDGE.

Captain,
Brigade Major,
25th Inf. Bde.

22nd December, 1917.
Issued at 4 p.m. through Signals to:-

Copy No.1. G.O.C.
2. Brigade Major.
3. Staff Captain.
4. Brigade Signals.
5. 2nd Lincoln Regt.
6. 2nd R.Berks Regt.
7. 1st R.Irish Rifles.
8. 2nd Rifle Brigade.
9. " 2nd Linc. R.
10. " 2nd R.Berks R.
11. " 1st R.Ir.Rif.
12. " 2nd Rifle Bde.

No. 13. 25th M.G.Coy.
14. 25th TM. Bty.
15. 23rd M.G.Coy.
16. 25th Field Ambce.
17. No.4 Coy. Div. Train.
18. 23rd Inf. Bde.
19. 24th Inf. Bde.
20. 8th Division "G".
21. 8th Division "Q".
22. War Diary.
23. Office.

AMENDMENT No. 1 to 25th INFANTRY BRIGADE ORDER No. 261.

Serial Nos. 7, 8, and 9 of Transport March Table issued with 25th Inf. Bde. Order No. 261 are cancelled and the following substituted :-

Serial No.	Date.	Unit.	Starting point. Place	Starting point. Time	From	To	Route	Remarks.
7	Dec. 25th	2/Rifle Bde.	Road Junction V.22.b.5.55.	7 a.m.	ACQUIN	ZELTMERIE	LUERES - LE UPPRE - SERQUES - TATINGHEM. thence as for Serials 1 to 6.	These units will join the main column at Road Junction, K.5.a.20.35.
8	ditto.	25/M.G. Coy	Road Junction V.15.d.0.4.	6.44 a.m.	WESTBECOURT	ditto.	ditto.	
9	ditto.	25/M.G. Coy	ditto.	6.48 a.m.	ditto.	ditto.		

Captain,
Brigade Major,
25th Inf. Bde.

22nd December, 1917.

MARCH TABLE for TRANSPORT of 25th Infantry Brigade Group.

Serial No.	Date	Units in order of march.	Starting Point.		To	Route	Remarks.
			Place	Time			
1	Dec. 25th.	1/3. Rajput Rifles.	Road Junction W.4.a.8.5.	8 a.m.	ZERMEZEELE	STEENVOORDE - ST.OMER - CLAIRMARAIS - NOORDPEENE - WEMAERS CAPPEL. thence as above.	1. Mounted representatives from each unit will report to the Brigade Interpreter at Road Junction W.4.a.8.5. at 8 a.m. to arrange billets at ZERMEZEELE.
2	do.	2/- Devons.	Road Junction Q.31.b.4.3.	7.25 a.m.	ditto.		
3	do.	25/Brigade H.Q.	Road Junction V.3.a.8.5.	7.14 a.m.	ditto.		
4	do.	2/Lincoln Regt.	ditto.	7.13 a.m.	ditto.		2. O.C. Column will arrange to reconnoitre a place for a mid-day halt for feeding and watering somewhere in the neighbourhood of CLAIRMARAIS. Other halts at the discretion of O.C. Column.
5	do.	25/Div. Sqdn.	Cross Roads V.5.c.3.5.	6.55 a.m.	L. WARDE		
6	do.	To 4 Coy Div. Train.	ditto.	6.59 a.m.	OUDEZEM.		ditto.
7	do.	2/Rifle Brigade.	Road Junction V.8.d.3.1.	6.17 a.m.	ACQUIN		ditto.
8	do.	25/L.G. Coy.	Road Junction V.15.d.0.4.	5.4 a.m.	WESTECCURT		ditto.	3. O.C. Column will issue such orders necessary for the march on Dec. 26th.
9	do.	25/M.G. Coy.	ditto.	5.7 a.m.	ditto.		
10	Dec. 26th.	25/Inf. Bde. 25/M.G. Coy. 25/L.G. Coy. 25/Fld. Ambce. Bde. Gov. Train.	ZERMEZEELE		WINNEZEELE area	STEENVOORDE - BOESCHEPE - thence as abc e. - POPERINGHE.	

To accompany 25th Infantry Brigade Order No. 261.

S E C R E T.
Copy No. 12.

25th INFANTRY BRIGADE ORDER No. 262.

Reference Sheets:- 27A. S.E. 1/20,000.
　　　　　　　　　　 36D. N.E. 1/20,000.
　　　　　　　　　　 28 N.W. 1/20,000.

1. Reference 25th Infantry Brigade Order No.261:
Personnel of 25th Infantry Brigade Group will proceed by rail on December 26th in accordance with attached Tables.

2. (a) The following Transport only will proceed by the second train detraining at VLAMERTINGHE:-

　　Per Battalion.　　　4 Cookers.
　　　　　　　　　　　　 1 Water Cart.
　　　　　　　　　　　　 1 Baggage Wagon.
　　　　　　　　　　　　 1 Mess Cart.

　　For M.G.Coy.　　　　1 Limbered Wagon.

　　Brigade H.Q.　　　　1 Baggage Wagon.
　　　　　　　　　　　　 1 Mess Cart.

　　Field Ambulance.　　1 Baggage Wagon.
　　　　　　　　　　　　 1 Limbered Wagon.

　　Trench Mortar Handcarts.

All other Transport will proceed by road on December 25th and 26th as already detailed in 25th Infantry Brigade Order No.261.

(b) All kits and blankets of Units will be carried on the second train.

3. Lorries will be supplied for conveyance of blankets and kits to entraining Station and from Detraining Station. Details will be issued later.

4. All personnel will arrive at entraining Station one hour, and Transport 3 hours before trains are due to leave.

5. 1st R.Irish Rifles will detail an Officer to superintend entraining. This Officer will report to R.T.O. at WIZERNES 2 hours before departure of Train No.1.
　　2nd R.Berks Regt. will detail an Officer to travel by Train No.1 and superintend detraining at detraining Station.
　　These Officers will be on duty during whole period of entrainment and detrainment, and will rejoin their Units on completion of duty.

6. 2nd Rifle Brigade will detail a loading party of 2 Officers and 60 men to report to R.T.O., WIZERNES 3 hours before departure of Train No.2 to load transport on that train. This party will proceed by this train to unload it at VLAMERTINGHE and will rejoin their units on completion of duty.
　　2nd Lieut. C.G.WHARAKER, 2nd Lincoln Regt. will superintend the entraining of transport at WIZERNES and will travel by Train No.2 to superintend detraining at VLAMERTINGHE.

7. Each unit will hand to the R.T.O. at WIZERNES, 1 hour before departure of train by which they are travelling, a complete entraining state showing numbers of Officers, O.R's. horses, vehicles, etc.

/8....

8. Lashings for securing vehicles to the trucks are supplied by French Railway Authorities. Units however must provide headropes for horses. Watercarts will be entrained full.

9. Supply arrangements will be as follows:-
   24th instant. Refilling of rations for consumption 25th and 26th instant.
   25th instant. Transport will march with own rations for 25th and 26th.
   Supply wagons will march empty and refill for consumption 27th inst. at WIMMERS CAPPEL about 2 p.m.
   26th instant. Units will entrain with rations for 26th.
   Supply wagons will deliver rations for consumption 27th on arrival in new area.
   27th instant. There will be a double refilling for Brigade Group in new Area to enable units to hold 2 days' rations in addition to the current day's rations and iron ration.

   Railhead on and after 26th instant will be at VLAMERTINGHE.

10. Billeting parties of all units, except 25th Field Ambulance and No.4 Coy, Train, will report to the Staff Captain at the entraining station at 6.30 a.m. 26th instant and travel by Train No.1. They should bring bicycles.
    Billeting party of 25th Field Ambulance will travel by Train No.2.
    Billeting party of No.4 Coy, Train will proceed by road with transport
    Details of accommodation in the new Areas are shewn in attached Table "C".

11. Ordnance will close at WIZERNES on 26th instant and open at VLAMERTINGHE on 27th instant.

12. Units will hand over all Area and Billet Stores (including paillasses) to incoming units or to Sub-Area Commandants. Receipts obtained will be forwarded to this Office.

13. Every endeavour will be made to settle all claims before leaving the Area. Any unit unable to do so will notify Claims Officer, 8th Division, giving particulars of claims still outstanding.

14. ACKNOWLEDGE.

                                                            Captain,
                                            Brigade Major,
24th December, 1917.   25th Inf. Bde.
Issued at 12 noon through Signals.

Copy No.1. G.O.C.
     2. Brigade Major.
     3. Staff Captain.
     4. Brigade Signals.
     5. 2nd Lincoln Regt.
     6. 2nd R. Berks Regt.
     7. 1st R. Irish Rifles.
     8. 2nd Rifle Brigade.
     9. QrMr, 2nd Linc. R.
   10. " 2nd R. Berks R.
   11. " 1st R. Ir. Rif.
   12. " 2nd Rifle Bde.
   13. 25th M. G. Coy,
   14. 25th T. M. Bty.

No.15. 23rd M. G. Coy.
   16. 25th Field Ambce.
   17. No.4 Coy, Div. Train.
   18. Entraining Officer,
      (1st R.Ir. Rif.)
   19. Detraining Officer,
      (2nd R. Berks R.)
   20. 2/Lieut. C.G. WORRAKER.
   21. 23rd Inf. Bde.
   22. 24th Inf. Bde.
   23. 8th Division "G".
   24. 8th Division "Q".
   25. War Diary.
   26. Office.

TABLE "C".

Location of units on arrival in New Area.

Date.	Unit.	Name of Camp.	Location.	Name of Transport Lines.	Location.	Remarks.
Dec. 26th.	HQ.25/Bde.	WIELTJE DUGOUTS	C.38.b.5.7.	YORK CAMP.	G.5.c.7.4.	In relief of 24/Bde.
	1/R.I.R. Ln. H.Q. & 2 Coys. 2 Coys.	CAPRICORN. CALIFORNIA.	C.19.d.5.6. C.25.c.3.8.	do. do.	do. do.	
	2/R.Berks.R. Bn.HQ & 2 Coys. 2 Coys.	JUNCTION. CALIFORNIA.	C.27.c.3.8. C.25.c.3.8.	do. do.	do. do.	
	2/Rifle Bde.	JUNCTION.	C.27.c.8.8.	do.	do.	
	2/Lincoln. R.	FASMAR.	C.27.d.5.3.	do.	do.	
	25/M.G.Coy.		H.7.a.2.9.		H.7.a.2.9.	Moves on Dec.27th to I.2.c.2.1. to be clear of H.7.a.2.9. by 12 noon 27th Decr.
	25/T.M.Bty.	WELSH.	C.27.c.5.5.			
	25/F.Amb.	MOATED FARM	H.2.d.8.2.	MOATED FARM	H.2.d.3.2.	
	No.4 Coy. Train.		G.5.a.6.6.			
	25/M.G.Coy.	PIONEER CAMP	C.27.c.8.0.	PIONEER CAMP	C.27.c.8.0.	Transport moves to I.8.a.5.c. on 28th Dec. Not to arrive I.8.a.5.3. before 12 noon 28th Decr.

TABLE "A" to accompany 25th Inf. Bde. Order No. 262.

Serial No.	Date.	Unit.	Starting Point. Place.	Starting Point. Time.	From.	To.	Remarks.
1	Dec. 26th.	1/R.Irish Rif.	W.4.c.1.1.	4.10 a.m.	ZUDAUSQUES.	WIZERNES Station.	Times in Column 5 refer to personnel only. Transport proceeding by second train must reach WIZERNES Station by 7 a.m.
2	ditto.	2/R.Berks.R.	Q.31.b.4.5.	5.0 a.m.	HORINGHEM.	ditto.	
3	ditto.	25/T.M.Bty.	ditto.	5.10 a.m.	BARBINGHEM.	ditto.	
4	ditto.	25/Bde.H.Q.	V.5.a.8.5.	3.0 a.m.	BOISDINGHEM.	ditto.	
5	ditto.	25/M.G.Coy.	V.32.b.45.55.	5.0 a.m.	WESTBECOURT.	ditto.	
6	ditto.	25/Fld.Ambce.	V.3.a.2.5.	5.30 a.m.	LA WATTH.	ditto.	
7	ditto.	2/Lincoln.R.	V.5.a.8.5.	7.0 a.m.	BOISDINGHEM.	ditto.	
8	ditto.	2/Ri...	V.22.b.45.55.	7.0 a.m.	ACQUIN.	ditto.	
9	ditto.	25/...	V.25.b.45.55.	7.10 a.m.	WESTBECOURT.	ditto.	

TABLE "B".

PROGRAMME OF ENTRAINMENT.

25th Brigade Group.
-o-o-o-o-o-o-o-o-o-

Train No.	Date.	Hour of Departure.	Entraining Station.	Unit	Approximate hour of arrival.	Detraining Station.	Remarks.
1	25th Dec.	7.0 a.m.	WIZERNES	25th Inf. Bde. H.Q. Signal Section. 2/R.Berks. Regt. 1/R.Irish Rifles. 25th M. G. Coy. 25th T.M.Bty.	10.0 a.m.	ST. JEAN.	
2	25th Dec.	10.0 a.m.	WIZERNES	Transport of Brigade Group as per para. 2 of Bde. Order No.262. 25th Fld. Ambce. Blankets and kits of Brigade Group.	1 p.m.	VLAMERTINGHE.	
3	25th Dec.	11.0 a.m.	WIZERNES	2/Lincoln. Regt. 2/Rifle Brigade. 23rd M. G. Coy.	2 p.m.	ST. JEAN.	

APPENDIX X

RELIEF ORDERS 30/12/17

SECRET  APPENDIX X   COPY No. 7

25th M.G. Coy Relief Orders No. 22

MAP REF.
PASSCHENDAELE
1/10,000

30th Dec. 1917

(1) The Coy will relieve 24th M.G. Coy in the line tomorrow morning 31/12/17

(2) A Sec & 2 Teams of D Sec. will constitute "A" Battery under 2/Lt HOOD
& will be at D.6.40.55;
B & C Sections will form "B" Battery under LIEUT LARKWORTHY
& will be at D.4.6.26.20.
2 Guns of 218th M.G. Coy will be at KOREK D.9.c.45.65.
1 Gun of D.Sec will be at WURST FARM. D.7.d.75.98.
These guns will be under the orders of 2/Lt LOCKHART.

(3) Sections will move off in the following order.
B & C Sections   4.30 am
A & 3 Teams of D Sec. 4.45 am.

(4) Guides will be at WATERLOO D.9.c.80.85, at 6.15 am as under.
3 guides for "A" Battery
3   "   " "B"   "
2   "   " KOREK.
2   "   " WURST FARM.

(5) Belt Boxes & Tripods will be taken over & a list showing distribution
will be forwarded to Coy H.Q. as soon as possible after relief

(6) All trench stores will be taken over & a list of same same forwarded to Coy H.Q.
as soon as possible after relief

(7) 2/Lieut PRITCHARD will arrange to convey guns, water etc. to WATERLOO
where they will be off loaded. Pack animals will move with the Sections
After off loading 8 mules will return to the SOMME DRESSING STATION.
to carry the guns of 24th M.G. Coy to WIELTJE.

(8) Upon completion of relief Coy H.Q. will be at D.10.b.20.65 approx.

(9) Completion of relief will be reported to Coy H.Q. by runner.

(10) The place where mules off load will be the ration dump.
Rations & water will be delivered there daily at 6.0 am.

Copy No 1 — O.C. A BATTERY
  "   " 2 —   " B   "
  "   " 3 — LIEUT RENNIE
  "   " 4 — 2/Lieut LOCKHART
  "   " 5 — 24th M.G. Coy.
  "   " 6 — 25th Inf Bde.
  "   " 7 — WAR DIARY
  "   " 8 — RETAINED

Signed
A Simmonds Capt.
Commanding 25th M.G. Coy

APPENDIX No 9

ORDERS FOR MOVE

25/12/17
to
27/12/17

"C" Form (Duplicate).
MESSAGES AND SIGNALS.

Army Form C.2123.

SM   EST   55

Service Instructions.

Handed in at N.B.T. .... Office .... m. Received .... m.

TO 25TH M G Coy

Sender's Number	Day of Month	In reply to Number	AAA
SC 225	25TH		

Reference 25TH Inf Bde Orders No 262 AAA you will travel by train No 2 tomorrow and detrain at VLAMERTINGE AAA your holding party will accompany you in train No 2 AAA you will reach the station not later than 9AM tomorrow AAA acknowledge AAA

FROM PLACE & TIME 25TH INF BDE

handed in at 3.30am

"C" Form (Duplicate).
MESSAGES AND SIGNALS.

Army Form C.2123

SM COPY

Service Instructions. NGF

TO 25th M G Coy

Sender's Number: SC222
Day of Month: 25

AAA

Refce this office no Q6/32 of D/24/12/17 send guide to bde HQs at 9pm tonight to take over lorry aaa this lorry will be available for you and 23rd M G Coy and can do 2 journeys aaa all kits must be at WIZERNES by 8am tomorrow aaa acknowledge aaa

FROM PLACE & TIME
addd 25th M G Coy repeated 23rd M G Coy for information
25th INF BDE

Army Form C. 2118.

WAR DIARY
or
INTELLIGENCE SUMMARY.
(Erase heading not required.)

Instructions regarding War Diaries and Intelligence Summaries are contained in F. S. Regs., Part II. and the Staff Manual respectively. Title pages will be prepared in manuscript.

VM 25

Place	Date	Hour	Summary of Events and Information	Remarks and references to Appendices
SHEET 28 N.W.	1/1/18		Strength and War Est. strength of 1 & 2 & 2.30 lay on strike on strong & contingents arrive	
			2 O.R. received from Base H.Q.R.	
	2/1/18		Lecture 10.15. Bath 2.30. rest continued from Base H.Q.R.	
	3/1/18		Same as on 2/1/18 H.Q.R.	
	4/1/18		Coy. were relieved in Battye Position by 33 M.C. Coy and moved into Reserve Camp at Winnezeele. L. Coy at H.Q.R.	APPENDIX VI Relief Orders
	5/1/18		H.Q. & Q. carried of Lewis at 11.30 a.m. Throughout the Whole day at 7 & 9.30, 30 at 12.30 for H.Q. 3 3. 2.O.R. & Lopital H.Q.R.	
			Coy. spent in cleaning guns & equipment etc. 1.O.R. & Lopital H.Q.R. 4 O.R. & Lopital H.Q.R. & 45 on leave U.K.	
	6/1/18		Coy. spent in cleaning camp etc. 1.O.R. on leave & U.K. 2.O.R. & Lopital 1.O.R. from old G. & Alert 10.R. from Base & W.Q. joined from 5th old G. Coy H.Q.R.	
	7/1/18		Coy. spent cleaning. Night out games for line & 3 hockey 15 teams 1.O.R. & Lopital 1.O.R. from hospital H.Q.R. 1.O.R. evacuated H.Q.R.	
	8/1/18		Coy. moved to Camp at YPRES. Relieved tomorrow at 8 a.m. Proceed to the line to relieve 24th B. Coy in close defence position. 2.O.R. evacuated 1.O.R. & Lopital 1.O.R. from line to U.K. H.Q.R.	APPENDIX XII Relief Orders
	9/1/18		Details were employed in building new entrenchments in the line & temporary camp. 2.O.R. to hospital. H.Q.R.	
	10/1/18		Same as on 9/1/18. 2.O.R. evacuated 1.O.R. from hospital. 1.O.R. from Base	
	11/1/18		Same as on 10/1/18. 2.O.R. wounded & C.C.S. H.Q.R.	
	12/1/18		Coy. was relieved in close defence position by the 23rd Batt. G. Coy & proceeded to Camp at YPRES & leaves all day.	APPENDIX XIII Relief Orders

Army Form C. 2118.

WAR DIARY
or
INTELLIGENCE SUMMARY.
(Erase heading not required.)

Instructions regarding War Diaries and Intelligence Summaries are contained in F. S. Regs., Part II. and the Staff Manual respectively. Title pages will be prepared in manuscript.

Place	Date	Hour	Summary of Events and Information	Remarks and references to Appendices
SHEET 28 NW	12/1/18		All E Coy to assist C.S.M. & 2 O.R. on leave to U.K. 10 officers & 1 O.R. from base to U.K. 1 O.R. for hospital. MKR	
	13/1/18		Cleaning guns & gun equipment. 2 guns were mounted for AA at T 2 c 2.8. 2 O.R. hospital. 2 O.R. from base to U.K. 1 O.R. to Retention Camp. MKR	
	14/1/18		Cleaning guns & gun equipment, working on Camp. 3 O.R. to hospital. 1 O.R. from hospital. 1 O.R. for base to U.K. MKR	
	15/1/18		Preparing guns etc. for line. 1 O.R. to hospital. MKR	
	16/1/18		Coy relieved the 24th M.G. Coy in the line on Basseux Posture. No games being in the line. 1 O.R. to hospital. 2 O.R. on casualty.	APPENDIX XIV Relief Order
	17/1/18		Details employed on fatigues & cleaning Camp. 1 O.R. from curves. 1 O.R. to hospital. 3 O.R. to hospital. 1 Officer. home to U.K. MKR	
	18/1/18		Same as on 17/1/18. 1 O.R. evacuated. 1 O.R. wounded. 4 O.R. to hospital. 1 Officer leave to U.K. MKR	
	19/1/18		Same as on 18/1/18. 2 O.R. to hospital. 1 O.R. wounded. MKR. 2 O.R. from ammo.	
	20/1/18		Coy was relieved by 227th M.G. Coy at 7 O.A.M. on Basseux Postune & proceeded by Lorry to STEENVOORDE AREA	APPENDIX XV Relief Order
	21/1/18		where Coy came under the orders of L/Col. SHERBROOK. D.S.O. 3 O.R. to hospital. MKR	
			Four offr & Coys were reorganised & the M.G. Batt was formed. Day was spent in fatigues & cleaning guns & equipment.	
			2 O.R. from Retention Camp. 2 O.R. transferred to 24th A. G. Coy. 2 O.R. evacuated to C.C.S. 1 O.R. to hospital. 1 O.R. home to U.K. MKR	
	22/1/18		Day spent in fatigues improving Camp & cleaning Rifles & Belt Boxes. 3 O.R. from leave. MKR	
	23/1/18		Day spent as on 22nd. 1 O.R. wounded. 4 O.R. transferred to 24th M.G. Coy. 1 O.R. from base. 1 O.R. from hospital. MKR	
	24/1/18		Day spent as on 23rd. MKR	

Army Form C. 2118.

WAR DIARY
or
INTELLIGENCE SUMMARY.
(Erase heading not required.)

Place	Date	Hour	Summary of Events and Information	Remarks and references to Appendices
	25/1/18		Day spent in cleaning guns equipment & improving Camp. 1.O.R. from hospital. 2.O.R evacuated. 3.O.R. leave to U.K. 1.Officer leave to U.K. H.T.R.	
	26/1/18		Day spent as on 25th. 2.O.R. for hospital. N.Y.R.	
	27/1/18		As per training Programme. 1.O.R course of cookery. N.Y.R.	APPENDIX XVI Training Programme
	28/1/18		As per training Programme. 2.O.R. Courses. H.T.R.	
	29/1/18		As per training Programme. 1.O.R. for course. N.Y.R.	
	30/1/18		As per training Programme. 1.O.R. from hospital. 2.O.R. from course. C.S.M. from leave U.K. H.S.	
	31/1/18		As per training Programme. Baths in the afternoon. H.S.	

A.R. Currie Lt.
O.C. 25th M.M. Cy

SECRET   COPY No 5

25th Machine Gun Coy Relief Orders

Ref Map.   8th January 1918
   PASSCHENDAELE
   ———————
   1/10,000

(1) The Company will relieve the 24th M G Coy in the line on the night 8/9 January

(2) <u>PASSCHENDAELE</u> guns Nos 1 + 2 situated at D6, b 45, 65 + D6, b 35, 72, respectively composed of 2 teams of D Section under 2/Lt LOCKHART

<u>MOSSELMARK</u> guns Nos 3, 4, + 5 situated at V30. C 70. 35. V 30, C 68, 40. V 30, D 25, 90. respectively composed of 3 teams of B Section under Lt. LARKWORTHY

<u>MEETCHEELE</u> guns Nos 6, 7, 8, + 9 situated at D5, b 35, 20, D5. b 29, 28, D4, D 80, 90. D4, D 75, 92 respectively composed of 4 teams of A Section under 2/Lt HOOD

<u>KOREK</u> guns composed of 2 teams of C Section who when in position will be under the orders of 218th M G Coy

(3) Guides for these guns will be at END of PLANK Road at 5 pm as under

   2 Guides for PASSCHENDAELE Guns Nos 1 + 2
   2   "   " No 5 GUN
   2   "   " MOSSELMARK GUNS. Nos 3 + 4
   2   "   " MEETCHEELE GUNS Nos 6 + 7
   2   "   " GUNS. No 8 + 9
   2   "   " KOREK GUNS.

(4) Sections will move off in the following order

   { PASSCHENDAELE Guns
   { MOSSELMARK   GUNS.   3.45 pm

   { MEETCHEELE   GUNS
   { KOREK   GUNS   4.0 pm

(5) Belt Boxes + tripods will be taken over + a list showing distribution will be forwarded to Coy HQ as soon after relief as possible

(6) All trench stores will be taken over + a list of same forwarded to Coy HQ as soon as possible after relief

(7) Transport. 2/Lt PRITCHARD will arrange to convey guns, water, etc to WATERLOO where they will be off loaded. Pack animals will move with their Sections. Where Pack animals off load will be the ration DUMP. Rations to be at this point at 6.0 pm each night.

(8) Upon completion of relief Coy HQ will be at D10, b52, 30

(9) Completion of relief will be reported to Coy HQ by runner.

    Copy Nº 1   O.C PASSCHENDAELE GUNS
    "   " 2   O.C. MOSSELMARK   "
    "   " 3   O.C. MEETCHEELE   "
    "   " 4   LIEUT. SPOONER
    "   " 5   24th M.G Coy
    "   " 6   24th Inf. Bde
    "   " 7   WAR DIARY
    "   " 8   RETAINED

    W Rumens Lt
    O.C 25th M.G. Coy

24th M.G. Coy.

SECRET.
COPY No. 9

25th INFANTRY BRIGADE ORDER No.266.

8th January, 1918.

1. The 25th Infantry Brigade will move to the WILTJE - ST. JEAN Area by march route on January 7th, 1918, and become Brigade in support, taking over from 24th Infantry Brigade.

2. All moves will be in accordance with attached March Table.

3. All details of relief will be arranged direct between Commanding Officers concerned.

4. All Area stores will be taken over.

5. The following billeting parties will be detailed:-
   Each Battalion   -   1 Officer and 6 other Ranks.
   25th T. M. Bty.   -   1 Officer and 1 Other Rank.
   25th Brigade H.Q. -   2 Other Ranks.

6. Two lorries will be at Headquarters, 25th Inf. Bde. BRAKE CAMP, at 8 a.m. on January 7th to convey these billeting parties to Camps in the WILTJE - ST. JEAN Area.

7. Brigade Headquarters will close at BRAKE CAMP at 5.30 p.m. and re-open at WILTJE DUG-OUTS at the same hour.

8. Completion of moves will be reported to Brigade Headquarters.

9. ACKNOWLEDGE.

                                            Captain,
                                         Brigade Major,
                                          25th Inf. Bde.

Issued at 4 p.m. through Signals to:-

   Copy No. 1. G. O. C.
           2. Brigade Major.
           3. Staff Captain.
           4. Brigade Signals.
           5. 2nd Lincoln Regt.
           6. 2nd R.Berks Regt.
           7. 1st R.Irish Rifles.
           8. 2nd Rifle Brigade.
           9. 25th M. G. Coy.
          10. 25th T. M. Bty.
          11. 8th Division "G".
          12. 8th Division "Q".
          13. 23rd Inf. Bde.
          14. 24th Inf. Bde.
          15. Bde. Supply Officer.
          16. 8th Div. Artillery.
          17. C. R. E.
          18. A. D. M. S.
          19. War Diary.
          20. Office.

MARCH TABLE with 25th Infantry Brigade Order No.266.

Serial No.	Date.	Unit.	From.	To.	Starting point.	Time of passing starting pnt.	Route.	Taking order from.
1.	4th January, 1918.	2nd Lincolns.	RED ROSE CAMP.	H.Q. & 2 Coys. CAPRICORN. 2 Coys. CALIFORNIA.	Cross Roads, H.8.a.45.80.	2.0 p.m.	VLAMERTINGHE – Road junction I.2.c.2.5. – St. Jean.	1st Sherwood Foresters.
2.		2nd R.Berks.R.	MIDLETON CAMP.	H.Q. & R C.P.	ditto.	2.10 p.m.		2nd North'n Regt.
3.		2nd Rifle Bde.	" " C.P.	H.Q. & 2 Coys. JUNCTION CAMP. 2 Coys. CALIFORNIA.	Cross Roads, G.6.d.45.20.	2.5 p.m.		1st Worcester Regt.
4.		1st R.Irish Rifles.	"B" CAMP BRAKE CAMP.	JUNCTION CAMP.	Rd. junction, G.6.a.19.29.	2.5 p.m.		2nd E.Lancs. Regt.
5.		25th T.M.Bty.	"B" CAMP.	WELSH CAMP.	Cross Road, G.6.d.45.20.	2.25 p.m.		24th T.M.Bty.

Units will halt every 10 minutes to the clock hour.

SECRET.   Copy No. 9

8TH DIVISION ORDER No. 251.

5th January, 1918.

1. 24th Inf. Bde. will relieve 23rd Inf. Bde. in the line on the night January 7th/8th.

2. (a) On relief, 23rd Inf. Bde. will proceed to the BRANDHOEK Area by light railway from WIELTJE under arrangements to be made by 8th Division "Q", and become Brigade in Divisional Reserve.

    (b) Hours of departure from WIELTJE will be notified later by 8th Division "Q".

3. 25th Inf. Bde. will move up to WIELTJE – ST. JEAN Area by march route on January 7th and become Brigade in support.

    Route. VLAMERTINGHE – Road junction I.2.c.2.3. – ST. JEAN. Head of column not to reach road junction I.2.c.2.3. before 3 p.m.

4. All details of relief will be arranged direct between Brigadiers concerned.

5. Trench Stores, Aeroplane Photographs, and Intelligence details will be handed over.

6. Two lorries will be at H.Q., 25th Inf. Bde. at 8 a.m. January 7th to convey billeting parties to Camps in the WIELTJE – ST. JEAN Area.

7. The following M.G. Co. Reliefs will be carried out on January 8th and night January 8th/9th:-

    218th M.G. Coy. will relieve 23rd M.G. Coy. on Barrage.
    25th M.G. Coy. will relieve 24th M.G. Coy. on Close Defence.

    On relief, 23rd and 24th M.G. Cos. will proceed to BRANDHOEK and YPRES respectively.

8. 8th Division "Q" will arrange for three lorries to convey 25th M.G. Coy. to YPRES in the early morning of January 8th. The same lorries will be at WIELTJE DUG-OUTS at 10 a.m. on that day to convey 23rd M.G. Co. to BRANDHOEK.

9. Completion of Machine Gun Co. reliefs will be reported to Divisional Headquarters and to 24th Inf. Bde.

10. ACKNOWLEDGE.

Issued at 2pm.

Lieut.-Colonel.
General Staff.

P.T.O. for distribution.

2.

Copies to:-
- No.1 Divisional Commander.
- 2 23rd Inf. Bde.
- 3 24th Inf. Bde.
- 4 25th Inf. Bde.
- 5 8th Div. Artillery.
- 6 22nd D.L.I.
- 7 23rd M.G. Coy.
- 8 24th M.G. Coy.
- 9 25th M.G. Coy.
- 10 218th M.G. Coy.
- 11 D.M.G.O.
- 12 C. R. E.
- 13 O.C., Signals.
- 14 "Q".
- 15 A.D.M.S.
- 16 Left Bombardment Group ⎫
- 17 39th Division. ⎬ For
- 18 50th Division. ⎬ information.
- 19 VIII Corps "G" ⎬
- 20 VIII Corps "Q" ⎭
- 21 A.P.M.
- 22 War Diary.
- 23 File.

SECRET.

Copy No. 9

8TH DIVISION ORDER No.252.

9th January, 1918.

1. 23rd Inf. Bde. will relieve 24th Inf. Bde. in the line on the night January 11th/12th.

2. (a) 23rd Inf. Bde. will proceed from BRANDHOEK Area to WIELTJE by light railway, under arrangements to be made by 8th Division "Q".

(b) Hours of departure and point of entrainment will be notified later by 8th Division "Q".

(c) On relief, 24th Inf. Bde. will proceed to the BRANDHOEK Area by light railway from WIELTJE under arrangements to be made by 8th Division "Q", and become Brigade in Divisional Reserve.

(d) Hours of departure from WIELTJE will be notified later by 8th Division "Q".

3. 25th Inf. Bde. will remain as Brigade in Support.

4. All details of relief will be arranged direct between Brigadiers concerned.

5. Trench Stores, Aeroplane Photographs, and Intelligence details will be handed over.

6. (a) The following M.G. Co. reliefs will be carried out on January 12th, and night January 12th/13th:-

   24th M.G. Co. will relieve 218th M.G. Co. on Barrage.
   23rd M.G. Co. will relieve 25th M.G. Co. on Close Defence.

(b) On relief, 218th and 25th M.G. Cos. will proceed to BRANDHOEK and YPRES, respectively.

(c) Machine Gun defence of the Sector as laid down in Appendix II of 8th Divisional Defence Scheme, will be put into operation as from 5 a.m. January 13th, 1918.

7. 8th Division "Q" will arrange for three lorries to convey 23rd M.G. Co. to YPRES in the early morning of January 12th. The same lorries will be at WIELTJE DUG-OUTS at 10 a.m. on that day to convey 218th M.G. Co. to BRANDHOEK.

8. Completion of Machine Gun Co. reliefs will be reported to Divisional Headquarters and to 23rd Inf. Bde.

9. ACKNOWLEDGE.

S. Adair
Lieut.-Colonel,
General Staff.

Issued at 8 p.m.

P.T.O. for distribution.

- 2 -

Copies to:-

No.	
1	Divisional Commander.
2	23rd Inf. Bde.
3	24th Inf. Bde.
4	25th Inf. Bde.
5	8th Div. Arty.
6	22nd D.L.I.
7	23rd M.G. Coy.
8	24th M.G. Coy.
9	25th M.G. Coy.
10	218th M.G. Coy.
11	D.M.G.O.
12	C.R.E.
13	O.C., Signals.
14	"Q".
15	A.D.M.S.
16	A.P.M.
17	Left Bombardment Group)
18	33rd Division
19	39th Division } For
20	VIII Corps."G". } information.
21	VIII Corps "Q"
22	War Diary.
23	File.

Secret   Relief Orders

Operation Order No 8
by
Capt. F.W. Robinson M.C.
Cmdg 23rd Machine Gun Coy.

1. The Company will relieve the 25th MG Coy in the close Defence positions in the line on the 12th/13th according to the following programme

Section No	Guns	Position	Gun Nos	Officer i/c	Guides at	Time
3	2	PASSCHENDAELE	1 & 2	Lt KNIGHT	WATERLOO	5-30 PM
2	3	MOSSELMAARKT	3, 4 & 5	2 Lt KENNEDY	ditto	ditto
3	2	MEETCHEELE	6 & 7	" WARBUTTON	ditto	ditto
1	2	1. LAAMKEEK / 1 BELLEVUE	8 & 9	" BRUCE	ditto	ditto
4	4	KOREK	10, 11, 12 & 13	" EVANS	25 MGC HQ	3-30 PM
1	2	HILL 37	14 & 15	" MUSSON	ditto	3 - PM
3	1	Coy HQ	16			
Coy H.Q.	—	LAAMKEEK	—	C.O.	WATERLOO	5-30 PM

Dress Fighting Order. Sandbag puttees, Greatcoats & ground sheets rolled bandolier fashion.

Teams 4 men per gun 1 NCO per Sub-Section.
No 5 gun will be i/c of a Sergeant.

Section H.Q. 1 Officer 1 Servant 1 Runner.

Rations & Water for 2 days will be taken into the line

Rations & Water for 15th and 16th for guns No 1 to 9 & Coy H.Q. will be at WATERLOO at 5-30 PM on the 14th inst. Empty tins must be sent back to transport lines.
For guns No 10, 11, 12 & 13 at JUNCTION of GRAVENSTAFEL & PLANK ROADS at 5 PM. for guns 13 & 14 at SOMME DRessing Stn at 4-30 P.M.

Feet Every man will take 4 cartridge cases of powder into the line, feet will be rubbed & socks changed daily under arrangements to be made by the 2 i/c.

Solidified Paraffin Will not be issued to 4 guns at KOREK and No 13 & 14 guns

Coy H.Q. Will consist of C.O. CO's Servant 2 Lt. BRUCE, Ptes SHAW & FIELD, 2 Section Runners, 2 men at BELLEVUE (Ptes ROBINSON and a man from No 3 Section) TOTAL 11.

Situation   LAAMKEEK D.10.b 50.30.

Communication   On completion of relief runners from the 25th MG Coy will guide 2 runners from 1 & 2 guns & 3, 4 & 5 guns back to Coy H.Q. where 2 runners will remain. 2 return to their Section.

These men will be used as runners for guns Nos 1 to 9. OC No 6 & 7 guns will report relief complete to Coy H.Q. his runner will return to Section H.Qrs. Similarly 2 men will be sent from KOREK and will return to their Section H.Qrs.

Hand Over

Nos 15, 14, 12, 13 & 16 will take 1 Tripod & 8 Belt Boxes per gun into the line. Officers concerned will arrange their carrying parties. Guns No 1 to 12 will take over tripods and belt boxes, obtain receipts and send lists of stores taken over to Coy H.Qrs as soon as possible after relief.

Reports Intelligence Summary, Indents & certificates that feet have been rubbed and socks changed daily will reach Coy H.Q. by 5-30 P.M. daily. Lists giving Map Ref true bearing of lines of fire of guns, S.O.S Lines etc will be sent to Coy H.Q. by 5-30 P.M. on 13th inst. All maps range cards etc will be taken over.

(Sgd) F. W. Robinson Capt.
O.C. 23rd MG Coy.

SECRET   COPY No.
   A
                    25th M.G. Company RELIEF ORDERS No. 28.
REF. MAP
   PASSCHENDAELE   15th January 1918
   —————
    10,000

① The Company will relieve the 24th M.G. Coy in the line on
   the morning of the 16th January

② Barrage Positions composed of 12 guns will be occupied as
   under
       A Battery   D4.b.10,35. Composed of A. Section under the
                                 orders of 2nd Lt HOOD
       B Battery   D4.b.30,20. Composed of C Section under the
                                 orders of Lieut WESTON
       C Battery   D4.b.50,05   Composed of D Section under the
                                 orders of 2nd Lt LOCKHART
       REAR GUNS   will be occupied by B. Section under the orders
                    of Lieut LARKWORTHY as under. H.Q will be at
                    D.9.d.94.97.
            No 16 Gun D.8.d.15.59 To be mounted for A.A. duty by day
            No 17 "   D.8.d.29.87
            No 18 "   D.8.c.15.98
            No 19 "   D.9.b.11.22.

③ Guides for the Barrage Guns will be at END of PLANK ROAD at
   5.30 AM. as under
            2 Guides for A Battery
            2   "   "   B   "
            2   "   "   C   "
         Guides for REAR GUNS will be at SOMME DRESSING
   STATION at 6 AM. as under
            1 Guide for No 16 Gun
            1   "   "   No 17 "
            1, "   "   No 18 "
            1   "   "   No 19 "

④ Sections will move off in the following order
            A. Section   3.30 AM.
            C.   "   3.40 AM.
            D.   "   3.50 AM.
            B.   "   4.30 AM.

⑤ Belt Boxes and tripods will be taken over and a list showing
   distribution will be forwarded to Coy. H.Q as soon
   after relief as possible

(6) All trench stores will be taken over and a list of same forwarded to Coy. H.Q. as soon as possible after relief

(7) Transport 2nd Lt PRITCHARD will arrange to convey 12 guns water etc to BELLEVUE and 4 guns water etc to SOMME DRESSING STATION mules will be off loaded at their respective destinations
Where animals off load will be the Ration Dumps
Pack animals will move with their Sections.
After off loading 6 mules will await at BELLEVUE and 2 mules at SOMME DRESSING STATION to bring out guns of 24th M.G. Coy.

(8) Upon completion of relief Coy HQ. will be at D14. b 10.05.

(9) Completion of relief will be reported to Coy. H.Q. by runner.

Copy No 1 O.C. A. Battery
 "   " 2   "   B.   "
 "   " 3   "   C.   "
 "   " 4   "   Lieut LARKWORTHY
 "   " 5   "   SPOONER
 "   " 6   "   24th M.G. Coy
 "   " 7   "   25th Infantry Brigade
 "   " 8   "   WAR DIARY
 "   " 9   "   Retained

15-1-18

A.K. Rumen, Lieut
25th M.G. Coy.

SECRET.   Copy No. 9

8TH DIVISION ORDER No.254.

13th January, 1918.

1. 25th Inf. Bde. will relieve 23rd Inf. Bde. in the line on the night January 15th/16th.

2. (a) On relief, 23rd Inf. Bde. will proceed to the BRANDHOEK Area by Light Railway from WIELTJE under arrangements to be made by 8th Division "Q", and become Brigade in Divisional Reserve.

   (b) Hours of departure from WIELTJE will be notified later.

3. 24th Inf. Bde. (less parties detailed for work on 15th January) will move up to WIELTJE - ST. JEAN Area by march route on January 15th and become the Brigade in Support.

   Route.   VLAMERTINGHE - Road Junction I.2.c.2.3. - ST. JEAN. Head of column not to reach Road Junction I.2.c.2.3. before 3 p.m.

4. All details of relief will be arranged direct between Brigadiers concerned.

5. Trench Stores, Aeroplane Photographs, and Intelligence details will be handed over.

6. Billeting parties of 24th Inf. Bde. will proceed to the WIELTJE - ST. JEAN Area by march route early on January 15th.

7. The following M.G. Coy. reliefs will be carried out on night January 15th/16th and day of January 16th:-

   218th M.G. Co. will relieve 23rd M.G. Co. on night 15th/16th on Close Defence.
   25th M.G. Co. will relieve 24th M.G. Co. on morning of 16th January, on Barrage.

   On relief, 23rd and 24th M.G. Cos. will proceed to BRANDHOEK and YPRES respectively.

8. 8th Division "Q" will arrange for -

   (a) Light Railway transport to convey personnel of 218th M.G. Coy. from BRANDHOEK to WIELTJE on the afternoon of January 15th.
   (b) Light Railway to convey personnel of 23rd M.G. Coy. from WIELTJE to BRANDHOEK Area on night 15th/16th.

   Details as to time of departure of trains etc., will be notified later by 8th Division "Q".

9. Completion of Machine Gun Co. reliefs will be reported to Divisional Headquarters and to 25th Inf. Bde.

10. ACKNOWLEDGE.

Issued at 4 p.m.

S. Adam

Lieut.-Colonel,
General Staff

P.T.O. for distribution.

2.

Copies to:-

No. 1 Divisional Commander.
2 23rd Inf. Bde.
3 24th Inf. Bde.
4 25th Inf. Bde.
5 8th Div. Arty.
6 22nd D.L.I.
7 23rd M.G. Coy.
8 24th M.G. Coy.
9 25th M.G. Coy.
10 218th M.G. Coy.
11 D.M.G.O.
12 C.R.E.
13 O.C., Signals.
14 "Q".
15 A.D.M.S.
16 A.P.M.
17 VIII Corps "G".   ⎫
18 VIII Corps "Q".   ⎬ For
19 Left Bombardment Group. ⎬ information.
20 33rd Division.   ⎬
21 39th Division.   ⎭
22 War Diary.
23 File.

SECRET.
Copy No. 9

25th INFANTRY BRIGADE ORDER No.267.

Ref. 1/40,000 sheet 28 N.W.
    "   28 N.E.
                                    14th January, 1918.

1. (a) The 25th Infantry Brigade will relieve the 23rd Infantry Bde. in the line on the night January 15th/16th.
   (b) Reliefs will be carried out in accordance with attached Table.
   (c) All details of relief will be arranged direct between Battalion Commanders concerned.

2. All Trench Stores, Aeroplane Photographs, Intelligence Details, Special Maps, Work in hand or proposed, will be taken over.

3. (a) The following will be taken up into the Line:-
       1 Pick or Shovel per man (except Lewis Gunners)
       4 Sandbags a man.
   These picks and shovels will be carried up instead of entrenching tools, will be considered as part of the man's equipment and will be brought out on relief.
   (b) Greatcoats will not be taken up into the Line.
   (c) Puttees will be worn for the march up to the Line. On arrival in the trenches they will be taken off and put round the waist, and sandbags will be worn on the legs.

4. The following distances will be maintained on the march:-
       Between Companies   -   400 yards.
       Between Platoons   -   100 yards.

5. (a) On the night of January 16th/17th the following Inter Battalion reliefs will take place :-
      2nd R.Berks Regt. will relieve 2nd Lincoln Regt. in the Right Subsector.
      2nd Rifle Brigade will relieve 1st R.Irish Rifles in the Left Subsector.
   On relief 2nd Lincoln Regt. will move back into Support and 1st R.Irish Rifles into Reserve.
   (b) Reliefs will not commence before 6 p.m.
   (c) All details of relief will be arranged direct between Battalion Commanders concerned.

6. (a) Completion of reliefs ordered in para. 1 will be reported by the Code Word "TRENCH".
   (b) Completion of reliefs ordered in para. 5 will be reported by the Code Word "FEET".

7. Brigade Headquarters will close at WIELTJE DUGOUT at 8.30 p.m. on January 15th and will reopen at CAPITOL, D.13.d.8.3., at the same hour.

8. ACKNOWLEDGE.

                                                           Captain,
                                                     Brigade Major,
                                                     25th Inf. Bde.

Issued at 3 p.m. through Signals to:-

Copy No.1. G.O.C.	12. Bde.Int.Offr.	23. 8th Div. "G".
2. Brigade Major.	13. 23rd Inf. Bde.	24. 8th Div. "Q".
3. Staff Captain.	14. 24th Inf. Bde.	25. War Diary.
4. Bde. Signals.	15. 116th Inf. Bde.	26. Office.
5. 2nd Lincoln Regt.	16. Right Brigade.	
6. 2nd R.Berks Regt.	17. C.R.E. 8th Div.	
7. 1st R.Irish Rifles.	18. C.R.A. " "	
8. 2nd Rifle Brigade.	19. A.D.M.S. " "	
9. 25th M.G. Coy.	20. 33rd Bde.R.F.A.	
10. 25th T.M. Bty.	21. 45th " "	
11. Bde. Supply Offr.	22. 218th M.G.Coy.	

SECRET.

ADMINISTRATIVE INSTRUCTIONS
issued in conjunction with 25th Infantry Brigade Order
No. 267, dated 14th January, 1918.

1. **ACCOMMODATION.**
If further accommodation is required for details, application should be made by Units direct to Area Commandant, Left Division, VLAMERTINGHE.

2. **TRANSPORT.**
Transport of Units will remain in present positions at YORK CAMP. Brigade Transport Officer will arrange to take over advanced pack lines at I.1.d.5.6., also 40 Pack Saddles from 23rd Infantry Brigade.

3. **RATIONS.**
(a) Units will take two days rations with them when they go into the line to-morrow. A train carrying rations for consumption 16th and 17th will leave EAGLE Dump at 6.30 a.m. to-morrow.

(b) Rations for consumption 18th will be delivered to units on the 16th instant. They will arrive by train at SPREE FARM about 2 p.m. and will be conveyed to BELLEVUE on pack animals - to reach there not later than 5 p.m.

(c) As the practice of cooking the tea at the Transport Lines and re-heating it in the Line, proved a success, it will be continued during the Brigade's tour in the Line.

(d) It is regretted that it is impossible to effect an increase in the present scale of issue of Solidified Alcohol as the present scale is only made possible by drawing on Army and G.H.Q. Reserves. The present scale works out about 50 8 oz. tins per Battalion.

4. **PICKS & SHOVELS.**
All picks and shovels required by Battalions in accordance with para.3 of Brigade Order No. 267 will be drawn from Brigade Headquarters, WIELTJE on morning of 15th instant.

5. **BLANKETS.**
Blankets, surplus kit, etc., will be returned to Transport Lines or Blanket Store at VLAMERTINGHE on G.S. Wagons which bring up the blankets of units of 24th Infantry Brigade.
It has been decided that each man should have a blanket when the Brigade entrains on the night of 18th instant. 6 Tents have been erected on the North side of the broad guage track opposite the Soup Kitchen at WIELTJE. Battalions will arrange therefore to store in these tents to-morrow blankets on the scale of 1 per man on trench strength. These blankets should be properly rolled and securely tied. Each Battalion will leave a storeman in charge of the blankets until night of 18th. Application should be made to Staff Captain, WIELTJE, who will allot the tents.

6. **SOCKS.**
Division are going to arrange for a supply of 5,000 socks over and above those now in possession of units. This should admit of one pair of socks being available at entraining point on night of 18th so that the men can change their socks in the train. These socks could be stored with the blankets at WIELTJE.

7. **TRENCH FEET.**
Units will carry out the treatment laid down in 8th Division Trench Foot Scheme to-morrow. Units will render without fail by 8 p.m. to-morrow a certificate to the effect that all men

have undergone the treatment and are in possession of two .303 cartridge cases full of camphor powder.

8. **AREA STORES, etc.**
All Area Stores, including gum boots and R.E. material, will be carefully handed over to relieving units, receipts obtained and forwarded to this office.

9. **S.A.A., GRENADES, R.E. STORES, etc.**
Arrangements for the supply of these are given in paras. 5 and 6 of Administrative Instructions dated 29/12/1917.

10. **CORRESPONDENCE.**
All correspondence on "A" and "Q" matters should be addressed to Rear Headquarters, WIELTJE DUGOUT. Correspondence of a similar nature issued from this Office will be sent to Units Orderly Rooms at the Transport Lines.

Captain,
Staff Captain,
25th Inf. Bde.

14th January, 1918.

TABLE to accompany 25th Infantry Brigade Order No. 237.

Serial No.	Date.	Unit.	From.	To.	To relief of	Starting Place	Point Time.	Route	Remarks.
1	Jan.15/16th	2/Lincoln Regt.	CAPRICORN	LINE, Right	2/Scottish Rifles	KANSAS Cross.	5.15 p.m.	IETJE - ST ANTHEIM Road.	Platoon guides at BELLEVUE at 6 p.m.
2	ditto.	1/R.Irish Rifles.	JUNCTION	LINE, Left	2/Middlesex Regt.	ST. JEAN Cross Roads.	4.45 p.m.	ST. JEAN - LITZENHOLE Road. No.6 Track.	Platoon guides for 3 Coys. at KRC-PRINZ at 5 p.m. - for Fourth Coy. at BELLEVUE at 6.45 p.m.
3	ditto.	25/T.M.Bty.	WHIGE	LINE	23/T.M.Bty.	ST. JEAN Cross Roads.	4.55 p.m.	IETJE - LITZENHOLE Road. or No.5 Track.	To follow 1 Coy 1/R.I.R. 6 Guides at BELLEVUE at 5.55 p.m.
4	ditto.	2/Z.Berks. Regt.	WHIGE	Support	2/Yorks. Regt.	Road Junction J.28.b.5. 5.55.	5.15 p.m.	IETJE - 2 Coys. Road.5. Track. No - 1 Coy. No - 2 Track.	To follow serial Nos.2 & 3. Platoon guides for 2 Coys. at KRC-PRINZ at 6.45 p.m. - for remaining Coy. 2 Coys. at BELLEVUE at 7 p.m.
5	ditto.	2/Rifle Bde.	CALIFORNIA	Reserve	2/Devon.R.	CALIFORNIA Camp.	6.0 p.m.	IETJE - BELLEVUE Road. or No. 5 Track.	To follow 2 Coys 2/Berks. Regt. Platoon guides at BELLEVUE at 7.30 p.m.

Post guides for Serial Nos. 1 and 2 will be provided at Headquarters of Coys. in the line.

SECRET.

Copy No ....

25TH INFANTRY BRIGADE ORDER No. 268.

Ref. 1/20,000 sheet 28 N.E.
     1/20,000 " 28 N.W.
     1/40,000 " 27.

16th January, 1918.

1. (a) The 25th Infantry Brigade will be relieved in the line on the night of January 18th/19th by the 86th Infantry Brigade, 29th Division, and will proceed on relief by rail to the WATOU Area.

   (b) All reliefs will be carried out in accordance with attached Table "A".

   (c) Details of relief will be arranged direct between Battalion Commanders concerned.

2. All Trench Stores, Aeroplane Photographs, Defence Schemes, Intelligence Details, work proposed or in progress will be handed over. Intelligence Maps and Special Maps will also be handed over, but all Trench Maps and other maps will be taken out of the line.

3. The 25th Machine Gun Company will be relieved on January 20th and night January 20/21st and will withdraw after relief to the new Area, under arrangements to be made by the D.M.G.O., 8th Division.

4. Completion of reliefs will be reported by the Code Word "BULLY".

5. For purposes of the move back to the WATOU Area the 25th Brigade Group will be constituted as follows :-

        25th Infantry Brigade. (less Machine Gun Coy.)
        24th Field Ambulance.
        No. 4 Coy., 8th Div. Train.

6. (a) Personnel of the Brigade Group will entrain at WIELTJE after relief on the night January 18th/19th :-
        First Train   - 9.30 p.m.
        Second Train - 11.30 p.m.

   (b) Transport of the Brigade Group will proceed by road to the WATOU Area under the Brigade Transport Officer on the morning of the 18th in accordance with attached table "B". Three vehicles per Battalion may be left behind for the provision of hot food for men coming out of the line. These will march to the WATOU Area on the 19th instant in accordance with attached Table "B" under orders to be issued by the Staff Captain.

   (c) All details of units, including Officers and Other Ranks from the Brigade Schools will accompany the Transport on the 18th.

7. Billetting parties will proceed to the new Area on the 17th instant. Detailed orders have already been issued on this point by the Staff Captain.

8. Each Battalion will detail 1 Officer and 4 N.C.O's (1 per Company) to report to the Staff Captain at WIELTJE DUGOUT at 8 p.m. January 18th to assist in the entraining. These Officers and N.C.O's will be responsible :-

        (i) For collecting and checking all picks and

/shovels....

shovels brought out by their own unit.

    (ii) For seeing that every man is issued with a blanket and a dry pair of socks on getting into the train.

    (iii) For seeing that every man has a hot drink from his own Battalion cookers before entraining.

9. The entrainment will take place at WIELTJE, about C.28.b.2.7. Cookers will be drawn up down ADMIRALS ROAD on either side of the railway. Blankets and dry socks have been stored in tents by the side of the railway at the entrainment point.

10. Brigade Headquarters will close at D.13.d.8.3. on completion of relief and will reopen in WATOU on arrival.

11. ACKNOWLEDGE.

                                            Captain,
                                         Brigade Major,
                                         25th Inf. Bde.

Issued at   through Signals to :-

        Copy No. 1   G.O.C.
                 2   B.M.
                 3   S.C.
                 4   Bde. Signal Officer,
                 5   2/Lincoln. Regt.
                 6   2/R.Berks. Regt.
                 7   1/R.Irish Rifles,
                 8   2/Rifle Brigade,
                 9   25/M.G.Coy.
               10   25/T.M.Bt.
               11   Bde. Transport Officer,
               12   Bde. Intelligence Officer,
               13   Bde. Supply Officer,
               14   218/L.3.Coy.
               15   23rd Inf. Bde.
               16   24th Inf. Bde.
               17   86th Inf. Bde.
               18   116th Inf. Bde.
               19   98th Inf. Bde.
               20   33rd Bde. R.F.A.
               21   45th Bde. R.F.A.
               22   C.R.A., 8th Division,
               23   C.R.E., 8th Division,
               24   A.D.M.S. 8th Division,
               25   A.P.M. 8th Division,
               26   8th Division, "G",
               27   8th Division, "Q",
               28   War Diary,
               29   Office,

RELIEF TABLE "A" to accompany 25th Infantry Brigade Order No. 252.

Serial No.	Date	Unit.	Relieved by	From	To	Route of Incoming Unit.	Coy. Guides. Place and Time	Platoon Guides. Place and Time	Post Guides. Place.	Remarks.
1.	Jan.18/19th.	2/Rifle Brigade	2/Royal Fusrs.	LINE, Left.	WATOU Area K.35.a.7.2.	WIELTJE - BELLEVUE Road - MALLARD X Roads.	A.D.S., SOHMT. 4 p.m.	MALLARD X Roads. 5 p.m.	For Right Co. at Coy. H.Q. For 3 remaining Coys. at VIRILE Farm.	1. Each Bn. will detail an Officer in charge of guides who will come with Coy. guides to meet incoming unit at SOHMT. 2. Times given for guides are those suitable for misty day with bad visibility. If day is fine and visibility good all times will be made half an hour later. If this alteration is made, units will be notified by the Code Word CLEAR. before 1 p.m. on Jan.18th.
2.	do.	2/R.Berks Regt.	10/Midx. Regt.	Support	WATOU Area K.30.c.4.0.	WIELTJE - BELLEVUE Road - MALLARD X Roads.	do. 4.45 p.m.	do. 5.45 p.m.	H.Qrs. of Coys.	
3.	do.	25/T.M. Bty.	86/T.M. Bty.	Positions near VEGETABLE Farm and BELLEVUE	WATOU	ditto.	do. (1 Offr.) 5.30 p.m.	BELLEVUE 1 Guide per gun. 6.30 p.m.		
4.	do.	2/Lancs. Regt.	1/Lancs. Fusrs.	LINE, Right.	WATOU Area K.15.d.5.6.	Road.	do. 5.40 p.m.	BELLEVUE 6.40 p.m.	H.Qrs. of Coys. in the line.	
5.	do.	1/R.Ir. Rifles.	1/Royal Guernsey L.I.	Reserve	WATOU Area L.7.d.7.5.	Road.	do. 6.30 p.m.	do. 7.30 p.m.		

TABLE "E" to accompany 25th Infantry Brigade Order No. 268.   TRANSPORT March Table.

Serial No.	Date.	Units (in order of march).	From.	To.	Starting Point Place	Starting Point Time	Route	Remarks.
1	Jan.18th.	2/Lincoln. Regt.	YORK Camp.	K.15.d.5.6.	Cross Roads G.4.d.3.4.	9.0 a.m.	POPERINGHE	1. 100 yards to be maintained between transport of units. 25 yards distance to be kept between every Section of six vehicles. 2. Brigade Transport Offr. will give orders for units to leave the column when nearing their billetting areas.
2	ditto.	25/Bde. H.Q.	ditto.	WATOU	ditto.	9.4 a.m.	ditto.	
3	ditto.	24/Fld. Amb.	G.5.d.7.3.	Q.7.b.9.1.	ditto.	9.8 a.m.	ditto.	
4	ditto.	2/Rifle Brigade.	YORK Camp.	K.35.a.7.2.	ditto.	9.12 a.m.	ditto.	
5	ditto.	2/R.Berks. Regt.	ditto.	K.30.c.5.0.	ditto.	9.16 a.m.	ditto.	
6	ditto.	1/R.Irish Rifles.	ditto.	L.7.d.7.5.	ditto.	9.20 a.m.	ditto.	
7	ditto.	No. 4 Co.Div.Train.	G.5.a.6.8.	I.13.b.1.3.	ditto.	9.24 a.m.	ditto.	
8	Jan.19th.	Vehicles left behind on 18th will march in same order as above.	YORK Camp	Respective Billetting Areas.	G.4.d.3.4.	—	POPERINGHE	To be clear of POPERINGHE by 1 p.m. on Jan. 19th.

Army Form C. 2118.

WAR DIARY
or
INTELLIGENCE SUMMARY.
(Erase heading not required.)

Instructions regarding War Diaries and Intelligence Summaries are contained in F. S. Regs., Part II. and the Staff Manual respectively. Title pages will be prepared in manuscript.

Place	Date	Hour	Summary of Events and Information	Remarks and references to Appendices
	1/2/18		9.0 AM Parade. 9.15-12.30 Infantry Drill, Gun Drill, Parade drill & stripping. 1 O.R. joined the company H/S	
	2/2/18		Company firing on the range 9.15-12.30. 2 O.R. leave to U.K. H/S	
	3/2/18		Church Parade. 2 O.R. leave to U.K. 2/Lt LOCKHART from leave to U.K. 1 O.R. from course H/S	
	4/2/18		As per training programme. M.T.P.	APPENDIX XVII Training Programme
	5/2/18		As per training programme. 2 O.R. hospital. N.P.R.	
	6/2/18		As per training programme. 1 Officer leave to U.K. 1 O.R. from leave. 3 O.R. from course 1 O.R. to course. P.E. 2 O.R. evacuated	
			L.C.E.S. 2 O.R. joined from Base.	
	7/2/18		As per training programme. N.P.R.	
	8/2/18		As per training programme. N.P.R.	
	9/2/18		Coy was inspected by Army Commander. 2 O.R. leave to U.K. 1 O.R. from hospital U.K.	
	10/2/18		Divl Sports. Camp & Parley Show 1 O.R. hospital. 4 O.R. from 47 Officers for leave to U.K. 1 O.R. from course	
			3 O.R. from base. N.P.R.	
Flêtre Belgium top N.W.	11/2/18		Coy by bus transport left STEENVOORDE at 11.15 A.M. & entrained at GODEWAERSVELDE. Coy detrained at BRANDHOEK & marched for night at camp sheets at 4.7 a 1.9. Transport arrived 2.15 p.m., 10 O.R. from base.	
			to U.K. N.P.R.	
	12/2/18		Coy's Transport passed off the coy at 9.0a.m. marched & camp sheets at C 26 D 99 Horses at & Coy's Supplies	

(A7883) Wt W80y/M1672 350,000 4/17 Sch. 52a Forms/C/2118/14 D. D. & L., London, E.C.

Army Form C. 2118.

WAR DIARY
or
INTELLIGENCE SUMMARY.
(Erase heading not required.)

Instructions regarding War Diaries and Intelligence Summaries are contained in F. S. Regs., Part II. and the Staff Manual respectively. Title pages will be prepared in manuscript.

Place	Date	Hour	Summary of Events and Information	Remarks and references to Appendices
IRISH FARM	12/2/18		1 O.R. to Hospital. 1 O.R. from hospital. 1 O.R. from Court F. Hill	
	13/2/18		Coy. Stand. Cleaning guns & equipment & refresher camp. 1 O.R. to hospital M.R.	
	14/2/18		Coy. employed on fatigues. 1 O.R. from hand Hosp. 1 O.R. evacuated M.R.	
	15/2/18		Coy. had baths. refit. musketry & drill & cleaning guns etc. 1 Officer & 2 O.R. & Guard joined. 1 O.R. to hospital	
	16/2/18		1 O.R. from hospital M.R.	
			Cleaning guns etc. Fatigues. 1 O.R. from H.U.K. 1 O.R. from hospital M.R.	
	17/2/18		As on 16th. 3 O.R. leave H.U.K. 1 O.R. from leave - France M.R.	
DEAD END	19/2/18		Coy. relieved 23rd M.G. Coy. – close defence positions. Details moved to Camp – YPRES. 1 O.R. to hospital. 1 O.R. from hospital M.R.	APPENDIX XVIII Coy Orders
	19/2/18		Details employed on fatigues & cleaning Camp etc. 1 O.R. to hospital M.R. 1 O.R. evacuated 1 O.R. from hand H.U.K. M.R.	
	20/2/18		Coy. employed on fatigues etc. 1 O.R. from leave H.U.K. 1 O.R. from hospital M.R.	
	21/2/18		Intr Section relief. Took place of guns in close defence. 1 O.R. att. evacuated. 1 O.R. from P.F. Cross. 1 O.R. evacuated H.U.K.	
	22/2/18		Coy employed on fatigues. Indirect fire on enemy parade E of VINDICTIVE X roads 7400 rounds. L't BONNER & 1 O.R. from U.K. 1 O.R. to Hosp. to U.K.	45
	23/2/18		Coy employed on fatigues. Indirect fire on enemy parade N of VINDICTIVE X roads 7000 rounds. L't RENNIE & 1 O.R. from U.K. 1 O.R. to Hosp.	45
	24/2/18		Details on fatigues. Company on the line relieved by 22nd M.G. Coy in close defence position. 2 O.R. leave U.K.	APPENDIX XIX Relief Orders
			1 O.R. evacuated. 45	
	25/2/18		Company to Listrett. Cleaning guns, fatigues. 2 O.R. from U.K. leave. 1 O.R. (attached) from hospital. 45	

Army Form C. 2118.

WAR DIARY
or
INTELLIGENCE SUMMARY.
(Erase heading not required.)

Instructions regarding War Diaries and Intelligence Summaries are contained in F. S. Regs., Part II. and the Staff Manual respectively. Title pages will be prepared in manuscript.

Place	Date	Hour	Summary of Events and Information	Remarks and references to Appendices
	26/2/18		Company on fatigues. Operations in case of emergency cells. 2 OR from UK leave. 1 OR to hospital	
	27/2/18		Company on fatigues. Baths in the morning. 1 OR to from fly camp	
	28/2/18		Company on fatigues. 1 OR leave to UK. 1 OR to course. 1 OR to hospital. 1 OR evacuated. 1 OR from hospital. 24 OR reinforcement	

H. Spooner Lt.
in OC 25th M.G.Coy

8th Divisional Machine Gun Battalion

Training Programme

for the period 2nd Feb 1918 – 9th Feb 1918

DAY	MORNINGS				AFTERNOONS	EVENINGS
	9.15 – 10.0	10.15 – 11.15	11.30 – 11.40	11.40 – 12.30	2.30 – 3.30	5.15 – 6.0
Sunday 3.2.18	Church Parade and Recreation					
Monday 4.2.18	Infantry Drill A & B	Gun Drill Companies on the Range	Revolver Exercises	Classes in Stripping, I.A. Cont. Jamms Belt filling and		Lecture to N.C.Os by Company Comdr
Tuesday 5.2.18	P.T. C & D	Gun Drill Companies on the Range	do	do	Lecture to Coy by Coy Comdr 2.30 – 3.0	Scouts Hut Reading Class by Lt Wills 218th M.G. Coy
Wednesday 6.2.18	Infantry Drill A & B	Range Drill Companies on the Range	do	do	Scouts Hut Reading Class	
Thursday 7.2.18	P.T. C & D	Barrage Drill Companies on the Range	do	do	Lectures by Platoon Commanders 2.30 to 3	Scouts Hut Reading Class by Lt Wills 218th M.G. Coy
Friday 8.2.18	Infantry Drill A & B	Range Drill Companies on the Range	do	do		
Saturday 9.2.18	P.T. C & D	Barrage Drill Companies on the Range	do	do		Scouts Hut Reading Class Lt Wills 218th M.G. Coy

NOTES (A) Reveille 6.30 AM daily ——— G.A. Parade 8 A.M. daily
(B) Special Courses have been arranged for Range takers, Signallers & N.C.Os.

SECRET   Copy No 8.

"C" Machine Gun Coy Relief Orders No 2.

1. "C" Coy will be relieved by "A" Coy in the line on the night of 24th - 25th.

2. Guides will be at WATERLOO as follows:-

   3.0 A.M. { 2 Guides from GOUDBERG TRENCH SECT. H.Q.
            { 2   "   MUSSELMARKT H.Q.

   3.15 A.M. 2   "   PILL BOX 83

   3.30 A.M. { 1 Guide each of 9, 10, 11, 12, 13, 14 Guns
             { 1   "   Advance H.Q.

3. Transport will wait for "C" Coy Guns at WATERLOO.

4. Inspite belts, belt boxes will be handed over and all information given to incoming teams & receipts obtained.

5. 1 Gun at No 14 and one Gun at No 9 position will be handed over.

6. A.A. positions at No 14 & 15 will be handed over.

7. On completion of relief "C" Coy will return to Batt Camp in YPRES.

              Copy No 1 O.C. "A" Section
                 "   2   "   "B"   "
                 "   3 Lieut CUFFE ADAMS
                 "   4   O.C. "D" Section
                 "   5   8th D.M.G.B.
                 "   6   "A" M.G. Coy
                 "   7   O.C. "B" Coy
                 "   8   Retained

24.2.18
                                                        H. Spence Lieut
                                                        Comdg "C" Coy
                                                        8th D.M.G.B.

8th, Division.

25th, Brigade.

2nd, Rifle Brigade.

November, 1915.

~~2 ARMY TROOPS~~

8 DIV

25

25 BDE

TRENCH MORTAR BTY

1915 JUNE to 1915 DEC

(447)

WAR DIARY
or
INTELLIGENCE SUMMARY
(Erase heading not required.)

Army Form C. 2118

25th Field Artillery
attached 5th Div.

Place	Date	Hour	Summary of Events and Information	Remarks and references to Appendices
In the Field	6/6/15	—	The battery proceeded to Reninghelst and billets and on same date to Headquarters 15th Infantry Bde at Zillebeke Lake	
	7/6/15		Right section came into action in the trenches with the Norfolk Regt, and the left section with the Bedford Regt	
	9/6/15		Lieut Hibbetson who came out with the battery for instructions returned to Headquarters on the morning of the 9th. On the evening of the 9th one man was killed and another injured	
	10/6/15		Lieut Ellis joined the battery from 5th D.A.C. The left section rejoined the battery and continued in action with the Norfolk Regt and the D.C.L.I. until the 15th, after which date no more ammunition was available.	

Peterson Capt R.F.A.
19/6/15

O.C. 25th L.H. Bty.

Army Form C. 2118

WAR DIARY
or
INTELLIGENCE SUMMARY 25th Trench Howitzer Battery
(Erase heading not required.) 28th DIV 2nd Army

Place	Date	Hour	Summary of Events and Information	Remarks and references to Appendices
	18/6/15		Battery came out of action and proceeded to billets near WESTOUTRE. Lieut Ellis was transferred to 29th T.H. Battery. Battery was now without any ammunition.	
	22/6/15		Changed billet, moving to farm E of WESTOUTRE	
	29/6/15		Proceeded to HOWITZER FARM near DICKEBUSCH, accompanied by the 33rd T.H.Battery. At the end of the month positions had been selected for the guns in the trenches of the 84th Infantry Brigade & objectives had been noted, but the Battery was still without ammunition	

B Gilpin
Capt RFA
Comdg 25th T.H. Battery

XXVIII

Army Form C. 2118

25–77 Forward HQ mg

WAR DIARY
or
INTELLIGENCE SUMMARY
(Erase heading not required.)

Place	Date	Hour	Summary of Events and Information	Remarks and references to Appendices
	July 1-19		Remained at Hazelbar Farm, Vlamertinghe, awaiting ammunition. Position were reconnoitred & selected in trenches opposite KEMMEL occupied by 84th Infantry Brigade	
	20		Moved in early morning to DRANOUTRE then proceeded to billets in farm between DRANOUTRE and WULVERGHEM.	
	21		Came into action in early morning in 85th Bde French trenches. Fired 9 rounds from same position in evening.	Ag 9/7/15
	22		Came into action with two guns on left of trenches occupied by British firing 8 rounds.	
	23		Fired 10 rounds from same position as on previous day	
	25		Came into action on right of 85th Bde trenches. Fired 4 rounds. 1 man killed & 1 wounded by enemy rifle grenade.	

B L Hanson Lieut
Comdg 25th TM By 1st Army

Army Form C. 2118

WAR DIARY
or
INTELLIGENCE SUMMARY
(Erase heading not required.)

23-7-17 74 Bty

Place	Date	Hour	Summary of Events and Information	Remarks and references to Appendices
	26. July		In action on left of 86th Brigade Trenches, fired 12 rounds.	
	29"		Fired 8 rounds from same position.	

7/8/15

B. G. Upton
Capt. R.F.A.
Comdg 25th T.H. Battery

WAR DIARY
or
INTELLIGENCE SUMMARY   23-7-71-71-685

Army Form C. 2118

(Erase heading not required.)

Instructions regarding War Diaries and Intelligence Summaries are contained in F.S. Regs., Part II. and the Staff Manual respectively. Title Pages will be prepared in manuscript.

Place	Date	Hour	Summary of Events and Information	Remarks and references to Appendices
	3rd			
	4th		Fired by night from E1 trench (E. Sinem) 18 heavy bursts 7 were blind.	
	4th		2Lieut R.E. Felton R.G.A joined the battery.	
	5th		Occupied position in "KINGSWAY" Communication trench (E. Sinem) Fired 3 rounds at enemy Sap opposite E15; present position unknown	
	8th		Fired 2 rounds at Sap opposite E15.	

10/8/15

Blackburn
Captain
Comdg 25th S.H. Batty

WAR DIARY
or
INTELLIGENCE SUMMARY

(Erase heading not required.)

Army Form C. 2118

25th T.H. Battery

Place	Date	Hour	Summary of Events and Information	Remarks and references to Appendices
	9.8.15		Fired 18 Light bombs from KINGSWAY (E1's Comm Trench) at dusk.	
	11.8.15		Half the Battery went into dug-outs near BURNT FARM.	
	13.8.15		2 N.C.Os & 10 privates & E. Surveys joined from T.H. school.	
	14.8.15		2 N.C.Os & 6 Gunners left the Battery & proceeded to T.H. school.	
			Map position of hill at T3 b 4.8.	

B.G. Alpin
Capt. RFA
Comdg 25th T.H. Battery

Army Form C. 2118

WAR DIARY
or
INTELLIGENCE SUMMARY   25th T.H. Battery.
(Erase heading not required.)

Instructions regarding War Diaries and Intelligence Summaries are contained in F. S. Regs., Part II. and the Staff Manual respectively. Title Pages will be prepared in manuscript.

Place	Date	Hour	Summary of Events and Information	Remarks and references to Appendices
	17/8/15		Fired 4 heavy & 42 light bombs at German fire Trench opposite E 15 (occupied by the Turks) in three series, one in morning, one at midday, one in evening. Position of billet T5 b 4.8. Advanced section T5 b 3.10 B.G. Upton Capt RFA Comdg 25th T.H. Battery 25/8/15	

Army Form C. 2118

25-7717 A/184

WAR DIARY
or
INTELLIGENCE SUMMARY
(Erase heading not required.)

Instructions regarding War Diaries and Intelligence Summaries are contained in F.S. Regs., Part II. and the Staff Manual respectively. Title Pages will be prepared in manuscript.

Place	Date	Hour	Summary of Events and Information	Remarks and references to Appendices
	29.8.15		The Battery did not fire this week. One gun & stores was transferred to 33rd T.H. Battery. One officer one N.C.O. & one gunner were despatched to 33rd T.H. Battery to instruct in drill of 1.5" T.H. Position of bullet T3 b 4.6. Advanced Section T5 b 3.10	B.L. Alpin Capt R.F.A Comdg 25th T.H. Battery

WAR DIARY or INTELLIGENCE SUMMARY

25th T.M. Battery

Army Form C. 2118

Place	Date	Hour	Summary of Events and Information	Remarks and references to Appendices
	30/9/16		2/Lt Felton was sent temporarily to command the 33rd T.M. Battery	

B.G. Upin
Capt. RFA
Comdg. 25th T.M. Battery.

Army Form C. 2118

WAR DIARY
or
INTELLIGENCE SUMMARY 25th T.H. Battery
(Erase heading not required.)

Instructions regarding War Diaries and Intelligence Summaries are contained in F.S. Regs., Part II. and the Staff Manual respectively. Title Pages will be prepared in manuscript.

Place	Date	Hour	Summary of Events and Information	Remarks and references to Appendices
	5/9/15		The Battery has not fired during the last week. B.W. T 3 b 4.6. Advanced Section T 3 b 3.10	

B Gilpin
Capt RFA
Comdg 25th T.H. Battery

5/9/15

Army Form C. 2118

WAR DIARY
or
INTELLIGENCE SUMMARY 25th T.H. Battery

(Erase heading not required.)

Instructions regarding War Diaries and Intelligence Summaries are contained in F. S. Regs., Part II. and the Staff Manual respectively. Title Pages will be prepared in manuscript.

Place	Date	Hour	Summary of Events and Information	Remarks and references to Appendices
	11/9/15		2Lt Felton & 2 men rejoined from 33rd Battery (T.H.) from which they brought one 3·7" T.H. Complete & a little ammunition for the same.	
	12/9/15		The Battery fired 25 heavy bombs at a ruined house opposite 84th Brigade Trenches, and also 10 3·7" bombs.	

Billets T3 b 4 8
Advanced Posh- T6 & 3·10.

R G Alpin
Capt RFA
Comdg 25th T.H. Battery.

H 00 19/9/15

Army Form C. 2118

WAR DIARY
or
INTELLIGENCE SUMMARY T.M. Battery 25-FZ

(Erase heading not required.)

Instructions regarding War Diaries and Intelligence Summaries are contained in F. S. Regs., Part II. and the Staff Manual respectively. Title Pages will be prepared in manuscript.

Place	Date	Hour	Summary of Events and Information	Remarks and references to Appendices
	17/9/15		Fired 4 heavy and 9 light bombs at ruined house opposite E2 trench Both htty Rifle line.	
	19/9/15		Fired 24 light bombs at trenches opposite E15 Trench	

B G Alpin
Capt RFA
Comdg 25th T.M. Battery

WAR DIARY or INTELLIGENCE SUMMARY 25th T.M. Battery

(Erase heading not required.)

Army Form C. 2118

Place	Date	Hour	Summary of Events and Information	Remarks and references to Appendices
	23/9/15		2 NCO's & 8 privates of E. Surry Regt. left the Battery and were replaced by 2 N.C.O.s & 10 privates of the Canadian Infantry. The Battery became attached to the 2nd Canadian Division.	

27/9/15

B. Alpin
Capt. RFA.
Comdg 25th T.M. Battery.

9/10/15

Army Form C. 2118

WAR DIARY
or
INTELLIGENCE SUMMARY 25th French Mortar Battery
(Erase heading not required.)

Instructions regarding War Diaries and Intelligence Summaries are contained in F.S. Regs., Part II. and the Staff Manual respectively. Title Pages will be prepared in manuscript.

Place	Date	Hour	Summary of Events and Information	Remarks and references to Appendices
	8/10/15		The Battery moved by night to DICKEBUSCH where on the following day it occupied hut/s	
	9/10/15		2Lieut Fuller returned from Temporary duty with the 33rd T.M. Battery.	

BLUMan
Capt RFA
Comdg 25th T.M. Battery

Army Form C. 2118

WAR DIARY
or
INTELLIGENCE SUMMARY — 25th T.M. Battery.
(Erase heading not required.)

Place	Date	Hour	Summary of Events and Information	Remarks and references to Appendices
	13/10/15		24 rounds were fired at crater opposite K1 Trench on VA Canadian Listening Post Avi. previous to the Infantry attack upon it. At the same time there was a general hostility bombardment along the whole of the 2nd Army front.	
	15/10/15		One action under Lieut Fuller moved into the VA Canadian Infantry Redt. area.	

B.U. Upton
Capt. R.F.A.
Comdg 25th T.M. Battery.

29.10

WAR DIARY or INTELLIGENCE SUMMARY

25th T. M. Battery

Army Form C. 2118

Place	Date	Hour	Summary of Events and Information	Remarks and references to Appendices
	24/10/15		Nothing of importance to report during last week. B.G. Upron Capt & O.C. 25th T. M. Battery	

WAR DIARY
or
INTELLIGENCE SUMMARY

25th T.M. Battery

(Erase heading not required.)

Army Form C. 2118

Instructions regarding War Diaries and Intelligence Summaries are contained in F.S. Regs., Part II. and the Staff Manual respectively. Title Pages will be prepared in manuscript.

Place	Date	Hour	Summary of Events and Information	Remarks and references to Appendices
	31/Oct/15		There is nothing of importance to record during last week.	

Ja 2/11/15

B Gilpin
Captain
Cmdg 25th T.M. Battery

WAR DIARY or INTELLIGENCE SUMMARY

Army Form C. 2118

25th T.M. Battery

Place	Date	Hour	Summary of Events and Information	Remarks and references to Appendices
			There is nothing of importance to record this week.	

B. Giffin, Capt. C.F.A.
Comdg 25th T. M. Battery

WAR DIARY
INTELLIGENCE SUMMARY 25th T.M. Battery

Army Form C. 2118

Place	Date	Hour	Summary of Events and Information	Remarks and references to Appendices
	10/4/16		One 1½" T.M. bomb lent to 33rd T.M. Battery for use in area of N.R. Canadian Inf. Bde.	
	17/4/16		This gun was returned.	

B. Gilpin
Capt R.F.A
Comdg 25th T.M. Battery

Army Form C. 2118

WAR DIARY
or
INTELLIGENCE SUMMARY 25th T.M. Battery
(Erase heading not required.)

Place	Date	Hour	Summary of Events and Information	Remarks and references to Appendices
	24/11/15		One 1½" T.M. Bed was sent temporarily to 35th T.M. Battery for use in reserve position. Two reserve emplacements were made in area of V.H. Avn. half hole & beds placed in them. B. Gilpin Capt. R.F.A. Comdg 25th T.M. Batty	

Army Form C. 2118

WAR DIARY
or
INTELLIGENCE SUMMARY 25th T.M. Battery
(Erase heading not required.)

Place	Date	Hour	Summary of Events and Information	Remarks and references to Appendices

There is nothing to report this week.

B.C. Ilvin, Capt RFA
Comdg 25th T.M. Battery

18/1/17

Army Form C. 2118

WAR DIARY
or
INTELLIGENCE SUMMARY
(Erase heading not required.)

25 B.T. M Bty

Instructions regarding War Diaries and Intelligence Summaries are contained in F. S. Regs., Part II. and the Staff Manual respectively. Title Pages will be prepared in manuscript.

Place	Date	Hour	Summary of Events and Information	Remarks and references to Appendices
	12.12.15		There is nothing to report during the past week.	

B. Yule
Major D: R.G.A.
Comdg 25th T M Bty

Army Form C. 2118

WAR DIARY
or
INTELLIGENCE SUMMARY
(Erase heading not required.)

Instructions regarding War Diaries and Intelligence Summaries are contained in F.S. Regs., Part II. and the Staff Manual respectively. Title Pages will be prepared in manuscript.

Place	Date	Hour	Summary of Events and Information	Remarks and references to Appendices
	16/12/15		The Section at Dickebush left their place for new Quarters at the TRENCH MORTAR GROUP, M24 A 83	
	17–19/12/15		New Emplacements were begun in front line trenches, in accordance with orders received from 5th Infantry Brigade. Preparation was carried out from these Emplacements	
	20/12/15			

Sutcliffe 2/Lt
25th Battery
T.M.

Army Form C. 2118.

WAR DIARY
or
INTELLIGENCE SUMMARY.
(Erase heading not required.)

25th T-M-Battery

Instructions regarding War Diaries and Intelligence Summaries are contained in F. S. Regs., Part II. and the Staff Manual respectively. Title pages will be prepared in manuscript.

Place	Date	Hour	Summary of Events and Information	Remarks and references to Appendices
	20/7/15		Moving of Battery's No 1 section from Neig. of Dug-outs in K 3 right - (just behind SP 13 well.) Transfer of ammunition (all) to K 3 right - and storing of new ammunition in Bomb proof shelter at SP 13 well. -	Ap. 1
	21/7/15		Building of new emplacement in J 4 and firing (3 Heavies) from K 3 gun -	Ap. 1
	22/7/15		Building of scrub house for section in dug-outs and bringing of 3 rounds of new ammunition from J 4. Resisting of emplacement in J 4. Reconnaissance of emplacement in J 10 and firing of two light-rounds from N 1 for registering purposes.	Ap. 1
	23/7/15			Ap. 1
	24/7/15		Enlarging dug-out cover for building of Battery's own dump, from which to store ammunition at Key at — 25 Run & Bubble stead Junction. 3 Heavies fired from J 4.	Ap. 1
	25/7/15		Our-for-by-Inspection by Gen. Capper of Inspector General 25th T-M-Battery	Ap. 1

Army Form C. 2118.

WAR DIARY
or
INTELLIGENCE SUMMARY
(Erase heading not required).

25th T Mortar Bty

Place	Date	Hour	Summary of Events and Information	Remarks and references to Appendices
	Dec 24th to 1st Jan		Emplacements were made in various parts of the brigade front and registration was carried out from all emplacements with satisfactory results.	Stf

Lieut W Johnson 2/Lt
3rd Tr Bn Buffs
25 TMB

1/2/1/18

www.ingramcontent.com/pod-product-compliance
Lightning Source LLC
Chambersburg PA
CBHW080823010526
44111CB00015B/2598